AMERICAN EDUCATION

Its Men,

Ideas,

and

Institutions

Advisory Editor

Lawrence A. Cremin
Frederick A. P. Barnard Professor of Education
Teachers College, Columbia University

AMERICAN EDUCATION: *Its Men, Ideas, and Institutions*
presents selected works of thought and scholarship that have
long been out of print or otherwise unavailable. Inevitably, such
works will include particular ideas and doctrines that have been
outmoded or superseded by more recent research. Nevertheless,
all retain their place in the literature, having influenced educational thought and practice in their own time and having provided
the basis for subsequent scholarship.

THE

SUNDAY-SCHOOL MOVEMENT
1780   1917

and the

AMERICAN SUNDAY-SCHOOL UNION
1817   1917

By

EDWIN WILBUR RICE

ARNO PRESS & THE NEW YORK TIMES
*New York * 1971*

Reprint Edition 1971 by Arno Press Inc.

Reprinted from a copy in
  The State Historical Society of Wisconsin Library

American Education:
  Its Men, Ideas, and Institutions - Series II
  ISBN for complete set: 0-405-03600-0
  See last pages of this volume for titles.

Manufactured in the United States of America

Library of Congress Cataloging in Publication Data

Rice, Edwin Wilbur, 1831-1929.
    The Sunday school movement (1780-1917) and the
American Sunday-School Union (1817-1917)
    (American education: its men, ideas, and
institutions. Series II)
    1. Sunday-schools--U. S. 2. American
Sunday-School Union. I. Title. II. Series.
BV1515.R5 1971   268   70-165728
ISBN 0-405-03717-1

THE
SUNDAY-SCHOOL MOVEMENT
1780   1917

and the

AMERICAN SUNDAY-SCHOOL UNION
1817   1917

By

EDWIN WILBUR RICE

President of the First Day or Sunday School Society; Honorary Editor of the
American Sunday-School Union; Member of the Phi Beta Kappa Society;
the National Geographic Society; the American Academy
of Political and Social Science, etc., etc., etc.

———————

PHILADELPHIA

AMERICAN SUNDAY-SCHOOL UNION

1816 Chestnut Street

FOREWORD TO THE READER

THIS work was not written to order; it has been a growth. My researches into the origin and principles of the modern Sunday-school began as a college graduate student in a pioneer service, about 1854. These researches have continued for an exceptionally long period of personal observation and service, in about every form and phase of the institution in America and Europe. Rare opportunities were providentially offered for years, especially by becoming the custodian of probably the largest and choicest collection of first-hand documents and material relating to the origin and early development of the movement that is to be found anywhere in America or the world.

It is significant that the greatest growth of the modern Sunday-school has not been where it started, but in America. The membership in the United States is easily double that of Great Britain, and equals that in all the other countries of the world.

A mass of historical material has been examined in collections in libraries and historical societies in the United States and Great Britain, and the important facts sifted for the benefit of the reader. Legions of excellent works have been issued on phases of the institution and along various educational, denominational, and other lines. These fragmentary treatises have increased the demand for a general work giving a comprehensive view of the institution: (1) as a great laymen's movement, (2) as promoting a spirit of Christian unity for service, and (3) as a great missionary agency for the universal spread of the gospel of Christ—making it a remarkable phenomenon in the progress of Christianity.

The modern Sunday-school was not new in its teaching, but was so new in form as to require a long campaign of education and a practical test of its value for a generation before it won the confidence of the public and of the churches. From the first, however, it was advocated by Christian laymen of different creeds, aided here and there by clergymen who had the grace to perceive, and the grit and greatness to declare, that Christ's kingdom was larger and more important than any one or a score of sects into which Protestantism had divided. Its success in any community depended upon uniting existing Christian forces in its support. The founders were forced, therefore, to seek a basis of unity in Christian service. They found it in declaring for a positive teaching of the essential truths of the Bible as held by all Christians, and in a neutral attitude on those doctrines upon which they differed. The majority of the modern Sunday-schools in the early days were formed on this basis.

3

It seems fitting, therefore, to present any comprehensive narrative of the origin and progress of the institution in sympathy with that broad spirit of Christian charity and unity in which it was conceived, and also from a union point of view. Moreover, in any account of the modern Sunday-school, the American Sunday-School Union cannot fail to be recognized for its prominent pioneer service in shaping the institution and in extending it to the multitude of those otherwise unreached by the gospel, and in preparing and providing literature and aids to Bible study on the same principle of Christian unity in which the Sunday-school movement was itself conceived. Nor would any account of the American Sunday-School Union be regarded as adequate or satisfactory that did not give a reasonably full sketch of the conditions and influences which preceded, in the providence of God, the forming of the Union. It should also include some record of the multitude of varied denominational and interdenominational activities which have followed, and in some measure have been stimulated by the mission and services of the Union— activities which it aimed to promote at home and abroad. For the American Sunday-School Union has not sought nor wrought for itself, but for the Master's sake and for the spread of Christianity. Well-nigh 100,000 of its Union schools in almost as many fields have voluntarily ceased to be Union, and gladly transferred their members toward the founding or strengthening of churches of Christ of all denominations, according to their preferences. The task confronting the Society is even greater now than at any previous period of its history.

The scope and structure of this book naturally grew out of these facts and conditions. Painstaking care has been exercised to note the important epochs and events of the Sunday-school movement. These have been derived neither from tradition nor hearsay, but wholly or chiefly from first-hand information. This has called for extended research, and for the wisdom and discrimination of many minds, that have generously responded to the call of the author. They have greatly lightened the task not only by suggesting what was of worth and value and of interest to be included, but also in the more difficult art of deciding what might be excluded from the narrative.

While the record of the multiplied pioneer activities of the American Sunday-School Union for one hundred years called for a generous space in the narrative, it has been the chief purpose of the author to present:

(1) A clear and concise account of the origin and progress of the modern Sunday-school in England and of Sunday-school organizations in Great Britain.

(2) The phenomenal extension of the institution in America and in other countries of the world.

(3) The great enthusiasm in lay and voluntary teaching which it developed, enlisting Christians of every class and creed.

(4) The production and free circulation of masses of religious literature, supplying city, village, and rural communities of all English-speaking countries and of many mission fields throughout the world.

(5) The remarkable number of Sunday scholars added to the churches, and the universal interest aroused by national and international conventions and associations and assemblies, denominational and interdenominational, making the Sunday-school a world-wide power in spreading Christianity.

But the Sunday-school has not yet enlisted the world in Bible study or Bible reading. Serious problems and immense tasks still confront the fulfilment of its high ideals. Though the institution has passed the experimental stage, it is yet comparatively in its youthful period. Its origin and achievements to the present may be chronicled; its history cannot be written while its great work remains undone. At many points, therefore, the narrative may seem to the reader fragmentary. No one is more conscious of this than the author. He asks the reader not to forget that the institution itself is still making history.

The author has throughout the volume endeavored to acknowledge his indebtedness to the multitude of authors of special works on Sunday-school development. Lest any should have been omitted, he makes this general acknowledgment here of his obligations to all those who have written so fully upon the various phases of Sunday-school work, and to all others who have with marked kindness and alacrity responded to his requests for information.

Thanks are particularly due to the librarians of the Historical Society of New York, of the Union Theological Seminary, of the Boston Public Library, of the State Historical Society of Ohio, of the Philadelphia Library, and to many other librarians and curators for their courtesy in the free use of documents in their respective institutions, and for their helpful aid in discovering the hidden riches stored in their published and unpublished records. Similar obligations are due to prominent workers in America and abroad for many facts and suggestions contained in their correspondence. The author has aimed to make particular acknowledgment of these in the body of the work.

Special appreciation and thanks must be given also to the managers of the American Sunday-School Union, without whose cordial co-operation and generous action in relieving the author from other duties this work could not have been prepared.

The volume has been enriched by the painstaking care with which William H. Hirst, Business Superintendent of the American Sunday-School Union, has collated and grouped the engravings and portraits.

The author highly appreciates the valuable criticisms and suggestions of the Editor, Rev. James McConaughy, Litt.D., and of Rev. A. J. R. Schumaker, Assistant Editor, who carefully read the work.

A like recognition is made of suggestions in respect to the structure and form of the work by Rev. Moseley H. Williams, Ph.D.; for statistics of missionary work furnished by Rev. George P. Williams, D.D., Secretary of Missions; for financial information and facts provided by John E. Stevenson, Treasurer, and for the careful proof-reading, while the book was passing through the press, of V. Winfield Challenger.

The ghastly conflict into which the nations of Christendom have been suddenly hurled painfully reveals to us the little progress of all Christian instruction in making obedient disciples of Christ in the nations. The forces of the church through the Sunday-school with its lay teaching have scarcely begun the very elementary work of properly interpreting and exemplifying the gospel. We have been playing at this herculean task. It must be more seriously grasped if we are to win the world in the name of our Lord and Master, Jesus Christ.

Should this effort to portray the origin, spirit, and method of the Sunday-school movement in its effort to unite the whole world in the study of the Bible aid in giving a more intelligent grasp of the problem to Sunday-school workers, the author will devoutly thank God that he has been permitted to have a share in promoting a world-wide searching of the Scriptures.

EDWIN WILBUR RICE.

May, 1917.

CONTENTS

7

THE

SUNDAY-SCHOOL MOVEMENT

AND THE

AMERICAN SUNDAY-SCHOOL UNION

SECTION I

ORIGIN OF THE MODERN SUNDAY-SCHOOL

WHAT inspired the modern Sunday-school movement? How came it to be? We may reverently answer—God inspired it; social conditions and the spirit of Christianity called for it.

What was the condition of society in the eighteenth century? Look at the picture of Europe as drawn by such judicious historians as Green, Lecky, and Lord Mahon. The titled classes were spotted with moral rottenness! Glance at English peasant life in that period. Are not the life and manners of masters an index of the character of the servants?

Rural England in the Eighteenth Century.—No one can intelligently grasp the great incentive to the modern Sunday-school movement without some knowledge of the physical, intellectual, and moral conditions of the masses in that day. The farming classes bulked large in rural England. They were poorly housed and not well clothed or fed. The rustic dwelling was rudely put together of stone or pebbles mixed with mud, with a mud floor, a thatched roof, a smoky atmosphere, and little warmth. The dwelling consisted usually of two rooms, made by a thin partition, sometimes of old sacking hung on a line, which also answered for drying garments. Windows for light were rare. Often the door and the large fireplace answered both for light and ventilation.

11

Geese, chickens, pigs, and people not infrequently found shelter in the same rustic dwelling.

The clothing was coarse; the commonest article being a smock, which was a sexless garment. It was worn by men as a wagoner's frock; women tied it at the waist and it became a gown. The freshness and size of it indicated the prosperity of the wearer. Shoes were luxuries, wisps of straw sometimes kept the feet and legs warm in winter.

Women did farm work and were expert in using the fork for turning muckheaps. They could make barley and oaten bread, baked on hot bricks, or cakes cooked in hot ashes, but they knew less about cookery in general than about field work. Potatoes were rare; often there were none at all. Bread, beer, cheese, and coarse meat were the chief articles of diet. The meals were served on a long table in a big kitchen. Sometimes three or four generations met there, seated on high-backed settles, or on the floor with the chickens and pigs. The most hilarious meal was the supper, when the day's work was done. Master and mistress, farm hand, maids and children ate salt pork or barley bread from wooden trenchers or metal plates and drank liberally of beer or cider. Candles were of split rushes, dipped in fat, giving a sickly light. The farm hand slept on barley straw in the garret, under the rafters or thatched roof, and made his toilet with the master, mistress, and maids at the water trough in the yard.

Illiteracy was common. There was no system of national or popular education; few attended an elementary school. There were not 3,500 public and private schools, it was said, in all England. A private school kept by a woman was called a "Mam" school, and if kept by a man it was called a "Gaffar" school. School hours were uncertain, often depending on the number of visits the master made to the ale house, or on the domestic engagements of the woman. She made bread, spun, washed, and heard the children say their a-b-c's at the same time. The man often kept his school and his business running together. He might be a shopkeeper or blacksmith, as well as a schoolmaster. He could cipher just a little and make some flourishes with a quill pen. Usually he stimulated the ideas of his pupils with the branches of a birch tree that grew near the school. Sometimes the school was attached to the church and taught by the vicar, whose "living" amounted to five pounds a year, with a cottage and an acre of land. His church was the schoolhouse; and one vicar, Robert Walker, had a spinning wheel within the altar rail and is said to have used the communion table as his desk. He was attired in a cloth cap, wooden shoes, and a long gray gown, spun by his own hand, with a leathern strap tied around his waist. He sheared his own sheep, fed his own hogs, and attended market fairs. Such is the picture drawn by historians of peasant life in Christian countries in Europe, just before the rise of modern Sunday-schools.[1]

The rural masses formed about two-thirds of the population of England in the eighteenth century. Their intelligence was not developed by their occupations; it was not easy to find a poor man who could read. Even the clergymen were poorly paid, unlettered, and seldom taught more than a catechism to the children. Ignorance and vice abounded among the lower orders in cities and towns, and the Bible was a neglected book. Hannah More says that in Cheddar, near the cathedral city of Wells, she found wealthy farmers hard, brutal, and ignorant, and saw only one Bible in all the parish—and that was used to prop a flower pot.[2]

The better classes sometimes patronized religion by attending cathedrals and churches in the towns. Lord Mahon says, "Throughout England, the education of the laboring class was most grievously neglected, the supineness of the clergy of that age being manifest on this point as on every other."

The reader will notice that these pictures are not drawn by bilious clergymen, nor by pious Sunday-school or theological writers—they are given by unbiased historians.

Out of this social condition—Christianity dying of respectability on the one hand and confronted by a seething mass of ignorance and nameless vices on the other—came the modern Sunday-school movement.

Robert Raikes.—The wretched condition of the working classes and of their children aroused the sympathy of Robert Raikes, a printer and publisher of Gloucester, England.

---

[1] On condition of wage-owners in England, 1830–1840, see G. M. Trevelyan, *Life of John Bright*, p. 58, ff.

[2] William Roberts, *Memoirs of the Life and Correspondence of Hannah More*, Two Volumes, New York, 1834.

Robert Raikes (1736–1811) inherited the trade of printer from his father, and began the modern Sunday-school movement in 1780, in Gloucester. His early biographers were fond of portraying his eccentricities. He was described by them as pompous, "a buck," a dandy, a faddist, and "Bobby Wild Goose." J. Henry Harris, his latest biographer, has given a more accurate and faithful portrait of Raikes, as a broadminded, far-seeing, philanthropic Christian, far in advance of his age. He had eyes trained to see, and a generous heart to sympathize with the suffering poor.

His first efforts were to secure a reform in the conditions of jails and prisons, rendering the life of a prisoner at least endurable. Failing in this enterprise, he began his new experiment of the modern Sunday-school, which swiftly gained a place among the most important of modern religious institutions. His mind was turned to this work by seeing from his window the neglected and ragged children playing, quarreling, cursing, and fighting, and hearing them use language too coarse to repeat.

One of the chief industries of Gloucester at that time was pin-making, at which the children worked as well as the parents. Seeing this sad waste of child life, Raikes began to ask himself why he should not begin reform with the children. "Is vice preventable? If so, it is better to prevent crime than to punish it. Can these ignorant masses be lifted out of this ragged, wretched, vicious state?" Thus Raikes discovered a great field for "botanizing in human nature," and "planting seed plots," to grow something worthy and respectable out of this seething "slum of moral filth."

He knew the children and their homes and their habits. It was useless to appeal to the parents; so he began directly with the children, in the belief that ignorance is the first cause of idleness and vice. He held that betterment could come to these children—these pin-makers and their homes through religious instruction alone.

His first school was in Sooty Alley, in 1780. The scholars were from the lowest strata of society. Some were from sweeps' quarters and the "Island," places of the worst repute. Some were so unwilling to come that he marched them to the school with clogs and logs of wood tied to their feet and legs, just as cattle were hobbled when grazing on the town commons in that day.

He rented a kitchen of Mrs. Meredith and paid her for it, and also for acting as mistress to these wretched children. She found the boys bad and the girls worse, and gave up her job in despair. The children were transferred to Mrs. Chritchley's house in Southgate Street, under another mistress. This building faced St. Mary de Crypt Church, and Raikes' house was also opposite. The children were required to come with clean hands and faces, hair combed, and with such clothing as they had, Raikes sometimes providing shoes and better clothes. Discipline was maintained, the boys being "strapped and caned" by Raikes himself. The girls were subdued in other ways. School was from ten to twelve o'clock in the morning. On Sundays the scholars returned at one, and after a lesson were taken to church. After church service they were taught the catechism, and sent home about five o'clock, charged not to play in the streets. Good behavior was rewarded by Bibles, Testaments, books, games, shoes, and clothing. The mistress was paid a shilling a day, which sometimes included the rent of the kitchen.

The teaching was not all done by the mistress. In the boys' classes (usually five in the class) the advanced pupils acted as "monitors" or teachers to the younger ones. So the voluntary principle was a feature of Raikes' schools. The girls were in classes in a separate room. They came, sometimes, with white tippets on their shoulders, and white caps on their heads, and they had "monitors" as special instructors. This mutual or monitorial system was applied by Raikes a decade before Andrew Bell or Joseph Lancaster proposed a similar system in day-schools.

Some writers on the early history of the Sunday-school movement have held that the credit of starting it should be divided with clergymen, but Harris has quite clearly shown that the vicar of St. Mary's did not take any personal interest in the schools, and Raikes himself declares that it was six years before the clergymen gave him any assistance. (Appendix, p. 439.)

The Rev. Thomas Stock, a rector in Gloucester and a relative of Raikes by marriage, had an entirely different view in respect to these schools. He consented to examine the progress made in Raikes' schools and to aid in discipline and decorum. He is also reputed to have started and superintended schools, but there is no evidence to show that he, in any measure, entered into the study of neglected child life, or contemplated making the modern Sunday-school a part of the organic work of the Church. The schools he had were parochial and for education in general. Raikes' movement aimed at popular religious education for the poor, the main textbook being the Bible. The Church had neglected the masses, and the masses had retaliated by neglecting the Church. Raikes faced this problem, and successfully made the experiment of redeeming the worst classes and cleaning up the slum life of that city, revealing first principles in popular religious education on the voluntary principle. Out of it grew a plan for national popular education.

Raikes' plan seems so simple to us now that many wonder why it was not begun long before. It must not be forgotten, however, that up to 1779 English law allowed no person to keep public or private school, or to act as tutor, who did not subscribe and conform to the Church of England. It was not until 1779 that the "Enabling Act" took full effect, which permitted dissenters to teach without such subscription.

Raikes evolved out of his studies and experiments these maxims:

1. Vice in the child is an imitation of familiar sights and sounds.
2. There is a time in the child's life when it is innocent. Then the faculties are active and receptive.
3. Good seeds cannot be planted too early.
4. The child takes pleasure in being good when goodness is made attractive.
5. The Sunday-school may be the instrument under God of awakening spiritual life in the poorest children and, supplemented by day classes, can form the basis of national education.

When he was satisfied that his scheme had passed the experimental stage, he made it public. His plan was explained to some distinguished guests—William Wilberforce, John

Wesley, and others, whom he took to his schools to listen to the children repeat prayers, sing hymns, and answer Bible questions. It is said they were astonished at the progress he had made with these ragged, ignorant children. A brief notice of his experiment was published in his *Gloucester Journal*, November 3, 1783. (Appendix, p. 437.) It was widely copied. *The Gentleman's Magazine*, issued in London by John Nichols, fully described the schools, inserting the letter of Raikes to Col. Townley dated November 25, 1783. In these ways the knowledge of the movement became widely known in Great Britain.

The primary aim of Raikes was to reach the poor and neglected children; hence the plan commended itself to many philanthropic and thoughtful persons, by whom it was warmly advocated.

The Voluntary Principle.—Contrary to the representations of the early biographers of Raikes (Lloyd, Power, Gregory, Pray, and others), and contrary to the popular notion, it has been clearly shown by Raikes' latest biographers that Raikes applied the voluntary principle from the first. (Appendix p. 438.) "The system," says Harris, "was founded on and supported by voluntary effort. Paid mistresses and masters were at first necessary, but they gradually disappeared. The monitors over classes were unpaid and voluntary from the beginning of his schools." The paid mistress or master of Raikes' schools was a superintendent. The strictly class teachers were unpaid, and voluntary examiners or supervisors, appointed or selected by Raikes, visited the schools to see that the instruction was given according to his wishes and to those of the supporters of the enterprise.

Experience soon proved that even the paid mistress and master made the system expensive and tended to limit its usefulness. If monitors, visitors, and others could be found to give their time, why might not persons competent for oversight as well, and thus all the instruction be secured without pay? The most important step in the founding of the system, therefore, was the replacing of the paid mistress or the paid master by voluntary masters, superintendents, and teachers. Raikes had used voluntary class teachers from the first, but he had paid the mistress partly for rent and partly for supervision. "The paid teacher, at first," says Harris, "was made responsible for the good behaviour, cleanliness, and ability of the children to read and repeat their lessons; then the work of the Sunday-school as a religious agency passed into other hands, whose work was purely voluntary."[1] This feature of wholly voluntary instruction and management adapted the Sunday-school to the needs of poor communities and parishes, and aided in its remarkable spread throughout Great Britain and America.

Raikes' Instruction.—The Bible was the center of Raikes' instruction. There was no public-school system and the masses were unlearned. Therefore he found it necessary to teach many persons to read in order to give them instruction in the Bible. One of his earlier books was called *The Sunday Scholar's Companion*. It was a little manual, compiled, it is said, by the Rev. Richard Raikes, and widely used in the schools formed by Raikes and others. It was surely in use in 1783, though the earliest edition now known is that of 1794. It passed through many editions and was issued up to 1824. Among other books used at this period were *A Copious School Book* and *A Comprehensive Sentimental Book*— the last containing the alphabet, spelling, moral and religious lessons, and stories and prayers adapted to "the growing powers of children."

Parochial schools used catechisms, creeds, and confessions, but Raikes and his followers used them only as secondary works, their chief textbook of instruction being the Bible. Herein was a radical difference between most of the early sporadic schools, previous to Raikes, and the modern Sunday-school movement which he started.[2] (Appendix, pp. 439 and 440.) It was a practical revolution in the system of instruction and gave much popularity to the plan. Not only did Raikes make a revolution by basing instruction upon the Bible, but he also made a marked change in the methods of instruction. Aside from applying the voluntary principle in teaching, he also applied the illustrative method. He gives a good instance of this himself.

---

[1] J. Henry Harris, *The Story of the Sunday-School*, p. 50.
[2] *A Comprehensive View of Sunday-Schools* was prepared by Jonas Hanway in 1786, a copy of which is in the possession of W. H. Groser of London. See Groser's *A Hundred Years' Work for the Children.*

"I was," he says, "showing my scholars, a little time ago, how possible it is for one invisible power to exist in bodies which shall act upon other bodies without our being able to perceive in what manner they act. This I proved to them by the powers of the magnet. They see the magnet draw the needle without touching it. Thus, I tell them, I wish to draw them to the paths of duty, and thus lead them to heaven and happiness; and as they saw one needle, when it touched the magnet, then capable of drawing another needle, thus when they became good they would be made the instruments in the hands of God, very probably, of making other boys good." Thus it is clear that Raikes understood from the first the illustrative method of instruction and intelligently applied it in his earliest schools.

Besides the books prepared by the Rev. Richard Raikes, and the two mentioned above which were prepared by Jonas Hanway, a philanthropist and noted traveler, the earlier schools had stories for the instruction and entertainment of children translated from the French and issued in 1787. Mrs. Trimmer compiled a manual for the use of Sunday scholars, and Hannah More issued a religious manual, entitled *The Mendig School Question Book*. But the chief manual, aside from the Bible, appears to have been *The Scholar's Companion*. The extant edition, 1794, has 120 pages divided into four parts. Part I has the alphabet and twenty-five simple lessons. The sentences are biblical, thus:

God is One.   The Lord is good to all.
God is love.   The Lord of Hosts is His name.
          The God of the whole earth, etc.

The other three parts of the book consist, chiefly, of passages from the Old and New Testaments, stating man's duty to God and to his neighbor. There is some history—the Creation, and the Fall and Redemption, and the observance of the Sabbath. The four parts are intended to be graded to suit the advance of pupils in knowledge.

Opposition to the Sunday-School.—In Great Britain there was a decided and, in some cases, bitter opposition to the Sunday-school itself. In America it was chiefly against the organized and Union type of the movement, as we shall presently see. In England the objection to Sunday-schools was that they were dangerous, demoralizing, bad institutions, and agents of the devil.

Hannah More and her sisters, who fostered schools among the poor, were condemned and their teachers persecuted by curates of the church, until she appealed to the bishop, gaining no redress beyond a diplomatic letter. Miss More says, "The aim of the curates was not merely to ruin the teachers employed, but to strike at the principles of all my schools and to stigmatize them as seminaries of fanaticism, vice and sedition."[1] They not only arrested her teachers, but assailed her personal character, charging her with hiring men to assassinate one of the clergymen, fomenting sedition, and even countenancing an attack on the king's life, and, finally, that she was in the pay of Mr. Pitt, and a prime instigator of French plots! The Bishop of Rochester denounced Sunday-schools and urged his clergy not to support them. The Archbishop of Canterbury received such attacks upon the new movement that he called the bishops together to decide what could be done to stop it. They believed it would injure the Church and would build up conventicles and dissenting chapels. (Appendix, p. 440.)

Some of the English nobility urged that if the vulgar were educated they would become supercilious, make poor servants, and want higher wages, and the higher classes would be embarrassed, if not obliterated. The worldly and tippling classes opposed the Sunday-school on the ground that it would end their amusements—games, cock-fighting, bull-baiting, wakes, revels, and tippling—and the publicans said it would destroy ale-houses and taverns. They tried to prejudice the people by telling them that Sunday-schools would take away their liberties and deprive them of all the enjoyments of life.

Advocates for It.—The sharp attack of foes served one good purpose; that of rallying friends to the support of the Sunday-school. It advertised the new movement, calling attention to its necessity and efficiency, and made the people think of the splendid opportunity it offered for the betterment of social conditions—physically and morally. While

[1] William Roberts, *Memoirs of Hannah More*, Vol. II, p. 63, ff.

this movement began *in* the church, it was by a layman, and was individual rather than ecclesiastical. It soon found some strong advocates among dissenters and churchmen alike. Rowland Hill answered, "In this grand design, we drop all names but Christ, and direct the children not to be dissenters from the Church, but dissenters from sin." John Newton, William Cowper the poet, Thomas Scott, John Howard the philanthropist, John and Charles Wesley, Bishop Porteus of Chester—later of London, the Bishops of Norwich, Salisbury, Llandaff, and the Earl of Salisbury, rallied to its defence and became hearty supporters. Even some ladies of fashion volunteered to become teachers. It progressed so rapidly that the queen herself gave it royal favor by sending for Robert Raikes and hearing the story of his work from his own lips.[1]

Organized Sunday-School Societies.—"Teach all the world the Bible; ask all the world to help us in the mighty task!" This was the inspiring word that gave spiritual power to the founders of organized Sunday-school societies. Filled by the Holy Spirit with a passion for teaching the Gospel of Christ, they conquered impossibilities.

The Sunday-School Society of 1785.—William Fox, a London merchant, astonished a monthly meeting of his brethren by proposing a society to teach all the children of the poor to read the Bible. Amazed by the magnitude of the proposition, deemed chimerical, they said, "We presume you would confine the plan to our Baptist denomination?" But Fox replied, "No, every person in the world should be able to read the Bible and we must call on all the world to help us."

Later Fox heard of the movement of Raikes, but claims that long before 1780 he had conceived the plan of universal education by a different mode. A correspondence with Raikes, however, changed his plan into that of a society for promoting the formation of Sunday-schools. Persons of different denominations, led by Fox, Henry Thornton, Jonas Hanway, Thomas Raikes, and others, formed the Sunday-School Society, in London, September 7, 1785. The full name at first was "The Society for the Support and Encour-

[1] J. Henry Harris, *Robert Raikes: The Man and His Work*, p. 128.

agement of Sunday-Schools in the Different Counties of England." As the work extended to Wales, Ireland and the British colonies, the name was changed to "The Society for the Support and Encouragement of Sunday-Schools throughout the British Dominions." It was popularly known by the shorter title of "The Sunday-School Society."

The novelty of the organization and the prominence of its founders brought it at once into popular favor, so that for some years it carried on a large work in Sunday-school extension. The method of the society was to lease rooms or buildings in villages or localities where the poor needed instruction, hire teachers, and maintain schools under rules adopted by the society, provide Bibles, Testaments, and other needed books gratuitously for the pupils, and have each school inspected by competent visitors; making all proceedings subject to the approval of a general committee composed of twenty-four persons, one-half of whom were from the Church of England, and the other half from dissenting denominations. In twenty-seven years it formed or aided 3,730 Sunday-schools, having a membership of 303,981; gave away 8,001 Bibles, 70,537 Testaments, and 329,695 spelling and reading books. It discontinued paid teachers in 1810, when it had expended 4,383 pounds, 15 shillings, 4 pence.

But it declined to change its methods, and its work gradually diminished. The founding of other societies and schools with voluntary teachers, and its refusal to sell rather than give its literature to schools, caused the income to decrease and rapidly exhausted its funds, until the society, after long struggles, voluntarily dissolved.

The London Sunday-School Union.—Under Raikes and the Sunday-School Society of 1785, the Sunday-school movement had been chiefly a philanthropic one. Now it began to emerge into a wider movement for religious education. In one school an earnest young worker, William Brodie Gurney, was astonished at the "improvements" he observed in another school. He learned that still other schools were better than either of these two, and he asked; "Why not get Sunday-school teachers together and improve the method of instruction, and stimulate others to open new schools in London?"

ENGLISH FOUNDERS

William Fox.

W. Brodie Gurney.

Robert Raikes.

William Groser.

W. F. Lloyd.

Mr. Gurney was scarcely twenty-five years old and his two friends hardly eighteen. They called a meeting in Surrey Chapel, where the famous Rowland Hill was minister, and formed the London Sunday-School Union, July 13, 1803. Paid teachers had been largely supplanted by voluntary ones, but instruction of the poorer classes was still the special purpose of the movement. The introduction of it into the churches was very limited and came only after weary waiting.

The chief purpose of the London Union was to improve Sunday-schools and thus promote some system in religious education. The Union was without a local habitation and did not hold an annual public meeting for nine years. Then they had a "breakfast" in the New London Tavern in May, 1812.[1] Not until fifteen years after its formation did it venture to rent part of a bookseller's shopwindow (44 Newgate Street) where Sunday-school supplies could be seen and purchased. Previous to this the Union met in schoolrooms or, more frequently, at the houses of the officers. As one of its chroniclers said, it was in a "peripatetic state," and its growth was slow.[2] In 1855 it erected a fine memorial building at 56 Old Bailey, London. About 1805 it reported four publications—a *Plan for Forming Sunday-Schools*, a *Guide to Teachers*, a *Catechism in Verse*, and a *Reading Primer* in two parts—all apparently pamphlets. That this was a day of small things was more apparent, however, than real. The Union kept faithfully in view its chief objects; namely, "to stimulate and encourage the education and religious instruction of the young;" "to improve the methods of instruction;" "to promote the opening of new schools;" and "to furnish literature suited for Sunday-schools at a cheap rate."

W. F. Lloyd, a talented young man who had achieved success in Sunday-school work, became secretary of the Union in 1811. Under his leadership the Union came into greater prominence and wider usefulness. He became personally responsible for the issue of *The Repository* or *Teachers' Magazine*, a periodical which was edited with such ability and wisdom as to attain a high rank with educators. The sys-

[1] W. H. Watson, *History of the Sunday-School Union.*
[2] W. H. Groser, *A Hundred Years' Work for the Children.*

tems of study and the literature of the London Union bore the impress of his judicious mind for nearly a quarter of a century. In harmony with its union or interdenominational character, publications were issued from time to time, chiefly of an elementary grade, for use in its affiliated schools. In London and throughout England, local unions were formed auxiliary to the parent Union, each of them being represented by a secretary and three members who, with twenty other members chosen on the committee at an annual meeting, directed the affairs of the London Sunday-School Union. Supplies were furnished at special prices to members of the Union, and grants of publications were made when its funds warranted. The formation of Sunday and adult schools was promoted, and also some aid given in housing and equipping them. The London Union also rendered important service in issuing suggestive plans for better Sunday-school rooms and, later, in loaning money, or granting aid toward making these improvements.

As early as 1810–15 its leaders discussed the adoption of theories of various educators, such as the mutual or "monitorial" system of Joseph Lancaster and Andrew Bell. But progress in this direction was blocked by a system of secular education proposed by Mr. Brougham, who inclined toward the views of Robert Owen, de Fellenberg, and others, and who placed small value upon Sunday-schools. In fact, he spoke of them in depreciating terms. If his plan prevailed, he said, they would be no longer needed. The defects of Brougham's scheme were attacked by John Foster in his famous essay on *The Evils of Popular Ignorance*, with such vigor and success that the plan failed to gain popular favor. But the agitation over it is said to have put back any public effort to remove the evils of popular ignorance for twenty— if not fifty—years, and seriously affected the progress of Sunday-schools.

The monitorial system of Joseph Lancaster was more popular and paved the way for the British and Foreign School Society in 1808. The somewhat similar system of Dr. Bell led to the organization of the National School Society in 1811. The latter limited religious instruction to the catechisms and creed of the Church of England, while the former excluded all catechisms and creeds, and required that the Bible only should be the basis of religious instruction.

About a decade later, the ingenious Lesson System of James Gall of Scotland became popular with the British Sunday-schools, displacing the learning by rote, the London Union strongly commending Gall's method. It was, however, sharply criticized for its deficiencies and partially supplanted by the Training System of David Stow. Stow exposed the fallacy of regarding *instruction* and *education* as one and the same. He noted the value of combining the interrogative, illustrative, and elliptical methods of teaching, and applied his principle to religious and moral, as well as to secular, instruction. These systems had advocates, but each of them was soon supplanted by other methods. The monitorial system of Lancaster, which was necessarily crude since it must use untrained teachers, fell into disuse in England and America. However, it had served the purpose of improving and extending the plan of unpaid or voluntary teaching in Sunday-schools.

The London Union, in common with other Sunday-school societies, considered the adaptation of some features of the so-called nature system, of Pestalozzi, the verbal and self-educative theory of Jacotot and the "spontaneity" idea of Froebel, culling some good features from each of these theories. During this period their lists of lessons changed from year to year and were largely empirical or experimental. Besides promoting teacher-training through circulating the works on principles of education by Henry Dunn, David Stow, Louisa M. Davids, and J. G. Fitch, the Union sustained training classes and had a "Sunday-School Union College for Teachers," which provided lectures, and had a temporary prosperity. This was followed by "Introductory," "Normal," and "Preparation" classes for teachers. The last proved more successful and satisfactory under B. P. Pask. Normal handbooks were issued later, and "Correspondence Classes" encouraged, including "Greek New Testament Classes," which became popular in the second decade of this century. A Sunday-school teachers' college was opened in Birmingham in 1900 by Dr. R. F. Horton, giving instruction in nine courses of study, including Bible history, Church history, Christian evidences, art of teaching, ethics, the English language, sociology and psychology.

Union Lessons.—About 1841 the London Union issued two series of Sunday-school lessons, with notes, questions and applications, but without the Bible text. One series was used in the morning session of English Sunday-schools and the other in the afternoon session. The helps were issued in a monthly tract of twelve pages. They did not provide reviews—weekly or quarterly—as the American Uniform Lessons of 1826 had done. They assigned such large portions of the Bible text for each lesson that they were better suited for advanced classes than for the main school, and were not widely used outside of England. Similar series of lessons were continued with changes and some improvements until the London Union adopted the "International Series," approved in America about 1872. This series, with some changes to meet English conditions, was continued into the present century. The British section of the Lesson Committee, appointed by the London Union, prepared a series of graded lessons to meet the demands of modern educators—a system differing from any of those proposed in America and limiting the grading by departments rather than by years. It also issues numerous lesson helps.

When the work of the Sunday-School Society of 1785 declined, the Union gradually took it up, including a mission for the extension of Sunday-schools on the Continent and elsewhere throughout the world. It was stimulated to do this by the zeal of Albert Woodruff, of America, who sought to introduce Sunday-schools into Germany, France and other countries of the Continent. This mission of the London Union has extended to India, China, and Japan, in co-operation with other associations abroad and in America. It prosecutes this mission by the employment of agents and special workers in the respective countries.

The International Bible Readers' Association (affiliated with the London Sunday-School Union) pledges its members to read a definite portion of the Bible daily. It claims about a million of such readers in nearly one hundred different countries. The London Union also maintains a reading room for teachers and a reference library and preparation classes for the training and qualifying of teachers in different centers in Great Britain. The society is chiefly supported by Independents or Congregationalists, Baptists, and Presbyterians. Its affairs are under the direction of a "Council" (formerly a General Committee), composed of persons selected from these denominations by the Council or by local Sunday-school unions. The Church of England and several Nonconformist religious bodies in Great Britain have separate Sunday-school societies in their respective denominations.

The London Union has always made a liberal use of the press. Besides the books heretofore mentioned, it early issued editions of Watts' *Divine and Moral Songs*, Ann and Jane Taylor's *Hymns for Infant Minds*, a tune book, and a juvenile harmonist, with collections for the young. Of periodicals, it approved the issue of Mr. Lloyd's *Sunday-School Repository* or *Teachers' Magazine*, first issued in 1813 as a quarterly and, in 1821, as a monthly, and adopted it in 1859. This, again, was succeeded by *The Sunday-School Teacher*, and in 1874 by *The Sunday-School Chronicle*, edited at first by the versatile Benjamin Clarke, and continued under the judicious Rev. Frank Johnson.

Of scholars' periodicals, *The Youth's Magazine* was issued about 1805, by Mr. Gurney, personally. From 1810 to 1830 scholars' periodicals were born and perished young, in sufficient numbers to fill a good-sized literary cemetery.

In 1832 *The Child's Own Book*, a serial publication, was begun at the low price of a half-penny a piece and continued until 1851, when it was supplanted by *The Child's Own Magazine*, a penny monthly. *The Bible Class Magazine* was commenced in 1848 and had a useful career; it was superseded by *The Excelsior* and then by *The Golden Rule*. *Kind Words* was founded in 1866, but in 1880 was changed to *Young England*, followed by *Boys of Our Empire* and *Girls of Our Empire*.

The London Union at its centenary in 1903 reported in its connection or affiliated with it 8,584 Sunday-schools, having 213,226 teachers and 2,252,497 scholars. In 1912 the Union reported loans to aid in school buildings amounting to 4,500 pounds, and benevolent contributions received on personal subscriptions and donations, 15,053 pounds, 10 shillings, 7 pence, exclusive of legacies and life memberships. It also received moneys on account of its general work amounting to 6,852 pounds, 2 shillings, 7 pence, and on account of various benevolent operations, such as the Bible Reading Association, home rests, lectures, children's homes, and the like, other sums which it appropriates to these various objects. In the second decade of the twentieth century the London Sunday-School Union counted 25,655 schools, 258,849 teachers, and 2,680,379 pupils in the United Kingdom, British colonies and India. The Church of England also reported a total membership in its schools (not in the Union) of upward of 3,500,000.

The Hibernian Sunday-School Society of Ireland.—The Hibernian Sunday-School Society was formed in Dublin in 1809, "to promote the establishment and facilitate the conducting of Sunday-schools in Ireland," by disseminating information, supplying spelling books and the Holy Scriptures at reduced prices, or by donation, and by "confining religious instruction solely to the sacred Scriptures or to extracts therefrom." The affairs of the society were conducted by fifteen members residing in Dublin. The receipts and expenditures the first year were upward of 450 pounds sterling. In 1816 the name of the society was changed to the "Sunday-School Society for Ireland." In the thirtieth year of its history, 1840, its receipts, including about 625 pounds from sales, were 3,245 pounds; over one-half of this sum coming from contributors in England. The total number of books and publications granted to schools in the thirty years was 605,740 Bibles and Testaments, 954,632 spellers, 5,964 *Hints for Conducting Sunday-Schools*, and over 400,000 class, roll, and minute books and alphabet cards.

The London Hibernian Society.—The above society must not be confounded with the London Hibernian Society, which was formed in 1806 in London. The Hibernian Society of London sustained three classes of schools; week-day, adult, and Sunday-schools. The founding and sustaining of Sunday-schools was incorporated into its work some years after its formation. In its twentieth report (1826) it claimed to have under its care 405 Sunday-schools, with 27,646 scholars.

This report throws some light on the conditions of the Irish population in that period: "Immense numbers of the Irish spend their Sabbaths at feasts or fairs, in fighting, wrestling, drinking, and other abominable practices, in which they mutually corrupt and are corrupted. By collecting the rising generation into Sunday-schools, they are not only restrained from such deteriorating practices, but are taught to read the Word of God, and are habituated from early years to keep holy this day."[1]

Neither of the foregoing societies should be confounded with the later *Sabbath-School Society for Ireland*, which has for its object to "promote and encourage the work of Sabbath-school teaching, especially in connection with the Presbyterian Church." This society was founded in 1862 in Belfast. By its fiftieth report (1912) there were under its care 1,037 schools, with 9,118 teachers and 81,928 scholars in "average attendance." Its receipts and expenditures for that year were upward of 10,000 pounds, chiefly from sales of publications. Its benevolent receipts amounted to about 675 pounds.

Church of England Sunday-School Institute.—The Church of England Sunday-School Institute was formed in 1843. Its object is "the extension and improvement of Church of England Sunday-schools." Its work is directed by a committee of about fifty persons, half of whom are clergymen and the other half laymen. It has about four hundred branch or local associations, holds institutes, issues publications, has teacher-training classes, examinations, and lectures. It provides a series of lessons and manuals on organization and teaching, school material and magazines, and has branches for the sale of the same. It offers to provide competent "deputations" to attend meetings of teachers, give lectures and training lessons, and visit Sunday-schools to suggest plans for their improvement.

In 1850 it issued for its schools a double series of lessons, with notes. Its serial lessons on "The Life of our Lord," by Eugene Stock (1870 on) were widely used in church Sunday-schools in England and were received with favor in other English schools and in America. Its lessons usually follow

---

[1] *Teachers' Magazine*, London, 1826, p. 216.

the church year. For a brief time it attempted to use the "International Lessons," but they did not prove acceptable to its schools and were abandoned. It provided a five years' course of lessons, based on the Bible and Prayer Book, and conforming to the church year. Since its formation, the Institute claims to have issued no less than one hundred and ten different sets of lessons. Its benevolent receipts in its Jubilee Year (1893) were 2,213 pounds and its receipts from sales and publications 10,863 pounds. It has held teacher-training courses of lectures and "training weeks" for teachers and intending teachers of both sexes, in the dioceses of England. Its Sunday-schools and Bible classes have a total membership of about 3,500,000. More than 1,000 persons have annually been enrolled for examinations as teachers. The confirmations of scholars from its schools have yearly exceeded a quarter of a million. Its yearly receipts from sales of publications have slightly decreased in the last twenty years.

The Wesleyan Sunday-School Union.—This organization was formed in England in 1875. It was merged into the Wesleyan Methodist Sunday-School Department about 1908. This is controlled by a "Council" of forty-five ministers and an equal number of laymen, which works through a smaller committee. The committee employs a competent person who gives special study to the improvement of its Sunday-schools. Grants are made to village schools of less than fifty scholars; other schools are aided in equipment and by examination of teachers' training classes, and conventions are held at various centers. This committee watches the results closely, and with some anxiety. In 1912 it reported: Wesleyan schools 7,565; officers and teachers, 130,516; scholars, 964,309; with members of Bible classes and brotherhoods, 122,836. The report adds: "It is discouraging to have, for six years in succession, to report a decrease in the number of our scholars of 12,443. It is high time that we most earnestly face the question, 'Why?'" The committee, in brief, ascribes the decrease partly to lack of interest, want of careful oversight and of systematic effort, and to the weakening of parental authority, the disregard of the Lord's day, and recent developments of Christian work. The graded plan was said to be gaining recognition. The report relates to the Wesleyan Methodist schools in Great Britain and Ireland, but not to those in the British colonies of America, Australia, Africa and Asia.

Sabbath-Schools in Scotland.—Sabbath-schools in Scotland are traced back to 1560, when part of the Lord's day was set apart for "catechising the young and ignorant." The churches laid the oversight of this work upon the ministry. The modern lay Sabbath-school movement followed. Thus the Edinburgh Gratis Sabbath-School Society was formed in October, 1796, with the proviso that its "schools be taught by members of the society without receiving any emolument or fee whatever." Similar schools were also formed in Aberdeen, Glasgow, and other towns of Scotland, chiefly however using catechisms in their instruction. The most active society for two generations was the Glasgow Sabbath-School Union, into which several previous organizations were merged in 1838. Out of this union came the Scottish National Sabbath-School Union, formed in 1898. Its objects are "to encourage, unite and increase Sabbath-schools and district unions in Scotland, improve the methods of conducting them, circulate information and give useful suggestions." The affairs of this union are conducted by twenty or more directors, annually elected, together with representatives from district unions. Its members include Sabbath-schools and unions in Scotland that send a report yearly to the national society, provided they hold the doctrines of "divine inspiration of the Holy Scriptures," "the deity and atonement of the Lord Jesus Christ," and "the personality and influence of the Holy Spirit." In the first decade of this century it had 1,746 schools, 29,307 teachers, and 295,590 scholars. It aims to promote the improvement of schools through normal training classes, by correspondence, by issuing works on child study, by conferences, examinations, reference and traveling libraries, by Scripture picture lending schemes, and by a monthly Sabbath-school magazine. It employs a traveling missionary and contributes toward the support of the foreign Sunday-school missionary in India. It encourages the formation of temperance societies, advocates better Sabbath observance and wider evangelistic services. The church of Scotland also has a committee which publishes *The Teachers' Magazine*, maintains examinations for both teachers and scholars, and issues schemes of lessons for the two large Presbyterian bodies of Scotland.

Sunday-Schools in Continental Europe.—The modern Sunday-school movement, which was so popular in Great Britain and America, has made slow progress upon the continent of Europe. Early in the nineteenth century, the London Sunday-School Union and the American Sunday-School Union made appropriations, from time to time, to aid in promoting popular Bible study in Europe.

Protestant countries of Europe maintain methods of religious education through parochial schools and churches, which in their estimation are quite effective and, along some lines, more effective, in creating Christian character than the modern Sunday-school. Religious training is not overlooked in these countries where Protestantism prevails.

In Germany, day-schools give general instruction in religion as well as in the sciences. This instruction may be based upon catechisms and general histories rather than upon the Bible. Nevertheless, it is instruction in religion in accordance with scientific school methods. In some parts of the German Empire illiteracy is less than in any other country of the world. The monks vigorously opposed the new learning of the Reformation era and the Roman Catholic influence is not counted favorable to the teaching of religion in the *Volksschule*. The Romanists desire to have their children instructed in the schools conducted exclusively by the church. The monks in the earlier period said, "The New Testament is a book full of serpents and thorns." A similar conflict in respect to principles of religious education took place in Switzerland, where it was a question whether the school should be denominational or not. A provision of the government finally stipulated that instruction in religion should be optional, as the parents of the children might decide. They were to be taught, however, by their parish clergymen, and the government teachers were not to interfere in that instruction.

In Roman Catholic countries the study of the Bible is rarely encouraged—generally discouraged. The people are urged to learn the peculiar forms of worship and doctrines of the Roman Church, through catechisms, elementary works, and parochial schools. Whatever we may think of their instruction, many in those countries esteem it satisfactory because it holds their children loyal to their particular forms of faith.

The modern Sunday-school movement was introduced into Sweden over sixty years ago by Lady Ehrenborg, who became acquainted with the system through the Crystal Palace Exhibition in London, in 1851. In this movement she was aided by Mr. Palmquist—a public-school teacher in Stockholm. The system has become more popular and grown with greater rapidity in Sweden, perhaps, than in any other continental country. It claims about 7,000 Sunday-schools, with 24,500 teachers and upward of 320,000 scholars.

In the Netherlands, Protestants are in the majority and are active, having had a Netherlands Sunday-School Union since 1865. It issued lesson helps, translating some of those on the International Uniform Lessons published by the American Sunday-School Union. It has upward of 2,000 schools, with 5,000 teachers, and about 214,800 scholars.

Owing to the political conditions in France and the peculiar religious controversies in that country, the modern Sunday-school has not advanced there in proportion to the efforts made for its introduction. The London Sunday-School Union appropriated money for the founding of a school by a French pastor as early as 1812. The first school in Paris opened in 1818. The second was founded by Dr. Monod in 1842, and the French Sunday-School Society was founded as early as 1857. This flourished for a time under the efforts of the late J. Paul Cook, who issued a Sunday-school magazine. The cause was further promoted, to some extent, by the efforts of Dr. McAll and his mission in Paris. Altogether France reports about 1,200 schools, with 7,000 teachers and 67,000 scholars.

The introduction of the modern Sunday-school into Germany began in 1834, but was promoted by the efforts of Albert Woodruff of Brooklyn, New York—a vice-president of the American Sunday-School Union—who succeeded in founding modern Sunday-schools there. He enlisted the London Sunday-School Union in a continental mission which included not only Germany, but France, Switzerland and Italy, and it has since extended to many other countries of the East. A Sunday-school convention was held in Berlin in 1891. The friends of the movement there claim about 9,000 schools, with 30,000 teachers and 950,000 scholars.

In Norway and Denmark, modern Sunday-schools were stimulated greatly, about 1877, by a native missionary employed by the London Sunday-School Union. They have taken more kindly to these newer methods than some of the other continental countries, having in Denmark about 1,400 schools, with 5,000 teachers and 92,000 scholars; and in Norway about 1,044 schools, with 6,000 officers and teachers, and over 106,000 scholars. In Italy, Austria, Spain, and Portugal, the modern Sunday-school movement has taken root, but its growth is necessarily slow in these papal lands. Recently there has been a marked awakening in Italy, under the influence of the Waldensian Society, the missionaries of the Methodist Episcopal Church of America, and the work of the late Mr. Van Meter in Rome. He was successful in securing a room formerly used by the inquisitors of the Papal Church, near the Vatican. In this room he had printed copies of the Gospels in vernacular and successive volumes of the *Scholars' Handbook* on the International Lessons, issued by the American Sunday-School Union.

In Russia and other countries of modern Europe, where the Greek Church prevails, Sunday-schools have been established in a few places. In other nations of the world, throughout Asia, Africa, and the Philippine Islands, the extension of the modern Sunday-school is dependent largely upon foreign missionary societies working in these lands. There is a growing Sunday-School Union on the continent of Australia, which promotes the formation of Sunday-schools under conditions more favorable than in some of the other countries, reporting about 8,000 Sunday-schools, with 53,000 teachers and 570,000 scholars.

In India the friends of Sunday-schools have struggled for years to promote Bible study in the face of almost insurmountable obstacles. Not the least of these obstacles is the great diversity of speech. The India Sunday-School Union aims to unite Christian workers in Bible study, and to direct their attention to the importance of educating the child. Weekly editions of Sunday-school lessons and helps are issued in upward of twenty languages and dialects. Thus the gospel message of Christ may be heard or read by British, Eurasian and natives—by many of the millions of Hindus—whether Buddhists or Moslems, in that great country, wonderful for the magnificence of its temples and for the intensity of the sufferings and sacrifices of its people, in trying to find and to worship an unknown God.

It is computed that the membership of the Sunday-schools of India is not less than 750,000. The whole number of Indian children under sixteen years of age is computed to be over 130,000,000. Nearly 140 missionary societies are proclaiming the gospel in India and are in sympathy with the purpose of The India Sunday-School Union. Over large sectional areas these various mission societies are coming into voluntary co-operation for the purpose of greater efficiency. The outlook for the progress of Bible study in that country is hopeful.

New Zealand has a society with 1,700 schools, about 10,000 teachers, and 120,000 scholars. The Fiji Islands report 1,000 schools, with a membership of 25,000.

The work in Africa is largely in the South African lands, where progress is being made. They report about 5,000 schools, 15,000 teachers, and about 200,000 scholars; in all Africa about 9,000 schools, 30,000 teachers, and 520,000 scholars.

Less progress is being made in Central and South America, since large portions of the population are Indian, and those that are white, or partially of the white race, are attached to the extreme wing of the Papal Church, discouraging modern Sunday-schools and generally forbidding the study of the Bible by the common people.

Instruction in Great Britain.—For the first fifty years of the modern Sunday-school movement, attention was given more to the theory of education, the development of methods, and the training of teachers, than to the careful preparation of suitable lists of lessons for Sunday-schools. The chief textbook used by Raikes and his associates has already been described (pp. 437, 438). Private and pay schools were sustained in the cities and villages of Great Britain at this period, but there was no system of public education for the rural districts.

One competent writer says: "Popular education in England made less progress than in any other Protestant country in Europe." It is also affirmed that education of the masses of England was almost entirely neglected prior to the rise of the Sunday-school movement.[1] Obviously, therefore, the leaders in this movement found it necessary to discover principles of popular education and instruction applicable to the condition of the masses at that period. The books of instruction were very simple; perhaps, to our modern sense, rather crude. Yet they had some clear views in respect to grading the instruction which is indicated by the textbooks in use in these early Sunday-schools. Thus, they advanced from the alphabet to simple words of one or two syllables, then to the more difficult grade, ending with the New Testament and Bible as books for reading lessons. The practice of committing passages of Scripture and verses of hymns to memory for recitation widely prevailed for a considerable period. Following this came some limitation to the lessons to be memorized, giving an opportunity for explanation and application of the truth. Thus the schools of London and some of the larger cities of Great Britain adopted the Bible lessons put forth in America with Judson's helps, and editions of *Judson's Questions* were issued for the use of other schools, as will be noted later under the history of the movement in America.

The London Sunday-School Union prepared its first annual list of lessons about 1840, and the next year began serial notes on the lessons. Similar lists were published by the London Union from time to time until it adopted the Uniform Lessons, afterward called "The International System of Sunday-School Lessons," in 1873. These were used together with a series of "Afternoon Lessons" for several years. This system was displaced in part by a series of graded lessons which aimed to adapt the selection of passages of Scripture to the ages of the scholars in the various departments of the schools. Another popular series of lessons in Great Britain was that prepared by Eugene Stock, widely used in the Sunday-schools of the Church of England, as already noticed, and these lessons gained in popularity among many dissenting schools of Great Britain. The Scottish Sabbath-schools have quite

---

[1] F. V. N. Painter, *A History of Education*, pp. 302–304.

uniformly followed the lists of lessons prepared under their own direction.

The British Sunday-schools very early aimed to improve their mode of instruction. They perceived that this could best be done by securing trained teachers. They found it essential to issue magazines and periodicals giving information in regard to practical methods pursued in the various schools throughout the kingdom and in presenting theories of education and pointing out how these could be adapted to the improvement of teaching in Sunday-schools. Thus as early as 1813, Mr. William F. Lloyd began the publication of a periodical called *The Sunday-School Repository* or *Teachers' Magazine*, first as a quarterly, then as a monthly, in 1821. This periodical was edited with much ability and had an important influence in unifying the system and methods of teaching in British schools. His periodical was merged later into *The Union Magazine*, and this again was followed by *The Sunday-School Teacher*, and *The Sunday-School Chronicle*, already mentioned. To apply the truths of the lessons for the scholars, other periodicals were issued and rapidly multiplied, so that after each lesson the truths imparted might be further impressed upon the mind to shape the conduct and life through incidents, stories, and various didactic articles, in simple language, suited, as was supposed, to the child mind.

In general British Sunday-school workers held to the theory that education should embrace the whole man; that physical, intellectual and religious training were all three necessary for a complete training of a person as a Christian. They discovered many obstacles and difficulties in the way of carrying out their idea, partly owing to the structure of society in a monarchial country, partly due to theories of education springing out of mediæval scholasticism, which Bacon, Milton, and later educators undertook to reform.

Voluntary instruction with unpaid teachers, the use of the Bible as a textbook, and the economical character of the Sunday-school movement made its expansion phenomenal, in Great Britain as elsewhere. A parliamentary census of England and Wales, in 1818, gave 5,463 Sunday-schools, with 477,225 scholars. A like census in 1833 put the membership at 1,548,890. An educational census of England and Wales in 1851 gave the number in Sunday-schools at 2,407,642, and this was 260,000 more than could then be found in the public and private schools of those countries.

The centenary of Sunday-schools in 1880 placed the number of Sunday scholars in Great Britain at 6,060,667, taught by 674,704 teachers. At the close of the first decade of the present century, there were 49,210 Sunday-schools in Great Britain and Ireland, with 712,625 officers and teachers and 7,425,957 scholars. In all Europe, so far as reported, there were 83,033 schools, 823,280 teachers and officers, 9,581,769 scholars.

These statements justify the assertion of the Great Commoner, John Bright, "I believe that there is no field of labor, no field of Christian benevolence, which has yielded a greater harvest to our national interests and national character, than the institution of Sunday-schools." [1]

Of the obstacles to its growth on the Continent it has been said—and perhaps with truth—that the state controls education too dominantly for the modern Sunday-school to grow. In fact, among all the Latin races, the Sunday-school is a "delicate exotic." It seems to require a large freedom, otherwise it withers or has a sapless growth. In fact, in some monarchial countries, it seemed to have greater obstacles at the beginning. Thomas Raikes, writing in 1787, said: "Sunday-schools flourish in England; in Scotland they are not wanted; in Ireland they are highly necessary."[2]

Whether under the empire or the republic, the Sunday-school has not found a congenial soil in France.

In Germany, the parochial schools, as already stated, led the majority of the people to consider the new movement not a superior one, and therefore unnecessary. In Roman Catholic countries, the voluntary, lay-teaching feature of the modern Sunday-school doomed it to exclusion. The so-called Sunday-schools, under Cardinal Borromeo, Archbishop of Milan, were catechetical and had little in common with the modern movement. The zealots of the hierarchy in the Greek Church were not favorable to the modern movement, although Catharine II

---

[1] *Church Sunday-School Magazine*, July, 1887, p. 572.
[2] J. Henry Harris, *The Story of the Sunday-School*, p. 125.

of Russia invited Mr. Raikes to St. Petersburg—an invitation which he declined—to explain the system.

Where it has made any headway on the Continent, it has been among the free Protestant churches, by missionaries from other countries, especially from Great Britain and America. Church and state customs have interfered with its proceedings and limited its extension. The European war (1914) broke in pieces plans of Sunday-school and mission work in Continental countries devastated by contending millions in the greatest conflict the world has ever known. (See International S. S. Lessons, British Graded Lessons, Teacher Training, Conventions.)

SECTION II

Toleration and Education in America.—"Tell me what you are learning and I will tell you what you are" is a new version of an old proverb that fittingly interprets the educational zeal of the founders of the American nation. However diverse their views on other matters, they were united in this—that education and religion were vitally necessary for the stability and happiness of any people. They also sought for freedom to worship God according to the dictates of their own consciences. Their ideal was civil and religious freedom, often rather vaguely practiced. Yet "liberty" was the one cry of Pilgrim and Puritan in New England, of the Dutchman in New York and New Jersey, of the Highlander and Huguenot in the Carolinas, of the Cavalier and the Churchman in Virginia, of the Romanist in Maryland, and of the German and Quaker in Pennsylvania. In theory and practice, the Quaker stood for larger toleration than did the others, "We are here for the Lord's sake," said Penn, in 1682.[1] Later his followers declared: "Our business here is not so much to build houses and establish factories . . . that we may enrich ourselves . . . as to erect temples of holiness and righteousness, which God may delight in." Of New York (then New Amsterdam) the directors wrote, "Let every peaceful citizen enjoy freedom of conscience."

As might be expected, therefore, the modern Sunday-school movement found more congenial conditions and fewer obstacles in America than in Great Britain. Pilgrim and Churchman alike made early provision for religious instruction and for the education of youth. While there was no system of free schools for the entire people, careful attention was given to general education and to the founding of colleges, as Harvard in Massachusetts, 1638, and William and Mary in Virginia,

[1] See *Penn and Religious Liberty*, p. 24.

40

1693. The State and the Church were divorced, but education
and religion, with the early settlers, went hand in hand. In
America the Sunday-school encountered some difficulties of a
type similar to those found in Great Britain. In the eighteenth
century there was a general decline in morals and religion.
This was checked, in part, by revivals under Edwards and
Whitefield in the north, and the Huguenots in the south, but a
wave of disturbing events—European skepticism and manners,
and general low morality—swept over the country in the
latter part of that century. Thus President Dwight of Yale
says, "France, Germany and Great Britain vomited the dregs
of infidelity upon us." Another writer testifies to a conspiracy
of infidels and atheists against religion, government, and
humanity, against truth and peace, order and liberty, which
"brought disorder and wickedness in every form . . . in
New England and in other parts of the world." Moreover,
formative American society felt the adverse influence of the
great writers in the Augustan age of English literature. A
noted American educator has pointed out the lack of any just
conception of education by these eminent literary writers of
that age.[1] The Pilgrims were more broadly tolerant than the
Puritans. Puritan writers in America, like those abroad, were
in favor of education for clergymen and the professions; the
Pilgrims favored general education of the common people also.
Gov. Winthrop was more liberal and tolerant than Cotton
Mather, and William Penn expressed greater religious toleration than Churchman or Puritan, but the Huguenot *practiced*
the broadest spirit of religious liberty in that era.

Dr. Samuel Johnson said: "A little learning to a poor man
is a dangerous thing"—a reflection from Pope's noted lines:

> A little learning is a dangerous thing;
> Drink deep or taste not the Pierian spring.

This statement is as offensive to reason as the simile is to a
teetotaler! Shakespeare describes the child as "creeping like
snail, unwillingly to school." Shenstone was merry over the
manners of a school-dame, and Goldsmith describes a schoolmaster as arbitrary and tyrannical, while Cowper appealed to
his age to treat private tutors with decency. Even Sir Walter

---

[1] Horace Mann, *Lectures on Education*, p. 225, ff.

Scott paints a person awkward in manner, careless of dress, a superstitious pedant—and names the pedagogue Dominie Sampson. Washington Irving, infected by a similar epidemic, caricatures the schoolmaster in his character of Ichabod Crane. All this shows the low ideal—or lack of ideal—of popular education and of the educator.

With all this ignorance and unpopularity, the modern Sunday-school movement had to contend, even in America. In face of it, however, American workers are given credit for successfully experimenting; while Great Britain adopted the results, so far as dissimilar social stratification made it possible.

Intelligent American educators were then sure of one thing —that the best way to displace ignorance, to develop public conscience, and to make intelligent and virtuous citizens, was to give thorough instruction in the Bible. They had a profound conviction of the importance of such instruction as a basis of stable government. They were apprehensive that the ignorance and consequent wretchedness that they knew prevailed in the cities of the Old World might easily be transplanted to the cities of the New. As a result of these observations and convictions, Christian philanthropists in different colonies of America, with a benevolent spirit born of this religious zeal, attempted to remove ignorance and misery and to better society through Bible study.

Early Sunday-Schools.—A careful investigation of first-hand records of Sunday-schools reveals that, like all great moral and religious movements, the modern Sunday-school idea existed more or less clearly in many minds and sprang up in many widely separated communities. Leaving out of consideration the parochial schools in the Middle and Southern states, and the parish schools of New England attached to the church, there were—parallel with these in many places—schools on Sunday in which the chief instruction was from the Bible. Some of them used catechisms also, especially in New England. John Cotton's famous catechism, entitled *Milk for Babes* (1646), was reckoned by Cotton Mather as *the* catechism of New England for fifty years after its publication. *The New England Primer*, like *The Bay Psalm Book*, indicates the kind of instruction given in schools on Sunday. But in other sections the instruction was more directly biblical than where either Cotton's catechism or the New England Primer was used. Therefore it is clear that there were schools in America, held on Sunday, previous to 1780, which were substantially similar in type to the present Sunday-school. It is generally conceded by American students of first-hand documents that such schools of a character like to those founded by Raikes, with all their essential features, were to be found in America long before his day. These schools had many of the features as well as the form common to the modern Sunday-school, which entitled them to be counted forerunners of the modern movement. True, they were sporadic instances. The movement by Raikes gave popularity to the new form and led to its almost universal adoption. Claims have been made for the early existence of many such schools. I need note only the following:

Norwich and Bethlehem, Connecticut; Roxbury and Plymouth, Massachusetts; among the Schwenckfelders, and at Ephrata, Pennsylvania; Philadelphia, under Zinzendorf and Mrs. Greening; and, perhaps, Savannah, Georgia, by Wesley. (Appendix, pp. 441, 442.) These schools were not merely to prepare persons for confirmation, church membership, or coming to the Lord's Supper, but to train or teach them how to live the Christian life.

Here and there a local church tolerated the modern Sunday-school in form and in fact for children of the church, but such cases were rare. Denominational organizations were jealous of their prerogatives. Ministers were the generally recognized leaders in religious instruction. Laymen, even in New England, had a secondary place, if any place at all, in conducting such instruction. True, there were teachers associated with the pastors in some churches of the early order in New England. This feature gradually developed into the toleration of intelligent and devout Christian laymen as aids in imparting religious instruction, not only in the family but also in the church. The idea and the principle spread slowly. Bishop White, on his return from England where he had gone to be consecrated as Bishop and had learned of Raikes' movement, was unable to introduce it into his "United Parish" in Philadelphia. The churches regarded it as an innovation and were suspicious of it, partly because of its English origin.

Americans were exceedingly jealous of an invasion of their religious liberty.

At first, therefore, this new scheme was rejected by the churches, though accepted by individuals as a philanthropic movement for the moral and religious education of all classes. It thus became largely a movement sustained by laymen, and upon a union basis; not opposed to, though not a part of, the organized work of the local church.

Organized Sunday-School Movement.—Herein is a striking illustration of the marvelous working of God's providence upon different minds in different places to prepare the way for the coming of his kingdom. When Raikes' movement first agitated England, America was in a tumult over questions relating to its civil government and the founding of the nation. The federation was weak and the new nation was in danger of being split into a dozen contending, petty states. Happily this was averted by the adoption of the Constitution in 1787. This peaceful conclusion gave an opportunity for Christian philanthropists to turn their attention toward the removal of ignorance and vice, and the education and betterment of the common people through religious instruction. Philadelphia was then the chief city of the country, having one-third more population than New York, and was likewise, for a time, the country's civil as well as commercial center. The religious toleration characterizing the colony founded by Penn was perpetuated by his followers and tended to promote the spirit of philanthropy and benevolence. This stirred the hearts of the citizens of Philadelphia to grapple with the problem of the moral and religious improvement of the young.

The First Day Society.—The lack of education of young persons who were apprenticed to trades was conspicuous. This not only hindered their efficiency as workmen, but led to various forms of vice and depravity. Most of these persons were children of indigent parents. Because of the lack of free public schools, they had not received instruction in early life. So Sunday, it was remarked, "was employed for the worst of purposes; the depravation of morals and manners."

It was apparent to the philanthropic persons who became impressed with these conditions that it would require a united effort of all the forces for good to succeed in the betterment of society as it then existed.   Benjamin Rush, M. D., who had been educated at Princeton and for a time was a member of the Old Third (Pine Street) Presbyterian Church (but had lapsed into Universalism), together with some friends and persons attached to other congregations in the city, proposed a meeting.   This meeting, which was attended also by Bishop William White (later he was chosen president), was held December 19, 1790, and it was decided by ten or twelve benevolent persons present to organize a society for the establishment of First Day or Sunday-schools.   A constitution was prepared and adopted at a meeting the following week, December 26, 1790; the purpose being to instruct the rising generation by teaching them "from the Bible" and "from such other moral and religious books as the society might, from time to time, direct."   As this constitution was presented and discussed, section by section, "read over, adopted by paragraphs, amended and finally agreed to"—this process consuming an entire meeting— it is evident that careful thought was given to the forming of this plan for the society.   There is no evidence in their records, nor any intimation given, that they copied the plan of Raikes in England, but as one of their number had been in England, doubtless it was not unknown to some of them.

The churches not being ready for such a movement, it was practically necessary to establish it on a voluntary and union basis.   Rooms were hired for holding its schools, and teachers or masters secured to conduct the schools, after the manner of the plan pursued in England.   Obviously, however, their plan was not merely to teach reading and writing; their real purpose was to improve the morals and the religious character of the "learners."   They insisted that all reading lessons should be from the Bible.   Even the primers and spelling books which they approved, consisted of words and short sentences from the Scriptures.

Nor did this First Day Society confine its labors to opening and conducting Sunday-schools on Sunday.   It had the wider purpose in view of promoting public, free schools for the state.   One of its first acts was to forward a petition to the Legislature of Pennsylvania declaring "that the proper education of youth is an object of the first importance, particularly in free countries, as the surest preservation of the virtue, liberty and happiness of the people." The directors called attention to the salutary effects of Sunday-schools already established, as proving that similar schools established at the public expense are "the most effective means of diffusing these blessings among the people."

The society adopted five rules for the government of its schools. The second required the teachers to see that pupils committed to their charge attended the places of public worship to which they severally belonged. The third rule required the scholars to come clean, and, "if guilty of lying, swearing, pilfering, indecent talking, or any other misbehavior, the teacher shall point out the evil of such conduct, and if that should prove unavailing, notify the visiting committee who, if they see cause, are to expel such delinquent from the school, in the presence of the other scholars." Rule four states the time when the schools are to be held, and rule five that a copy of the rules are to be posted in each schoolroom and read and explained once a month to the scholars, "also whenever the teacher shall see occasion."

The records of the society tell of some of the lads who steadily attended the schools and received premiums for good behavior and improvement in their studies, and have since "become opulent and respectable members of the community." Many of the directors of this society were conspicuous in public affairs. Benjamin Rush was a signer of the Declaration of Independence and prominent in temperance reform. Matthew Carey, as a liberal Roman Catholic, stood in high repute among his fellow citizens. Dr. Benjamin Say, Dr. William Currie, Joseph Sharpless, Thomas P. Cope and Capt. Falconer were noted for their interest in public affairs.

It is worthy of note that some years later the state of Delaware instituted free schools for the education of children on Sunday; those schools to expend not exceeding twenty cents for every white scholar taught. About a score of schools was soon founded under that act, and the state appropriated nearly $200 a year to each county for the maintenance of such Sunday-schools.[1]

Bishop William White was retained as president of the First Day Society for about forty-six years. Peter Thompson,

[1] *Report of Commissioner of Education*, 1896, 1897, Chapter IX.

Jr., was the first secretary. Several schools were opened for girls and for boys which were held from eight o'clock to ten o'clock on Sunday morning and from four, or half-past four, to six o'clock in the afternoon. The masters were to receive, for forty scholars, thirty pounds a year colonial currency (or about eighty dollars), but as each of the schools speedily reported upward of one hundred scholars, the salary was increased to forty-five pounds, or $120, per annum for each master. To stimulate the pupils in learning, it was agreed either to issue or to purchase "small moral books to be let to the scholars or given as premiums." Among the books so purchased were: *Doaley's Fables, Barbauld's Songs, Beauties of Creation, Catechism of Nature, Powers of Religion, Economy of Human Life, Watts' Songs, Whole Duty of Woman,* and *Fruits of the Father's Love,* besides Bibles and Testaments. They studied economy of administration; for when several designs for a society seal were offered and the amount required for the designs exceeded what they thought prudent to expend, they rejected them, and selected a simpler seal with a Scripture text which they put, for brevity's sake, in Latin, *Licet Sabbatis Beneficere* (It is lawful to do well on Sabbath Days).

The persons forming the First Day Society were of different faiths, yet, aside from Bishop White the president, no reader of their records of today could tell to which of the several denominations the respective members of that society belonged. Their religious differences were so put aside and they were so fully agreed in their zeal for "the religious improvement and good education of youth" that they worked together as one body of benevolent Christians.

In the first twenty-three years, the benevolent receipts of the society were $9,186.49, and its expenditures $9,133.01. It also had legacies amounting to about $1,550, which were funded. It taught, gratuitously, 2,127 youths in the first ten years of its existence. Early in the nineteenth century, the system of Sunday-schools with voluntary teachers became so wide-spread that the First Day Society decided to discontinue its paid schools, which it did before 1819, and voted to expend the income of its funds in aiding schools in Philadelphia and vicinity which were conducted upon the new plan of voluntary, unpaid teachers. The aid consisted chiefly in appropriating publications of the Sunday and Adult School Union or of the American Sunday-School Union—a work still continued. The First Day Society is, therefore, the oldest existing Sunday-school society in the world.   Its charter was granted in 1796 and it has continued for over 125 years, and still maintains its organization intact, with a board of twelve visitors and a president, vice-president, secretary and treasurer that manage its affairs.   It has been closely affiliated with the American Sunday-School Union for a century, most of the members and officers being also in responsible positions in the Union.

The Voluntary System.—The churches in their organic capacity continued for some time to regard the Sunday-school movement not as a church institution but as a philanthropic effort to improve the moral condition of the ignorant and neglected classes outside of the church.   Some ecclesiastics declared that it was a wicked use of holy time to hold such schools on the Sabbath day.   It is said that a young woman of the First Congregational Church in Norwichtown, Connecticut, had gathered a number of children for instruction on Sunday and that the pastor of the church, when passing the building, shook his ivory-headed cane at it, with honest indignation declaring: "You imps of Satan, doing the Devil's work." [1] Thus the spirit of Christianity awakened activities in its members that some ecclesiastics conscientiously felt compelled to condemn.   The preachers proclaimed the gospel; and the laity interpreted and applied it literally and logically—more broadly than did their teachers.   The instance in Connecticut does not stand alone.   In a large number of places throughout the United States, at that period, churches would not allow the Sunday-school a place in their buildings.

As in England, so here in America, the expense of paid teachers was too great to be continued, and voluntary teachers were absolutely necessary for the general success of the new movement.   So great grew the "craze" for voluntary teaching that paid teachers were almost discredited.   In the wild zeal for it, a leader as intelligent as John Angell James declared: "Hireling teachers can scarcely be expected to possess either the zeal or the ability of those who now engage in the work

---

[1] Henry Clay Trumbull, *Yale Lectures on the Sunday-School*, p. 128.

from motives of pure benevolence. Gratuitous instruction was an astonishing improvement of the system."

The erroneous conclusion of this writer is obvious, for it would exclude the best educators in nearly all our religious and intellectual institutions of the present day, including clergymen. Nearly a generation passed, however, before the church would generally tolerate this Sunday-school movement. Some advanced educators now think that modern Sunday-schools will not make decided progress in religious education until they return to some system of paid and thoroughly trained teachers, as well as paid superintendents.

Even the plan of Dr. Andrew Bell and of Joseph Lancaster —the voluntary, mutual and monitorial system of instruction —failed fully to recommend Sunday-schools to the church. Raikes had earlier applied this monitorial and voluntary plan, so they were not the originators of it. By it, the new movement was made possible and popular throughout Britain and America—but outside of the church. It enlisted the laymen in an active effort to promote the kingdom of Christ. While winning lay members to its advocacy and support, it caused many in the ministry to look upon this feature as an invasion of their particular prerogatives and so they continued to stand aloof from it, or simply to patronize it, as a scheme to be tolerated when used for the betterment of the ignorant and lower classes. It was not, in their view, a movement desirable in the organized work of the church. This was particularly true in the churches of Scotland.

Why the Early Movement was Union.—It is now a piece of forgotten history that for about forty years after the founding of the modern Sunday-school movement the schools were virtually compelled to adopt the non-denominational or union plan. The organized church generally either opposed the scheme or believed that to make it an integral part of the church would debase the divine plan, by a mere man-made appendage. It was imagined by some that the supporters of the Sunday-school imperilled or impaired the influence of the church. Even so late as 1812, the famous Stockport School of England felt it necessary to justify its adherence to the union principle in these plain words: "While party dissension runs high, . . . attached to no particular sect, our plan comprehends whatever is excellent in all."

The spread of schools on the union principle was phenomenal. The common people took to them gladly. While catechism recitation was sometimes counted irksome, Bible study was popular. Wherever union schools were fostered, a wave of religious revival usually followed in the community. For these reasons, the prevailing type of early modern Sunday-schools was forced to be, for nearly half a century, on the union plan. This was particularly true in America. These new schools sprang up not merely in cities, but in provincial towns and in the rural districts. Religious journals of England and America recorded marked revivals of morals and religion, following the spread of Sunday-schools in the early part of the nineteenth century, as well as the birth of great Bible, tract, and missionary institutions for the spread of the gospel. Nor were such schools on the union plan confined to cities or to rural districts; they were and are that form of Bible study best adapted to reformatories, benevolent homes, houses of detention, jails, penitentiaries, and other penal institutions of the state and of the federal government. They are equally well adapted to army posts, naval and life-saving stations, and to all government organizations where the religious instruction must be non-sectarian.

Not only were early Sunday-schools necessarily on the union basis; they continued to be the most successful form of Bible study in conditions such as have just been indicated. Their wonderful growth and marvelous spiritual power were in a large measure due to the faithful teaching of the Bible and to that visible unity for which the Master prayed: "That they all may be one . . . that the world may believe that thou didst send me." (John 17 : 21.)

The rapid increase of local union Sunday-schools and classes and the need for information in respect to the best practical modes of conducting them, naturally suggested the value of co-operation, if not combination, of the various local organizations into a wider advisory and administrative body. It was necessary, however, to proceed with great caution in this matter. Denominational lines were drawn very sharply and often the controversies over theological doctrines and modes of church worship and of church polity were keenly discussed, sometimes with no little acrimony. Federation of churches was out of the question and, by many, would have been counted a compromise of the truth. The association of local schools was therefore purely voluntary, and care had to be taken not to interfere with the internal management of the schools. But the spirit of co-operation and union was coming rapidly into popular favor.

Union Society of 1804.—As early as 1804, a number of women of different denominations formed a "Union Society" for the education of poor female children in Philadelphia. This society gave attention to the religious training and instruction of girls. It is worthy of note that all the persons managing this society were women; twenty-six of whom applied for an act of incorporation, which was granted them in April, 1808, by the state and the supreme court, with the affirmation that the women were "citizens of this commonwealth." This society prospered for several years, having upward of three hundred children in one school who "on entering the school knew nothing beyond their alphabet; and many were ignorant even of that." They were taught to read, write and sew. They also committed to memory "large portions of Holy Scripture, many devout hymns," and were instructed "in such catechisms as were most approved of by their parents."

This society held public examinations annually, when premiums were "awarded to such of the scholars as excelled" and monthly private examinations, attended by the subscribers and donors, were also provided, that the supporters might witness the "effects of their liberality."

The Evangelical Society.—Persons belonging to different congregations in Philadelphia, in 1808, formed a society at the house of Archibald Alexander to promote "the knowledge of and submission to the Gospel of Jesus Christ among the poor in this city and vicinity,"[1] by providing chapels, school buildings and schools, and holding mission and other evangelical services.

Sabbath meetings were held for adults and for children also. At the latter services, children and youth recited passages of Scripture which had been committed to memory, together

[1] *Constitution of the Evangelical Society.*

with portions of hymns and questions from such catechisms as the parents approved. These services were open and free to all classes. The society obtained a charter in 1812.

An important fact in its history was the visit of Rev. Robert May (a missionary going to India for the London Missionary Society), who for a time (1811–12) conducted a school, gave monthly lectures, and held evangelistic services in Philadelphia and vicinity.[1]

Mr. May was familiar with the modern Sunday-school methods of England, and imparted much information concerning them to the evangelistic workers in Philadelphia. He popularized in America the system of awards to children for committing their lessons known as "the ticket currency," which consisted of red and blue and other tickets of Scripture, to which were attached different nominal values, and which were given for perfect attendance, good conduct and for excellent recitations.

Besides these services which the Rev. Robert May rendered in lectures and in holding religious services for adults and for children, he also conducted a Sunday-school on Sundays, according to the modern methods. Of this school he kept a record himself, stating the order of the exercises, showing that it was on the school system and taught by voluntary teachers similar to the methods pursued in Sunday-school now. (Appendix, pp. 444, 445.) This record of Mr. May's, in his own handwriting, is preserved among the archives of the American Sunday-School Union.

Mr. May left so marked an influence upon the Christian workers of Philadelphia that the writer of the first report of the Sunday and Adult School Union, five or six years later, erroneously assumed that the first suggestion of Sunday-schools in America upon the modern plan was due to the visit of Mr. May. This claim cannot, however, be maintained in view of other first-hand documents. He did propose the establishment of Sunday-schools on the modern method in a letter dated July 29, 1811, and addressed to the Evangelical Society. That society recommended the plan, but left the execution of it to its respective committees. Mr. May formed and conducted a Sunday-school while continuing to supervise the society's

[1] *Minutes of the Evangelical Society*, 1811–12.

evangelistic services. But Sunday-schools, in the modern
form, were begun in Philadelphia and elsewhere years before
Mr. May's visit.

Thus there is good authority for a Sunday-school on the
modern plan at Pawtucket, Rhode Island, in 1797, founded by
Mr. Collier, then a student in Brown University and afterward a Baptist clergyman at Charlestown, Massachusetts.
This school was favored by Mr. Slater, proprietor of the factories in Pawtucket, and it was attended by many of the opera-
tives in the mills. It was for both secular and religious instruction. A Sunday-school on the modern plan was also formed
about 1803 in New York, by Mr. and Mrs. Divie Bethune and
also by Mrs. Bethune's mother, Mrs. Isabella Graham. As
early as 1809, a Moral Society was founded in Pittsburgh,
Pennsylvania, for the suppression of vice, reformation of manners, and to promote useful knowledge. A member of this
society suggested that its objects could best be carried out by a
Sunday-school. Such a school was opened in September of that
year and attended by about 240 children and adults.

Church Schools.—Between 1810 and 1815 the beneficial
effects of this Sunday-school movement began to make an impression upon organized churches in different places. Churches
began to allow Sunday-schools to be held in their church buildings. But where the schools were interdenominational or
union, and were reaching families attached to various religious
creeds, this was deemed unwise, and, as in the case of the
Evangelical Society above noted, the offer of rooms in the
churches was declined on the ground that it would give the
school a sectarian bias. This, of course, would limit its widest
usefulness, when it professed to be conducted on a union basis.
In other cases, when the churches favored the movement,
schools were formed under distinctive denominational supervision.

Instances of this kind of school are recorded previous to the
War of 1812. There was not, however, any wide-spread movement in the churches favoring schools in the church until
the close of that war. Then they spread rapidly, not merely
in centers and cities like Philadelphia, New York, Boston,
Baltimore, Albany, Charleston, Pittsburgh, and other large
towns, but throughout the country in the smaller villages in

nearly all the then well-settled states. Organizations sprang up in many places outside of these great centers, as in Maine, New Hampshire, Massachusetts, Connecticut, New York, New Jersey, and even as far west as Ohio and Indiana and in the Southern States. These schools, however, continued practically to be either independent of the church or an appendage to it, rather than recognized as an organized part of local church work. This was due largely to the peculiar sentiment prevailing in the churches themselves. For many in the church still questioned the wisdom of accepting the modern Sunday-school as a part of the church's work.

Hence Sunday-schools were of necessity maintained in partial or total independence of church control, although often held in the churches. Even a generation or so later, when the church "came to itself," it did not apparently realize its mistake, except to discover that these schools in the church should properly be conducted and controlled by the church. It sharply censured Sunday-school workers for not at first heartily assenting to such control. The church leaders forgot, or were entirely ignorant of, the fact that their predecessors in the early history of the Sunday-school movement had not welcomed the schools, and had thus kept them outside for more than a generation. The schools had so long been in the habit of managing their own affairs, and of providing for their own support, enforced by this sentiment of the church, that it required an educational campaign of long continuance to undo and correct this habit and, smoothly and satisfactorily, to bring even church Sunday-schools into organic harmony with the church. And the school was long left to pay its own expenses after it came under church control. This will appear from the discussions constantly recurring in the earlier Sunday-school conventions.

Why Organized Unions.—The present generation needs to be reminded of the material and civil conditions of the country from 1810 to 1820. The United States had been in a feverish excitement and turmoil incident to the war (1812–15). Peace had come, and with it increased attention to education and religion. Attention was also given to improved facilities for communication and transportation, neither of which were abundant nor rapid at the best. "Swift packets" between

America and Europe were sailing vessels requiring from three to five weeks for a trip. Postage on letters was prohibitive to all except well-to-do persons. The rates (there were nine rates) were from six cents for under thirty miles to twenty-five cents for over four hundred and fifty miles, "for one piece of paper," and an extra rate for every additional piece of paper. The mails were usually carried by stage or on horseback. Information on the progress of the Sunday-school movement was subject to these serious handicaps in communication and transportation.

Nevertheless considerable information of value had filtered through the country relating to this new movement of Sunday-schools with voluntary unpaid teachers, and news of the benefits which had resulted from various successful efforts to plant and sustain the same in many different places. The churches were beginning to appreciate the value of this agency and, though only a minority was yet convinced of the wisdom of adopting them as a gospel agency in the churches themselves, their popularity was rapidly gaining ground among the laymen.

The most important forward movement in this direction was made in New York City, stimulated by the practical experiments in Philadelphia. Several local Sunday-school associations were formed and were vigorously promoting the cause in various regions about Philadelphia some time before 1816. New York City claims the credit of being the first large city to have permanent organized societies for promoting Sunday-schools on the voluntary plan. In accord with the custom of the time, the organization there was two-fold; one for females, and another of a general character for males or for both sexes.

Sunday-School Union Societies in New York.—Mr. Eleazer Lord of New York spent several months in Philadelphia in the early part of 1815. While there his attention was drawn to the then novel subject of Sunday-schools. Two or more of them, with voluntary, unpaid teachers, he especially observed with their methods of procedure; secured copies of their books, and studied how the institution originated in England. Returning to New York in the summer, he devoted the autumn and early winter to visiting clergymen and prominent laymen of different denominations, calling attention to this movement, which was new to them. He interested Dr. John M. Mason, who proposed a public meeting for the formation of a society to promote the organization of Sunday-schools on this plan.

Mr. Lord found many objections to this proposal. He appears to have been very diligent and tactful in meeting the difficulties thrown in his way, in answering objections, explaining methods, harmonizing conflicting views, allaying fears, and urging the claims of the neglected children and youth upon the attention of Christian laymen and clergymen. Some of the objections are interesting to note. It was pleaded that it would be cruel to confine the little ones (who had been in school during the week) on Sunday, when they ought to be free to roam for their health. It was urged that this work, requiring in some cases the teaching to read, would profane the Sabbath and make it a day of labor instead of rest; that it would be an infringement of parental prerogative, for God had appointed the parents to train the children; that it would interfere with the rights of clergymen who ought to catechize the children— in fact, that the whole scheme was impracticable; suitable teachers could not be found; it was a novelty and it would fall to pieces; and "it would be harmful as bringing too much of a lay influence into a work which was strictly ecclesiastical and clerical." But with patience, prudence, kindness, and some concessions to prejudices and infirmities of good men, the preparation for such a meeting was completed early in the winter of 1815.

Mr. and Mrs. Divie Bethune of New York spent part of 1801 and 1802 in England, and had noted the progress of Sunday-schools in Great Britain. Mrs. Bethune and her mother, Mrs. Isabella Graham, had opened a Sunday-school in New York in the fall of 1803, at the house of Mrs. Leech, in Mott Street, and carried it on at their own expense. They also formed two other Sunday-schools for poor children and, later, founded a school for adults in Greenwich in 1814, shortly before Mrs. Graham died. Out of these schools came a plan to form a female society to establish Sabbath schools. (Appendix, p. 445.)

Mr. Lord and his associates deferred the carrying out of their proposal "in courtesy" to this movement, so that the female union was organized a month in advance of the other

union.   The women in New York, under the leadership of Mrs.
Bethune, had read Dr. Pole's history of adult schools and had
received various publications in regard to Sunday-school union
societies in England from Mr. Stephen Pruest of Bristol, in
December, 1815.   They were also familiar with the movement of the women in Philadelphia, and with the formation of
societies in that city which, as they gallantly say in their
report, had "outrun their sisters in New York in this useful
work." [1]

Stimulated by these various facts, they proposed a union of
all denominations in the city, which was favored by a few.   On
January 24, 1816, a number of women met in the lecture room
of the Wall Street Church, New York, and held a meeting
again at the same place on January 31st, which was more fully
attended, and formed the "Female Union Society for the Promotion of Sabbath-Schools," the objects being: "To stimulate
and encourage those engaged in the education and religious
instruction of the ignorant; to improve the methods of instruction; to promote the opening of new schools; to unite, in Christian love, persons of various denominations engaged in the
same honorable employment."   Among the six rules adopted
for each school were: "The object of the school shall be the
education and religious instruction of children not under six
years, and female adults who cannot procure those benefits
during the week;" "No children belonging to any other
Sabbath-school shall be admitted."   Mrs. Divie Bethune was
chosen first directress, and Miss Mumford secretary, and its
affairs were placed under the direction of a committee of ten,
together with the officers.   Before the end of the year, this
society reported under its care 21 schools, 250 teachers, 3,163
scholars.[2]

One week later, a notice in *The Commercial Advertiser* of
New York called another meeting to be held in the assembly
room of the City Hotel, on Broadway near Cedar Street—
Divie Bethune presiding.   The constitution and rules for the
organization of the New York Sunday-School Union Society
were perfected, and adopted at a subsequent meeting in the
same place, February 26, 1816.   At this meeting, the Rev.

[1] *First Annual Report*, 1817, p. 5.
[2] See *Constitution and Rules*, 1816.

Dr. John M. Mason presented "one of the most powerful and eloquent and touching appeals" upon the purpose of the society. The organization was completed by the appointment as president of Mr. Richard Varick, who had been for twelve years (1789–1801) mayor of New York, Mr. Eleazer Lord as secretary, with a committee of twenty-one members who, with the officers, had the management of its work. The objects of the society were thus stated: "To encourage and assist those engaged in the superintendence and instruction of Sunday-schools; to promote the establishment of new schools; to improve the methods of teaching; and to unite . . . persons of different religious denominations in this benevolent undertaking."

By the end of the first year, they reported twenty-eight schools under their care, with "no less than 3,000 scholars." At first, they used the lessons compiled by the London Sunday-School Union, comprising sketches "of sacred history and precepts and promises of the Bible."

The society assured the public that its work would not detract from the usefulness of the public free schools of the city, but rather increase the attendance upon those schools.[1] This society and the Female Society appear to have worked in perfect harmony, one with the other, for several years, stimulating greatly the formation and the efficiency of early Sunday-schools. The New York Sunday-School Union Society recorded also a long list of other places (twenty-five or more) throughout the country in which Sunday-schools had already been established at this date. The London Union's lessons do not appear to have been used long; for in the third report the committee are gratified by the "almost innumerable verses, chapters and even whole books which have been committed to memory by the learners, and recited in the schools." Several instances are known of individual boys having repeated thirty to forty chapters, comprising entire Gospels, at one time. "Some schools report an average of five thousand verses of Scripture committed per quarter or 20,000 in the course of the year, besides hymns, sketches of sacred history, and ordinary lessons." No wonder that this crowding of the memory and the memorizing of such a large number of verses and

[1] *First Report*, p. 15.

hymns became a hobby, producing, as some physicians alleged, the disease called hydrocephalus (water on the brain).

While this objection to the craze for memorizing a large number of verses was very general, there were evidently some notable exceptions. For so sane and scholarly a man as Rev. Dr. James W. Alexander testifies, when advanced in life, "that for one verse that I know by heart, I wish I knew a hundred." He was a "learner" in a Sunday-school in the days when memorizing was a habit, that is, from 1812 to 1816. Looking back, after forty years, upon this period, he gives it as his sober judgment "that if a pupil must forego one or the other—the explanation of the meaning by question and answer or the possession of a text in his memory verbatim—he had better let go the former." [1] He evidently was not afraid of "water on the brain" in consequence of too much memorizing of Scripture!

Some of the foremost educators, judges, and rulers of the country were at one time or another interested in Sunday-school work through the New York Union Society and, after a dozen years or more, it absorbed the Female Society, carrying forward the united work in the city with great vigor for more than fifty years. Among the many forward movements which it had the honor to suggest, were "A system of select uniform lessons," with *Judson's Questions* thereon, which it firmly claims "did more for Sunday-school efficiency than can be calculated." It was foremost in the introduction of Sunday-school circulating libraries. It was one of the earliest in the field (under Father Seton) for the organization of graded infant schools. It was conspicuous for having public examinations of scholars and of teachers, and of lectures and meetings for teachers. It threw all its influence in favor of a special Sunday-school hymnology and suitable music for children. It early suggested a national Sunday-School Union.

The New York Female Sunday-School Union Society became an auxiliary to the Sunday and Adult School Union, and thus an integral part of the national society, before the Sunday and Adult School Union changed its name to the American Sunday-School Union in 1824. It is significant also that the New York (Male) Sunday-School Union Society later became

---

[1] James W. Alexander, *American Sunday School*, p. 119.

auxiliary to the same union. Thus New York and Philadelphia workers were closely interlocked in laying the foundations of this national enterprise.[1]

Similar combinations of Sunday-schools in other centers than Philadelphia and New York were urged and completed with more or less success, as in Boston, Hartford and New Haven, Albany, Utica, Princeton, Baltimore, Charleston, Columbia and Pittsburgh.

A Larger Union.—The rapid multiplication of schools and of local combinations of schools created a desire for a closer bond of union.[2] The desire for some general medium of communication—some central bureau of information upon methods, progress and improvement of Sunday-schools—began to appear in various parts of the country. At first this conception was dim and vague, but it gradually took on definite form and found varied ways of expression through different workers. It was early discussed by the educators and supporters of Sunday-schools in Philadelphia and vicinity. The plan of schools associating together for their common improvement and progress seems to have been specially promoted in that city. It was rapidly spreading, also, in New York and elsewhere, leading to the formation of the two societies already described. The zealous efforts of the workers in Philadelphia, which had so stirred the mind of Eleazer Lord, had earlier worked out the formation of a number of smaller organizations or co-operative school societies "on such principles as would not interfere with the actual independence of the individual societies" or schools. The call became strong for a wide co-operation in the common cause. This feeling found public expression, so far as the records show, among the members of the "Male Adult Association" of 1815, in Philadelphia. Having considered this subject, that association appointed a committee "to confer with the different Sunday and Adult School Societies in the city and suburbs to ascertain their views upon the expediency of forming a general union society."

Sunday and Adult School Union.—The first form suggested for this union or association was stated in a preamble and thirteen articles, and bears the official signature of representatives

[1] See *Society Reports, New York Sunday-School Union*, 1817 to 1866; also Isaac Ferris, *Semi-Centennial*, 1866.
[2] For a list of these associations and schools, see *Appendix*, pp. 447–451,

from at least ten local societies. Two of the representatives were women, besides a male representative from a "female association." While the "Adult School Association" promptly began to foster and found schools, its members appear also to have industriously discussed and considered making the society more compact, and giving it a broader outlook and field of operation. From the idea of an "Association of Philadelphia" managed by an "acting committee," the proposition was soon enlarged to that of a general union, embracing all Sunday-schools. This was probably due in part to Mr. Divie Bethune of the New York Sunday-School Union Society just formed, who attended one of the three meetings held in Philadelphia in the month of May to perfect the organization of the Sunday and Adult School Union. He described the plans, benefits, and success of the New York society at some length. Changes were also doubtless further due to the popular sentiment in favor of unpaid teachers and of introducing the Sunday-school into the churches. Rapid progress was made along these lines, which British workers observed, and credited to the fact that America had the benefit of England's experiments and experiences, and therefore formed organizations upon a "superior plan."

During May, 1817, the constitution of the Union was frequently amended, copies were ordered to be printed, and the Society adjourned to meet at the call of the "acting committee." The next recorded meeting was a delegated one, attended by representatives of eleven Sunday-school associations and societies of different denominations, and held at the northwest corner of Fourth and Vine Streets, Philadelphia. This meeting elected Samuel J. Robbins, President; E. W. Seeley, Vice-President; Joseph Nagel, Second Vice-President; John P. Bankson, Corresponding Secretary; James Henderson, Recording Secretary; Hugh de Haven, Jr., Treasurer. There were no representatives from the Society of Friends, nor were there any clergymen present at any of these meetings, so far as the records show. It was clearly a movement exclusively by the laity. Membership in the society was limited to those who signed the constitution, "and acknowledge the leading doctrines of the Bible." [1]

---

[1] Article I, Constitution.

Why workers like Bishop White and the Friends who were actively interested in the First Day Society failed to take part in the organization of this Union for sustaining Sunday-schools by voluntary teaching is not definitely stated. Some infer from the records that they favored segregated church schools, or schools with paid teachers, and were not favorable to mixed schools on the new plan for all children, including those within and outside of families attached to the church. Whatever may have been the reason for their failing to share in the formation of this new union, it is a fact that Bishop White was foremost in forming the Philadelphia Protestant Episcopal Sunday and Adult Society late in that year. One ecclesiastical historian says that this society "did not accomplish very much." [1] But it had periods of singular activity, not only in controversy respecting methods, but also in developing individual workers. It had a somewhat checkered career. A generation later came "The American Church Sunday-School Institute."

The early history of this movement indicates divided views among the ecclesiastics and the clergymen. Some were in full sympathy with the new movement, others stood aloof from it or were in doubt of it. This appears also from the fact that the committee of the Sunday and Adult School Union did not find it easy to secure a minister of ability to give an address or discourse on the purpose and objects of the new Society, by which the members desired to enlist the public in the cause. Finally one was secured and the Society also presented an address to the public in a circular letter. The presentation of its purpose to the public served to clarify the conceptions of the members themselves regarding the work. This soon found an expression in their changed constitution, and in the introduction of features to promote the Society's efficiency as well as economy. After repeated discussions and changes, and in anticipation of securing an act of incorporation which was proposed, the direction of the association or union (for both terms were popularly applied to it at first) was placed under a "board of twelve managers," elected annually by ballot, and of "two representatives from each school society." It

[1] Rev. Oscar S. Michael, *The Sunday-School in the Development of the American Church*, p. 89.

PRESIDENTS

Alexander Henry, 1817–47.

Hon. John McLean, 1848–60.

John A. Brown, 1861–73.

Robert Lenox Kennedy, 1873–81.

Hon. William Strong, 1882–95

Morris K. Jesup, 1896–1908.

was also stipulated that "clergymen of different denominations, whose school societies were attached to the Union, were honorary members with the right to vote." While the objects of the Society remained substantially unchanged, the internal structure was modified in some respects. As indicating a wider outlook, the title of the Society was changed from that of the "Association of Philadelphia" to the "Sunday and Adult School Union." Philadelphia was recognized as the headquarters, but the Union's operations were to extend "to towns and villages in the country," there being, apparently, no limit to its field in this respect. The name *Philadelphia* was not in the title in the constitution nor in the charter.

Under the amended constitution, a new election was ordered in December, 1817, and twelve managers were chosen by ballot out of thirty-six persons who were nominated. This was also a delegated meeting, representatives being present from eleven associations and societies. In addition to these twelve managers, there were also "two representatives from each school society."

At the next meeting of the managers in January, 1818, the officers elected by ballot were: Alexander Henry, President; John Claxton, John Welch, Edward Thompson and Thomas Latimer, Vice-Presidents; John P. Bankson, Corresponding Secretary; John C. Pechin, Recording Secretary; and Hugh de Haven, Jr., Treasurer. This meeting was held in Van Pelt's schoolroom. The president of the late organization, Mr. Robbins, was present and stated the object of the meeting, and read the revised constitution. The delegates presented their certificates. Three additional Sunday-school associations were admitted before the close of the meeting, so that there were fourteen associations and societies of different denominations represented in revising and perfecting the constitution of the Society, including the change of name from "Association" to "Union." An act of incorporation was to be applied for by a committee. The recording secretary was instructed "to call upon the relatives of the late secretary to obtain such books and papers belonging to this Society as may have been in his possession, and to record the minutes of all the meetings of the Society which have not been entered."[1] The successive

[1] *Minutes*, January 14, 1818.

and varying acts of the Society are confusing to the reader, though the records appear to have been written up with reasonable accuracy. The confusion is due, largely, to the uncertainty of all who were feeling their way cautiously to the formation of a new institution.

Seven Years of Formative Work.—Having a wider outlook and field of operations and having made the organization more compact by the change of name from "Association" to "Union," the Sunday and Adult School Union addressed itself vigorously to its real mission. The Rev. Mr. Parker, a clerical member of the Society, speaking at its first anniversary, affirmed: "This Union, however, but recently formed, is fast advancing to the full attainment of all that it originally proposed. It has occasioned the establishment of some schools and it has given a powerful impulse to others; it has commenced printing tracts, spelling books, tickets, alphabetical cards, and other items. The advantages of its consolidated funds, its combined zeal and its united wisdom have clearly appeared." He added, "The primitive spirit of harmony and union is reviving; and I believe that missionary societies, Bible societies, and Sabbath-school societies are to be honorably instrumental in bringing about that enlarged, cheerful and universal co-operation in the work of the Lord, which is so devoutly to be wished." Similar sentiments were expressed by the Rev. Dr. Staughton, and also by Mr. Bayard of Princeton, New Jersey, who asserted that the efforts and results exhibited in the report of the Union proved "the happy influence which Sunday-schools exert on the intellect, the morals, and the happiness of society; and it will be the germ of future and progressive good to places and periods now unknown." Dr. Staughton rejoiced that Sabbath-school labors were gratuitous; that "to combine for such instruction is the duty obvious to everyone," and generous recognition was made of the work of women in missionary and Bible institutions who were ready "to instruct the ignorant and clothe the impoverished."

Mr. Bayard also announced his firm conviction that "Sunday-schools are in the order of Providence," and that "the invention of stereotype plates, the establishment of auxiliary institutions of Lancastrian schools, and more particularly of Sunday-schools, have most efficiently contributed to diffuse the cheering beams of revealed truth through the most distant regions of the globe."

With stronger emphasis, the benefits and advantages of the Union were recognized in 1820, in an address by the Rev. Dr. John H. Rice, of Virginia, who eloquently declared, "It is delightful to witness the healing of those divisions, which have so long been the reproach of the Christian name, and have so deeply injured the best interests of the Christian cause." "Your report exhibits," he said of the Union, "the operations of a cheap, extensive and efficient charity. When I say a *cheap charity*, I mean to affirm that the sum of money expended on Sabbath-schools does, in this way, purchase a greater amount of good than can be procured, perhaps, in any other way whatever." "I may state the sum expended last year at about $3,000, while the number of pupils in your various schools is nearly 20,000. This makes the annual expense of each scholar less than twenty cents. In what other way could an equal amount of good be effected with no greater expenditure?" "But it is also a most extensive charity."

The Rev. Dr. Ezra S. Ely also added his testimony in commendation of the principles of the Union, "When the Pine Street Sabbath-School Association was formed, there were but three or four communicants among the teachers; but now all, except one, are professors of the religion of Jesus." The Rev. Dr. J. J. Janeway and the Rev. Gregory Townsend Bedell, D. D., in like manner, heartily commended the work of Sunday-school teachers and of the Union.

The same year, British workers, through the London Sunday-School Union, voiced their general surprise at the growth of the work in America. The London Union, in 1820, declared:

> In the United States of America the progress of Sunday-schools has been truly astonishing. The friends of education there had not to work their way through such difficulties as the early promoters of Sunday-schools in England. They possessed the advantage of British experience; they at once perceived the great benefit of union, and by commencing on this superior plan they have made more rapid progress than in England, considering the comparatively short time in which they have been established. Sunday-schools are formed in almost every considerable town and village. They have extended to the savages and the Indian tribes, and have spread particularly among the blacks.[1]

[1] Report *London Sunday-School Union*, 1820, *Sunday-school Repository*, Vol. IV, p. 435.

American readers of today may share in the astonishment of the English workers that for seven years the Sunday and Adult School Union should begin each report with joyous notes of prosperity. At first it had about a dozen affiliated associations, but closed its first year with fourfold that number and, by the end of the seventh year, it enrolled over 720 schools, associations or societies, located in seventeen different states, with over 55,000 members connected with its work through auxiliaries. The progress of the Society in the seven years is indicated by the following summary from its annual reports. This table shows that from having a few associations in one city and its suburbs, it speedily reached national proportions and attained a national reputation:

	Schools.	Teachers.	Scholars.
1817–18	43	556	5,970
1818–19	129	1,431	12,306
1819–20	227	2,653	19,481
1820–21	313	3,724	24,218
1821–22	402	4,197	31,297
1822–23	513	5,012	37,993
1823–24	723	7,300	49,619

Its Literature and Results.—The Union was foremost among the agencies issuing suitable publications for Sunday-schools, beginning with a small volume entitled *Little Henry and His Bearer*. In the second year, it issued over 50,000 copies of books, including 10,000 Sunday-school hymn books, besides 10,000 alphabet cards, 10,000 copies of the Ten Commandments, and 450,000 blue and red Scripture tickets. In its fifth year, it issued about 90,000 books, besides 25,000 hymn books, 8,000 school books, 173,000 tracts, and 500,000 blue and red Scripture tickets. This list of publications steadily increased in variety and in numbers. The Society aimed to supply every kind of Sunday-school requisites required for the efficient conduct of the schools. It also provided a suitable literature for distribution among the families who were without, or had a scant supply of, religious reading. So great was its activity that the Religious Tract Society of Philadelphia voluntarily handed over its work, influence, and publications to the Union, which also distributed pamphlets and tracts and other religious literature suited for individuals and families.

In their activities for extending Sunday-schools and providing them with literature, the managers of the Union were
especially careful to note how far these means attained the
end at which the Union really aimed—the making of Christian
character.   Repeatedly, year by year, they record revivals in
different portions of the country, reporting remarkable spiritual results in the number of teachers and learners who were led
to profess their faith in Jesus Christ and were added to the
various local churches in the vicinity of the schools.   They
note with joy the marked moral and religious improvement in
many communities.   A fair specimen of these reports is this
one, cited from a section in New Jersey:

> No sooner were schools commenced in destitute places than
> a change was visible in the morals of the children and the in-
> habitants of the neighborhood.   Profane swearing, intemper-
> ance, and Sabbath breaking, which formerly prevailed to an
> alarming extent, in a great measure ceased. . . . This was not
> all; from a number of reports of schools belonging to this
> Union, it appeared that many teachers and scholars have been
> made the recipients of divine and saving grace.

Statements of a similar character are found on almost every
page of the reports from the 700 auxiliary societies and schools
connected with the Sunday and Adult School Union.

Broadened Service.—It is worthy of note that the leaders in
the Sunday and Adult School Union did not limit its mission
to the founding and fostering of Sunday-schools.   The managers appointed a special committee on the "suppression of
vice and immorality," to investigate the prevalence of those
evils and to co-operate with existing agencies in proposing new
methods for more effective restraint and suppression.[1]   This
committee made frequent reports of its work and of its success.
The Union also called attention to the profanation of the
Sabbath and appointed a committee to enlist the co-operation
of the evangelical societies and other institutions for promoting
better observance of the Sabbath Day.[2]

As an indication of its wider outlook in the distribution of
the Scriptures, as well as in the teaching of them, the Board
asserted: "It is the primary object of this Society to contribute towards the establishment of Sunday-schools *throughout the country*."   Hence it placed various publications at the

[1] *Minutes*, February, 1819, and May, 1820.   [2] *Minutes*, December 3, 1818, ff.

disposal of Mr. Bacon, who was agent for the Bible Society, suggesting that he might distribute them in families and communities.   He thus became a missionary agent of the Union, as well as of the Bible Society of Pennsylvania.[1]   The managers said: "if we are enabled to continue the active exertions of a faithful agent, an abundant harvest may be gathered."

For the greater efficiency of the work, the Union arranged to employ Robert Piggot as depository agent, paying him at the rate of $350 a year for a room for the depository, and for so much of his time as might be required to attend to the duties of the agency.[2]

The managers of the Union conceived that their mission was as broad as the command of the Master to every creature of whatever race, color, or country.   This is indicated by the delight with which they speak of thirteen schools for the instruction of Indian children.   Three of these were in New York state, four in the Cherokee nation, one among the Choctaws, two among the Chickasaws, one in Indiana, two in Arkansas and one in Missouri.[3]

From the first the Union had in its connection schools for the education of the negroes.   A further evidence of the breadth of its mission is given in its efforts to extend the advantages of the Sunday-school to the rich as well as to the poor.   They said:

> Your Board has witnessed with regret the prevalence of an erroneous sentiment respecting the principles of Sunday-schools. It is this—that they are intended only for the poor.   This has arisen from the improper application of the principles of gratuitous instruction.   These schools are intended as much for the affluent as the indigent.   The great object is religious instruction; it is, indeed, given without money and without price—is it, therefore, of no value to those who have the means and who, if it were vendible, would secure it by purchase?

First Sunday-School Missionary.—Finding that voluntary representatives and workers required to be supplemented by an intelligent and more expert worker, they employed, in 1821, the Rev. William C. Blair as Sunday-school missionary. He traveled about 2,500 miles, mostly on horseback, visiting six states, from Pennsylvania to North Carolina, founding

[1] *Minutes*, September, 1819.   [2] *Minutes*, June, 1819.
[3] *Fifth Report of the Sunday and Adult School Union*, 1822, p. 8.

sixty-one Sunday-schools, visiting thirty-five others, reviving twenty, and establishing six tract societies and four adult schools within one year. He began this work August 4, 1821, going in company with the treasurer of the Union on his first tour. Another friend journeyed with him for several weeks, but most of his work was accomplished alone. He made a full report of his labors, expressing his great regret that owing to temporary illness he could not accomplish more and could not pass more leisurely through different counties of these states and establish schools in every neighborhood. He closed with this significant statement, "There ought to be eight or ten Sunday-school missionaries in every state."[1]

The labors of this first missionary were so satisfactory that the Society adopted paid missionary workers as a permanent agency. Thus in May, 1824, it states: "From former experience of the beneficial effects of the labors of Sunday-school missionaries, the managers have employed during the last year two missionaries; the Rev. Timothy Alden, President of Allegheny College, and Mr. M. A. Remley." President Alden rendered services for that year and the next with very beneficial results, reporting in February, 1824, that he had formed Sabbath-schools in all directions, having added to the number connected with the Union forty-seven, "mostly new schools, established where such institutions had never before existed." He adds, "More than a thousand children and adults (and of the latter several are married women) are now receiving instruction in these little seminaries of gospel science."[2] He notes the astonishing achievements of "two little girls, not nine years old, who in the course of one year have recited the whole of the New Testament—and many have recited several thousand verses each."

Mr. John P. Bankson, corresponding secretary of the Union, resigned in January, 1820, partly on account of ill health, but mainly because he wished to devote his life to missions in Africa, where he died soon after. A year before his resignation, when the Union's report for May, 1819, had been completed, Mr. Bankson requested the privilege of adding this clause, "That zealous minister of Christ and faithful friend of Sunday-

[1] *Fifth Report of the Sunday and Adult School Union*, 1822, pp. 59, 60.
[2] *Seventh Report of the Sunday and Adult School Union*, 1824, p. 67.

school children, *who had the honor of introducing the present system of Sunday-schools into the city of Philadelphia and even into the United States,* has finished his labors and gone to his reward: the Rev. Robert May is dead." Without investigating the accuracy of this statement of Mr. Bankson, the Board admitted the clause in italics into its report. There is abundant evidence in other records to show that Mr. Bankson was misinformed, and that Sunday-schools on the "present system" existed in the United States, and even in Philadelphia, long before the visit of Mr. May in 1811. The inaccuracy of this statement has been pointed out many times, and it has been proved to be erroneous by succeeding, as well as preceding, records and narratives relating to the early history of the Sunday-school movement in the United States.

The activity of the Sunday and Adult School Union created a desire for a name which would indicate the national co-operation among Sunday-schools which already existed in fact. This found frequent expression in various parts of the country between 1818 and 1823. The way was providentially prepared for it in a remarkable manner. Co-operation of local unions in various centers of the country further promoted the idea. Organizations in England, Scotland and Ireland gave increased definiteness to the conception of a union national in name as well as in fact.

Spirit of Christian Unity.—The beneficent influences of Christian unity were not wanting in Philadelphia, even in the seventeenth century. A church was organized in 1698, preceding the First Presbyterian Church on Washington Square —the earlier church having been born in a spirit of Christian brotherhood. Foremost pastors and educators noted the growing unity among Christians, so happily voiced by Dr. Rice of Virginia, already quoted. This found voice in a definite suggestion for a union national in name by the New York Male Sunday-School Union, in 1820. In its annual report, it affirmed that there was a growing harmony among Christians and Sunday-school workers, and pointed to the magnitude of the work accomplished by the Sunday and Adult School Union within three years, in support of its statement and to local unions in New York, Baltimore, and other cities of America. The proposal was in this forceful language:

Your committee cannot forbear intimating the great benefit which would result from a union embracing all the Sunday-schools of the United States, on a plan in some respects similar to the American Bible Society. Equally catholic in its principles and simple in its design, the Sunday-school system would be equally benefited by such a union. The vast amount of facts and information which could then be embodied with precision, and presented annually to the public, would afford a powerful and irresistible appeal to their patronage and support. Your committee do not perceive that any serious obstacle exists to prevent the prosecution of this enlarged plan, and we would rejoice if this hint should lead to the opening of immediate correspondence with the principal societies of the United States for this purpose.

After pointing out some of the achievements of the London and Irish Sunday-School Unions, it presented this strong economic argument in favor of its proposal:

In addition to the strength and consequent superior efficiency of combined efforts, your committee will add one other result which they hope will have its full weight upon all such as have hitherto, with the most upright intentions, opposed a general union: that is, the great *saving of expense*. On the disjointed plan, the expenditure is twice, in some cases three times, as much as it would be were the funds of all united. The cost of books, it is well known, is proportionately less as the number of copies is increased. That which would cost six cents in a single society may be had for two or, at most, three cents, in a large edition, such as a general union would require. And when we consider the increased power which this gives for extending the blessings of the system, it is believed that no other argument will be wanted to convince the candid, liberal, and humane mind of the utility of such a union as your committee have deemed it their duty to recommend.[1]

Later the New York workers recognized that the Sunday and Adult School Union had become national in scope, and required a change in name, and for other unions to become auxiliary, to be what they had outlined in their recommendation. And this was done.

Nor was the New York Male Sunday-School Union alone in its advocacy of this federation. The Sunday-School Union Society of Charleston, South Carolina, also affirmed:

Sunday-school unions are designed to concentrate the temporal and spiritual powers of men into one grand stream, which will, in no small degree, bear away on its mighty bosom the moral darkness and wickedness of our world and usher in the

[1] *Report New York Sunday-School Union Society*, 1820, pp. 16, 17, 22.

millennial day. We hope to see this union extend until their circles be united and the glory of the world shall fill the whole earth.[1]

The Princeton Sabbath-School Society of New Jersey, already an auxiliary to the Sunday and Adult School Union, comprising eighteen schools and over a thousand learners, seemed to have had a vision of a larger union, as expressed in its fifth annual report—a report which is quoted with approbation by the managers of the Sunday and Adult School Union. This New Jersey society declared:

> Permit us to express the wish that the association, of which it is our privilege to form a part, may continue to flourish and extend its genial influence till that happy day shall arrive when one mighty union shall be formed embracing in its limits the people of every language and of every land.[2]

Here is not only a vision of a world Sunday-school union, but a prophecy of it a century in advance of its fulfilment! All these suggestions concentrated in and upon the existing Sunday and Adult School Union, as having now attained a national scope.

Early Modes of Instruction.—Religious instruction in families, schools, and churches was as various as were the religious creeds in the American colonies. The earliest modes of instruction were brought over from the home lands. There was no uniformity, and very little unity in either creed or instruction. Churchman and Dissenter retained each his distinctive views and modes of worship, practically little changed by transportation across the Atlantic. Puritan and Presbyterian had allied forms of maintaining church and parish schools and imparting religious instruction in the family. Their methods differed widely, however, from those of the Churchman and Cavalier of Virginia, from the Hollanders of New York and from the Huguenots of the Carolinas. The Quakers of Pennsylvania were quite opposed to forms—whether in worship or in religious service. They regarded all ordinances, like baptism and the Lord's Supper and an appointed, paid ministry, as perversions of religion; their instructions sprang from a conviction of an "inner light." Whatever was really forceful in

[1] *Report of the Sunday and Adult School Union,* 1823, p. 55.
[2] *Ibid.,* p. 42.

their religious teaching was largely expressed orally and by example.

Puritan and Pilgrim alike in the early days in New England had family religious instruction through catechism, questions and answers, or in some interrogative or didactic form. One of the earliest of catechisms among the Puritans and Pilgrims was that by John Cotton, already named, which was famous for more than two generations. It was euphoniously entitled, *Milk for Babes, drawn out of the Breasts of Both Testaments, Chiefly for the Spiritual Nourishment of Boston Babes in either England; but may be of like use for any Children,* . . . *by John Cotton, teacher of the Church of Boston, New England.* It was issued in London in 1646. Cotton Mather calls it, "The Catechism of New England," and fifty years after its issue says, "The children of England are to this day most usually fed with this excellent catechism." It contained sixty questions and answers which became familiar as household words in New England, and it was made a part of the famous *New England Primer* in the next century, thus continuing its popularity for more than a hundred years.

The educators and the ministers of that day are generally looked upon as a very somber class, little given to humor. But it is said that a conceited friend of John Cotton was boasting of his insight into the Book of Revelation, when Cotton very modestly said, "I must confess myself to want light on these mysteries." His friend went home at once and humorously sent John Cotton a pound of dipped tallow candles —the common light of that day!

For a hundred years *The New England Primer* was counted "the school book of Dissenters in America," and for another hundred years was frequently reprinted. It is represented to have had a sale of over three million copies, besides numerous editions in England and Scotland, even into the nineteenth century. Later, the *Westminster Shorter Catechism* (1647) was used with that of Cotton in the homes of the eastern colonies. In the first decade of the nineteenth century appeared the famous *Evangelical Primer* of Joseph Emerson. The *Heidelberg* (1563) and *Anglican* (1549) *Catechisms,* and the still earlier catechisms of Luther (1529) were also used by their respective followers in America. Their use was so firmly established in these communions, that when the new Sunday-school movement—to teach direct from the Bible—appeared in America it was exceedingly difficult to displace the catechisms, or even to put side by side with them the Bible lessons.

In early American Sunday-schools, simple and somewhat crude plans of instruction were adapted from the Raikes' schools and the London Sunday-School Union (1803). An attempt was made, roughly, to grade the classes according to the attainments of the scholars. The six grades which were common in the Sunday-schools in England (1780–1790) were reduced to four grades in the early American schools. Twenty years later, British schools adopted similar departmental grades, named infant, elementary, Scripture and senior. It was necessary in England to teach many learners to read in order that they might read the Bible. This was true in America also up to the introduction of the system of free public schools. In the lowest grade were those who were taught the alphabet and words of one syllable; in the next grade were those who, while unable to read, could spell out some words in two or more syllables; in the next advanced grade were those who could read, but only indifferently and with hesitation; and the highest grade was composed of those who could readily read in the New Testament.[1]

The supplies used in the Sunday-schools were the alphabet on cards and a simple spelling book especially prepared for the Sunday-school which contained also reading lessons; all the sentences being taken from some portion of Holy Scripture, while the "spelling lessons" were words taken from the same portions of Scripture. Moreover in all the grades it was particularly required of the teachers, and the learners were especially enjoined, to give attention to religious instruction a certain portion of the time during each session of the school. Only a part of the time was to be spent even in learning to read or in mastering the alphabet. Nor were they to trespass upon that time of religious instruction to recite verses of Scripture or hymns.

Memorizing Era.—The prevalence of catechetical instruction was so great that it seems to have been impossible to overcome it except by stimulating the scholars to memorize hymns

---

[1] Louisa Davids, *The Sunday-School*, 5th edition, p. 384.

and verses from the Bible. This ran to a great extreme and became not merely a hobby but almost a craze. Scholars and schools entered into rivalry to see which could report the largest number of verses memorized and recited. This custom began early in the century, about 1804 or 1805, in the earlier schools, and continued for upward of fifteen years. During this period, Sunday-school reports are full of such records as these: "One of the children has committed to memory the four Gospels. Two others have recited the first three books of the New Testament, and one of them one hundred and seven, and the other one hundred and five, hymns." Another school which was held in the evening reports that "most of the scholars are attentive, diligent and grateful, and recite at least one hundred verses of an evening." Again, "large portions of Scripture are recited. Two girls in six successive weeks recited 8,336 verses." Still another one, not to be outdone by others, reports, "One girl has recited from the commencement of the Bible to Isaiah, another all the New Testament and several books of the Old Testament."

Nor were they all children. One school reports that the scholars are from the age of seventeen to seventy-eight years, and that they recite Scripture every Sunday evening and "repeat at a time from one to eight chapters in the New Testament." One person, seventy-eight years old, who did not know a letter in the alphabet on entering the school, was taught to read with facility and to write a decent hand. Another tells of one scholar who recited "all of Dr. Watts' psalms and hymns, besides fifty out of other books, in three Sabbaths," and at another session of the school, "the same scholar recited 1,752 verses of Scripture." And to show the impartiality of the instruction, another school reports that a colored woman recited, at one lesson, "570 verses of Scripture."

Scores of pages could be filled with similar reports from the early schools in regard to the remarkable cases of memorizing Scripture and hymns and the various catechisms.[1]

Rewards and Penalties.—The system of rewards and punishments of those early schools was also interesting. They were quite varied, but the following was a general system which

---

[1] *Reports, Sunday and Adult School Union,* 1818–1822; *Sunday-School Repository,* etc.

prevailed for nearly a decade in the early part of the last century. Tickets, with passages of Scripture printed with a border on thin red and blue pasteboard, were used for rewards. In the highest classes no reward was given except for good recitations—a blue ticket being given for every six verses of Scripture memorized and recited, and the same for every page of catechism. In the next grade a blue ticket was given to each scholar who was present at the roll-call, and for every hymn recited, a similar ticket. In the beginners' classes a blue ticket was given for punctual attendance and for good behavior also. Six of these blue tickets were equal to one red ticket, and one red ticket was counted worth half a cent in value, to be redeemed every three months with religious books and tracts suited to the capacity of the child.

On the other hand, there were penalties as well as rewards. Children of the highest class absent at roll-call forfeited one blue ticket, and, for neglecting to recite a lesson, a similar penalty. Also, if absent from the morning or the afternoon session, without a satisfactory excuse, they forfeited another ticket, and still another if they behaved improperly in church. Similar penalties for absence were imposed upon the lower classes, and for bad behavior, whether in church or in school.

No favor was shown teachers or superintendents. A teacher who was absent at roll-call in one of the early Sunday-schools was fined twelve and one-half cents for each offence. Superintendents were punished with *double* these penalties for similar offences.

Teaching Methods.—Of the modes of instruction in the early period of American Sunday-schools (1780–1820) it may be affirmed that the lessons and the methods were in a crude and formative condition. In fact the theories of education in general were in a state of evolution. There was an effort to adapt the instruction to the varying conditions of the communities, and of the learners. The first schools in America, as well as in Great Britain, were primarily for the ignorant and neglected. Only a small percentage of this class could read, for American free public school systems had not yet come, and many people were too poor to send their children to pay schools. It was absolutely necessary in many cases to teach not only the youth but adults to read, if they were intelligently to grasp the truths of the Bible. This could be done in but few cases on week days, because the adults and older children were required to labor six days to earn their daily bread. Sunday was the only opportunity they had to learn, even to read, with the exception of those who might do so on week-day evenings. The number who could take advantage of the week-day evenings was limited, and most of these were too tired from their long daily labors to attend evening classes or to receive religious instruction. But, as we now send medical missionaries to the heathen for their physical betterment and, through this ministration aim to reach them with the gospel of redemption, so, in the early times of Sunday-schools, Christian philanthropists used the Sabbath time to teach the poorer class to read, that through this means they might know for themselves the message of salvation. Great care was taken regularly to present the saving truth of the gospel to these learners at each session of the school. From the earliest time of the new movement, the teachers were enjoined to spend a definite portion of the session giving oral religious instruction in talks, in lectures and by personal appeals to the learners. Hence, the first mode of instruction in the Sunday-schools in America, as abroad, was largely oral, and closely allied to what was later termed "the lecture system."

This lecture system was accompanied by catechetical lessons—teaching by means of questions and answers—and was followed by the era of memorizing Scripture, hymns and catechisms. When it was carried to such an extreme as to require from one to three hours to hear the verses which a single scholar had committed, this system of cramming the mind, unnatural and forced, was held to produce "hydrocephalus," as before stated, and the popularity of the plan waned.

It is evident, long before this point was reached, that the managers of the Sunday and Adult School Union, while glad to have the children store up in a reasonable manner the truths of the Bible in their memory, felt sure this cramming system and parrot-like recitation could not be the most beneficial. They clearly saw a better way, and tried a better mode of instruction. Various methods were introduced in different localities and soon there emerged a more satisfactory system of efficient instruction in Sunday-schools, as we shall presently see.

American Sunday-School Union.—"The modern Sunday-school movement began with teaching youth to spell out the words of Scripture; it has been busy ever since teaching them to spell out the meaning and spirit of those words," as I suggested in a previous treatise.[1] It marked a significant crisis in the progress of Christianity. The American Sunday-School Union is closely related to this movement in America. To present an adequate view of the origin and work of this Union, it has been essential to consider the early history of Sunday-schools.

"The idea of a *national* society had, for several years, engaged the thoughts of the friends of Sunday-schools in various parts of the country. The Sunday and Adult School Union had already become national in its scope; it lacked only the proper name. After correspondence on this subject, a plan was distributed for consideration, and delegates from various and distant societies were invited. Letters commending the object were received, leaving the matter to the Sunday and Adult School Union; no delegates from distant Unions are recorded as present.[2] At this meeting, "the whole subject was referred (finally) to an annual meeting of the Sunday and Adult School Union." Of that Union of 1817 it was then asserted, it "has already extended its happy influence over a large portion of the states; and, although not in name it was in fact, a National society. It furnished a broad and sure foundation upon which to erect a superstructure that should be in name, as well as in fact, a National institution." It "now offers its advantages to all smaller Sabbath-school associations of every name, in every part of the world."[3]

In accord with the general sentiment thus widely expressed, the Sunday and Adult School Union, at its annual meeting, ratified the previous action of its managers, considered and approved a constitution for the "American Sunday-School Union," and agreed to change its name and to transfer "the

---

[1] *Century of Sunday-School Progress*, 1899, p. 6.
[2] For list of auxiliaries and schools that united in change of name see *Appendix*, pp. 447–451.
[3] *Report, Sunday and Adult School Union*, 1824, p. 89.

funds, books and property of the Sunday and Adult School Union (amounting to about $5,000), contributed chiefly by the citizens of Philadelphia, to the American Sunday-School Union." This constitution was prepared by a committee of the Sunday and Adult School Union and adopted by its managers and members, thus changing the *name* of the Union to the "American Sunday-School Union."

It completed the organization by the election of managers and officers. The officers of the Sunday and Adult School Union were chosen as officers of the American Sunday-School Union, and managers of the former union were re-elected, also further indicating that this was, in fact, only a change of name.

The location, objects, membership, principles or basis of union, and the field of operations of the latter, were substantially the same as those of the former society. (Appendix, p. 452.) The records and notices of these proceedings indicate a change of name in accord with its scope and character, rather than the institution of a new society. This change was ratified by a public meeting, May 25, 1824.

"By common consent Philadelphia became the seat of the American Sunday-School Union." Why? Because: (1) the Sunday and Adult School Union "was the largest institution of the kind in our country," already national in fact, having auxiliary or affiliated unions in seventeen of the twenty-four states; (2) it was centrally situated, closely connected with the then western states; and (3) Philadelphia was a chief city and an important center for the whole country.

Objects.—The objects of the American Sunday-School Union stated in its constitution "are to concentrate the efforts of Sabbath-School Societies in the different sections of our country; to strengthen the hands of the friends of religious instruction on the Lord's Day; to disseminate useful information, circulate moral and religious publications in every part of the land, and to endeavor to plant a Sunday-school wherever there is a population." The members declared "that the Society is composed of citizens of several religious denominations, embracing within its plans and objects all ranks, sexes and ages in our country." [1]

Twenty years later (1845) when the Union finally obtained

---

[1] Charter, *Plain Statement of Facts*, 1828, p. 6.

a charter under its present title, in consequence of its experience, the "objects" were combined, and concisely stated in a *reverse* order, thus: "The object of this corporation is to establish and maintain Sunday-schools, and to publish and circulate moral and religious publications." [1]

Basis.—The fundamental principles of the Union were clearly set forth in substantially the same terms in successive reports and official documents of the Society from 1817 to 1845. These were "the essential truths of Protestant Christianity held in common by all Evangelical denominations." Full and explicit statements on this point were repeatedly made, setting forth this fact exclusively and inclusively. Thus it was asserted that the basis of union required "no sacrifice of principle; no compromise of duty; no interference with the internal management of smaller associations," but did require that "all discordant elements must be banished," and that "union with Christ and union with each other form the basis of the American Sunday-School Union." [2]

Before the Evangelical Alliance was formed, the Union issued this statement, which is substantially the same as that which was afterward adopted in nine articles as the doctrinal basis of the Alliance.[2] As Christian laymen, the managers of the Union declared their belief that they could teach "the essential truths of our common faith, without reasonable offence to anyone touching matters of unessential importance." While loyal to the denominations to which they respectively belonged, yet, as Christians, they asserted "we can maintain the integrity of our relations to our respective churches and communities, while we can unite to teach the truth that Christ taught and as plainly as he taught it." They further affirmed, in terms almost identical with those set forth later by the Evangelical Alliance, that their basis included the doctrines of "the supremacy of the inspired Scriptures, as the rule of faith and duty—the lost state of man by nature, and his exposure to endless punishment in a future world—his recovery only by the free, sovereign and sustaining grace of God, through the atonement and merits of a divine Redeemer, and by the influence of the Holy Spirit—the necessity of faith, repentance and holy liv-

[1] *Act of Incorporation, Section 2.*
[2] *American Sunday-School Magazine*, July, 1824, p. 5.
[3] *Report Evangelical Alliance*, 1846; Schaff, *Creeds of Christendom*, Vol. 3, p. 827.

ing, with an open confession of the Saviour before men, and the duty of complying with his ordinances of Baptism and the Lord's Supper—in these doctrines we find the essential and leading truths of the Christian system; in the reception of these doctrines we agree, and with God's help, we endeavor to teach and inculcate them on all whom we can properly reach."[1] They confidently asserted that their experience in the Union "has satisfactorily demonstrated that the grand leading principle on which this National Association of the friends of Sabbath-schools was originally based—an union of the great and cardinal points of Christian belief, is as practicable in operation as it is noble in principle; and time has but the more firmly cemented that bond."[2]

Members and Management.—The American Sunday-School Union at first stipulated that each subscriber of three dollars annually "shall be a member;" each subscriber of thirty dollars at one time "shall be a member for life." Also "members of auxiliary Sunday-school unions or societies, paying three dollars and making an annual report," were "entitled to vote at all meetings of the Society." The terms of membership in the Society continued substantially the same for twenty years. When the act of incorporation was secured in 1845, the terms of membership were modified so that "every person being a citizen of the United States, who shall contribute annually three dollars to the funds of the Society, shall be a member so long as such contribution is continued," "and every person being a citizen, as aforesaid, who shall contribute thirty dollars within three years shall be a member for life," provided, "his name has been reported to and approved by the Board." Thus it will be seen that any citizen of the United States, no matter what his nativity, sex, color, or condition, may become a member of the Society or corporation and have a voice in its meetings and a vote in the election of managers on the same conditions.

The affairs and funds of the Society are under the direction of a board of officers and managers. By the first constitution the officers and thirty-six managers must be laymen, but "clergymen whose school societies are attached to the Union

---

[1] *Brief View*, 1st Ed., p. 5; *Sunday-School Pioneer*, p. 13; *Historical Sketch*, p. 17; *Report*, 1844, p. 57.
[2] *Historical Sketch*, p. 9; *Report*, 1828, p. 5. See *Appendix*, pp. 452–454.

shall be entitled to vote in the board of managers." "Officers of Sunday-schools auxiliary to this Society, shall be ex-officio managers." This provision placing clergymen and officers of Sunday-school unions on the board of managers was evidently soon discovered to be cumbersome. The Union, in a year or two, had nearly four hundred auxiliaries and more than a thousand school societies attached to it, which might have given it a board of management of several hundred persons, making it not only unwieldy, but practically inefficient as an executive board or a deliberative body. Hence, in 1826, and later when the charter of incorporation was secured from the state in 1845, the management of the Society's affairs was limited to a board "consisting of a president, vice-presidents, a corresponding secretary, recording secretary, treasurer, and thirty-six managers, twenty-four of whom shall reside in the city of Philadelphia or its vicinity." The managers were at first arranged in three groups; to serve one, two, and three years respectively, but they were eligible to re-election for three-year terms. It was further provided, "the officers and managers shall be laymen and shall be elected by ballot." The managers were given power to elect all officers of the Society, to fill vacancies in their own body, and to adopt such other measures as may, in their opinion, promote the objects of their association.

While all the managers were to be laymen, this did not prevent the Society from bringing to its aid clergymen and educators in every department of its work. Ministers and biblical scholars were employed as writers, authors, editors, and missionaries or agents—giving the Union the advantage of the ablest, wisest men of affairs to conduct its operations and also the benefit of the most learned and experienced scholars and educators in every department of knowledge and in every field of biblical interpretation.

The practice of the Society shows that the term "laymen" was interpreted in the narrow and strict sense of the people in distinction from the clergy; not of people as distinct from *all* professional classes. Thus "laymen" would be all persons not clergymen or preachers recognized by their respective denominations.

In the Society's business procedure, the members of the

VICE-PRESIDENTS

Hon. James Pollock, 1855–90.

Jay Cooke, 1870–1905.

B. B. Comegys, 1891–99.

John H. Converse, 1894–1910.

J. W. C. Leveridge, 1895–96.

Society were the corporation, and they annually elected managers for three years, or to fill unexpired terms thereof. The managers elected the officers annually, and appointed the standing committees. The editor, secretary of missions, missionaries and all other workers were nominated by the respective committees. They may be either laymen or clergymen, but they must be elected or approved by the board.

The board of officers and managers of the Union were also empowered "to appoint such other officers not herein before provided for as may be necessary; to provide for and regulate the admission of persons being citizens of the United States as members of the corporation, and to make all other laws and regulations necessary to the good government of the corporation and not repugnant to the constitution and laws of the United States or of this commonwealth."[1]

The managers are elected by ballot, at the annual meeting of the life and annual members who form the corporation. The Society must ratify any sale or transfer of property approved by the board, or any change in the charter, to make the same valid. The act of incorporation by the state of Pennsylvania places the Society in the class of benevolent institutions. It, therefore, has neither stock nor stockholders, the property being held in trust by the corporation for its benevolent objects. The managers serve without salary or compensation, esteeming it a work of love and a service for the Master. The officers (except the treasurer, who gives bonds for the faithful performance of his duties) also have served the Society without compensation, and even the onerous duties of the treasurer were performed by Christian business men for over fifty years without salary.

The board of managers distributed the direction of its operations among four standing committees: on publication, on missions, on finance, and an executive committee. These committees consider various plans and operations and recommend measures, from time to time, which to be valid must be approved by the entire board.

The members of the Society or corporation are watchful in regard to maintaining a fair proportionate representation from different evangelical denominations, not only upon its

<hr />

[1] *Charter*, Section V.

board but also upon each of the committees, of such as are willing to co-operate and sustain the work of the Society and to see that no one denomination has a preponderating influence therein. Its publications are specially guarded, since not more than three members of the committee on publication can be of the same denomination, and even then nothing shall be printed or published or sold by the Society, or at its expense, to which any member of the committee shall object.[1]

The uniform purpose of the Society has been, and is, to publish and distribute its literature at cost, or on the smallest margin above cost. The profit, if any, has been and is set aside for the improvement of its publications, for their gratuitous distribution to those who may be unable to purchase them, or for its benevolent work.

It will appear from the foregoing basis and statements in respect to the structure of the Society that the American Sunday-School Union is not to be classed strictly as *un*-denominational in membership, since all its members and workers are connected with, and active members of, some particular church. It cannot, of course, be called *anti*-denominational, for these members, as individuals, support and are in good standing in their respective denominations. In some sense it is *inter*-denominational, but not in the sense in which that term is often used, viz., to imply a body composed of representatives officially appointed and recognized by ecclesiastical authority.

The American Sunday-School Union is rather a voluntary union of individual Christians, of different religious views and creeds, co-operating for the purpose of promoting religious education through Bible study and the establishment of Sunday-schools. It is not a union of churches, nor does it aim to form churches of any particular denomination. It leaves church organization to the discretion and decision of the communities where its Sunday-schools exist.

Big-hearted, consecrated men of affairs, representing the Church of Christ of every name, seeing the multitudes who neglected the Church and religion, were guided by the Spirit to unite in the great mission of teaching the truths of the Bible to those who were otherwise unreached by the gospel.

---

[1] *By-Laws*, Article VII.

It is significant that the managers of the Union, in their first report, recognized their responsibility to submit a report of their proceedings not to the public, but to the *members* of the Society. This point they distinctly state in the opening sentence of their first report. Various clauses in subsequent reports indicate that this first statement was neither an oversight nor an inadvertence, but a candid conviction of the managers in respect to the parties to whom they were chiefly responsible.

Scope and Field.—The managers of the Union, from 1817 on, surveyed and defined the scope and field of their work with the marvelous clearness of seers, and described the unreached communities with such vivid accuracy as to arouse and startle the public conscience. Existing agencies, apparently doing their utmost, left an immense field in the country without gospel instruction. The educational work which ought to be done by the family, the ministry, and the state, was not to be lessened or overlapped. Thus the Union repeatedly emphasized the duty of parents to instruct their children so as to promote stalwart moral and Christian character. The managers declared, "We have no wish to relieve parents of their awful charge. We rather wish they may feel loaded with the burden." To the many non-religious families, and to the indifferent among professing Christian and church members, they had a mission to persuade and stimulate them more faithfully to give religious instruction in their homes. They proposed, also, to provide and to introduce family religious instruction where it was not given.

Nor did the Union aim to overlap, in any sense, the work of the ministry or of the organized church. The proclamation of the gospel by preaching, except in such communities as were unreached by the local church, was no part of the great Union Sunday-school work. On the other hand, their aim was to bring to the attention of the local church and its ministry, communities that had been overlooked and which might receive the preached gospel, and to aid them in doing it. The Union sought out those unreached communities, usually outside of cities and large towns, and in the open country, where the people were so divided in nationality, in speech, in religious prejudices, or by irreligious views, that a successful organization for the study of the Bible could be secured only upon the basis of our common Christianity.

Public Schools.—Again they defined the field of Sunday-school operations for the Union and marked it off from that of the common school. Everywhere they proposed to stimulate the state, to provide free public schools, to teach the elements of a physical and intellectual education under government support. This would relieve the Sunday-school from the burden which it early had of teaching so many illiterates to read in order that they might themselves study the Bible.

This careful defining of the scope of the Union's work made it quite improbable that there could be overlapping of its work with other agencies of the church. It made the Union the forerunner of the churches, opening a way for them more successfully to follow.

Thus the Union found that its scope was not narrow nor was its field small. The population of the United States in 1824 was between ten and twelve million. Of these about three million were between four and sixteen years of age. It was computed that not more than one hundred thousand of this number were members of existing Sunday-schools in 1824, and this was considered a very liberal computation. To this number out of Sunday-schools, immigration was adding rapidly. A large proportion of these immigrants were non-evangelical, so that the thoughtful in the churches were alarmed. It was said that the population would double in twenty-five years and that the number under religious instruction should have been ten times as great as it was.

With courage and large optimism, the managers addressed themselves afresh to the problem before them, proposing vigorous advances along several lines at the same time. Realizing that every worker required proper tools with which to work and proper information in regard to his work, the Union sought anew:

(1) To gather and to disseminate information in respect to the best methods of religious education, to provide thorough equipment for Sunday-schools, systematic courses of Bible lessons, and religious literature.

(2) To develop leaders in different communities who should organize the workers into local, county, and state unions,

enlisting voluntary helpers and employing skilled missionary superintendents.

(3) To encourage communities in organization and in service for the above purposes, to offer them the best facilities for securing literature and every kind of equipment, at or below the cost of production.

Hence the managers put all their energies, at first, into the preparation of a lesson system, dictionaries, commentaries, manuals, lesson-helps, primers, texts, tracts and requisites for the full equipment of Sunday-school and family study, besides issuing a variety of periodicals for teachers and scholars, and creating a body of juvenile religious literature sufficient to supply any and every community with a suitable library.

Systematic Survey.—The managers of the American Sunday-School Union improved the system of gathering information from all the schools affiliated with it, and from other schools. A system had been pursued by the Sunday and Adult School Union which the managers enlarged and improved. A special question blank for reports was issued covering four pages of large legal-cap paper, upon the margin of which they printed forty-two questions, asking for information in regard to the local union and schools, and the condition of the community. These questions were classified in several groups, calling for a census of the school or schools in the Union, giving the name, location, officers, number of teachers and scholars of each sex, and the time when each school was held, as well as how the school was controlled; the number of scholars in each of three grades, the number of teachers and scholars who had made profession of faith, how the expenses of the union or the school were provided, the interest parents and pastors took in the school, how often it was visited by a minister of the gospel, whether it had a concert of prayer, what methods were taken to increase the interest in the school, and the influence of the school or schools upon the families and neighborhood where held. They further asked if there were other neighborhoods without Sunday-schools or churches, how many and where they were, and how they might be supplied, the character of the literature used or read in the neighborhood and in the school, and finally the obstacles or difficulties to the prosperity of the school or union. If the report came from a local union, they were asked to give the census of each school connected therewith.

In this survey, they further sought trustworthy information in regard to education generally—the character of the common schools, the method of teaching, how the school was housed, how the scholars were rewarded—and instances of remarkable providences connected with the work in any way, or with the community.

When we recall the scant facilities for transportation, having neither telephones, telegraphs, railroads, nor steamboats, and the slow and costly mails—each letter or piece of paper costing from six to twenty-five cents for transmission—and discover that they secured reports from every one of the then twenty-four states, and also from territories of the United States, and moreover extended their outlook and their gleaning of facts to British America, the West Indies, South America and to most of the countries of the Old World, Sunday-school workers of today may well be amazed at their admirable scientific methods, and at the thorough information which these industrious laborers of about a century ago were able to collect.

The returns of this survey led the managers to declare they "felt more deeply than ever the immensity of their work;" and they strove "as they were able, to proportion their exertions to the wants of our growing country." [1]

With Christian patriotism, they affirmed that the virtue and prosperity of a nation like ours depended upon implanting in the hearts of the people those principles which alone can qualify them to be good citizens, and they were sure that only so could the nation be preserved from "that ruin with which it will be overwhelmed, should vice and infidelity loosen the restraints of virtue and make our population a turbulent mass of moral pollution." [2]

Again they announced, as the result of their survey:

> Our country still spreads before us a wide uncultivated field. . . . The meager provision which she makes for juvenile education must be more and more enlarged until all her children may learn with equal privilege the rudiments of a common education. . . . Were each of our separate legislatures to make a provision, as wise and ample as have some of them, for

1 *Report*, 1826, p. 3.　　　　　　2 *Ibid.*, pp. 15, 16.

early education, the necessity of Sunday-schools would not be superseded. Their aid would then be required to make the young thoroughly acquainted with the Word of God, because, although the good old custom of reading the Scriptures at the beginning and close of school still obtains in some places; yet, generally, the Bible is a book almost wholly excluded from our common schools and if read at all, rarely, with the solemn reverence and fixed attention which become an assembly of young mortals.[1]

Family Instruction Aided.—In respect to the charge often made in those early days, and sometimes repeated now, that Sunday-schools interfere with family instruction, the Union said:

> Our Society has always deprecated the tendency of Sunday-schools to lessen the sense of parental responsibility and to devolve the whole duty of the religious instruction of children on strangers. . . . On the contrary, the Christian responsibility of parents is greatly increased by the multiplied assistance which the teaching and reading furnished by Sunday-schools give to the due performance of their duty.[2]

Church Relations Urged.—Again this survey brought to the attention of the Society the frequency with which the denominational Sunday-school was independent of, or loosely allied to, the church. It led them to make the following declaration:

> Sunday-schools need more—much more—of the co-operation and countenance of churches and their pastors. It is an erroneous opinion that the instruction given in these (union) schools interferes with the rights, or relieves the duties of parents or pastors. And it should be distinctly understood, as it has been repeatedly and distinctly avowed, that the American Sunday-School Union does nothing, and desires nothing, that shall prevent the inculcation of truth, as it is held by the parent or pastor of any evangelical denomination. . . . It avoids everything distinctive in doctrine, discipline and worship which is a controversy between the denominations, it teaches nothing contrary to those distinctive doctrines, but simply leaves to the pastors and officers of churches and to the parents of the children all the opportunities and facilities for instructing them in the truth as they regard it, which they could all enjoy if the institution of Sunday-schools was unknown.

It even claimed to increase and multiply the facilities for instruction a thousand-fold. While favoring the closest relations between the denominational school and the church, it

---

[1] *American Sunday-School Magazine*, 1824, Vol. 1, p. 2.
[2] *Report*, 1838, p. 19.

still left the pastor and church to determine "by their own conduct and measures, how close and mutually advantageous shall be its connection with Sunday-schools."

It is clear, therefore, from the repeated utterances and practices of the Union, that it regarded its work as that of a pioneer of the churches of every name—as a vanguard preparing the way for their coming in the newer settlements—as an auxiliary agency for reaching mixed communities in the older states. It aimed to keep alive in such places a vital, living Christianity, by inculcating its essential and fundamental doctrines.

Sunday-school statistics based upon careful information secured by the Union through "a general survey of Sunday-schools throughout the world," led the managers to compute the Sunday-school membership in 1825 at 857,905, exclusive of those in the United States. During the year there was reported an increase abroad, chiefly in Great Britain and Ireland, of 194 schools, 670 teachers, and 25,722 pupils. In view of this increase, it was estimated that the number of pupils abroad was 900,000. In the United States, the Union computed there were 180,000, making "a grand toal of 1,080,000 Sabbath scholars in the world." The managers add: "This sum, though large, is only the 1,050th part of that portion of the population of this earth who, were proper means employed, might be brought under the influence of Sabbath-school instruction." [1]

Three Lines of Work.—In view of the general survey of conditions, the Union proposed to make definite advances along three related lines:

(1) Educational: by providing a system of lessons, a decidedly religious juvenile literature, a complete equipment for the school, and definite information upon principles and methods of teaching.

(2) Organization: by promoting teachers' meetings in the local school, by forming county and state unions among schools and teachers for inspiration, counsel, and mutual improvement.

(3) Extension of Sunday-schools: by employing general agents and missionaries and providing a medium of communication for and between all Sunday-school workers.

[1] *Report*, 1826, p. 13.

The managers affirmed that one of their acts was to establish the *American Sunday-School Magazine,* a monthly journal devoted to the interests of the cause. This journal had been projected and planned by the Sunday and Adult School Union in 1823, and an editor had been found in Mr. Frederick W. Porter of New York, a young man experienced in editorial work. The American Sunday-School Union also purchased *The Sunday-School Repository,* which had been issued for a short time by the New York Sunday-School Union. It was urged that a magazine of this kind, properly conducted and supported as a medium of intelligence and information—a repository of useful and able discussions on Sunday-school operations, and containing plans, views and reports of conferences in respect to the cause—would not only be a witness to the world of the value of Sunday-schools, but would increase their moral and physical strength by cementing them together in the common work.

The Union also promptly provided a monthly publication for the pupils. The teachers of the New Haven Sabbath-School Union (in connection with the Sunday and Adult School Union) had planned a small monthly periodical called *The Teachers' Offering* or *Sabbath Scholars' Magazine,* in November, 1823, intended "as a monthly reward book for punctual attendance, correct recitation and good behavior." This periodical the Union purchased in 1824, and changed its title to *The Youth's Friend.* This was enlarged in its scope to include "a great variety of excellent reading for children." It was a sixteen-page magazine, each monthly number illustrated with engravings and supplied with inspirational reading for the home.

In rapid succession the Union issued circulars and pamphlets urging Sunday-school workers to organize local, county, and state unions, suggested a suitable constitution and plan of procedure in forming the same, issued rules and regulations for the efficient management of schools, proposed systems of rewards, published instructions to aid teachers and to guide the librarian in the use and in the keeping of a library, set forth schemes for rewarding and interesting scholars, and in various other ways provided information which indicates the complex organization of Sunday-schools of that day.

Campaign of Education and State Organization.—But the Union did not trust to the printed page alone. Union leaders bent their best energies to select and send forth able instructors and lecturers who explained the system of modern Sunday schools. They sought men qualified to introduce better principles and methods of instruction, with sufficient force and magnetism of address to inspire a deeper and wider interest in the cause at the various centers of population and influence in the country. Some of these men were leading educators in the state and in colleges and higher institutions of learning. A number *gave* their services to the cause, others were paid a moderate salary for devoting all their time and energies for a part or whole of the year to this laudable work. These campaigns of education were sufficiently vigorous to arouse zeal and stimulate enthusiasm in Bible study and in religious education greater than America had ever before witnessed.

Thus the American Sunday-School Union entered upon a nation-wide work, with a vision, a system, and enthusiasm hardly surpassed in the present century. This may be indicated by these earnest words:

> Let us dig deep and lay the living stones on the sure foundation. Let pious parental care, or infant schools for the little ones conducted by wise and tender matrons, prepare the way for the Sabbath-schools. Let Bible societies furnish the Word of God to be read; while our schools give a taste for reading the best things, and teach all in early life to search the sacred Scriptures. Let missionary societies send forth the heralds of the Gospel with these Bibles in their hands, to be explained and applied to those who in Sabbath-schools have become familiarly acquainted with them; and finally, let all Christians do their duty in supplicating the influences of the Holy Spirit in their convincing, enlightening, vivifying, and purifying power.[1]

Thus these seers of a century ago had a vision of bringing together all Sunday-school and Christian educators into one great world Sunday-school union. Not only that, but they also had a wider vision of bringing into close relations and proper articulation, one with the other, all the activities and organizations in the Church of Christ; a world co-operation and federation of all Christendom, of whatever name, joining together for the one great purpose of unitedly proclaiming to every creature the gospel of the kingdom, until it shall tri-

[1] *Report*, 1827, p. xii.

mphantly cover the earth and Christ shall reign as King, to
whom "every knee shall bow," and whom "every tongue shall
confess to the glory of God the Father."

A vigorous campaign of instruction was also carried on, not
only by the general agent but by missionaries (six of them)
employed in 1824 "to establish new Sunday-schools; visit old
ones; revive, animate and encourage such as were languishing;
organize auxiliary unions; explain the objects of the Society
and . . . extend its influence and usefulness." [1]   Besides
these, special agents were sent out on important missions;
men of eminence who were volunteers and unpaid workers, to
organize the Sunday-school forces.   Thus the first state Sunday-school union organized was at Londonderry, New Hampshire, September 9, 1824.   A delegated meeting was called,
through correspondence of the American Sunday-School
Union, which commissioned the Rev. Gardiner Spring, D. D.,
of New York, to attend the convention as a delegate from the
national Society.   Representatives from the various counties
were present, and the state union was organized with Daniel
Dana, D. D., president; Hon. Joshua Darling, vice-president;
John H. Church, D. D., corresponding secretary; Rev. J.
Curtis, recording secretary; and John W. Shepard, treasurer;
with six managers and a secretary in each county, completing
the organization. [2]

The second state to form such a union was Connecticut—
a state which then and since has been counted as foremost in
educational activities.   Those who took part in this second
state Sunday-school union were men of national reputation.
Nathaniel W. Taylor was president; Lyman Beecher, secretary; and others among the officers were Timothy Dwight,
Joel Hawes, and Samuel Mervin.   Those who are familiar
with the history of that period in Connecticut will recognize
these names as among the foremost men in the state, and it
implies that they regarded the formation of a state union as "an
era in the history of moral improvement in Connecticut," and
"an object worthy the high character of the state."   They held
that "Sabbath-schools have accomplished great things, but
they may accomplish much greater good by increasing their

[1] *Report*, 1825, p. 7.
[2] *Report*, 1824, p. 7; *Sunday-School Magazine*, Vol. I, p. 123.

number and improving their plans. . . . We may reason
ably expect that the genial influence of these institutions will
be felt in all our cities and towns and villages."[1]

The enthusiasm created for organization was so wide-spread
that, within eighteen months from the change of name, the
American Sunday-School Union had nearly four hundred
auxiliary unions in twenty-two of the twenty-four states, nine
of them being state unions. The demand for juvenile literature which it had created exceeded all expectations, requiring
the printing of 90,000 pages per day in 1825. In addition to
this, it issued a large quantity of periodical literature and over
600,000 red and blue Scripture tickets per year. It continued
its survey of the whole field, besides sending out reports to be
returned to it from thousands of schools, gathering information
in respect to the numbers, prosperity, methods of instruction,
and increase of its schools, year by year, for several years.
These reports were made on large blanks with the forty-two
questions printed along the margin and space for full replies,
as already described.[2]

The Union also at once began to provide elementary works
for use in the schools, beginning with the *Union Primer*, which
was edited and compiled by a member of the Board (Joseph H.
Dulles, a Yale graduate), who presented the same to the
Society with the stereotype plates from which it was printed,
and which speedily attained a circulation of well-nigh a million
copies. So great was the activity of Sunday-schools and the
call for reading matter that in 1825 the Union reported over
900,000 copies of different publications issued, besides periodicals. In 1827 it reported 1,616,796 copies, making a total
in three years of 3,741,849 copies of publications.[3] *The American Sunday-School Magazine* speedily reached a circulation
of 2,500 copies a month, and *The Youth's Friend* 10,000
copies.

The managers were even more assiduous and careful in
respect to the quality than they were in regard to the quantity
of works issued. They sought to convey "the most important
truths in a pleasing form; adapted to the minds of young
people," so that "they have been read with avidity by thou-

[1] *American Sunday-School Magazine,* 1824, pp. 187, 188.
[2] *Report,* 1826; *Appendix,* p. 1.
[3] *Report,* 1827, p. iii.

ands of persons who have little taste for any other religious
books."[1]

The Committee of Publication created by the Sunday and
Adult School Union was enlarged and given more important
duties by the American Sunday-School Union. The managers observed with regret "that improper books are too generally placed in the hands of youth—books abounding with
foolishness, vulgarity, and falsehood, or otherwise deficient in
relation to their moral influence." They therefore were desirous "not only of furnishing their own schools with suitable
books; but of introducing such books into schools, of a different description, and rendering them so abundant as to force
out of circulation those which tend to mislead the mind and to
fill it with what must be injurious to it in subsequent life."
They regarded this of "importance equalled only by the value
of character in this world, and the soul's everlasting welfare
in the next," so they endeavored "to increase the number and
size, and to elevate the character of their publications."[2]

SKETCHES OF PROMINENT WORKERS

Alexander Henry (1766–1847).—First President of the American Sunday-School Union, 1818–1847.

In a century of Sunday-school service, since its first complete organization—1817–1917—the American Sunday-School
Union has had seven presidents. Mr. Samuel J. Robbins
rendered good service from July to December, 1817, as temporary president, in framing the basis and first constitution of the
early Union of 1817–1824.

The founders of this organized movement were men of deeds
rather than words. They desired as a leader a man with clear
vision, high personal character, sound judgment, and commanding influence. They found Alexander Henry to possess
these qualifications in an eminent degree, and elected him as
president of the perfected organization. Mr. Henry was a
prominent merchant, philanthropist, and Christian citizen. He
had achieved success in business, and twice retired therefrom;
first in 1807, but when the war of 1812 impaired his fortune, he
re-entered business, to retire again in 1818 still a compara-

[1] *Report*, 1827, p. iii.   [2] *Report*, 1826, p. v.

tively young man. After some months of consultation wit
the various school organizations then in Philadelphia an
vicinity, a preliminary organization, with Mr. Robbins, a
temporary president, paved the way for a Union, of which M
Henry was unanimously chosen permanent president. H
brought to the task sagacity, prudence, and long experienc
When the Sunday and Adult School Union was enlarged an
its name changed to the American Sunday-School Union, h
was re-elected to this position of honor. He was a mod
presiding officer. From 1818 to 1847 the record shows that h
presided at every anniversary of the Union except that of 184
when prevented by the illness which ended his life. He was
model chairman also in his self-restraint. He rarely or neve
took the time of the meeting to make a speech, althoug
qualified to present the work in a clear, perspicuous and forcib
manner. He was an inspiration as well as a leader and unde
him the Union work made marvelous progress. The wisdom
enterprise, judgment, and prudence which had enabled hin
twice to amass a fortune in the mercantile business were carrie
into his management of organized Sunday-school work. H
combined expanded views with judicious plans and a vigorou
execution of them. While attached to his own church, and
liberal supporter of it, he was also an ardent lover of Christia
unity and urged that principle in the plans of the Union fo
nation-wide evangelization. His early training qualified hin
for this great work, as the following sketch will show.

Alexander Henry was born in County Down, Ireland, Jun
15, 1766. His mother was left a widow when he was two year
old. He was given a good education, being prepared under
tutor to enter a university, and then was to go into professiona
life. The sudden death of his tutor turned his attention to
mercantile career. In 1783, when the independence of Amer
ica was conceded by treaty, he and an elder brother planned t
emigrate to America and the land of Penn. His brother, fallin
into a love affair about that time, abandoned the trip. Bu
Alexander came alone, bringing a few guineas, a small stock o
hosiery, and some products of Irish looms, with letters of recom
mendation to a mercantile firm in Philadelphia. This firm
promptly engaged him at two hundred and fifty dollars a year
His talent and ability for business were so conspicuous that ir

two months the firm placed him in charge of a branch store at thirteen hundred dollars a year. Then, owing to a bank becoming embarrassed, Mr. Henry decided to go into business for himself, and such was the confidence reposed in him by his friends at home that in less than seven years he was overrun with consignments from the best commercial houses in England and Ireland.

Mr. Henry united with the Second Presbyterian Church of Philadelphia in 1803, and threw himself with zeal into religious work. He became a teacher and then an officer in the Sunday-schools of that day and was active in schemes of public education, serving as president of the Board of Education of Philadelphia for about sixteen years.

Under his administration as president of the American Sunday-School Union, it conceived and carried out some of the greatest enterprises in its early history, including the Limited Lessons, and the Mississippi Valley and other great missionary enterprises, which are noticed elsewhere. His associates held him in enthusiastic esteem, "for his expanded views, his judicious execution of well-selected plans, his great personal influence, and his liberal supplies of pecuniary aid." "He was counted a good theologian, sound in the faith, fixed in his religious belief but charitable toward those who differed from him." He was generous in his benevolence; among other things he purchased a large stock of wood for many years, which in winter he distributed to the needy. Before there was a general tract society in this country, he purchased tracts in England and distributed them, and secured the writing of new ones at his own expense. He paid for the education of young men for the gospel ministry and was counted among the first in this country to engage in instruction in modern Sunday-schools. Among educators of large vision, he was highly esteemed.

His youngest daughter, Mary Henry, became the wife of Samuel Austin Allibone, LL.D., a distinguished bibliographer and the editor for ten years (1868–1878) of the American Sunday-School Union's publications. His great grandson (of the same name) has held for many years the responsible position of secretary of the Presbyterian Board of Publication and Sabbath School Work.

Joseph H. Dulles (1795–1876).

Among the founders of the American Sunday-School Union there were business and professional men who, by their college and university training, were specially fitted to render important service in any educational scheme like that projected by the Union. Of these Joseph H. Dulles easily stood in the front rank. He and his associates knew how to bring the operations of the Union into an effective system.

Joseph H. Dulles was born in Charleston, South Carolina, February 7, 1795. His father, a merchant, immigrated from Dublin, Ireland, to Charleston, South Carolina, and was taken prisoner by Sir Henry Clinton at the siege of that city. The son graduated from Yale College in 1814, and was engaged in mercantile and religious enterprises in Philadelphia for about sixty years. He was a close friend of the Rev. Dr. Thomas H. Skinner, Sr., of the Rev. Dr. James P. Wilson, and of Albert Barnes, and of many other theologians and educators who were interested in the work of the Union. He was an officer successively in the Fifth, First, and Calvary Presbyterian Churches of Philadelphia.

He became a manager of the Sunday and Adult School Union in 1823, and urged that the name be changed to the American Sunday-School Union. He was a member of the committee which drew up the constitution and by-laws of the Union under its present name, and advocated measures which promised to secure marked progress in the Sunday-school cause in America. Thus he advocated the publication of *The Sunday-School Magazine*, the first American periodical for Sunday-school teachers; and aided in selecting F. W. Porter as its editor, in 1824. He called attention to the need of a new building for the Society's use in 1825, and that year compiled the *Union Primer*, of which millions of copies were circulated. He suggested, and was sent to secure, Frederick A. Packard, a successful lawyer of Massachusetts, as editor of the Society's publications in 1828, and was active in planning the Mississippi Valley Enterprise of 1830, and also aided in starting the publication of a *Sunday-School Teachers' Journal* weekly, the first of its kind in the world. His reputation among national Sunday-school workers is indicated by his being a delegate to the First National Sunday-School Convention of 1832, and honored by an appointment on the Committee of Business and Inter-rogatories, with John Hall, John Wiegand, James B. Longacre, and Frederick W. Porter. This committee appears to have been the most important one in the conventions of 1832 and of 1833, inasmuch as it had the selection and presentation of the various topics and matters to be considered by the convention. These were believed to represent the most advanced methods in Sunday-school work attainable at that time.

Although Mr. Dulles was constantly pressed with the cares and responsibilities attending an active business, he found time to project and aid in carrying into effect various measures for the advancement of the Sunday-school cause. His literary training qualified him to prepare and repeatedly revise or re-write the *Union Primer*, and also material for a *First Reader*, both of which were printed with engravings, and the plates and copyrights were generously presented by him to the Union. Though a pioneer in the American Sunday-School Union, he was one of the few men who ever aimed to keep fully abreast of the progress of the times, rarely looking back, but always look-ing forward for improvements. He always welcomed and ad-vocated new measures when they promised larger results.

He put his work before himself. Thus it was characteristic that his last request should be that none of the societies with which he had been connected take any *public* notice of his death. His associates, however, recalled his long and valuable service, his earnest devotion, his profound foresight and his unostentatious liberality to a society which he regarded as a leading agency in evangelizing the country. He closed a long and useful career on March 12, 1876.

Francis Scott Key (1780–1843).

Mr. Key was a lawyer, statesman, orator, patriot and poet. He attained national distinction as counsel in some of the no-table historic cases before the United States Supreme Court, and was given a delicate diplomatic mission to adjust troubles between the Creek Indians and the immigrants to Alabama, which he settled to the satisfaction of all parties. During the war of 1812, Mr. Key was sent with a flag of truce to the British Admiral to secure the release of Dr. Beams, a fellow-townsman of Key's, whose home was in Georgetown, District of Columbia. The British Army was bombarding Fort McHenry, one of the defences of Baltimore, and Key was detained on the fleet and compelled to witness an all-night assault on the fort. Worn out and overcome by anxiety, he longed for the day, and when dawn came by the aid of a spy-glass he saw the United States flag still floating over the fortress; his joy flashed forth in the poetic lines which have become a great national anthem, "The Star Spangled Banner."

Mr. Key was an earnest Christian, a teacher of a large Bible class, and prominent in the conventions of the Episcopal Church. He was chosen a manager of the American Sunday-School Union in 1824, and continued for a number of years to take an active interest in the Society's work, presiding at a great meeting in Washington in 1830, to promote the extension of Sunday-schools in the valley of the Mississippi. He was active and successful in interesting senators, diplomats, justices of the United States Supreme Court, and members of Congress in that enterprise, and secured the attendance of several of them, including the Hon. Daniel Webster, to make addresses at that meeting.

SECTION III

UNIFORM LIMITED BIBLE LESSONS

MOST of the Sunday-school lessons previous to 1820 were either from the catechism or were verses from the Bible or from hymns chosen and memorized by the scholar.

Memorizing Era.—This system or lack of system was chiefly repeating, in a parrot-like manner, what had been committed to memory. Scholars were permitted to choose any part of the Bible or any hymn, and were encouraged by rewards to commit to memory as much as they could. It was evident that the scholars did not understand the meaning of much they were thus repeating. There was little time for explanation or application of the lesson. Even when the sessions of the school were two hours or more in length, they were too short for the teacher to hear the scholars repeat all that had been memorized. A verbal memory was abnormally developed—and the mind crammed to its utmost capacity.

A remarkable example of this gigantic memorizing was that of "Blind Allick" (Alexander Lyons), of Stirling, Scotland. James Gall and others testify that he could repeat the entire Bible or any verse or chapter, if a single clause were given to him, and could also tell where it was found. But if he were asked to quote a verse in proof that man was a sinner, or any verse to tell how he was to be saved, he was totally at a loss for the verse. His memory tenaciously held the words, but his mind utterly failed to grasp the sense. True, the excessive memorizing of verses was rather an abuse of a good thing than the right use of it. Harm was in the excess, and not in the thing itself. Nevertheless educators pointed out better and more scientific methods of instruction. It, however, was an experimental period in educational work.

Educational Theories.—The foremost educators were still feeling their way through theory and practice toward some satisfactory principles. Of the practical experiments along broader lines only those need to be noted that were on trial in advanced schools, and among educators during this memorizing era. Lewis Baldwin, principal of a young ladies' school in Philadelphia, after giving a trial to a plan which he had conceived for imparting religious instruction on non-sectarian lines, upon the essential doctrines of religion and salvation, prepared and published, in 1816, *The Biblical Interrogatory*, or questions explanatory of sacred history, prophecy, etc., covering the most interesting portions of the Old and the New Testaments. It was designed for use in families and schools, as he quaintly says, "to facilitate the acquaintance of the rising generation with these precious oracles of God." His questions were printed without answers, but references to Scripture are given after each question to aid the teacher and scholar in finding the answer. This is a small 18mo. volume, of over 300 pages, and has chronological and other tables. The work was commended by several of the most prominent ministers of different denominations in Philadelphia. About the same time *Lessons for Bible Classes* were prepared by the Rev. Dr. John McDowell, which attained a circulation of 100,000 copies in ten years, when it was revised and re-issued by the American Sunday-School Union for advanced Bible classes.

Uniform Limited Lessons.—While these and many like works were prepared upon the Socratic plan of teaching, they were quite different in their methods from the ordinary catechism. They followed the fundamental principle of the modern Sunday-school movement, namely, "basing all lessons directly upon the Bible, and sending the teachers and the scholars to that volume rather than to creeds and man-made statements of the truths of the word of God." As already stated, the Sunday and Adult School Union did not encourage cramming the memory, or the parrot-like recitations which prevailed in 1817. As wise builders, they proposed to have their work constructive rather than destructive, and therefore did not denounce the prevailing system, but rather undertook to displace it by what seemed to them a far more intelligent and improved mode of instruction.

From 1820 to 1823 the number of advanced schools which dissented from this excessive memorizing steadily increased in different parts of the country. To exclude the unprofitable plan of committing large portions of Scripture to memory without religious instruction, a system providing lessons of from ten to twenty Bible verses to be used by all the schools was conceived and tried by several, but notably by two of the schools connected with the New York Sunday-School Union Society. This Limited Lesson System commended itself at once to the best Sunday-school workers in New York, and was speedily introduced into most of their schools. It was adopted by the American Sunday-School Union, and recommended for use in all its auxiliaries, then comprising a majority of the schools in the United States. A list of the lessons, with the dates on which they were to be studied, was provided, so that absent scholars might learn the lesson in course. The *same lesson text* was to be used in *the whole school*, with the possible exception of the infant class not able to read, and in a few cases, of advanced Bible classes, which already had adopted a scheme of lessons that covered a large portion of the Bible. This system of study was further urged for use in all schools, and was generally adopted, making it, therefore, a "Uniform System of Lessons."

To facilitate the use of this new scheme of uniform lessons, different teachers' helps were issued, adapted to the main school and to several grades—the germ of the multitudinous Sunday-school helps of today.

Aids on Lessons.—The aids for teachers and scholars on this early uniform system of lessons were based upon the educational theories of the first quarter of the last century. They comprised leading features of lesson helps developed by the uniform system fifty years later (1872). It is therefore worth while to sketch their origin and character.

Sunday-school workers of Great Britain and America developed systems of instruction quite independently of each other, partly because of the lack of communication between the two countries, but chiefly because of the different conditions of the people and families that were to be instructed. An examination of the systems of lessons provided for early American Sunday-schools, impresses the worker of today with the wisdom, far-sightedness, and fairly accurate pedagogical knowledge of those early educators. In some respects they

were a generation in advance of their age; their ideals anticipated many of the features of the advanced methods current
in the twentieth century.   During the catechism, and spelling-
book, and memorizing eras of the early Sunday-school movement, individualism reigned almost supreme; each scholar was
separately taught the alphabet, each more advanced scholar
recited his own lesson.   Some have designated it the period
when the "graded-lesson theory" ran wild, for, as a rule, each
scholar had a special lesson.   Classes there were, in name, but
classification was for discipline rather than for instruction.
There was neither uniformity nor federation in the teaching
work.

Dissatisfaction with such a fragmentary and individualistic
system increased in America and forced the workers (even
though not expert educators) to cast about for some better
one.   It was obvious that the lessons must be limited, even
for memorizing, to admit proper school or class instruction.
Truman Parmele of Utica, New York, proposed a list of
selected lessons from the four Gospels and the Acts, in 1823,
and issued helps upon them.   The questions were few—some
calling for thoughtful study in addition to memorizing the
lesson.   His work was named *Questions on the Historical
Parts of the New Testament*, designed for Sabbath-schools,
by Truman Parmele, a superintendent of the Utica Union
Sabbath School.   (Appendix, p. 456.)   The preliminary
issue consisted of lessons covering the first three chapters of
Matthew and was intended "merely to give the teacher an
idea of the manner in which he should proceed in his explanation."   It also contained an outline of the lessons upon the
entire Gospel of Matthew and upon most of the Gospel of
Mark.

Early in the same year, S. W. Seton, familiarly known as
"Father" Seton, and William A. Tomlinson, of New York,
arranged a scheme of lessons, *without questions*, for general
use in all the classes of their schools.   These were passages of
Scripture covering the leading events in the life of Christ.
"Father" Seton was well-known as an expert infant or primary
class instructor in the public schools.   Their system is thus
described: "They have arranged select portions of Scripture
for every Sabbath in the year, comprising from ten to twenty

RECORDING SECRETARIES

John C. Pechin, 1818–21.

Abraham Martin, 1825–28

Frederick A. Packard, 1829–59.

M. A. Wurts, 1861–81.

John S. Hart, 1860

Richard Ashhurst, 1883–93.

J. M. Andrews, 1894–1910.

SUPERINTENDENTS OF DEPOSITORIES

George S. Scofield.

Alexander Kirkpatrick.

verses each, one of which portions is announced each Sabbath to the whole school and all are engaged the following Sabbath in receiving instructions from the *same lessons*. Each scholar is supplied with a printed card containing the selection, the lessons [being] numbered in order. The scholars are required to read the portion during the week and after receiving instruction on it, to commit it for recitation. . . . These lessons are chronologically arranged, so as to embrace all the leading incidents of the gospel in due order." The pastors gave a weekly lecture to the teachers on the lesson for each Sabbath. It was also the topic at the monthly concert.[1]

This system of lessons attracted wide attention and was enthusiastically adopted. An association of teachers in New York declared, by formal resolution, October, 1824, "that the lessons for recitation in Sabbath-schools should be selected and previously explained by the teachers." It issued the same year a list of seventeen select lessons, on slips or cards, to be used for a few months from January 1, 1825. But in March, 1825, the American Sunday-School Union printed a list of select lessons for one year in card form, which comprised studies on the life of Christ.[2] Their object was to give schools in other cities than New York, and in smaller towns, an opportunity to test the new system of study. The list numbered the lessons, cited the passage of Scripture (not printing the text), and gave a title to each lesson. The lists were divided into four parts, one for each quarter of the year, and printed *without question, note,* or *comment.* This first annual list comprised forty-nine lessons, the other Sabbaths being given to the quarterly examination of the scholars. The select or limited Scripture lessons, from 1824, appear to have been quite different in the number of lessons for the first and second annual courses, and also in the length and in the character of the topics selected. Thus the number of lessons for the first annual course is variously given at forty-nine in one list, forty-seven in an announcement, and, later, forty lessons for the year, and even thirty-eight and thirty-six in other lists.[3]

The system was successfully introduced into Sunday-

[1] *Report New York Sunday-School Union Society,* May, 1825, p. 14.
[2] *Sunday-School Magazine,* 1825, p. 83.
[3] *Report,* 1826, pp. 92, 110, 111, 112 *Appendix;* 1827, pp. xxvii, xxviii, 25, 26, 119, 120 *Appendix;* 1826, p. 25. See *Appendix,* p. 457, for reference to the Selected Lessons used during previous years.

schools in New York, Philadelphia, Boston, Albany, and elsewhere. Wherever tried, it proved satisfactory and aroused great enthusiasm.

The second year's course of select uniform lessons followed and was issued with the first year's course—the two comprising eighty-nine lessons; forty-nine in the first course, and thirty-six or forty in the second. Of the second year's course of only thirty-six or forty it was said: "The course is intended to occupy every Sabbath through the year, excepting the first Sabbath of every month and one Sabbath in every quarter, which should be given to reviewing the lessons and an examination before the pastor of the church."

A general call for this system of lessons made it evident that the "select uniform system" had won the day. In response to the wider call, the list was again carefully revised and re-issued; the first course of lessons was reduced to forty. Of this revised course they said: "The useful effects, as exhibited in the few schools that have fully tested it, left it in no way doubtful that the general adoption of it would be conducive to the rapid improvement of other schools. . . . The design of the system is to exclude the unprofitable plan of committing large portions of the Scripture to memory *without religious instruction;* and to introduce a method whereby the scholars shall receive particular instruction on *all* that they commit to memory. . . . A list of the lessons, with the date of those Sabbaths on which they occur, is provided for the superintendents conducting the schools and the ministers engaged to lecture on the lessons. . . . Similarly, some cards are printed for the use of the scholars, so that when absent they may read and learn the lessons in the course. . . . The number of lessons is forty, being ten for each quarter. The last Sabbath in the month the lessons are omitted for the purpose of giving other religious instruction."

This custom of assigning one Sabbath each month to reciting proofs in answer to monthly questions prepared by the Union, and of giving instruction on the Ten Commandments and in the catechism, prevailed in the New York schools. Again, the American Sunday-School Union, in issuing the revised system and list, suggested that schools should spend one Sabbath each month in a review, thus providing fifty-two lessons for the fifty-two Sundays of the year. The schools were left free, however, to conduct a review once each quarter as before, and to give the other Sabbaths to special lessons on the Commandments, on the peculiar doctrines of each church, or in the church catechism.

The American Sunday-School Union expressed the hope that the new system would be adopted by all its auxiliaries [practically, it was] and by all Sabbath-schools in the whole country. Thus the projectors proposed to secure *uniform* lessons. Already the hope was expressed "that this plan will very soon be so systematized that *every school* may be furnished with the *same lesson*—that thus every teacher and every scholar may be occupied upon the same subject at the very same time."[1] Here was a Uniform Lesson System for all schools, on the wise plan of freedom in using it, for the entire school, giving an option for other special lessons for the Infant Class, and advanced lessons for higher Bible Classes, but offered for *all* to use at the same time.

Judson's Questions.—To facilitate the study of this new *uniform* system of lessons the New York Sunday-School Union, in connection with the American Sunday-School Union, issued a series of questions on the selected Scripture Lessons, prepared by Albert Judson, who was for some time employed in the extension and improvement of Sunday-schools in New York.

The first set of helps was in two volumes of about 200 pages each, each volume covering the forty lessons, for a year's study, and being noted as part of a "five-year" cycle of lessons. The list of lessons with titles was inserted at the end of the volume. The Scripture text was not printed except in special editions at the end of the volume. The first year's course as revised began with the lesson on the appearance of the angel to Zacharias and included the history of the events of our Lord's life, death, resurrection and ascension, and was counted the "historic course." The second year's course included lessons on the parables and teaching of our Lord. Every lesson was limited to from fifteen to twenty-five verses. Volume III, the third years' course of lessons, was announced as ready, June 1, 1828.

To aid the teachers in grading their instruction to the

[1] *Report*, 1826, p. 9.

needs of the scholar, there were three grades of questions in each lesson. The first was designed to be plain and easy; the second of less simplicity, requiring more thought and leading the teacher and his pupil to inquire into the meaning of the text; the third was still more difficult and general in scope, extending to passages in different parts of the Bible bearing upon the same subject. Interspersed with these were questions relating to the geography, customs, and oriental coloring of the medium through which the truth was presented. At the end of the volume were plans and suggestions upon conducting public examinations of the scholars at the end of each quarter, and an "Address to Teachers" on their duties, and urging fidelity therein.

The plan was warmly commended by nearly all of the foremost ministers of every evangelical denomination in New York, Philadelphia, and other large cities. It was endorsed by Dr. James Milnor, Dr. J. M. Matthews, Provost of New York University, Dr. Gardiner Spring, Dr. Henry Chase, Dr. Archibald Maclay, and others, of the Baptist, Dutch Reformed, Methodist Episcopal, Presbyterian, Protestant Episcopal, and various other churches.

This system of lessons and these helps and fresh works of exposition on the Bible marked a new era in Sunday-school progress. One leading educator declared, "At once instruction became more intelligent, more thorough, and more effective." Those using it said they "observed the working at the time and noted how, at once, new character was given to the institution, that it truly was a *congregation of Bible schools.* Teachers of little or no experience, however, required brief notes on the lesson to use in class work. These were also provided. There were, in fact, at least three helps which appeared about the same time from three different points of view and, as Chancellor Ferris noted, were entirely independent of one another. In addition to the one by Parmele and that by Judson, already noticed, a third was issued entitled *A New Series of Questions on the Select Scripture Lessons for Sabbath Schools,* by a superintendent, who was understood to be Harvey Fisk. He knew of Judson's questions, and says, "Some will ask, 'Why publish a new series, since Judson's have been so extensively approved?'" His answer is, "We think the new series will be far better adapted to promote the success and prosperity of Sunday-schools in the country." His preface implies that he thought Judson's helps too difficult for the average rural school. The two, however, were soon after combined into one.

Of the new lesson system and its helps it was further declared: "Not a point of interest or importance is contained in a given portion of the Word of God but may be brought out, and the scholar is constantly advancing in the knowledge of divine truth, and, if he completes the whole course, [five years], his knowledge of Bible history, geography, biography, biblical antiquities, and what is essentially momentous of scriptural truth, will be very extensive."

Art of Questioning.—Moreover, they had this to say on the Socratic mode of teaching Scripture: "The plan aims to secure some right understanding of the Scripture study. For this end it requires the teachers to make use of simple and various questions—questions suited to compel attention to every minute point, to excite and draw forth thought and to awaken the moral sensibility of the heart. Few teachers are qualified to discharge this duty without help. All are aided by a judicious directory in their own preparation."

The two kinds of helps upon the same scheme of lessons—that by Judson and by Fisk—were combined, revised, and re-edited, and issued by the American Sunday-School Union. But, before this, the demand for Judson's helps had been far in excess of the supply—7,000 copies of the first volume were issued in New York, and were found utterly inadequate. The American Sunday-School Union purchased the right to issue 50,000 copies of the first and second volumes. This failed also to meet the demand. Several editions were rushed through the press in America and large editions were immediately reprinted in London by the Religious Tract Society for use in English schools. Fisk's helps were recognized as containing some features wanting in Judson's, and so, with the cordial consent of the respective authors, Mr. Fisk was chosen to combine the best features of the two into one. This combined system was revised by the editors and the committee of the American Sunday-School Union and became the forerunner of the *Union Questions.*

It was called a compilation, "by Harvey Fisk in conjunction with the authors of the previous helps," and "revised by the committee of publication of the American Sunday-School Union."

It will be seen, therefore, that the first issue of the famous *Union Question* volumes was based on this system of select, uniform lessons, the Bible texts being those already selected and approved by educators entirely independent of Mr. Fisk, and of any of the question or other helps on the texts for study.

The purpose of Fisk's later work was tersely stated: "The great object of a book of questions is to excite the mind to a careful and thorough examination of the Scriptures. When the mind is once aroused and then led forward in the right course, it receives no benefit by being burdened with too many questions. This sentiment is imbibed from long practice in this mode of examining the Scriptures." To guard against "parrot teaching" and "parrot reciting," this caution is added, "Too many questions also render the instruction mechanical and prevent the teacher from the exercise of his own powers." The new helps were graded and, at the same time, were so framed as to meet the needs of all Sunday-school teachers as well as of all those who gave instruction in families—practically, for a Home Department. Thus, under family instruction, it was said in the preface to the first volume, "Some families are so situated that their children cannot be connected with any school. Some parents who are thus situated have already introduced this system of teaching their children on the Sabbath, either before or after the time of public worship." Here is a *Home Department* early established in connection with the first system of uniform lessons.

Moreover, a book of questions alone was found to be inadequate also as a help upon the new system of lessons. In response to wide calls, the *American Sunday-School Magazine* and other journals began to furnish notes and comments on the same system of lessons, with added illustrations and applications. Specimens of a lesson system ascribed to James Gall found their way to this country and explanations based on his plan were prepared and issued. These comprised a five-fold form of treatment of each lesson text; that is, teachers' helps in five distinct forms of (1) narrative, (2) questions,

(3) explanations, (4) symbols, and (5) practical lessons, which were issued week by week upon the same lesson text. Many other forms of helps were issued, but those already described give a fair idea of the multiplex aids provided for Sunday-school teachers who used this early, select uniform lesson system. Many others in more permanent form and of wider scope followed.

Bible Dictionaries.—Even these multiplied aids only partially met the widespread need. Progressive teachers desired something further than mere notes and comments, excellent as they were. There were calls for a comprehensive but inexpensive dictionary of the Bible and for similar aids in Bible geography, Bible history and biblical antiquities, portable maps of Bible lands, and a cyclopædia of manners, customs and habits in oriental lands. These added requisites the American Sunday-School Union undertook to provide, securing a foremost scholar to edit a dictionary of the Bible,[1] and another to prepare a work on biblical antiquities,[2] and a third on Bible geography,[3] and others on history—biblical and ecclesiastical—so that, as these were forthcoming rapidly, the new system of uniform lessons produced a library of auxiliary books bearing upon Bible study. Furthermore, the new system required special study and preparation on the part of superintendent and teacher in respect to methods of instruction, and speedily works on theories of education, applicable to Sunday-schools, were called for; since it was difficult for those who had little mental training to master expositions of Scripture and to have facility in teaching and impressing the Scriptural doctrines. As Chancellor Ferris tersely put it: "The searching into the deep meaning of the sacred volume called for other auxiliaries. Commentaries were required by teachers, or some substitutes. As few teachers could buy them, this want was met by the lectures of many a pastor, who made the select lessons the subject of his weekly exercise."[4] "And then appeared in rapid succession, Nevin's *Jewish* (biblical) *Antiquities*, and the *Bible Dictionary* of the American Sunday-School Union." Chancellor Ferris adds, "The select lessons requiring the question book, and that demanding the

---

[1] Archibald Alexander.   [2] John W. Nevin.
[3] J. H. and J. W. Alexander.   [4] Isaac Ferris, *Memorial Discourse*, p. 46.

expository works, marked an era in Sunday-school instruction."

The system called forth a multiplicity of helps and grades of exposition, as well as question books. "The American Sunday-School Union," said Chancellor Ferris, "has most successfully carried out the propagation of question books. It has thirty-four distinct books of different grades, namely, eight for young children, five manuals of instruction for young Sunday-school classes, fifteen question books proper for Sunday-schools, and six question books for Bible classes."[1]

In New York City alone, nineteen pastors delivered weekly lectures on the select lessons for the ensuing Sabbath, during the year (1826). An evening school for teachers was also recommended.[2]

The history of the evolution of the early Select Uniform Lessons is somewhat surprising to the reader of today. The idea sprang up spontaneously in various widely separated schools. The details of the system varied somewhat and the introduction and use of the lessons during the trial years (1824–1828) overlapped, as might be expected in any new scheme, in the process of evolution and introduction. But each successive list tended to improve the scheme.

Five-Year Lesson Cycle (1827).—This select uniform system took more definite form in New York, where S. W. Seton, W. A. Tomlinson, and Anthony P. Halsey, as a committee, associating with themselves the Rev. Albert Judson, prepared an outline course of lessons to be put before the public. As a result of trial schemes for some time, a course of five years' lessons was decided upon; the first year comprising the mission and life of our Lord, the second year studies upon the parables and teachings in the Gospels, for the third year it was first proposed to study the Epistles and the founding of the Church as given in the book of Acts, but this was changed to studies in the Old Testament for the third and fourth years, including Genesis and biographies of prominent persons therein. The course concluded with studies in the book of Acts for the fifth year.

---

[1] Isaac Ferris, *Memorial Discourse*, p. 47.
[2] *Report New York Sunday-School Union*, 1827, p. 6. *Appendix*, p. 457.

Many changes were made also in the number of lessons from year to year, as already stated. In the first year's course, as announced, there were forty-nine lessons, and thirty-six in the second. But after the trial years the number of lessons was made forty in each year's course. The other twelve Sabbaths in the year were given to reviewing or to the teaching of catechisms and other lessons at the option of the school. This *Five-Year Cycle* of Selected Scripture Lessons, with Judson's Questions for the Second Annual Course of Instruction, was issued early in 1827, by the American Sunday-School Union and ran through several editions within that year.

Union Questions—Nine-Year Cycle.—The earliest helps on the lessons were those already described, by Judson, Parmele, Fisk and others. The most prominent of them being those by Judson. Judson's were twice or thrice rewritten, various improvements being added and more attention was given to the grading of the instruction. Early in 1828, the best features of these several helps were combined and issued under the title of *Select Questions,* by the American Sunday-School Union.

A still further revision and improvement followed in the grading in *Union Questions,* to aid teachers in adapting instruction to scholars. The cycle of the lessons was extended from five to seven years and eventually to eleven years, with a twelfth year devoted to a general review and comprehensive view of the entire Bible. The helps and *Union Questions* upon the system of uniform lessons were repeatedly revised, before the First National Sunday-School Convention of 1832, and immediately after it, by John Hall (afterward Rev. John Hall, D.D., of Trenton), who was aided, in the final revision of the *Union Questions,* by a company of about fifty leading educators to whom proofs of each volume were sent for revision and suggestion. So numerous and radical were many of these corrections that each volume had to be completely rewritten from these corrected proofs. The reputation of this system of uniform lessons of 1826 and onward, and of the lesson books thereon, is indicated by the circulation which they attained, running into hundreds of thousands of copies and totaling some millions.

Public Examinations.—In some cities where the select Scripture lessons were introduced, public examinations were held.

It is recorded that the workers in the schools tried to avoid all parade and distinction among the scholars. The school was, however, brought into the church and given a place in front of the pulpit or in the galleries, sometimes in six, eight, or ten divisions. The questions were asked by the pastor from the pulpit and this exercise was followed by a short address, interspersed with appropriate hymns. The churches were thronged on such occasions and "the audiences were astonished to see how well the pupils understood what they had committed to memory and the promptness and animation with which they answered the questions." These public examinations were held once a quarter, or at other stated seasons, and served to make the Sunday-school work more widely known and to increase its popularity.

This uniform lesson system speedily revealed the scarcity of competent teachers. To remove this difficulty and to give a thorough acquaintance "with the uniform system of instruction" and with the best plan of teaching a class, the Union proposed the establishment of a school for teachers, which should be conducted either by the wisest and most experienced of those engaged in the work, or by experts.[1]

To recapitulate the features claimed for this system: (1) it was "a uniform series" of lessons—it distinctly proposed to displace the earlier schemes which overlapped one another, such as alphabetic, spelling and reading, memorizing and "parrot recitation," the "story plan," and the lecture form of instruction, as well as all other "Babel" systems of lessons; (2) it was a system of study comprehending the Bible—it first included five annual courses of lessons and then was extended to seven and nine, and finally eleven years of study; (3) it specially provided for reviews—weekly, monthly and quarterly. It also provided for public examinations before crowded assemblies. It gave an opportunity for definite instruction upon the various doctrines peculiar to each denomination of Christians; (4) it was intended for national use, being recommended by ministers and leading educators in different denominations, and its universal adoption was expected, and practically attained. The Massachusetts Sunday-School Union reported its general use. *The New Jersey*

[1] *New York Sunday-School Union Report*, 1827, p. 7.

Journal said it was used everywhere in that state where the plan could be obtained. The demand exceeded the supply. Other states reported gain in efficiency by its use and predicted that it would soon overspread the land, a prediction which was practically fulfilled; (5) it called forth and was accompanied by numerous graded helps, some of which have already been described.

In 1876 *The Sunday-School Times* published a description of this plan and called attention to the similarity of the features of that plan and the International Sunday-School Lessons of 1872 that were then in use, and said: "When the new features of the present system of lessons [of 1872] are clearly pointed out, it will be time to resume the discussion who was their author."

The benefits of the system appeared in not merely the wider knowledge of the Scriptures, but also in wide-spread revivals of religion throughout the country. It was said that the circulation of one series of helps based on this early scheme of uniform lessons was computed to be equal, annually, to about seven-tenths of the entire number of teachers then engaged in the Sabbath-schools of the United States. It was also widely used in Canada and the same lessons were introduced into the Sabbath-schools of England through reprints by the London Religious Tract Society. So it became the first international system of Bible study. The religious journals of the day reported news of the revivals and accessions to the church from schools in nearly every part of the land where these uniform lessons were used. This system increased a general demand for commentaries and other aids to Bible study, and is said to have led many biblical scholars to put the results of critical learning in more popular form, such as *Barnes' Notes*, and other like works.

Relation to Public Instruction.—Sunday-schools were, and are, deeply indebted to the theories of great educators and to public education for some of their best features. On the other hand, public schools have been greatly aided by the Sunday-school movement. The debt was great to Sunday-schools, but it has been amply paid and with generous interest.

Intelligent founders and friends of the early Sunday-school movement gave careful study to the various theories of education which had been put forth and which were current in their time. There were several fundamental questions to be settled: What is essential in education? What is the scope of instruction? What are fundamental principles in education? Besides these, emerged other important primary questions on methods of instruction. These could not be settled merely by public discussion or by a convention or by philosophic speculation. No body of men coming together could theoretically settle the principles of this institution; they must be developed out of experience. Bodies of men, however wise, cannot *make* principles; they may *discover* and *declare* them.

The development of the principles of education was gradual. It is not straining the facts to say that nearly every system of education that had been and was current received careful consideration by leading Sunday-school workers in the first fifty years of its history. Each theory was studied, sifted for practical features, and examined in a severely critical manner, because all theories of education were then in a fluid state. Their perception of this condition was stated in the following terse terms: "The system of public instruction is essentially retarded by the want of qualified teachers and suitable books." Again they asserted: "The mass of uneducated or miseducated mind is already appalling and is increasing." "Where education has the largest number of liberal and enlightened friends, . . . even there we find the prevailing modes of teaching exceedingly indifferent and mechanical.[1]

Inductive Theory.—This judgment was not the result of a superficial examination. Many were familiar with the inductive or deductive principle suggested by Bacon, and the outlines of education proposed by Milton and Locke. The theory of education proposed by Pestalozzi came early under their critical study. In fact, one of the earliest notices of that system in English was made in a Sunday-school journal, the criticism being based on a study of the French edition, before an English translation appeared. Elaborate notices of the man, his work, and his views were given in religious and Sunday-school teachers' journals. He was recognized as "a useful and true philanthropist," but they discovered faults as

[1] *Report American Sunday-School Union,* 1831, pp. 25, 26.

ell as virtues in his system. They said, "Nature was the
goddess of the scholastic temple reared by Pestalozzi." Yet
they showed a candid and judicial spirit in adding, "The
religious faith of the man has little to do with his system. . . .
forms no good reason for despising his methods." From
many of his visionary theories they sifted those that they
counted sensible and substantial and applied them to instruction in the Sunday-school so far as they thought teachers could
be made to understand and turn them into practice.

Theory of Spontaneity.—Froebel's idea of spontaneity was
also examined because it was regarded as more devout than
that of his master, Pestalozzi. They said his religion began
in nature, but he recognized God in nature and man. They
criticized his system as irreligious in a large sense because it
began with nature instead of beginning with God. But the
principles which he suggested as applied to child growth and
spontaneous development also were suggested as valuable in
Sunday-school instruction.

The Word Method.—The popularity of Jacotot's word
method of teaching pupils to read attracted their attention.
Jacotot's rule seemed to be to tell the pupil nothing, explain
nothing, insist upon nothing, affirm nothing. The pupil was
to be a self-educated person. One maxim of his was, "Learn
something thoroughly and refer everything else to it," and
another sensible maxim was, "We are not learned merely because we have been taught; we are learned only when we have
retained." Of course it would follow, "To forget is the same
as never to have learned." Here, again, the Sunday-school
workers of that day discerned a system of nature carried to
its logical extreme, and amounting well-nigh to a mass of
negations, if not to practical agnosticism. Jacotot put some
of his views in startling form. Thus he held, "Real learning
is not the offspring of hireling teachers." The chief value of
his maxim in Sunday-school work was that it could be turned
as an argument in favor of voluntary, unpaid teachers.

The Monitorial Theory.—Again the monitorial and mutual
systems of Andrew Bell and of Joseph Lancaster were gleaned
to enrich, if possible, the methods of instruction in Sunday-
schools at that early day. Dr. Bell's system was turned to
support sectarian or church instruction only, though that was

not a necessary feature of his system. Lancaster's plan w.
turned the other way; so far as moral instruction was to
inculcated, it was to be based only upon the Bible. He wou'
exclude the teaching of all creeds and denominational pec'
liarities from his system. As he visited this country, h
system was tried and for a time was said to have had '
powerful collateral influence upon the history of Sunda*
schools."[1]

Lesson Theory.—More marked and practical was the s
called lesson system of James Gall. But Gall was charge
with lack of knowledge of the child mind. His plan was sai
to be copied from, but inferior to, a similar one outlined b
Thomas Lyle in 1675, and later by David Stow. Some c
the critics were severe enough to say that Gall's system pos
sessed "neither philosophy nor common sense," while th
earlier writers were pronounced "philosophical." Gall
system was introduced into America with high praise, but i
did not win great favor. Some of his works were offered t
the American Sunday-School Union, and some features com
mon to the earlier lesson system, in a revised form, were com
bined with other features to form the five-fold lesson helps o
the early uniform limited lessons for Sunday-schools (1826
1850).

American schools made the same objection to Gall's systen
that those in England had done, to wit, the absence of in
struction except on words, and the employment only of direc
catechetical questions, and that the multitude of practica
lessons in his system distracted the child's attention and pre
vented him from gaining clear ideas.[2]

Training Theory.—An advance over Gall's system was pre
sented by David Stow in his *Training System*, first issued be
fore 1830. He pointed out that telling was not teaching; tha
teaching or instruction was not training the child as a whole
Mere instruction does not lead the child to make the truth hi
own. Stow's *Training System* was popular in England fo
nearly thirty years, but it failed to obtain any wide popularit
in America. The leading defects of the system appear to b
a lack of adaptation except to the youngest infant classes

[1] *Sunday-School Trachers' Magazine*, 1831, pp. 425–483, ff.; *Sunday-School Journal*
1832, *passim*.
[2] H. Clay Trumbull, *Teachers and Teaching*, pp. 178, 183–186.

he necessity for having a separate room for each class, and
he want of a proper book of explanations for the teacher's
use.

The "Verse-a-Day" Plan.—Of the "Verse-a-Day" the editor of *The Sunday-School Journal* (Union) says: "It is a simple
plan of leading the whole community to a knowledge of the
language of the Bible in detached portions. . . . There are
obvious and insuperable obstacles to the introduction of the
verse-a-day system into the Sunday-schools as a course of
instruction, and it will be especially undesirable at this moment,
when the evidence is flowing in upon us from every side 'that
the use of the selected lessons has been found a principal means
of promoting extensive revivals in Sunday-schools.'" In
fact, about all the space that could be allotted to lesson explanation was given to comments upon the selected lessons
which were often quite numerous. Thus, in Lesson 12, for
1831, there were twenty paragraphs—each paragraph giving a
distinct application of some teaching of that lesson in addition to extended explanation.

These Sunday-school leaders had a clear vision of the whole
field of education. They believed that any system of education was defective which did not include moral and religious
instruction and training as its crown. In this they had the
approval of some of the leading public educators who insisted
on the need of training the entire child nature to produce a
stable character. Thus the then superintendent of schools in
Connecticut declared: "Any course of instruction is imperfect which does not embrace the harmonious development of
the whole nature of the child. . . . There are a vast number
of children in the state who are not gathered into the Sunday-
school. . . . The common school is the only institution which
reaches them, and any serious defect there is vital, as regards
those who have no other means of education."[1] Moreover,
these leaders declared, "Moral education with the great mass
of citizens is a question of reduction of taxation," or perhaps,
"with the wealthier class it is a question of security" of life
and property.[2]

It is obvious from these statements that great educators
contributed no little to the structure of Sunday-schools and

---

[1] *Report*, 1841, p. 14.   [2] *Report*, 1836, p. 20.

their principles and methods of teaching. It is equally evident that Sunday-schools have had a strong influence upon public education by giving it stronger fiber and vitality. They have been mutually helpful to each other and can continue in a large measure harmoniously to work toward a satisfactory education of the whole man. Statesmen who aided in forming the educational systems in the middle western states testified to the popular sentiment for public schools, awakened by the pioneer Sunday-schools.

Bible Doctrines.—In connection with the course of study projected by the Union, it is to be noted that in their intense zeal for their peculiar faiths some have criticized its teaching. While commending in general the good work of the American Sunday-School Union, they insinuated that it taught only a "milk-and-water gospel" and thus developed a kind of "jelly fish, spineless" religion. The Union has answered this baseless charge by pointing to the sweeping revivals of religion which have taken place wherever its schools have been planted, and to the number of reported conversions in its schools (thousands every year), yielding a larger percentage of persons confessing Christ, proportionately, than were reported by most of the churches in those denominations from which these criticisms came. It has further answered this charge by pointing to the fact that the federation of Protestant churches for co-operation and work rests upon the same principles that were the basic foundation of the Union and of the Evangelical Alliance in 1846, and of the modern Federation of Churches. That for a century the Union has taught the essential doctrines of the gospel held in common by all evangelical churches: "The doctrines which Christ taught and as plainly as he taught them," and that because of this adherence to the fundamental truths of salvation the divine blessing has followed the teaching in their schools with remarkable revivals of religion. Their annual reports afford abundant proofs of these statements.

In the first decade of the twentieth century it notes that 98,659 professed conversions were reported (besides thousands uncounted) and 1,062 churches of different denominations followed from the schools it planted, and that 305,000 copies of the Scriptures were provided for homes found without the

TREASURERS

Hugh De Haven, Jr., 1818–26.

Paul Beck, Jr., 1827–39.

Herman Cope, 1840–57.

Levi Knowles, 1861–74.

Richard Ashhurst, 1881–1907.

Bible, showing that the same blessed results continue to crown its efforts.

Perhaps the American Sunday-School Union owes a part of its Christian spirit to its environment.   It was born in Philadelphia.   A fundamental principle of the colony was religious toleration, which opened the way for co-operation in Christian work.   At a time when the Puritan was punishing or expelling heretics, and the Churchmen of Virginia were fining schismatics because their children were not baptized in the Episcopal Church, and when they made it unlawful for anyone to teach the young, even in a private family, Penn and his associates in Philadelphia were insisting upon liberty of conscience for all to worship God according to their own faith.   A century later some came into the colony bringing a spirit like to that in Virginia and New England.[1]

The uniform lessons were continued in the *Union Questions*, through a cycle of five and seven years successively.   This first series of question books was again revised and ran through one or more successive cycles of five to seven years in schools of different denominations, as well as in undenominational or Union schools.   Thus they were commended as the best then known by the first and second National Sunday-School Conventions of 1832 and 1833, and again by the National Convention of 1859 the Union was requested to revise and re-issue these questions as still well adapted to the advanced departments of most of the Sunday-schools through the country.

The generation of pupils in Sunday-schools from 1840 to 1865 was accustomed to the use of question books in some form.   The prevailing custom was to choose series of lessons upon which the books of questions were available.   For instruction in doctrines peculiar to each denomination dependence continued to be placed upon catechisms, and particular Sundays were designated for this purpose for schools using the *Union Questions* also.   In the latter part of this period, previous to 1865, the larger denominations urged the putting forth of a series of lessons specially intended to include the doctrines peculiar to each denomination.   This broke up the uniformity of lesson study throughout the country and

[1] *Penn and Religious Liberty*, p. 25.

created a crisis. In the period that immediately followed there appeared what was termed "the Babel Series" of lessons.

The lessons prepared by the London Sunday-School Union for use in Great Britain, from 1842 on, were used to a limited extent in some of the larger schools of America. Independent lessons chosen by the larger schools themselves, as suggested by this London series, were adopted and in use among schools in different parts of our country. This system was largely topical.

The *Union Questions* of the national Society were followed by a series of explanatory question books and lessons on the New Testament chiefly, while the Methodist Episcopal Sunday-School Society issued, or adopted widely, Orange Judd's *Lessons for Every Sunday in the Year*, from 1862 to 1865. In 1866 *The Sunday-School Teacher* of Chicago prepared a series of lessons which became widely popular. Many adopted the series of *Berean* lessons by John H. Vincent, or the *Westminster* series by Henry C. McCook, or the series by Allibone and Newton known as the *Explanatory* series of lessons. These series were used simultaneously in different sections of the country. They were the connecting link between the early Uniform Lessons before described and the later Uniform Lesson Systems from 1872 to the present time. A sketch of this latter Uniform Lesson System will be found in another section.

SKETCHES OF PROMINENT WORKERS

Archibald Alexander, D.D., LL.D. (1772–1851).

Few men of his time had a wider influence upon the religious life in America than Archibald Alexander. He was a careful, not to say profound, thinker upon many subjects relating to religious education. The highest tributes of respect and veneration were paid to his memory by leading evangelical workers of all denominations. His wise counsels were often sought and always cheerfully given, and highly prized by the founders of the American Sunday-School Union. His singularly astute treatise *Vindication of Sunday-Schools*, and on the improvement and enlargement of plans of instruction, prepared for the American Sunday-School Union, won the Society a multitude of friends and had no small part in shaping its polity. He commended the Society strongly because in conducting its Sunday-schools it knew "no sect but Christianity and no creed but the Bible." His discussion of the character of the literature that should be provided for Sunday-schools, particularly the proportion of fiction, was judicious and convincing. It is also noticeable that he proposed a system of improved, graded instruction for Sunday-schools. He believed that biblical instruction should include all classes from the infant of two years to the man of one hundred years; that all might be properly classified in six different grades or classes, and grouped in about three departments. His first two grades or classes would include what are now called "Beginners," and "Primaries"; his third, youth until completing the adolescent period; and his other three grades, persons in the later adolescent period to old age. He would solve the rural problem by having the younger classes instructed early in the day. The adults should meet after the morning church service for departmental study, under the direction and inspection of the pastor and other qualified persons. This would displace and solve the problem of a second church service and sermon. It may surprise some of the present generation who are discussing "departmental lessons" to discover that here in 1829 this versatile scholar clearly outlines the germ, if not the plan, that is outlined in our day by Lesson Committees.

Dr. Alexander also prepared for the Union the first comprehensive, compact, and scholarly dictionary of the Bible in America, which was issued in so cheap a form as to be available for teachers of the most limited means.[1] He was president of Hampton-Sidney College, Va., 1797 to 1806; pastor of the Third Presbyterian Church, Philadelphia, Pa., 1806 to 1812; and professor in the Theological Seminary, Princeton, New Jersey, 1812 until his death in 1851. During his pastorate in Philadelphia, he enlisted laymen in plans for instructing children of the poor, and in sustaining a society for promoting Bible study. His view was: "the entire church should be a great Sunday-school, and that all should be disciples or teachers." He was an acute and careful student of human character, and attained great skill in the analysis of its many

[1] *Suggestions in Vindication of Sunday-Schools*, 1829 and 1845, pp. 9, 17–23, and 23–27, and *Reports of the American Sunday-School Union, passim.*

phases as related to religious emotions and conduct, which made him a successful instructor and a helpful writer of works for preachers and teachers.

Hon. Willard Hall (1827–1875).

Our British friends were greatly surprised that the Sunday-school cause in America should early receive the support of eminent merchants, judges, legislators, and statesmen of national fame. A typical specimen of this class was the Hon. Willard Hall of Wilmington, Delaware, justice of its supreme court, and manager and vice-president of the American Sunday-School Union for about half a century—1827–1875. His activity and commanding influence in the movement were so prominent that he was unanimously chosen president of the Second National Sunday-School Convention at Philadelphia, May, 1833. His legal training, combined with an acute, candid and judicial mind, qualified him to defend the principles and methods of the Sunday-school movement at an early day when, added to the great and effectual door open to it, it had "many adversaries."

Thus the American Sunday-School Union was attacked along three lines: first, for calling the attention of the public to the immoral and hurtful literature placed in the hands of youth. This the Union aimed to force out of circulation by the introduction of new and better books. It was alleged that the Union thus interfered with the liberty and rights of readers and of publishers who were issuing these hurtful and immoral books. Judge Hall defended the right of the Sunday-school movement to carry on a warfare against such harmful literature, and caused the great majority of honest publishers voluntarily to sign a declaration commending the Union in thus creating a taste for good reading and promoting morality. The second charge—which seems humorous if not almost silly in these times—was that the Union and the Sunday-school movement attempted to proselyte the young in favor of some one denomination. Judge Hall made short work of this indictment by showing that the Union was working in the interest of *all* evangelical churches and had no new denomination to set up. It was the glory of the Society that it opposed sectarianism and proclaimed the principles of evan-

gelical Christianity. The third accusation in those days—
that it aimed to become a political power in the state—was
made to seem ridiculous under the trenchant treatment of
Judge Hall. He was always true and loyal to the best interests of the cause and the present generation owes him a debt
of gratitude for his skilful and abundant labors. Pamphlets
giving his arguments and pleadings in justification of this
work on a Union basis had a large circulation and a wide influence in correcting misapprehensions, removing prejudices,
and winning support. The judicial candor and high character
of the author and his full and lucid presentation of facts
carried conviction to the intelligent and fair-minded public.

Theodore Frelinghuysen, LL.D. (1787–1862).

Among the early supporters and counselors of the American Sunday-School Union Theodore Frelinghuysen, educator,
statesman, and scholar, stands in the foremost rank. He was
an officer during its infancy and continued in that capacity
for thirty-five years. His wide learning, his keen mind and
his statesman-like views made him an influential personage
in all measures tending to alleviate human misery and misfortune and to give better conditions to the wage-earner and
a healthier state to society. He was, from early life, a teacher,
and then superintendent, in a Sunday-school, counting it a
greater honor to fill these positions than to be a senator of the
United States, a position which he also filled to the satisfaction of his fellow-citizens. He was invited to a responsible
position in the service of the American Sunday-School Union
at an early day, but a field of usefulness opening to him in the
United States Government caused him to decline the Union's
offer. However, on public occasions he always advocated
its interests with force and eloquence, and gave it the benefit
of his professional abilities and counsels to the end of his life.

He was unanimously chosen president of the first National
Sunday-School Convention in New York in 1832, where
representatives from fourteen states and four territories, including many very capable men from different sections of the
country, were present. The novelty of this assembly, the
topics discussed, the eminence of the speakers, the enthusiasm
of the delegates, and the consecrated spirit that prevailed in

the convention, marked it as an epoch in the progress of the Sunday-school movement in America.

Perhaps Mr. Frelinghuysen's farsighted and well-balanced views were never better expressed than in an eloquent address at the anniversary of the American Sunday-School Union in 1835. In a broad and statesman-like manner, he forcibly declared that Sunday-schools, while laying the foundation of public and private integrity and intelligence, provided the strongest preservation of our liberties and of our rights and the best guarantee for the peace and good order of society, and that they therefore deserved the patronage of the statesman as well as the Christian. He is one of the great and good men who will long be remembered for wise, self-sacrificing and blessed service rendered to his fellow-men.

John Hall, of Trenton, N. J. (1806–1894).

At the anniversary of the American Sunday-School Union, held in Trenton, New Jersey, in 1890, there occurred a memorable scene—the Rev. B. W. Chidlaw of Ohio, held up before the audience a time-stained commission which he had received fifty-four years before, signed by the venerable John Hall. The pioneer missionary and the old-time secretary had never met until brought together at this anniversary. As the two remarkable workers shook hands, Dr. Hall humorously remarked, referring to his signature, "I can write better than that now."[1]

John Hall was born in Philadelphia, August 11, 1806, educated at the University of Pennsylvania, from which he was graduated in 1823, and was admitted to the practice of law in 1826. In 1832 he gave up law practice to devote his life to Christian work, becoming a manager and, later, a special secretary of the American Sunday-School Union. He was office editor of *The Sunday-School Journal* and of *The Youth's Friend*, revised the first five volumes of *Union Questions*, and outlined the preparation of seven other volumes of the series. He wrote and compiled several other works for the Union, and aided in directing the missionary operations of the Society, signing the commission of Dr. Chidlaw in 1836. The knowledge and training which he obtained in the service

---

[1] *Sunday-School World*, 1890, p. 263.

of the Union qualified him for the gospel ministry, and he was settled as pastor of the Presbyterian Church in Trenton, New Jersey, in 1841, a position which he retained until called home at the ripe age of 88 years.

Besides preparing several works for the American Sunday-School Union, he was the author of a number of other works published by the Presbyterian Board of Publication, delivered a course of lectures in Princeton Theological Seminary and, for a time, filled its chair of pastoral theology, and received his degree of Doctor of Divinity from Princeton University in 1850.

Dr. Hall, besides possessing a commanding personality, was esteemed an able scholar, a vigorous and careful writer, and an instructive and impressive preacher.

SECTION IV

OPPOSITION TO SUNDAY-SCHOOLS AND TO UNIONS

WHEN Christians are awake and revivals are abroad, the devil is said to get busy. When Sunday-schools in America began to achieve success, opposition became pronounced. The Sunday-school was born of the spontaneous impulse of individual Christians of different creeds—primarily and voluntarily a union movement. It was not favored in the early days by any ecclesiastical body. It was not begun by any resolution or decree of a church council. It was not, at first, admitted into the churches, but was held in private houses or halls hired for the purpose, as heretofore stated.

Why Opposed.—The opposition appeared in three or more phases: (1) Against the purpose and plan of the Sunday-school; (2) against its introduction into the church; (3) against the principle of union, upon which schools were early founded and conducted.

As in England, so in America; in some quarters it was regarded as a desecration of God's house to hold a Sunday-school within it. It seemed to some a desecration of the Sabbath to teach the ignorant to read, even to the end that they might read the Bible for themselves. This latter objection prevailed widely in America, even so late as 1817, when in a public meeting in New York a speaker alluded to it in this forceful language: "An objection has been frequently made to this institution [the union Sunday-school] on the ground that to teach the poor to read on the Sabbath is a breach of that holy day. . . . A breach of the Sabbath to teach the vicious and illiterate to read and to value their Bibles! A profanation of the Sabbath, through the medium of the Scriptures, to dispel the mists of ignorance, and to open the floodgates of divine light on the regions of moral darkness! To break the fetters of transgression by the all-powerful agency of the Word of the holy God!"

128

Others hesitated to favor the Sunday-school because, in their view, it would interfere with family religious training. They held that family instruction had divine sanction, but they incorrectly inferred that it would be obstructed by "such a man-devised agency" as a Sunday-school. Dr. Thomas Chalmers had forcibly answered this sophistical and false view by showing conclusively that the Sunday-school would have a beneficial and not a baneful influence on family instruction. His answer was reprinted and widely circulated in America.

Again some evangelistic workers, like those who were associated in the Evangelical Society in Philadelphia (1809–1811), looked with suspicion upon this new movement. Like the evangelistic workers in London, they said the Sunday-school was good as far as it went, but it did not go far enough. "We need," said they, "an institution to teach practical religion in more decided and definite forms." So they stood aloof, or patronizingly permitted it. Some opposed the Sunday-school because they thought it was too sectarian in character, while others said it was too latitudinarian. The same criticisms were later made upon the American Sunday-School Union. Still others apprehended a union of church and state and a political domination that would be destructive to the liberties of the people. Most of these objections seem trivial now, although a few of them are still whispered in certain circles.

But in the face of this opposition, Sunday-schools were constantly visited by singular and remarkable revivals of religion which uplifted the poor and ignorant and worked moral revolutions in communities. This was a significant mark of divine sanction. Thus attested, they gradually won their way into Christian favor and into the various churches.

Opposition to Organized Union.—There is a bit of history long since forgotten which illustrates the opposition, misrepresentation, and persecution to which the friends of the Union were treated about a century ago. Because some ecclesiastics feared these schools would prove detrimental to denominational progress, they would not allow them in the church. Hence most of the early Sunday-schools were conducted on the union basis from necessity, until they demonstrated their beneficent purpose and won popular favor.

When the American Sunday-School Union asked th
Legislature of Pennsylvania for an act of incorporation unde
its present name the request developed bitter opposition
The Union simply desired to be made *legally* responsible fo
its debts, and for the carrying forward of its benevolent wor
in a more public manner. This request was made in 1824
and 1825, and again in 1827. It was signed and endorsed by
foremost citizens of Philadelphia, including business men an
leading book publishing houses.

Readers now will hardly believe that the request was hel
up because of a formal remonstrance against it by person
professedly "liberal" in religion, and by some connected with
"orthodox" faiths. These opponents conceded a high personal character to the citizens who formed the Union. They
insisted, however, that the institution was dangerous; that it
threatened the liberty of the people; that it concealed its
real purpose, and underneath an ostensible aim to promote
education there lurked a great plot "to subject the consciences
and persons of the free citizens of this United States to the
tyranny of an ecclesiastical domination"; "that numerous
highly respectable associations are openly proscribed" [the
Sunday-School Union was evangelical and aimed to unite all
persons in its work who accepted the fundamental Bible doctrines held in common by all evangelical denominations];
"that the children brought into these schools are to be instructed . . . in the illiberal and narrow views of men";
and that the "necessary results of incorporating it will be a
monopoly, both spiritual and temporal, alike repugnant to
the genius of the Constitution and destructive to the future
exertions of many enterprising individuals."

The Society had had a charter from the courts under its
earlier name, in 1819. Then it was young and not so widely
conspicuous. It is quite obvious that the "many enterprising
individuals" who opposed it included some who were gaining
a living or making money by dishonest and questionable occupations—the liquor interest, gamblers, and other persons
whose business might be imperiled by the teaching of Sunday-
schools.

Charter Remonstrants.—This "remonstrance" was followed
up by a remarkable appeal "To the People of the State of

Pennsylvania" on the "Alarming Progress of the American Sunday-School Union!" This document, reminds one of the sophistries and specious arguments of the Liquor Trust to save the liquor traffic from being abolished by the righteous indignation of the people. These foes to the charter of the American Sunday-School Union found pliant politicians in the Senate. The speeches of two senators who opposed granting the charter have come down to us. One asserted that if this charter were granted in a few years the Union might become such a powerful institution that any politician who was an infidel would find "his political life terminated"—a remarkable testimony to the efficiency of Sunday-school instruction even in those days!

Moreover, the granting of the charter was attacked upon strangely contradictory grounds. One urged that it be not granted "to this potent engine of *clerical* usurpation"; another that it should not be granted because the reverend clergy were *excluded* from the Union, and laymen only controlled it. It was insinuated that there was a very crafty plan, like the proverbial cat, concealed in this Union meal; that, by excluding the clergy, the friends of the Union tacitly confessed the danger to religious liberty from that quarter. One of the senators sought to strengthen his argument against the Union by asserting that "the respectable sect—the Methodists . . . were not in favor of the Union. . . . They disliked national societies for religious purposes."[1] The speeches of both senators were reprinted in the *New York Christian Advocate and Journal* of that day, with sympathetic editorial remarks which led five managers of the Union, who were also prominent members of the Methodist Episcopal Church, to send a specific correction of some mis-statements and a denial of certain alleged facts in the speeches, upon which the editorial remarks were based. Thus the five members denied "any preponderating influence of any one denomination in the councils of the American Sunday-School Union. Were such the fact, they would have discovered it," they asserted, "since the majority of them had been managers of the Society since its first organization, had generally attended the meetings, and had taken part in its discussions

[1] *Legislative Proceedings*, February 7, 1828.

and had voted on the questions presented." They further asserted their belief that "this hostility to the Union sprang chiefly from a real opposition to all Sabbath-schools, and to the essential doctrines of the Bible itself."

It is little wonder that the legislators became befogged and failed to grant the charter. Happily, the American Sunday-School Union was able to carry forward its work as a voluntary organization for twenty years without a charter. Then another set of lawmakers came to the front and, moved by strong public sentiment, not to say shame and indignation, cheerfully granted the charter in 1845.[1] (Appendix, pp. 461, 462.)

This opposition will not seem so strange when one recalls the religious history of that period and the sharp, often bitter, controversies that prevailed over creeds and dogmas. These controversies engendered unchristian feeling, albeit they sprang from a sincere conviction of truth as some saw it. Naturally, those who were contending for denominational teaching believed that religious instruction of the children should be strictly along the lines of their particular church creeds.

However, when Sunday-schools were visited with the revivals already noted, and were enthusiastically sustained by the common people, it was somewhat remarkable to note the change of view on the part of some later leaders. Some of them, with singular blindness to the humor of it, even sought to claim the credit for originating this movement, because some of the founders were *lay members* of their church. This appeared, they thought, to give them a kind of original patent on the origin of the movement and in some cases they claimed that the American Sunday-School Union was founded by the church, and forgot that their predecessors had stoutly opposed it. Thus a writer in the Protestant Episcopal Church claims that the Sunday-school movement began in that church, and he would imply that it, rather than individuals should be credited with the founding, among others, of the American Sunday-School Union.[2] Some writers of the Methodist Episcopal Church have asserted that the earliest Sunday-

[1] See *Christian Advocate and Journal*, 1828; *Episcopal Watchman*, 1827–29; *Church Register*, 1828, for passing statements; Brownlow's *Address*, 1831; *The Charter—Plain Statement of Facts*—1828.

[2] *The American Church Sunday-School Magazine*, 1904–05; also Rev. Oscar S. Michael, *The Sunday-School in the Development of the American Church*, p. 69, ff.

school in America was established by a bishop or preacher of that church. Other writers in the same church declared, in earlier days, that the Presbyterians founded the American Sunday-School Union and were aiming to make it a national organization strong enough to cause Presbyterianism to be established in America by law.[1] The Congregationalists also, among others, have been credited with being *accessories* before the fact, since their faith was said to be an easy solvent of all creeds.

Perhaps it was only human to expect that an organized union of Sunday-schools would meet with decided opposition. The spirit of federation and comity and co-operation is even yet on trial and is not an accomplished fact.

The American Sunday-School Union was confronted by another opposing phase, springing from the diversity in evangelical churches. If Union Sunday-schools continued to teach and emphasize the *essential* doctrines of the Bible, the non-essentials which divide the churches might be overlooked, and there might follow a dangerous lowering of the denominational fence. To overcome this, and to emphasize denominational views, a decided movement for the organization of denominational Sunday-school unions was started, each denomination forming one for itself. Thus in 1826 a union of all the Protestant Episcopal Sunday-school societies was projected in Philadelphia, under the leadership of Bishop White, which resulted in the formation of the Protestant Episcopal Sunday-School Union. Bishop White had been in sympathy with the founding of the First Day or Sunday-School Society in 1790 for teaching the ignorant and neglected classes outside of the church. But in 1817 when it was proposed to form the Sunday and Adult School Union to reach children inside, as well as outside, of the churches, he threw his influence in favor of a denominational union. Probably similar influences led to the formation of the Methodist Episcopal Sunday-School Union in the same year. Similar organizations were formed also by other denominations.

This multiplication of Sunday-school unions naturally confused the public mind. It was not easy to distinguish the one from the others, and communications and contributions in-

[1] W. G. Brownlow, *Sunday-Schools*, 1831, p. 20, ff.

tended, for example, for the American Sunday-School Union sometimes found their way to one of the denominational Sunday-School unions, and vice versa. Some worldly people smiled over what they counted the shrewdness of denominational leaders in appropriating the name "Sunday-School Union" to their denominational organizations. Of course this embarrassed the American Sunday-School Union more than other early unions because it was the national Society of this name. Yet it rejoiced that the denominations were aroused actively to look after the children within their respective churches.

The opposition to the American Sunday-School Union was ultimately turned, by the blessing of God, to its advantage. It constrained some of the ablest and most godly men in several evangelical bodies to come out in open defence of the Union's work on the union principle, as the Hon. Willard Hall of Delaware, Hon. Theodore Frelinghuysen and Archibald Alexander of New Jersey, Lyman Beecher of Massachusetts, the Breckenridges of Kentucky, and hosts of other leading men. They were loyal to their denomination, but they were Christians first, and then denominationalists. Moreover, the common people in America proverbially love *fairplay*. They might care little for religion, but because they wanted every person and institution to have a fair chance in this free country, especially those aiming to do good, they generally favored the American Sunday-School Union having a "square deal" at the hands of the people.

In religious, as in civil, matters, history repeats itself. There are periods of ecclesiastical high tides, followed often by popular waves in favor of co-operation, of comity, and unity in religious work. The zeal for founding Sunday-schools and for uniform lessons in 1826 brought about a little later, as we shall presently see, a great wave in favor of co-operation and union, which gave efficiency to these efforts. There began to dawn on earnest souls, a conviction that a disunited Protestantism, and a divided Christianity could never conquer the world for the Christ. Later there followed again an ecclesiastical high tide for teaching "distinctive doctrines," for using "denominational literature," and for making very young children familiar with the "peculiar phraseology"

MANAGERS

Joseph H. Dulles, 1823–75.

Lewis R. Ashhurst, 1839–73.

George H. Stuart, 1848–73.

Alexander Brown, 1857–93.

J. Livingstone Erringer, 1863–1905.

John R. Whitney, 1873–1905.

of the religious faiths which the workers respectively represented. Such high tides of ecclesiasticism prevailed before the origin of the modern Sunday-school. They have continued all through its history at irregular periods, and have exerted a powerful influence upon its progress. A broad statesmanlike view of this history inclines one to say, it is better to have agitation than stagnation. But it is best to have all Christians banded together for the conquest of the world for Jesus Christ.

SKETCHES OF PROMINENT WORKERS

James Waddell Alexander (1804–1859).

James Waddell Alexander, son of Archibald Alexander, was a teacher and preacher of exceptional natural gifts, qualifying him to illustrate practical ways to use the diversified truths taught by his father. He was a warm advocate of the work of the American Sunday-School Union, as educator, pastor, and author. He wrote upward of thirty volumes for teachers and youth, which were issued by the Society. They were conspicuous for their versatility of style and the diversified topics treated. His *American Sunday-School* was an eminently practical work upon the position, management, and influence of that institution in American life, and was frequently quoted by writers and workers. His *Good, Better, Best* was an exceedingly suggestive volume upon three ways of aiding the poor and the ignorant to make the most of their lives. His *Carl, the Young Emigrant* forcibly brought to the attention of the American people the religious instruction which should be given to the young immigrants pouring into America from every nation of the world. Other volumes pointed out practical ways of religious training, and stimulated many a young lad to make the best and most out of his life. His contributions to religious education along these four, and other great lines, were among the most valuable of their day. His *Scripture Guide*, and *Biblical Geography*, which he prepared jointly with his erudite brother, Joseph Addison Alexander, were valued for their concise and accurate information, and for nearly a generation were the companions of his father's *Dictionary of the Bible* and of Dr. John W. Nevin's *Biblical Antiquities*, all of which were issued by the Union.

Abraham Martin (1793–1880).

The life and labors of Abraham Martin, better known as "Father" Martin, were closely interwoven with the early progress of the Sunday-school cause in America for two generations. Mr. Martin was one of the founders of the earliest schools organized with voluntary teachers in Philadelphia. It was then, as now, the banner city in Sunday-school activity. Previous to 1800 a mixed plan prevailed in Sunday-schools of having one or more paid superintendents or supervising teachers with other teachers volunteering to give their services without pay. This mixed system was not satisfactory and was superseded by the schools choosing superintendents as well as teachers who would serve on the voluntary plan. With all his earnestness, young Martin was discreet— as young persons in those days were compelled to be in religious work. If too energetic and forward, they were regarded as officious, and often reminded of what was counted their proper place in the rear of the Lord's hosts. But young Martin's zeal was contagious, and his activity irrepressible. He gradually won his way, through good service, into the various small Sunday-school organizations, and was a delegate from the Galilean Society (Reformed Dutch) to the representative meeting called to consider the formation of the Sunday and Adult School Union in 1817. The records show that he was enthusiastic in persuading prominent citizens to join in the support and management of that society, although he does not appear to have accepted any official position in it. But when that earlier union was changed into the American Sunday-School Union in 1824, Abraham Martin became recording secretary for about four years—1825 to 1828.

His energy and abilities secured him a call to supervise an "Infants' Retreat" in Germantown, Pa., where he had the care of over two thousand little ones. Later he was the representative of the Sabbath Association. These societies he served for nearly twenty years, until 1851. He then resumed his activities in special Sunday-school service, becoming a manager of the American Sunday-School Union in 1852 and until his death, November 8, 1880. His tact and devotion in Christian work led to his appointment as a lay Sunday-school evangelist, a service which he had undertaken as a voluntary worker before 1820, and which he resumed in the last fifteen years of his life, being sustained by a special fund created by his friend, Robert Lenox Kennedy of New York.

Mr. Martin was versatile and resourceful, ready for any emergency and alert to promote every advance in Sunday-school methods. Thus, in 1817, when juvenile religious books were sought for publication, Mr. Martin laid a package of carefully selected English works before the managers of the Sunday and Adult School Union, from which their first book, *Little Henry and His Bearer*, by Mrs. Sherwood, was selected and republished as the pioneer booklet of the Union, to be followed by millions of copies of similar juvenile books within a few years.

He was likewise alert and successful in Sunday-school extension. As lay evangelist of the Union, he reported assisting in the organization of over one hundred mission schools, out of which had grown twenty-six churches, some of them being very prominent, and modestly added, "many persons have been converted therein."

John Wanamaker gives this reminiscence in a letter to Dr. Rice:

"You may not remember that Bethany Sunday-school owed its inspiration to a boy who attended a convention called by the American Sunday-School Union to awaken an interest in establishing mission Sunday-schools in Philadelphia. I was that boy, and the result of it was, two weeks later the same boy came down to the American Sunday-School Union and found Mr. Abraham Martin to advise with him as to the best locations in the city. Through "Father" Martin, Edward H. Toland suggested the southwestern section of the city, which had largely been given up to the scope of rangers. It was there that Bethany Sunday-School began, and it is there that Bethany Sunday-School, with its church of 3,400 members, still holds the fort."

Father Martin was a stimulating speaker, and schools of all denominations in the city welcomed him. Hundreds of persons recalled with delight his clear, ringing voice and charmingly simple manner. He was accustomed to hold up a small red book, about an inch square, which he called the smallest book in the world, entitled *Small Rain,* filled with the most precious messages from God's Word. The secret of his power was in the simplicity of his faith, the fervency of his prayers, and his exceptional generosity. He was known to pledge and to give a thousand dollars at a time out of his small income. He won confidence by his meekness and his simple-hearted, yet tactful and devoted spirit. Did controversy or friction arise in any deliberative meeting, he would spontaneously lead in prayer, and speedily the bitterness would disappear and the spirit of harmony and love be restored in the assembly. He was an inspiration to his associates, who cherished the memory of his humble and blessed service as an efficient workman who "needeth not to be ashamed."

SECTION V

RELIGIOUS literature for the Sunday-school was a necessary adjunct to its permanence. One of the biggest problems that confronted the workers was to develop religious literature adapted to American youth.

Juvenile Literature in 1800.—At the beginning of the last century children's books of that kind in general circulation were few, even when such works as *The New England Primer*, *The Pilgrim's Progress*, *Robinson Crusoe*, and Webster's spelling book were included. This is the testimony of such witnesses as President Humphrey of Amherst College, Dr. T. H. Gallaudet of the Deaf and Dumb Institution, Hartford, and others who were young in those days and later came into national prominence. Dr. Gallaudet, for instance, says that a dozen books of this type could be found only by counting several primers and toy books, like *Glass Slipper*, *Goody Two Shoes*, *Blue Beard*, and *Who Killed Cock Robin?* J. R. Case of Philadelphia testified that *Jack the Giant Killer*, *Puss in Boots*, *Cinderella*, and similar toy works, exhausted the literature for children in 1800. This was the result of an inquiry by Frederick A. Packard made in 1850, as editor of the Union's publications. (Appendix, p. 462.)

It is evident from Dr. Packard's inquiry, however, that the eminent persons he reached had not been familiar with some of the children's books which were in existence, in their childhood. It is computed that between 1744 and 1802, John Newbery and his successors published about "three hundred volumes," of which two hundred were classed as juveniles by him. These so-called "volumes" were mere primers, which Newbery secured through the editorial aid of Dr. Samuel Johnson, Oliver Goldsmith, and others. There is a tradition that Goldsmith roomed on the upper floor of Newbery's house for a time, and wrote, among other things, the *History of Giles Gingerbread, Goody Two Shoes, The Way to be Happy*, and various other short stories intended to please the little ones. They did not please the hypochondriac temper of Dr. Johnson. A number of the works which Newbery put forth in England were reprinted in "pirated editions" by Isaiah Thomas of Worcester, Massachusetts. He was, however, a "beneficent pirate," for he adapted many of these English works to America, by putting them into a "more colloquial phrase." They did not gain much circulation in America, however, until about 1810 to 1830. Nor were many of them distinctively juvenile: not a few of them were nursery rhymes. Dr. Johnson did not favor them. He said, "Babies do not want to hear about babies. . . . They like to be told of giants and castles and of somewhat which can stretch and stimulate their little minds."

So too, the neurasthenic bacchanalian bachelor, Charles Lamb, ranked these same nursery rhymes as English "Classics," and cursed the graded and more sensible works of Mrs. Barbauld, Mrs. Trimmer and their "whole crew." Neither of these ancient critics, who were childless themselves and based their opinions on observing their neighbors' or borrowed children, would be accepted as authoritative, if they were living in this generation. Students of child development, now would laugh such critics "out of court." The Newbery works may have been *"nursery* classics" in that age, but justly deserved the speedy oblivion into which the irritable bachelor lamented they had disappeared even in his lifetime.

Clearly, therefore, a juvenile literature of a religious type must be evolved, and a taste and demand for it created. The magnitude of this task can hardly be conceived now, flooded as we are with millions of volumes intended to interest the young. The managers of the Union had trained minds, children of their own, and also a clear vision and decided conviction in respect to the kind of literature needed. They said: "In the days of our fathers and even in the childhood of some middle-aged persons among us, entertaining and instructive little books of a religious tendency were few indeed; and when a youth had perused Janeway's *Token for Children*, *The Pilgrim's Progress*, and *The Holy War*, where could he

EDITORS

Frederick A. Packard, LL. D., 1829–67.

John Hall, 1832–38.

John S. Hart, LL. D., 1858–60.

Richard Newton, D. D., 1867–77.

S. Austin Allibone, LL. D., 1868–78.

find another volume, except the Bible, in which experimental religion is attractively exhibited in the forms of colloquy and narrative?" Janeway's *Token* and Bunyan's *Holy War* would fail to attract youth now!

They grappled with and mastered the great task—at least in their own estimation. Some will marvel that, in a single generation, a juvenile literature was produced that was so widely read as to work a complete revolution in the reading habits and in the moral taste of a large portion of the American people. The rules adopted were radical and would be deemed drastic in their severity in these days. But to them it seemed necessary to purify and to keep pure the reading for the young. Their first rule was to secure works of a thoroughly evangelical character. They said, "The broad impress which we wish all our books to bear is that of vital, active, elevated piety, leading children to the knowledge and fear of God, and to a cheerful observance of all his commands." They had a vision of danger in creating an appetite for new books because they are new. The appetite might become abnormal by indulgence. They sought to obviate this danger without losing the good in it, by presenting such literature as would give instruction as well as be interesting—literature the children would read and remember.

Parents and children alike, however, had to be waked up and informed so as to judge more accurately of the true nature and character of books and literature suitable for child reading. They further insisted that this literature for the young should be true to fact and to nature. They say, "It is never to be forgotten in the composition of children's books that language which is simple enough to clothe a child's thoughts is not too simple to express the conception of an angel."[1]

Character of Literature Demanded.—They, in fact, required four things of the literature: *First*, it must be clearly and absolutely of a moral and religious character; *second*, it must be graded and adapted to the capacity of the growing mind of the child; *third*, it must be of a high order of style and fairly good *literature;* and *fourth*, the books should be American and for American children. They declared, on the last

[1] *Report*, 1831, p. 21.

point: "We have no need to go abroad for subjects and scenes of interest. American divines, statesmen and benefactors—American mountains, forests, prairies and rivers—American history, hopes and prospects—may surely furnish subjects enough of grateful, profitable and interesting contemplation to American children."[1]

The managers of the American Sunday-School Union had a feeling similar to that which forcibly impressed Dr. Oliver Wendell Holmes forty years later. He graphically described the difficulties to understand in his youth some of the current books for children. Thus, "It is a great misfortune to us of the more elderly sort," he wrote, "that we were bred to the constant use of words in English children's books, which were without meaning for us and only mystified us.

"We were educated, you remember, on Miss Edgeworths' *Frank* and *Parents' Assistant;* on *Original Poems*, and *Evenings at Home*, and *Cheap Repository Tracts*, [Hannah More]. Then we found ourselves in a strange world, where James was called Jem, not *Jim*, as we always heard it; where a respectable but healthy young woman was spoken of as 'a stout wench'; where boys played at *taw*, not marbles; where one found cowslips in the fields, while what we saw were buttercups; where naughty schoolboys got through a gap in the hedge, to steal Farmer Giles' red-streaks, instead of shinning over the fence to hook old Daddy Jones' baldwins; where Hodge used to go to the alehouse for his mug of beer, while we used to see old Joe steering for the grocery to get his glass of rum; . . . where there were larks and nightingales instead of yellow-birds and bobolinks; where the robin was a little domestic bird that fed at the table instead of a great, fidgety, jerky, whooping thrush.

"What a mess—there is no better word for it—what a mess was made of it in our young minds in the attempt to reconcile what we read with what we saw!"

The facilities of transportation now in some measure decrease the misfortune of youth in Dr. Holmes' day and in the period when the Sunday-School Union was formed, as some Americans by travel become somewhat familiar with British scenery and habits. But it is still true that the mass of youth

[1] *Report*, 1831, p. 20; also *Appendix*, p. 463.

in America would not easily understand phrases, habits and scenery springing out of British society and surroundings. Some works are so cosmopolitan in spirit as to be widely understood, but the mass of literature for a nation's need, and especially for its children's need, should spring out of the nation's life and have its color and setting in the national scenery and customs.

Of course these conditions called for a radical departure from methods then current with editors and publishers of literature. It required a revision of works already issued, and often a revision and change of original works prepared expressly for the public.

Probably for these reasons the books and literature of the American Sunday-School Union were issued anonymously for many years. Their character was certified by the imprint of the Society and the statement on the title page of each work that it had been "revised by the committee of publication"; or, if it was an original work, they stated that it was "written for the American Sunday-School Union, and revised." When the author's name was placed on the title page (which was rare), as in the case of the *Vindication of Sunday-Schools*, by Archibald Alexander, D.D., and the *Dairyman's Daughter*, by Legh Richmond, the works were printed without alteration, or, if changed, the consent of the author was secured. (Appendix, pp. 463, 464.)

They invariably adhered to this custom as announced to the public in 1824. A few years later they say: "No book has received the imprint [of the Society] but with the consent of at least *three* members of different denominations of Christians; and in no instance has a publication been ordered against a single dissenting voice. Nor has this harmony been preserved with difficulty, and only by the aid of imposed restraints on the freedom of thought and discussion. It has flowed from a union of feeling, arising from the influence of common motives and the impulse of a common aim."

Thus the Union iterated and reiterated its intention in respect to the character of its literature. All its works must contain "Gospel truth," "free from gross errors," "in pleasing form"; must be "thoroughly biblical and evangelical," "popular in style," while "pure in tone, serious rather than sensational;

filled with the spirit of the Word"; not the spirit of the world
Yet they must be adapted to the progressive development of
child mind as apprehended in that era, and must be thoroughly American in their coloring and environment: their
illustrations drawn from what American children actually
saw.

Moreover, besides awakening a taste for this literature by
making it attractive with engravings and bright thinking, the
purpose was to increase a demand for it by putting it at a very
low price, selling it to the public without profit, often even
below cost.

Fiction or No ?—A strong controversy prevailed in regard to
certain classes of literature, whether they should be excluded
or included as works healthy for young children.   This con-
tention was especially sharp in regard to works of the imagination and of fiction.   Many moralists, pastors, and some
Sunday-school societies insisted that all fiction should be excluded.   To the managers of the American Sunday-School
Union this rule seemed strict and drastic, for it might exclude
The Pilgrim's Progress and indeed, might prevent the Society
from reprinting the story of the Prodigal Son—both of which
are certainly in the region of the imagination as to literary
form.   Therefore in regard to works of the imagination, the
Union required that they should be in "strict accordance with
truth and nature."   "This quality," they say, "is as effectually
preserved in *The Pilgrim's Progress* as in the *Life of Washington*—in the story of the *Prodigal Son* as in the history of Stephen's martyrdom."[1]

They put the matter thus: "The principle which would
exclude from children's libraries every book which gives false
or unnatural views of life, character, or duty," should be
scrupulously applied to all literature.[2]   They recognized how
toy books and primers had appealed to the imagination of the
young, and they considered how gradually and carefully they
must proceed.   "A transition too sudden and bold from the
silly stories, the very titles of which disgrace the annals of
education, to such books as *Sketches from the Bible* and *Anna
Ross* might defeat the whole object."   "It was a prodigious
leap for a child to pass from *Robinson Crusoe* to the *Life of*

[1] *Report*, 1831, p. 23.   [2] *Ibid.*, p. 24.

Henry Martyn and from *Mother Goose's Melodies* to Taylor's or Watts' *Hymns* as sources of moral improvement."[1]   Nevertheless they succeeded in aiding the child to pass from one to the other without taking a kangaroo leap.

The literature which they sought to develop was of widely varied types.   It included history, biography, travels, conversations, narratives, poetry, hymns and songs, discourses and didactic teachings; in short, it was a comprehensive and real literature for the young.

Engravings Appeal to Eye-gate.—Nor did the Union overlook the importance of the eye-gate in gaining attention to various forms of truth and increasing the impressions it might give through the use of skilful engravings.   It early employed special artists and engravers and designers who used their best skill in designing and producing engravings for its publications in what was then an attractive mechanical style; engravings which were adapted to the substance and literary forms of the works which it issued.   Of course the contrast between those pictures—of two or three generations ago—and those of the present time, indicates forcibly the progress of art in making juvenile literature attractive.

It was recognized that much of this literature must be suited to the domestic circle and the home.   But it must also be of a character which would justify its circulation through the Sunday-school, and therefore, for the most part, by implication, proper to be read on the Sabbath Day.   In some sections of the country, however, where the extreme Puritan idea prevailed, it was counted difficult to develop a literature of a type sufficiently religious or pious to pass the approval of those holding extreme Puritanic views, and at the same time make it sufficiently attractive to be read by the young.   While the Union desired to issue works of the highest possible religious type, it had the clear sense and discrimination to aim to produce works that would be read.

Moral Works.—Moreover, it sought to provide a clean and helpful literature for those communities remote from towns and from any public library (and public libraries were not common in the earlier days).   To this end it issued, in connection with the London Religious Tract Society, sets of books

[1] *Report*, 1830, p. 13.

written in attractive and instructive style for the young, on a wide variety of topics not strictly or wholly religious. Thus these works presented the facts in respect to the stars and astronomy, but in a reverent rather than in a skeptical spirit. The Union issued an original *Life of George Washington*, with a particular design to present prominently "those moral and religious traits in the character of Washington which constituted his highest and most honorable distinction." This work was written by a niece of a signer of the Declaration of Independence, Anna C. Reed, an accomplished literary woman; and the work, though published without a name, was translated into over twenty languages in a few years and had a circulation probably unequalled by any other life of the Founder of the American Republic.

Libraries for Schools and Families.—The Sunday-School Union, before 1824, had issued under its first name about eighteen works. The first book published by it, in 1817, was Mrs. Sherwood's *Little Henry and His Bearer*. By 1830 the American Sunday-School Union had issued over 6,000,000 copies of Sunday-school works, 200 bound volumes for libraries, started a *Teachers' Magazine*, and two other periodicals, expended annually over $76,000 in promotion of the cause, had in its connection 6,000 schools, 60,000 teachers, and over 400,000 scholars, and one-half of its schools reported in 1833 that 2,607 teachers and 6,121 scholars had professed Christ in that year alone.

But this circulation of literature was gained on a benevolent, rather than on a commercial basis. It was then counted as wise to promote religious education through the printed page as by the living missionary. Gifted and philanthropic workers entered with spirit into the purpose of the Union because they saw the large opportunity for good, and they cheerfully contributed some of their best work to promote so excellent an object. Many of these works delighted readers for more than a generation. They enabled the small rural communities to have a free circulating library on a plan at once simple and effective. The origin of the plan has been ascribed to Benjamin Franklin. As early as 1827, free circulating libraries were popular, so that it was said, "It is now common for Sabbath-schools to enjoy the benefits of an interesting and instructive

ibrary." The plan was for a school to secure voluntary contributions for the purchase of books to make up such a library
on the understanding that every one should be allowed to
take books out without pay. It proved a successful scheme for
creating a taste for good reading and in promoting popular
education. It was computed that a sufficient number of
volumes were issued within a few years to give at least one
book every two weeks in every home in the republic. In
fact, towns and districts were induced to found free circulating libraries, because of the popularity of this scheme of free
circulating Sunday-school libraries.

Referring to the multiplication of some classes of books
purporting to be for Sunday-schools, the Union said: "Many
of them are calculated to do irreparable mischief. Some will
be found to contain the most unnatural and unscrupulous
views of Christian character; others again studiously avoid
so much as an allusion to the religious relations and obligations of parents. Some strenuously advocate the peculiar
views of a denomination on whose patronage they depend,
and others would have children to believe that religion itself
is nothing but a system of conflicting creeds and imposing
dogmas. In a word, some inculcate nothing that is right, and
others everything that is wrong." These strong words indicate how careful the managers of the Union, and especially
its committee, were in guarding against circulating improper
works.

Juvenile Hymns and Songs.—The American Sunday-School
Union not only aimed to provide a juvenile literature, but it
sought to displace the rollicking and ribald songs by cleaner
and purer lyrics set to attractive music. It was a common
proverb then, "The devil has all the popular songs." Practically there were no moral songs or hymns of note for children
in 1800 to 1810, except the small collection of Watts' *Divine
and Moral Songs*, Roland Hill's *Divine Hymns in Easy Language*, and Jane and Ann Taylor's *Original Hymns for Sunday-
Schools*.

There were collections of hymns for children a century
earlier, but those of any importance issued from 1700 to 1800
could be counted on the fingers of a person's hand. Foremost
among them stands the little book by Isaac Watts. His

Songs for Children was among the last of his lyric writings.
It is remarkable that half a century before the rise of the
modern Sunday-school, a batchelor and semi-invalid should
have composed hymns for children which were joyously sung
by the little ones for more than a century, and which made
them better and wiser for the singing. Mother love in its
tenderness finds one of its best expressions still through the
simple rhythmic strains of the "Cradle Hymn." The most
forcible lesson against quarreling was taught by the quaint
verses of "Let Dogs Delight," and a lesson of industry was
happily taught in the song of "The Busy Bee." These songs
were not written for the Sunday-school, yet it is rare to find
such vigorous moral lessons, so happily and strongly expressed, in modern Sunday-school hymn books.[1]

Divine Hymns in Easy Language, by the famous, but eccen-
tric Rowland Hill, were designed as an appendix to the valuable songs for children by Dr. Watts (as the author says)
and were intended to be used by Sunday-schools of his day

[1] Critics since the days of Isaac Watts have differed widely in their estimate of his
life and works. Although his theology was regarded as having a liberal tendency in his
own age, he had a dismal view of human nature. It has been said of him that tender as
he was toward children he regarded them with a sort of compassionate shudder. Thus
he writes:

"What young ferments of spite and envy, what native wrath and rage sometimes are found in the little hearts of infants and sufficiently discovered by
their little hands and their eyes and their wrathful countenances even before
they have learned to speak or to know good and evil."

Again he says:
"Cast a glance at the sports of children from five to fifteen years of age; what
have all these little toys and fooleries in them that would be fit for young angels
dressed in flesh and blood? Would so many years of early life have been
wasted in such mean and trifling diversions by a race of holy and rational
beings? and how much early iniquity and mischief in thought, word and
action is mingled with these sportings among the younger tribes of mankind,
God only knows."[2]

Some excuse for these seemingly harsh words may be found in the fact that Watts
was a precocious but broken-in-health youth. Real childhood he can scarcely have been
said to have ever had. C. J. Abbey, in *Religious Thoughts in Old English Verse,* p. 352,
speaks of Watts' *Songs for Children*—some of them—as exciting a smile. In other instances they are tinged apparently with the gloom of a part of his theology. But, as a
whole, they well deserve the favor they have gained. Their homely simplicity com-
mends itself to children and clings to their memories. They are likely long to outlive
many verses which are far superior to them as compositions and which might be thought
more attractive to the young. . . . Among the moral songs . . . is the Cradle Hymn,
beginning

Hush, my dear, lie still and slumber.

Like many of Watts' hymns there are lines in it which might well be spared, but, as a
whole, it is quite equal to George Wither's

Sleep, Baby, Sleep.

and Mr. Palgrave justly says of it that few child-pictures have been drawn in words and
color of more perfect tenderness.

[2] Burder, *Works of Isaac Watts,* London, 1810, Vol. VI, pp. 72, 86.

'or so small a book, the range of subjects was wide, and it annot be charged with lack of clearness or with sentimenality, or misty or vague doctrine respecting sin and salvation. Thus, the natural progress of the child from one sin to another s forcibly if not very elegantly put in rhyme:

> The little wretch whose lying tongue
> Can whisper to another's wrong,
> Will other mischiefs quickly dare,
> And soon be found to curse and swear.

He evidently held to the possibility of child depravity, and hus portrays a quarrelsome child in song:

> But oh, what a horrible sight,
> When children, with anger and rage,
> Like lions, will quarrel and fight,
> While none can their anger assuage.
>
> Old Satan is then very nigh,
> Delighted that thus they have shown
> A murdering spirit; and why?
> Because 'tis akin to his own!

Very plain and blunt were the teachings of sin and salvation of those old songs. Perhaps our modern children's hymn writers might gather profitable hints by the study of these old collections!

The conditions remind us of a wise writer who said, "Let me make the ballads of a people and I care not who makes the laws." The songs of the ale-house and of the brothel were too common on the streets and often crept into Christian homes through the children. It was a gigantic but necessary task to change this. Some of the sweetest lyric writers and some of the best musical composers gave their ripest skill to the production of hymns and tunes in this new field. The charming melodies of Lowell Mason, and the rhythmic songs of Thomas Hastings and other musical writers, were composed for the young, and issued by the Union as worthy forerunners of the gospel songs that now fill our land. A simple manual on the art of singing by E. Ives was issued by the Union to teach the young to sing by note, as well as by rote. Music lessons for infant classes were also issued in large numbers. Collections of psalmody and of hymns followed the issue of an elementary book, *The Union Minstrel*, edited by Thomas Hastings for the use of juvenile classes. Successive editions and series of *Union Hymns* were issued by the hundred thousand, containing songs and tunes that pleased the ear and presented lofty ideals of life. These soon came into popular favor and were sung everywhere. So popular did these new juvenile songs, introduced through the Sunday school, become that they quite swept the low, rollicking ribald songs from the streets, if not from all assemblies of youth.

The first *Union Hymn Book* was repeatedly revised and issued in large editions of 20,000 or 30,000 copies—250,000 before 1846. In response to a call for similar hymns suitable for teachers' meetings, the Union issued a special collection containing a large number of hymns adapted for the use of teachers and teachers' meetings.[1] A *Two-cent Hymn Book* was issued, adapted for "Houses of Refuge," and other charitable institutions, and distributed by the tens of thousands of copies.[2]

The Society met with some serious difficulties in attempting to introduce juvenile songs widely into rural Sunday-schools. In that day the strolling "singing master" was a conspicuous character. Sometimes he was nearly as conspicuous for his lax morals and his use of stimulants as he was for his mastery of music. Probably some teachers and Sunday-school superintendents may have found it difficult to teach after the singing, as the New England minister did at the close of a very badly sung psalm. It was rendered so wretchedly that he read another to the choir and said to them, "You must try again, for it is impossible to preach after such singing."[3] But in the face of ignorance and of difficulties, the better class of juvenile hymns and songs won their way in city and country.

These successive battles and victories marked epochs in Sunday-school progress worthy of permanent record. These began soon after the origin of the modern Sunday-school movement, for praise and song were a necessary and efficient aid in giving that movement success.

[1] *American Sunday-School Magazine*, 1826, p. 384.
[2] *Report*, 1846, p. 20.
[3] *Ameircan Sunday-School Magazine*, 1826, p. 235.

Modern evangelists have found that a service of song appeals to all, of whatever religious creed or opinion, and carries
the gospel message with irresistible power to the heart.   In
devout songs there is rarely a discordant theological note.
Hymns by devout authors and composers—by Romanists, as
Bernard of Cluny, Faber and Newman; and by Anglicans, as
Heber, Alford, Ken and Keble; and by Calvinists, as Watts,
Toplady and Bonar; and by Arminians, as the Wesleys—are
made the messengers of truth; the hearers never thinking of
the peculiar creeds of the authors, but only of their devout
spirit and their consecrated lives.   So, in the earlier coming
together of persons in the Sunday-school movement, hymns
and tunes were chosen from all available sources that were
adapted to the religious development of the young.

In this pioneer service for the young, the American Sunday-
School Union had a large share.   As in lesson systems, so in
juvenile hymnology, there have been successive periods, each
introduced by a marked epoch or crisis.   When the modern
Sunday-school movement began, there were few if any hymns,
aside from those of Watts and of Jane Taylor, suited for use
in children's gatherings.   This was particularly true of moral
and religious songs; they were meager in quantity and not
high in quality.   This battle for betterment continued for a
generation.

Professor John S. Hart, LL.D., an eminent educator and
Sunday-school editor, out of his experience in Sunday-schools
in the first part of the last century, tells of "the grim and pon-
derous tune to which we youngsters were solemnly exhorted
to trail our voices, while a hymn of equally unattractive character dragged its slow length along.   The singing was a religious duty, to which we were expected to give heed, and which
we tried faithfully to discharge, as we would have tried to
submit cheerfully to an amputation, had circumstances required it; or as we would have walked to the school, if necessary, bare-footed through the snow, as one boy actually did
rather than forego his privileges."   He adds: "The music
suited to persons advanced in life is no more suited to children
than would be the measured and solemn gait of these aged
persons.   Childhood is jubilant, and quick in its motions.
. . . If the music is really to take hold of the feelings of

children, it must be simple, quick and lively in its general movement."[1] He points out the danger of an opposite extreme of providing for children trivial music or words that degenerate into slang, flippant, bordering only on the profane or what might be fit for a picnic or a circus, but not for a religious service.   There were certain tunes and words—"rude irreverent, fit only for clowns." It is unwise, in trying to escape from the dreary solemnities of a doleful, long-metered lugubrious hymn, to rush into the other extreme.

But in America, as in England, Sunday-school workers were compelled, at first, to make the best selection they could from existing hymn books.   These proved so inadequate that an insistent demand was made for original hymns and tunes better fitted to reach the youthful mind.

At the early anniversaries of the Sunday-School Union few suitable hymns were found.   Hymns by W. B. Tappan, Willis Gaylord Clark, and Dr. W. A. Muhlenberg, and other recognized hymn writers were composed to be sung at the annual meeting of the Society, and were, with spirit.   The American Sunday-School Union issued a selection of existing hymns in 1819, following the testing of some of them by printing them on separate sheets or cards for use in various Sunday-schools. While several thousands of this first hymn book were issued, it was apparent that the hymns were too mature and too "stiff" for the young.   They might be suited to persons of advanced years anticipating death and stepping into the grave.   Indeed, the characteristics of some hymns were so marked as to cause the irreverent to say that they were "well fitted for those pious young children in 'memoirs' " (too common then), wherein "all good little children died young." This fault was early recognized, "It has been found very difficult to meet the various wants of those for whose use these hymn books are designed."

The American Sunday-School Union also secured the writing of many new hymns for youth.   It issued manuals of hymns and music, including *A System of Instruction in Music* for the young.   Thomas Hastings wrote *Juvenile Psalmody,* issued by the Western Sunday-School Union of New York— an auxiliary of the American Sunday-School Union—in 1827.

[1] John S. Hart, *Thoughts on Sabbath Schools*, p. 93.

This was designed to furnish a concise system of learning to sing sacred music, "so simplified in its character as to be easily reduced to practice on the monitorial plan" of teaching. It was followed by a larger work, entitled *Manual of Instruction in American Sunday-School Psalmody*, by E. Ives, Jr., whose work embraced principles of musical education growing out of actual experience "in the instruction of about five thousand pupils." The lessons were so constructed "that children who have learned to sing by rote may, by an ordinary singer, be taught in one hour to sing a hymn scientifically."

That the young should understand the meaning of the hymn was early recognized by Sunday-school leaders. To carry out this rule, however, required hymns that the child could understand. Few such hymns were in existence, as already noted. To supply this lack the Union further encouraged the production of new hymns as well as the most careful gleaning from all the old ones—whether used in the church or elsewhere. These were published in successive "collections of hymns"—well nigh a dozen of them—of different types and sizes, and as fast as they were found unsatisfactory, the defective and weak ones were weeded out.

In this early period, stages or steps in the development of the child mind were recognized. Thus, a selection of hymns for infant classes was issued; another for the main school of the adolescent age; a third for senior and Bible classes; a fourth for teachers' meetings, and a fifth containing special hymns and music on temperance, and for Christmas, anniversaries, and other special occasions. Thus the educational principles upon which the Society planned its system of Bible study were applied to its hymn books. In all this service, Sunday-school educators were pioneers, since songs for the young, whether social, educational, or religious, did not exist as a class. Before this period, the children were compelled to join as best they could in church hymns and in the social songs written and intended for grown people.

Another marked epoch was when the Society provided evangelistic hymns and music suited for revivals and prayer-meetings. Nettleton's *Village Hymns* failed to meet the need, outside of New England. Among the earliest popular compilations of this kind was one made by a committee of the

Young Men's Christian Association and published by the American Sunday-School Union previous to the great revival of 1857 and 1858. *Union Prayer Meeting Hymns* was published in a variety of editions with some new tunes, but for the most part those of a familiar and of a standard but popular type.

As the principles of education were better understood and the development of the child mind more clearly defined, there came a call for hymns and especially for music expressive of gladness, lively feeling and joy, characteristic of youthful minds. It was clearly seen that neither the old music, nor the words, quite suited the lively treble of the voice of youth. The words should not be unintelligible on the one hand, nor meaningless doggerel on the other. The music should not be doleful or "dragging," nor should it be frivolous, but expressive of the cheerful and happy spirit of childhood. As these ideas emerged there was a call for an advance along these lines, marking another period in the character of Sunday-school hymnology. It first appeared in connection with *Sunday-School Anniversaries*—a series of half a dozen chiefly original hymns and tunes written by foremost authors and composers for these occasions. They speedily became so popular that hymns and tunes of a similar type were called for in all the devotional services of Sabbath-schools. Authors, composers, and publishers combined to flood America with compositions, taking advantage of this popular idea, which amounted almost to a craze.

To stem this craze for quantity—something ever new, even if doggerel and light music—and to displace it with something that would be more reverent and instructive, the American Sunday-School Union invited the Rev. Dr. Charles S. Robinson, a recognized authority in hymnology, and Theodore E. Perkins, a musical composer of note, to prepare a book of a more devout spirit of praise and worship for Sunday-school use, and, at the same time, to retain "as many of the familiar and popular pieces of the best authors as was consistent, with a fair number of fresh tunes and hymns of real worth," blending the old and the new together. Dr. Robinson had already attained fame as a compiler of *Songs for the Sanctuary*. His *Calvary Songs* included many of the evangelistic pieces made widely popular by the revival workers, Ira D. Sankey, D. L. Moody, P. P. Bliss, and others.

The Society had already prepared the way and created a taste for a book of this class by its previous *American Sunday-School Hymn Book*, and the *Sunday-School Hosanna*, which were among the pioneers in this second period or epoch in juvenile hymnology.

These two movements, namely, modern evangelistic meetings and the Sunday-school, are credited with contributing largely to the volume, if not to the quality, of American hymns. The popular demand was so great that doubtless a large number were produced under this pressure which fairly came under the criticism since made, that "the majority of these hymns are such that their continued use is not to be desired, while the quality of the music to which they are sung is even poorer than that of the hymns."[1] The Union recognized this increase in quantity and decrease in quality, and endeavored to turn the movement so as at least to improve the quality.

Of some earlier and famous hymn writers, as Watts, Addison, Doddridge, and Steele, it has been said they did not create high-class lyrics. Literary critics count their productions as only fair examples of the influence of the poetical school of Pope. But they did express the new and growing spirituality of evangelical religion. Cowper, Newton, Toplady, and Charles Wesley opened a new era of deeper spirituality in Christian experience, and of improved lyric merit. They wrote lines suited for singing, as all lyrics are not. These lines expressed the emotions of the Christian mind, and thus became endeared to the Christian heart. For a lyric is the creation of a poetic imagination; a Christian hymn is that also, plus the inspiration from a devout communion with God.

It could not be expected that the character of evangelistic and Sunday-school hymns should rise above that of general church hymnology. It ought, however, to attain at times at least a high order of merit, and it surely did. Note the modern hymns of Bonar, Ray Palmer, Fanny Crosby, C. Wordsworth, P. P. Bliss, Matheson, and many others. It was the aim of the American Sunday-School Union to bring Sunday-

[1] George W. Gilmore, in *Schaff-Herzog Encyclopedia.*

school songs and music up to this high standard. The Union spared neither labor nor expense to accomplish its aim. It was not ambitious to produce bulky volumes; it sought rather to sift out the standard and the best of the popular hymns and tunes which had worthily won a place in the hearts of all evangelical Christians. On this plan it issued *Union Hymns*, *The People's Hymn Book*, *Calvary Songs*, *Hymnal for Primary Classes*, *Favorite Hymns*, and similar collections, all of a moderate size. In preparing the *Hymnal for Primary Classes*, the guiding purpose was "to have every hymn and exercise teach the love of Jesus, some scriptural truth, and some important moral principle which, once fixed in the minds of children, might ever influence their lives." The material of these works was gleaned from every available source; some of it was original, written to suit children's voices, "to be sung in unison." The collections were published at a price which would place them within the reach of all.

In making these improvements the Union did not depend upon a single author or composer. Thus in one of the later of its works, *Favorite Hymns*, upward of 200 of its missionary and evangelistic workers in all parts of America were asked to furnish a carefully sifted list of 200 hymns and tunes most widely used and most highly valued in their respective fields. These lists were collated, and from them were again sifted upward of 150 hymns and tunes which appeared oftenest in these lists. This collection was found to contain a large proportion of the spiritual hymns which were the heritage of Christendom, and comprised the best compositions of the widest and most famous lyrics and music writers, ancient and modern. Thus the American Sunday-School Union has diligently sought to contribute its share of service in this field of juvenile hymnology, improving the quality and also stimulating young Christians to higher ideals in spiritual living.

There is still room for improvement in the quality of hymns for praise and worship, in the Sunday-school. Many so-called hymns are not suitable to be so sung; they are not even passable lyrics, but only rhymes or doggerel. The songs of Watts and of his school have had a dominant influence over hymn writers for nearly two centuries. He hit the popular level of his age, but as an educator in taste his

verses "were not the happiest."[1]   Verses for use in worship
are abundant as the leaves of the forest, true hymns are
rare as flawless diamonds.   For a hymn is the lyrical expression of prayer, praise and holy meditation not only, but
in rhythm and harmony suitable to be sung.   It is not simply
the poetry of emotion, but of devotion—the unrolling of
great waves of feeling, of irresistible power and of unfath-
omed depths.   The ideal juvenile hymnology will express
all varieties of mental and spiritual growth in harmonies
appealing to the mystic heights and depths of the spirit
filled with a childlike faith in a Heavenly Father.   We wait
with patience for the ideal Sunday-school hymn book.   One
of the glories of an ideal work of this class will be that it can
voice the deepest truths of our holy religion in the simplest
language and free from doctrinal controversy.   It will reveal
the harmony of all fundamental religious truth.   It is an
interesting confirmation of this millennium of Christian unity
that the old hymns endeared to devout souls are the language
of the universal human heart, though the authors were often
champions of theological disputes.   Thus, hymns by Arians
churchmen, Catholics (Roman and Greek), Calvinists, Methodists, Lutherans, Moravians and many Chinese creeds are
now found in the hymnals of seven leading evangelical denominations.

Periodicals, Early Period.—The Sunday-school movement
early met with indifference and opposition.   The indifference
was partly due to ignorance or lack of proper information
concerning the purpose and methods of the institution.
The managers of the Union declared that some new effort
was required to give an impetus and wise direction to Sunday-
schools if they were to achieve success or even to make any
real progress.   This information was needed along several
different lines.

(1) Specific instructions were required on organization and
conduct of Sunday-schools and also upon the organization of
groups of schools in unions, co-operating with one another in
a common but limited field.

(2) A common medium of information was necessary between the various schools and unions scattered over the

[1] F. M. Bird, *Hymnology.*

country in order that whatever new methods were tried and found successful in any place might be conveyed to another. Thus the schools would be stimulated to improve not by speculative theories, but by actual methods, which had been put into practice and somewhere, at least, had stood the test of use.

(3) Information must further be given constantly upon the various modes of extending Sunday-schools into new fields by agents, missionaries, auxiliaries, churches, and voluntary workers, creating an interest and stimulating each of these into activity in every part of the land.

American Sunday-School Magazine.—To accomplish these ends, it was proposed to issue a general periodical. In 1823, *The American Sunday-School Magazine* was projected, but the issue of it was delayed until a competent editor could be found. A committee of the Union searched for several months and reported that the difficulty, not to say impracticability, of finding a person meeting the views of the Society in all points was great, yet they had found a young journalist in New York (Frederick W. Porter), who was distinguished for zeal in Sabbath-schools, a man of piety and evangelical principles, willing, at the end of his engagement in New York, to come to Philadelphia. Mr. Porter conducted the magazine monthly from July 1, 1824, for a few years, until Frederick A. Packard gave up a large and promising legal practice to devote his life to the preparation of religious literature for the young, at the call of the American Sunday-School Union. The increasing demands for the Union's literature within five years required Mr. Porter to give all his time to the management of its circulation and to the direction of its missionary work.

The object of the magazine was, broadly stated, to promote the three lines of work already indicated. It proposed to give a summary record of Sabbath-schools "in all parts of the world," to present the best methods of conducting them, to discuss questions relating to their management, to notice the literature, to treat of education, to give hints on training children in the fear of the Lord in the family circle, and to illustrate all these subjects by authentic facts, tending to exhibit the power of divine truth in a form to encourage parents and Sunday-school teachers, and to stimulate all to take part in the religious education of the rising generation.

It will be seen that their purpose was to cover the whole field of education as related to religion. It was not limited to teachers or workers, but was for all friends of the cause of religion, whether in the church, society, or the family.

Several similar periodicals were issued about the same time in Boston, Hartford, New Haven, New York, Utica, Princeton, and other places, but only for local circulation. *The American Sunday-School Magazine* had a wider outlook, taking on a national character and treating the progress of the movement in a more general way, suited to readers in different parts of the country. It aimed to do for America what *The Sunday-School Repository or Teachers' Magazine* of England attempted to do for Great Britain. It was issued monthly from July, 1824, each page being eight and one-half by five and three-quarter inches (the type page six and three-quarter by three and three-quarter inches), thirty-two pages in each number, with illustrations, maps, plans of rooms, etc., giving 384 large pages of reading matter yearly for $1.50.

Simultaneously with the regular monthly issues of the magazine, the Union sent out a great variety of publications at irregular intervals, giving information along all three of the lines of work above indicated. Thus letters, circulars, appeals, instructions, regulations and rules were poured forth from its presses with almost bewildering variety and quantity, such as *Directions for Forming and Conducting Sunday-Schools* (12 pages); *Hints to Aid in the Organization and Support of Sabbath-Schools in the Country; Plans and Motives for the Extension of Sabbath-Schools; An Address to the Citizens of Philadelphia;* another *To the Friends of Sunday-Schools in the United States; System of Internal Regulation for Sunday-Schools; Plan of Proceeding in the Formation of Auxiliary Sunday-School Unions,* and a constitution and by-laws for the same; *Hints on the Establishment of Sunday-School Depositories; Yearly Course of Select Scripture Lessons for Sunday-Schools; Annual Reports from Auxiliary Societies,* and *Suggestions in Vindication of Sunday-Schools.* Publications on the design, importance, and various other phases of the Sunday-school movement were repeatedly and fre-

quently issued in circular or pamphlet form and were gratuitously distributed by the tens of thousands over the country.

These numerous documents, along with the periodical
magazine—which was accompanied by an illustrated smaller
periodical for children, entitled *The Youth's Friend*, and a
third one, *The Infant Magazine*, for beginners—aroused
public interest in the cause of Bible instruction so that even
more full and systematic information was urgently demanded.
The workers wanted more detailed news and information in
regard to new plans and methods of instruction, and desired
reports of the character of the many experiments suggested
and introduced by those who were widely scattered through
the country and were thinking of novel expedients characteristic of every new movement. So there was a call for a
periodical more frequently issued and more of the character
of a newspaper.

Weekly Sunday-School Journal.—This agitation stimulated
the Union to project the issue of a large folio periodical each
week, and a prospectus and specimen number of *The Sunday-
School Journal and Advocate of Christian Education* was issued
November 24, 1830. The projectors of this mammoth
journal (for that period) announced that it would be issued
each week, beginning January 5, 1831. They declared that
the subject of religious education "had become a distinct and
interesting department of general intelligence and inquiry,"
making it indispensable to have this information presented in
a popular form; that "a weekly paper was found to be the
most efficient and least expensive mode of diffusing this information." It allowed scope "for general and familiar discussions and illustrations of all subjects connected with the
cause," and gave an opportunity "for greater variety and
quantity of matter than could be furnished in any other form
at the same price."

Moreover, the object of this benevolent institution, the
Sunday-school, was so important that it could not be assigned
any secondary place. This point was forcibly stated: "If to
instruct the ignorant, awaken the careless, and guide the inquiring, is the legitimate office of the Sunday-school teacher;
if to enlighten the mind, sustain the spirit, elevate the hopes,
alleviate the woes, and convert to God the soul of man, are

the legitimate results of Sunday-school instruction," it could not take a secondary place.

This new weekly journal was a newspaper-folio in form, of four pages, each page fifteen by twenty-one inches, five columns to the page, in close, but clear type. It presented news in regard to the progress of Sunday-schools from every state, with an occasional peep at their progress throughout the world. Every phase of the problem of education, as related to religion, was discussed. Special attention was given to prominent theories of leading educators which were then receiving the attention of the public and of the learned throughout the country. Full accounts of experimental plans and methods pursued in different schools in different parts of the country were given. Nor did the editors forget whatever would stimulate workers to improved plans and to an earnest inculcation and application of biblical truth in the formation of character. Nearly every number contained an engraving quite worthy of the artistic skill of those days, however crude it may seem to us now.

This journal also contained explanations and applications upon the Select Uniform Limited Lessons, which were then in use. These were entirely different from the "Helps" in the Union Questions which were also upon the same select Bible texts. The Moravian plan of "a verse-a-day" committed to memory was also noticed, and for some time the seven verses for each week appeared in full in one of its columns. Altogether the journal was not only equal to, but in advance of the average weekly newspaper of that day in regard to its information and Sunday-school news, as well as in respect to the available material relating to education, the lessons, and the various principles or methods applicable to Bible instruction. It published full reports of the first and second National Sunday-School Conventions of 1832 and 1833, held, respectively, in New York and in Philadelphia.

This weekly Sunday-school teachers' periodical was among the earliest of its class, if not the first weekly teachers' paper of its kind, issued in America or in the world. It attempted to throw light upon the systems of education which were then in an unsettled, formative condition.

The *Journal* brought into comparison the views of foremost educators of that period, which proved an excellent way of showing their diverse and even contradictory character. The editors and writers attempted to bring some clear order out of this confused discussion. They appealed to the public to support the *Journal* and the American Sunday-School Union. "If the friends of liberty and religion will stand by it, and sustain it with generous hearts and open hands, its field of usefulness and benevolent exertions will extend farther and farther until it shall embrace all the inhabited portions of the globe; and its duration and means will be measured only by the existence and wants of a sinful, dying world." Surely a wide outlook and a far vision were theirs!

The reports of state and county conventions were given with such frequency and fulness as to create a desire for a national convention. This was proposed by a resolution of the managers of the American Sunday-School Union and first published in the *Journal* in 1832. (This will be noticed more fully under *Conventions.*)

The *Sunday-School Journal* continued to be issued once a week from 1831 to 1835, at two dollars per year. Then, for financial reasons, it was issued only every other week, and the price reduced to one dollar per year. In 1843 the size of the page was reduced and it was offered to schools at the extremely low price of twenty-five cents per year. It was furnished at this popular price until 1859, when it was succeeded by *The Sunday-School Times*, and later by *The Sunday-School World.*

Juvenile Illustrated Periodicals.—This class of religious literature was a creation of the first quarter or half of the nineteenth century. The early juvenile illustrated periodicals were tiny affairs. Great Britain, in the early years of the Sunday-school movement, industriously put forth periodical literature in greater abundance than books. Several of these small papers for children were published by private enterprise. One of the pioneers in this field was *The Youth's Magazine*, edited by W. B. Gurney of London. It was a "popular and high-class monthly," primarily not for Sunday scholars but for young people in general. A small periodical of this class, called *The Sunday-School Child's Repository*, was issued

AUTHORS

Archibald Alexander, D. D., LL. D.

James W. Alexander, D. D.

Henry A. Boardman, D. D.

John Hall, D. D., of New York.

Philip Schaff, D. D., LL. D.

Edwin Cone Bissell D. D.

for a brief period from 1815 at Southwark, a part of London, and Mr. Gover soon after started a similar magazine which also was discontinued when the Religious Tract Society began *The Child's Companion* in 1824. According to Mr. William H. Groser, secretary of the London Sunday-School Union, about a dozen monthlies for young people were issued in 1825, varying in price from one penny to four pence each. The London Sunday-School Union Report for May, 1824, gives a list of fifteen "periodicals for Sunday scholars," but two or three of them do not seem to belong exclusively to that class, and two or three others belong, properly, to the educational rather than to the religious field. Most of them shared the fate of educational and literary magazines and periodicals begun in the latter part of the eighteenth century —they were short lived. This was specially true of literary magazines and periodicals in America. For out of a list of about 275, given in *The American Encyclopedia*, including American, English, French, German, and some other European languages in the various branches of learning—and that lived up to 1860—scarcely eighteen were begun before 1820. Many of these, in fact, were annals or journals of scientific or other societies and not properly magazines, reviews, or literary journals. The short lives of these journals and their ephemeral character might be expected in the development of a new class of periodicals in any country. There was, perhaps, less mortality among the juvenile illustrated periodicals in America than among other kinds of periodical literature, whether in America or abroad.

When the Sunday-school was founded the call began to be insistent for periodical reading matter of a moral and religious type, suited to the young. One of this class had been started in New Haven, called *The Teachers' Offering*, a tiny affair, which was bought by the Sunday-School Union in 1823 and continued under the title of *The Youth's Friend and Scholars' Magazine*. Its circulation quickly jumped from fifty copies at the first issue to 3,000, and then to 10,000, and soon to 13,000 for each issue. Its motto or keyword was "Buy the Truth and Sell It Not." It was issued monthly and covered sixteen small book pages, with one engraving each month. In reviewing it, a New York paper urged every parent to watch with what joy the children would hail its arrival. The reviewer suggested that the periodical should come in the child's "own name," and be his own paper, and adds: "The matter contained in this work is of a purely moral or religious character, and presented to the young reader in a style suited to his capacity. The engravings will be highly acceptable, and, what is still more important, almost every young person can find means to defray the expense of taking it." It was continued for over twenty years, when it was superseded by the larger and far more pretentious quarto or folio, *The Youth's Penny Gazette.*

The *Gazette* began in 1842 and was issued every other week at the marvelously low price of twelve and a half cents per annum when forty copies or over were taken, and marked a new era in juvenile illustrated periodicals for Sunday-schools. It claimed to contain intelligence "of the most various and interesting character," and facts and suggestions respecting Sunday-schools, missions, the temperance reformation, "and such expositions of prevailing errors and delusions as shall aid the teacher and interest the pupil in their common duties." It had several engravings in each number, one sometimes taking a whole page. It speedily attained a large circulation which it continued to hold for upward of fifteen years, when it was followed in 1859 by *The Sunday-School Banner* and *The Sunday-School Gazette.* They, in turn, were followed by *The Child's World* and other papers described later. The *Penny Gazette* claimed to be the pioneer in this class of folio, illustrated papers for Sunday-schools in America.

Infants' Magazine.—The Union not only made provision for the wants of the teachers and of youth, but it also took note of the wants of the little ones and aimed to furnish suitable reading for them in *The Infants' Magazine*, a small paper especially prepared to meet the tastes and capacities of the "wee ones" in the Sunday-school and in the home. It had engravings appealing to the eye, as well as interesting matter to be read to those who were yet unable to read for themselves. This little periodical was issued monthly by the American Sunday-School Union from 1829 to 1834, and was a pioneer of that class of religious papers now so abundant, aiming to interest the youngest children, beginning with the Cradle Roll.

Periodicals, Middle Period.—The great revival of 1857–59 gave a new impetus to the development of the Sunday-school. It aroused fresh enthusiasm in the systematic study of the Scriptures through infant, juvenile, adult, and Bible classes and teachers' meetings. This increased attention to Bible study called for better communication among its workers, such as might be afforded by a weekly teachers' journal. Such a periodical had been issued for a few years following 1830, as heretofore noticed, but it had been discontinued from lack of adequate financial support. Such a journal, broad in its outlook, not only helpful to teachers but encouraging the extension of Sunday-schools and discussing, in an evangelical spirit, means for giving greater life and efficiency to Sunday-school instruction through reports of proceedings of Sunday-school conventions and of the success of various forms of Sunday-school effort, reviews of religious literature of interest to workers—not overlooking successful methods of family instruction; in short, a journal free from denominational or sectarian bias, it was believed would be welcomed and well sustained.

The Sunday-School Times.—These considerations led the American Sunday-School Union to start *The Sunday-School Times* in January, 1859, securing John S. Hart, LL.D., an eminent educator, as editor, and I. Newton Baker as his assistant. It was considered advantageous to have a special editor for a teachers' journal of this scope and for the preparation of periodicals for the young which the Society continued to issue.

The Sunday-School Times was issued in newspaper form, each page about fifteen inches by twenty inches—each number a folio of four pages, at one dollar per year, single copy, or 100 copies for seventy dollars, to one address. It was ably edited, and warmly welcomed by a large number of Christian workers throughout the country. The Society, however, discovered what many private publishers experienced before and since that date; that the founding of a new weekly religious journal was an expensive experiment. The embarrassed condition of the Society's finances, together with the distracted condition of the country, led the managers of the Union after two years (in 1861) to transfer this publication to private parties (John S. Hart and others). By this transfer, it was believed that the paper might retain most of its old friends and gain more new ones in denominational schools, sufficient to give it adequate support.

It gradually won its way in influence under Dr. Hart, succeeded by Mr. Baker, and was later ably sustained by John Wanamaker as publisher, until it was again transferred in 1875 to H. Clay Trumbull and the Sunday-School Times Company, ranking among the foremost Sunday-school journals in the world.

In place of *The Sunday-School Times* thus transferred to private parties, the Union planned and issued another teachers' paper similar to *The Sunday-School Journal*, and the magazines which were issued by the Union from 1824 to 1859. Teachers and workers in rural and Union schools for which the Society cared, required and would sustain a journal adapted to their need if it could be furnished at a price within their means. Such a periodical the Union issued in March, 1861. As the title *Sunday-School Journal* first used by the Union had been appropriated by a denomination, the Society named this teachers' periodical *The Sunday-School World*. In taking this title it was intended to include whatever would be of interest to all workers in the Sunday-school and in the family interested in religion and the study of the Bible. It was issued monthly at fifty cents for a single subscription and forty cents in clubs. The size and shape were adopted with reference to binding at the end of the year, the page being eight by ten inches, sixteen pages or more in each number. The editing of the periodicals was again placed under the charge of Dr. Packard, as in 1858, and continued so until his death in 1868, when the Rev. Richard Newton, D.D., was appointed editor of the periodicals and Samuel Austin Allibone, LL.D., editor of the book publications. *The Sunday-School World* continued to be of the form and size noted until 1872, when the size of the page was considerably increased and other changes made, to be noticed hereafter.

New Illustrated Periodicals.—When *The Sunday-School Times* was begun in 1859 (a revival of *The Sunday-School*

Journal of 1831, in fact), changes were made in the juvenile periodicals also. *The Youth's Penny Gazette*, a folio which had been issued every alternate week since 1842, was followed in 1859 by *The Youth's Sunday-School Gazette*, issued once a month. It appeared in a new dress, on more expensive white paper, with a greater number of engravings, though somewhat smaller than those which had appeared in the *Penny Gazette*. The matter was intended for youths somewhat older than those who had been readers of the former paper. The *Gazette* was issued in clubs—100 copies to one address for eleven dollars.

At the same time, the Society published *The Sunday-School Banner* every week for children and youth under the teen age. It was about the same size and style as the former *Penny Gazette*, and was offered to schools as a weekly, a semi-monthly, a monthly, or three times a month: 100 copies, monthly, eight dollars; semi-monthly, sixteen dollars; three times a month, twenty-four dollars; weekly, thirty-two dollars a year. The topics treated in these juvenile papers were moral and religious for the most part, though the scope was much wider than that of its predecessor, *The Penny Gazette*. Articles relating to nature studies and similar subjects were frequently presented in its columns, and without tacking on a moral lesson at the end.

These two papers were discontinued in 1861 and were followed by *The Child's World* in 1862, issued semi-monthly; 100 copies at twelve dollars, or monthly, six dollars. The Civil War, which increased the cost of everything, compelled the Society to double this price. This paper was adapted in its matter to interest and instruct the young in the same way as *The Sunday-School World* was adapted to adults. The special feature of this *Child's World* was that the fourth folio page was suited to children just beginning to read and was printed in large type, with illustrations. It speedily attained a circulation greater than any of its predecessors in their palmiest days, and continued to have this circulation of more than 200,000 copies a month under Dr. Packard and Dr. Newton's editorship.

The periodical was adopted as a medium of information because it gave a large amount of reading matter at a very small price. The managers frequently called attention to this fact. Thus, it was said: "If all the reading matter distributed (through the three periodicals) in the form of sheets was circulated in book form, it would be equal to the issue of 1,280,357 pages in a day, or to 466,150,000 pages a year." Or, they put it in another way, "The amount of reading matter sent out in our periodicals is equal to an issue of 1,747 copies daily of *Pilgrim's Progress*." [1]

Periodicals, Later Period.—In 1872 *The Sunday-School World* was enlarged and reconstructed as to the arrangement and the kind of material furnished in it. The new Uniform Sunday-School Lessons were begun that year, as elsewhere described. New features were adopted. Expositions of the Sunday-school lessons were furnished by the Rev. John Hall, D.D., who had recently come to New York from Dublin; fresh gleanings from the Holy Land were furnished by the editor, Dr. Richard Newton; practical suggestions on methods of conducting and teaching in Sunday-schools were furnished by the normal secretary, Rev. H. Clay Trumbull; and a condensed record of progress of Sunday-school work at home and abroad by the assistant editor, Edwin W. Rice; besides special discussions on timely subjects from recognized biblical scholars.

These articles and discussions in *The Sunday-School World* embraced the principles and methods of teaching; approved modes of opening, conducting, and closing Sunday-schools; the classification of scholars; the proper management of primary, intermediate and adult classes; the selection and distribution of libraries; the right conduct of teachers' meetings and children's services, and whatever else related to the work of the Sunday-school and religious instruction in the home.

Material relating to the missionary work of the Society was also presented in a monthly supplement which contained an acknowledgment of the donations received for the support of that work from month to month. These supplements sometimes extended to eight pages quarto, in addition to the sixteen large quarto pages of the regular issue.

The plan of studying the lessons presented in *The Sunday-School World* had several new features. The entire Bible

---

[1] *Report*, 1859, p. 54.

text of the lessons was printed, with references and verses to be memorized, and a central truth. Explanations of difficult words were given, and the leading truths of the texts were tersely presented, with explanations, to exhibit the full scope of the lesson and enable the teacher with directness and fidelity to apply it to the life and conduct of the pupils.

These helps upon the lessons in the *World* were not designed to be taken into the class and read, but to aid the teacher in the preparation and right understanding of the lesson before he met his class. To aid him in discovering whether he had a reasonable grasp of the truth, suggestive points or topics that might be turned into questions were added, to each of which a definite answer must be given by the teacher or the pupil. These tests would enable the teacher beforehand to find out whether he had a sufficient mastery of the Bible lesson to teach it intelligently.

Closely related to the lessons in *The Sunday-School World* were treatments of the same lessons for the scholars in several grades (see below).

These improvements in the *World* led to a marvelous increase in its circulation, speedily attaining a yearly issue of about a half-million copies.

The Sunday-School World signalized the beginning of a new seven years' course of International Lessons in 1880 by changing its form from that of a sixteen-page quarto to an octavo magazine of thirty-six pages and upward, with an engraved cover. The readers gave gratifying proof of their appreciation of this change. The copies were bound at the end of the year and preserved by friends in different parts of the country. The editor, Edwin W. Rice, had associated with him from 1879 the Rev. Moseley H. Williams, a Yale graduate, who had previous experience as a journalist and pastor. *The Sunday-School World* continued under the leadership of these two editors and their assistants for over thirty years, various new features being introduced as conditions and changes arose in the progress of biblical and religious education.

Among these new features were: (1) A series of articles by the American Revision Committee explaining the purpose and character of the Anglo-American version of the Bible then in progress. The topics upon which the public desired information were indicated by Editor Rice, who, with the co-operation of Dr. Philip Schaff, secured the treatment of each topic by an accomplished scholar of the American Revision Committee who had given a life-study to that particular subject. The articles (nineteen of them) were republished in a book, and had an important influence in preparing the way for an intelligent reception of the revised version of the Bible when it was first issued in 1881. The leading papers of the country found them a rich source of information.

(2) A second new feature was giving light from Oriental manners, customs, and archæological research, upon the Bible lesson each week by such specialists as Prof. George E. Post of Beirut, John T. Haddad of Damascus, Selah Merrill of Jerusalem, Explorer F. J. Bliss of Syria, and many others— a line of Bible interpretation which was soon adopted by other teachers' journals.

(3) A third feature was a series of papers on child development by Rev. Moseley H. Williams, with other lines on principles and methods of teaching by Dr. Addison P. Foster. Alice W. Knox advocated the new class system in primary work, and John B. Smith contributed a superintendent's review of the lesson.

(4) A fourth feature was suggesting applications and illustrations of special truths under each lesson.

(5) Sketches of epochs in the history of the Sunday-school movement by the editor, Edwin W. Rice.

Periodicals for Scholars.—A special system of lesson helps adapted to the pupils was developed in harmony with the studies for teachers in *The Sunday-School World*. Hitherto the pupils had received little aid in Bible study except through catechisms and question books. Out of his experience and observation Editor Rice conceived of a system of periodicals intended to awaken the interest and aid all grades of scholars in Bible study, one which would be adapted to the successive stages of mental development of learners.

This system of helps started with *The Primary Lesson Paper*, giving the story of the lesson, things to remember, and questions and answers in the words of the Bible text for instructing little ones.

The Intermediate Lesson Paper had the text, central truth and daily readings, with a sketch of the lesson, questions, and applications, calling for some reflection. The *Advanced Lesson Paper* for more mature minds added an analysis of the truths of the text, and called for the practical lessons to be drawn from the text.

To aid in retaining these truths a *Scholars' and Teachers' Quarterly Review Paper* was issued, showing the scholar how to review the studies of the three months, and a similar quarterly, called *The Superintendent's Review Paper*, was published to aid the superintendent in making a three months' review of the lessons in the whole school. With *The Superintendent's Review Paper* was issued a large *Review Wall Chart*, printed in bold type, so that it could be read by all in an ordinary schoolroom.

The graded lesson papers for scholars were appreciated and created a desire for a bound volume. So the *Scholars' Handbook* on each year's lessons was issued in parts (1874–1889). This was recognized as the scholars' commentary. It contained the Bible text in paragraphs, a sketch of events omitted in the course of the lessons, a description of places, persons, and customs, and brief explanations and suggestions, with illustrations, maps, blackboard outlines, and charts; in fact, a complete help for scholars. The *Handbook* was adopted and translated into Dutch by the Netherlands Sunday-School Union. An edition in Italian was also issued at Rome and a Protestant Episcopal edition adapted to the church year was issued for several years (1878–1880).

Rice's *Handbook* created a call for *The Scholars' Companion* (1878–79), which he also edited. This was a monthly, giving fuller explanations, studies, notes, tests of study, and pictures, with answers to such questions as the pupils would be likely to ask. It was in square quarto form, eight pages, at twenty cents a year, single copies.

The Scholars' Companion was followed after two years by *The American Sunday-School Union Quarterly* (1880), issued in larger quarto form than the *Companion* and illustrated, and presenting the lessons for three months in one number, at twenty cents a year.

The increased interest in Sunday-school study awakened a

demand for a similar help for the younger scholars, so *The Primary Quarterly* was issued, printed on pink-tinted paper, a square quarto, with enlarged type and original engravings illustrative of each lesson.

Illustrated Reading for the Home.—*The Child's World*, which succeeded *The Youth's Penny Gazette* of 1842, was published continuously from 1862 to 1881, when it was succeeded by two papers, to increase the interest in religious reading in the home. The Union began (1881) *The Picture World*, with large type, and prepared specially for the very little ones. It was a folio, eight-page paper, in four parts, so that it could be cut, and a part distributed every Sunday. For the older boys and girls the title of *The Child's World* was changed to *The Youth's World*, and the matter adapted to those of somewhat more mature taste. It contained sketches of Scripture events, studies in nature and music, and stories by popular writers. In January, 1882, two new illustrated periodicals were added: *The Illustrated Treasury of Knowledge*, devoted especially to information concerning God's wonderful works in Nature as revealed by modern science and explorations; and *Truth in Life*, a temperance paper, showing the manifold nature of God's physical laws and the importance of obeying them.

In January, 1883, a fourth illustrated paper of similar style and price, entitled *The Sunday Hour*, was issued, containing Scripture biographies, popular accounts of explorations, and studies in Bible lands with pictorial illustrations. Thus each of these papers had a distinct field and presented attractive reading for the home, helpful in developing moral and religious character.

The development of these changes and the increased interest which they brought to the illustrated periodicals were chiefly due to the skill and discrimination of the assistant editor, the Rev. Moseley H. Williams, Ph.D.

In January, 1888, *The Illustrated Treasury of Knowledge* and *Truth in Life* were merged in *The People's Paper*, a semimonthly, to meet a call for a low-priced illustrated periodical. In 1891 the Union was asked by many children, "Why not get a paper every time we go to Sunday-school?" In response to this the Union began that year the publication of an illus-ated periodical called *The Young People's Paper*, a weekly, printed on toned paper in good type and filled with illustrations, stories, and material intended to enforce Bible truths in the home.   At the end of the year (1891) *The Youth's World* and *The Sunday Hour* were discontinued; *The Young People's Paper* was improved and *The Picture World* was made more attractive for the little ones.

In January, 1913, *The Sunday-School World* was enlarged and improved by adding comments on the daily Bible readings on an original plan, prepared by the Rev. F. B. Meyer of London.   Besides special expositions of the Bible lessons suited to adults, as presented by Rev. James McConaughy, who had been added to the editorial force, other helps suited to boys and girls, with suggestions to teachers of younger children, were also provided, in addition to the features which had previously been given, such as illustrations from life, and lights from the Orient furnished by residents in Bible lands, so that the Bible could be read "through Oriental eyes."

Further important changes were made in the editorial force in March, 1915.   The Rev. James McConaughy was elected editor of the Society's publications, to succeed Dr. Rice (now honorary editor), and the Rev. A. J. R. Schumaker, assistant editor, in place of the Rev. Moseley H. Williams, Ph.D. (retained as honorary assistant editor).   Other changes followed in fulfilment of the purpose of the American Sunday-school Union ever to provide a sound, evangelical, and interesting Sunday-school literature.

The learned expositions provided in *The Sunday-School World* by Prof. Ozora S. Davis, D.D., were reinforced by many new writers, presenting the truths of the lessons in forms adapted to aid teachers in the various grades of Sunday-school instruction.   Blackboard outlines and suggestions for superintendents were also presented by experienced workers.

Appreciation of these improvements was shown by a marked increase in the circulation of the *World* and the Society's series of helps.   The issue of a periodical for home study, entitled *Sunday-School at Home*, was begun in July, 1915.   The *Union Quarterly* was more closely adapted to the needs of older boys and girls and to adults, and in January, 1917, the *Primary Quarterly* was restricted to the needs of younger scholars up to nine years of age, and a *Junior Quarterly* begun for those from eight to twelve. One feature of the quarterlies is the handwork, besides many suggestions to teachers of these grades, added to the material for the pupils and a better typographic appearance, and in the *Sunday School at Home* special pages of reading matter for those following the Sunday-school lessons, with hints on methods of organizing and developing home study. A careful revision was made also of the *Little People's Lesson Pictures* and of the picture roll. All these changes and improvements increased the usefulness of these periodicals, but rendered them more closely fitted to the classes for which they were designed.

The Young People's Paper, weekly, was filled with more original designs and engravings, and with reading matter for young persons, while *The Picture World*, also issued weekly, met the requirements of children of a younger age, including a story of the Sunday-school lesson told in simple language and illustrated by incidents from real life, with correspondence with children from different parts of the country occupying several pages each month.

These and other improvements marked the advent of the centennial year of the Society's history in 1917.

SKETCHES OF PROMINENT WORKERS

Frederick Adolphus Packard, LL.D., Editor and Secretary (1829-1867).

More than to any other one man the shaping of the early literature of the American Sunday-School Union was due to Frederick A. Packard. A lawyer, a man of affairs, an accomplished scholar, an indefatigable worker, and a humble-minded consecrated Christian, he gave his life to the formation and upbuilding of the Sunday-school cause in America. To miss the inspiration of his honored career and his life would be a great public loss. Mr. Packard was born in Marlborough, Massachusetts, September 26, 1794. His father, pastor of the church in that town, and his mother (a Quincy) were lineal descendants of old Puritan families. The son was educated at a noted school of his uncle's in Wiscasset, Maine, and graduated at Harvard College with the honors of his class in 1814. It is significant of the bent of his mind and of his

.earning that his commencement oration was in the Hebrew language. He studied law in Northampton and entered the profession in Springfield, Massachusetts. He was also the editor and proprietor of *The Hampshire Federalist* in 1819, a predecessor of *The Springfield Republican.*

His religious views and life were shaped under the influence of Dr. Samuel Osgood, and also by Judge John Hooker, whose daughter, Elizabeth Dwight, he married in 1822. He was connected with the Sunday-school of the Congregational Church of Springfield and chosen superintendent in 1827. It is said that he took peculiar interest in selecting books for the library of the school. His literary taste and his earnest piety made him a good judge of the best reading for the young.

In these three forms of service he gained a high reputation, so that in 1828 he was sent as a delegate to attend the anniversary of the American Sunday-School Union. By his wisdom and force of thought he made so favorable an impression upon that meeting that the Society soon sent one of its managers (J. H. Dulles) to secure him for the position of editor of its publications. This call involved giving up bright prospects and an assured income as a lawyer, and a removal from among his friends and those of his family to a strange city, to an untried work, on a limited income. But it was a service in which he might become widely useful in promoting the religious education of the young of the nation. After a thoughtful and prayerful consideration of the call, he regarded it from God and accepted it. He held that position for nearly forty years, discharging its duties with singular discretion, scholarship, and ability. With the exception of two years of the period from 1829 to 1867 about every publication bearing the Society's imprint, to the number of upward of 2,000, were carefully examined and in one way or another bore his editorial impress. Several that had the largest circulation and the widest usefulness were the product of his versatile mind.

Most of the annual reports of the Society for twenty-five years were prepared by him under the direction of the managers, while he also bore a full share in the plans for the distribution of its literature and in projecting its splendid missionary enterprises for the extension of Bible schools in the older states and throughout the new West. He exerted an important influence on the public-school system of several of the states, and in reforming, to some extent, the prison discipline, acting as editor of a journal on that subject for a number of years. His sane views on education and his skill in discipline, together with his ripe experience and genial personality caused him to be twice invited to become the president of Girard College. Although this had the attractions of a large salary and better residence and increased social advantages he declined to leave what he had chosen to be his life-work.

His catholicity of spirit was shown by the pleasure which he took in worshiping not only in the Clinton Street Congregational Church of Philadelphia, but, after that was disbanded, with equal pleasure in the Presbyterian, and later in the Episcopal Church. He became a pew-holder in the latter but always retained his membership in the church of his first love and choice.

Perhaps in no other period of his life were the wisdom and grace of his Christian character more conspicuous than when unpleasant differences among the managers of the Union led to a suspension of his duties for some months preceding the Civil War. This act gave greater grief to his friends than to him, for they missed his counsels in regard to the future of the Society's operations. No one can read his private correspondence with managers of that period without being profoundly impressed with the depth of his Christian character, his courtesy, and his loyalty to the work which kept out any shade of bitterness from his spirit. Happily, some of the opposition withdrew, harmony was restored, and Dr. Packard resumed his editorial work. The wisdom and spirit of the course pursued by his friends in the Board commanded the confidence and support of the members and supporters of the Union generally throughout the country.

Out of this experience, which imparted a mellowness and ripeness to his Christian character, he wrote *The Higher Rock*, wherein he graphically presents some of the fundamental and profound truths of the Christian life.

Mr. Dulles, a lifelong friend in the Board of Managers, paid this tribute to him:

No society was ever blessed with a more devoted, energetic, able and indefatigable officer; nor has the great cause of Christian education ever had a more zealous and intelligent advocate. . . . He came to it in its infancy; and, bringing with him a clear and sound judgment, a vigorous and cultivated intellect, a heart alive to the great interests of humanity, and a conscientious devotion to his work, he was enabled by his studies, his counsels at the Board and the productions of his pen, to exert the most powerful influence in promoting the objects of this Society and making it the means of shaping the views and characters of four successive generations. Almost every book on its catalogue has been subjected to his thoughtful and careful revision; and among them are many, by no means the least excellent, of which he is the author.

Among the most useful and important of his works are: *The Teacher Taught, The Teacher Teaching, The Union Bible Dictionary* (1855), *The Higher Rock*, and *Life of Robert Owen.* Not less important were his frequent contributions on public education, on prison discipline, and upon the extension and management and improvement of Sunday-schools. In the latter field he was recognized as a master thinker in his day.

Dr. Packard's view was that all publications of the American Sunday-School Union should be prepared and edited impersonally, since he regarded the Society's imprint as more weighty than any individual name. He made a very few eminent authors exceptions to this rule. Probably this view was partly the fruit of his own modesty, for he shunned every species of publicity, none of his useful works bearing his name, with perhaps one or two exceptions.

During the last few months of his life he was a great sufferer from the distressing nature of his disease (a cancerous affection of the lip), which shut him in a dark room. He passed to his reward November 11, 1867, at the age of seventy-three, confidently trusting in the grace of his Redeemer.

Hon. James Pollock, LL.D. (1810–1890).

James Pollock was vice-president of the American Sunday-School Union for thirty-five years, 1855–1890. He had the distinction of having presided over a greater number of business meetings of the Society than any other officer excepting Alexander Henry. Mr. Pollock was eminent as a statesman, jurist and governor, a popular and forcible speaker, and an exemplary Christian worker. A country boy, born in

Milton, Pennsylvania, September 11, 1810, he graduated at Princeton College in 1831, entered the profession of law and rose rapidly to distinction, first in his native state and later in the nation. His sterling integrity and Christian patriotism caused him to be chosen governor of the state. While director of the United States Mint in Philadelphia, he suggested placing the motto "In God We Trust" upon the national coin, which was done. His ability and broad culture were recognized by two colleges bestowing upon him the honorary degree of Doctor of Laws.

For years he was the head of a large Bible class and superintendent of a Sunday-school. His prominence in this work caused him to be chosen, from among many notable men, as president of the third National Sunday-School Convention, Philadelphia, 1859. His enthusiasm and wisdom in promoting religion is well illustrated by a speech of great fervency which he made when presiding at an anniversary of the American Sunday-School Union in 1855. Interpreting the name of the Society to signify patriotism, religion and love, he flashed forth his thought in these burning words:

> Citizens of America: Have you ever stopped to think where you are, what you have been, and what is your destiny? There is a national Christianity, . . . an American conscience, a great American heart; that heart, that conscience must be touched, must be enlightened with the glorious truths of the Bible ere they can feel and realize and know the responsibilities they owe to their country. . . . American! Every association that surrounds that name pleads eloquently the cause of the American Sunday-School Union. . . . As an instrumentality it comes to the American heart, to the American conscience; it comes, as it ought to come, to the young heart in all its innocence, in all its joyousness; it comes to the child in its mother's lap; to the son just beginning to realize that he may be a man; to the daughter, that she may possibly be released some day from the cares and anxiety of her mother; it comes to that class who, above all, are to be the glory and upbuilding of our country—the children!

His humility was sometimes shown to be quite equal to his greatness. When Chief Magistrate of the state, he was called to preside at a meeting of the Sunday-School Union where the hope was expressed that the influence of the religious magistrate of the state would ever be found on the side of truth and righteousness. Mr. Pollock responded to this spontaneous esteem with words of warm appreciation and with deep feeling:

> I feel and, in the presence of my God, desire to realize my accountability to him.   .   .   .   While I regard the approbation of my fellow-man, give me, oh, give me the approbation of an approving conscience, and I will feel happier and prouder than amid the loudest plaudits that ever fell from the lips of an admiring world.

He was always eager to do the Lord's business, with earnestness and dispatch—sometimes approaching to haste and abruptness—but with a depth of consecration which those who knew him best appreciated, while conscious of the power of his masterful mind and loving heart.   He filled fourscore years with blessed service for his fellow-men.

John Seely Hart, LL.D. (1810–1877), **Editor of Periodicals** (1858–1860).

Dr. John S. Hart, educator, editor and author, of New England ancestry, was born at Stockbridge, Massachusetts, January 28, 1810; graduated at Princeton College 1830, where he became professor of ancient languages and later of rhetoric; was principal of the Philadelphia High School and of the New Jersey Normal School.

Among many educational works of which he was author, are *Thoughts on Sabbath-Schools, Sunday-School Idea*, and a treatise on rhetoric.   He also edited, for a brief time, the Pennsylvania *Common School Journal* and *Sartain's Magazine*.

His wide knowledge of literature and his experience as an educator led the American Sunday-School Union to choose him as editor of its periodicals in 1858.   He edited *The Sunday-School Times*, first issued by the Union.   In 1861, he resigned as editor of periodicals of the Union, becoming the proprietor of *The Sunday-School Times*.   This he continued for some years on his own responsibility, until he sold it to J. C. Garrigues, from whom it was acquired by John Wanamaker, and then by Henry Clay Trumbull and The Sunday-School Times Company.   Mr. Hart suggested many improvements in the Union's literature.   The more important of them were carried out in the face of great financial obstacles.   He was progressive in his educational ideas, an acute thinker, a tactful and winning teacher of the young, and an earnest and exemplary Christian.

Richard Newton, D.D. (1813–1887), **Editor of Periodicals** (1867–1877).

Dr. Richard Newton attained a world-wide reputation as a Christian worker and writer for youth. "The Prince of Children's Preachers," was the title given him by Charles Spurgeon of London. Dr. Newton was born in Liverpool, England, 1813; graduated at the University of Pennsylvania; studied theology and entered the Protestant Episcopal ministry; and was rector in three important parishes in Philadelphia from 1840 to 1887. For years he preached sermons to children at intervals, usually once a month. These sermons were published in about thirty volumes. His material for them and for his other books was gleaned from every source, making it encyclopædic in scope. In this he was aided by one of his family who was a wide reader, and clipped or copied from current literature, newspapers, books, and every source, anecdotes and facts which were collected in a series of scrapbooks, indexed by subjects. To these Dr. Newton had resort whenever he wished illustrations upon any subject that he was called to treat. He wrote for the American Sunday-School Union *Illustrated Rambles in Bible Lands*, *Five-Minute Talks for the Young*, and other works, as *Heroes of the Early Church* and *Heroes of the Reformation*, which had a wide circulation. His largest work was *The Life of Jesus Christ*, illustrated. His books were translated into more than fourteen languages.

As editor of the periodicals of the American Sunday-School Union for about ten years he skilfully presented the simple truths of the gospel in attractive and illustrative forms, and gave a clear gospel-note to the periodical literature of the Union. While reverential and dignified in manner, there was nothing somber or gloomy in his teachings. He always presented the Christian life to the young as a cheerful, glad and happy one; not only as the way to be saved, but the only way to make this life worth living. Though devoting most of his time to pastoral and not to editorial work, he was an inspiring guide always to the office editor and force, in shaping and arranging the periodical material.

Samuel Austin Allibone, LL.D. (1816–1889), **Editor** (1868–1879).

Born in Philadelphia and for years engrossed in business, his controlling passion for books led Dr. Allibone to achieve first rank among American bibliographers. His *Dictionary of Authors* was a monumental and standard work, giving notices of 46,499 authors of England and America, filling three volumes, each of a thousand closely printed pages. A list of the works of each author is given with a verdict thereon gleaned from many critics.

Dr. Allibone was book editor of the American Sunday-School Union, from 1868 until 1879, broken by a year's absence in Europe. He wrote four improved and explanatory question books for the Society on the Gospels and the Acts, an *Index to the New Testament*, and a *Union Bible Companion*, and edited many other works for the Union. He was a wide reader, an industrious worker, and a frequent visitor to hospitals and prisons, to which he carried the gospel message. He always had religious pamphlets or tracts in his pocket, giving them discreetly on the street, in the cars, and wherever opportunity offered. In an age of literary pretense, he did not disdain to serve his Master by scattering tracts containing the words of life in very plain and simple forms. He made a comprehensive and admirable classification of all the publications of the Union, showing that while its issues were on religious subjects, the largest proportion of them were instructive, vigorous, and substantial works, rather than homiletical, or works of fiction.[1] Died at Lucerne, Switzerland, September 2, 1889.

John Hall, D.D., New York (1829–1898).

No man had a greater influence than Rev. Dr. John Hall of New York in the marked advance made in Bible and Sunday-school study in America when the Uniform Lesson System of 1872 was adopted. As soon as the committee of fifteen publishers had agreed upon a series of lessons in 1871, Dr. Hall was promptly secured to prepare the expositions of the lessons for the American Sunday-School Union. His reputation as a biblical scholar, his popularity as an expository preacher, his experience in preparing similar lessons abroad as editor of *The Evangelical Witness* of Ireland, pointed him out as emi-

[1] S. D. McConnell, D.D., *In Memory of S. Austin Allibone, LL.D.*, 1890.

nently qualified for aiding in the introduction and promotion of the new Uniform System in America.

For fifteen years with rare fidelity, firmness, and scholarly compactness of thought and expression, he presented the meaning of the Bible Lessons in *The Sunday-School World* to the instruction and delight of teachers and scholars on both sides of the Atlantic.

Dr. Hall was among the first three named on the Lesson Committee by the International Sunday-School Convention of 1872, and with them selected lessons and wrote expositions not only for the preliminary year 1872, but through two complete cycles of study. These Uniform Lessons and his expositions were foremost in promoting a remarkable advance—almost a complete revolution—in the form and character of Sunday-school study; and the advance and popularity of the system became a marvelous phenomenon in the history of American Christianity. The circulation of *The Sunday-School World* and the Society's biblical helps was speedily trebled (about half a million a year).

Dr. Hall not only rendered great services to the cause by preparing these expositions for the lessons, but also in heartily and ably presenting the work of the Union in prominent cities, East and West. With singular ability and earnestness, he became a tower of strength in advocating its missionary and publication work, greatly strengthening the Society and increasing its benevolent operations. During his ministry, his church was a generous friend and a very liberal contributor to the support of the Union; a legacy of upward of $80,000 came from members of his church. His best thought for the formation of a *Christian Home* and how to maintain it, was worked out in a volume published by the Society, which was widely circulated and was also a favorite wedding gift. The impulse which he gave to evangelical Christianity will long be felt, not only in America but throughout the world.

Henry Clay Trumbull, D.D., LL.D. (1830–1903), **Missionary and Normal Secretary** (1858–1875).

In the galaxy of distinguished Sunday-school workers of the last half of the nineteenth century, few attained the prominence and wielded such an influence as Henry Clay Trumbull.

Endowed with rich natural gifts, fiery in temperament, imperious in manner, alert in mind, acute in judgment, and working at a high tension, he was a conspicuous leader, proud to be counted a Puritan of Puritans.   Spiritually trained under Dr. Joel Hawes, Charles G. Finney and Horace Bushnell, and associated for some years in mission work with "Father" David Hawley, his success in missions led to his call for a wider work among teachers in Connecticut, and by the American Sunday-School Union in August, 1858.   His seventeen years' service was interrupted by a call as chaplain during the Civil War, from 1862 to 1865, but he continued to hold the Society's commission during the interval.

He was as active with his pen as in person, writing six thousand letters within four years, making one thousand addresses, visiting five hundred schools, besides forming seventy-five new ones, and through his earnest and impetuous manner multiplying himself over and over again by stimulating others to a like service.   Returning from the army, he was chosen secretary of missions for New England and Normal secretary of the American Sunday-School Union; was a prominent leader in the missionary conference at Chicago in 1866, influential in the National Sunday-School Conventions, and a voluminous contributor to the Sunday-school magazines and journals. He was the author of numerous biblical and Sunday-school works; chief among the latter were: *Yale Lectures, Teachers and Teaching,* and *Individual Work for Individuals.*   He resigned his position with the American Sunday-School Union in 1875 to become editor and proprietor of *The Sunday-School Times,* in which position he continued to the end of his life.

He retained the warmest interest in the work of the Union, asserting that he first gained an idea that the Bible was a book for children to know from *The Child's Scripture Question Book,* published by the Society, and when he began to teach in the Sunday-school found "the helps prepared by the Union in advance of those of any other organization, at least in this country."   At the Seventy-fifth Anniversary of the Society under its present name, he gave this weighty testimony:

I speak with emphasis and earnestness of our indebtedness in this country to the idea and agency represented by the American

Sunday-School Union for most of what we have in our peculiar civilization, and of our social, moral, and religious prosperity among the nations of the earth.[1]

Richard Gay Pardee (1811–1869).

Mr. Pardee was prominent among the sagacious lay workers in the Sunday-school cause. A farmer's boy, with limited education in the common schools, but carefully trained in business, he carried system into every form of Sunday-school work which he undertook. He was a descendant of Elder Brewster of the Mayflower, and married Rebecca Camp. The Camps were a family noted in Connecticut for their benevolence and interest in the Sunday-school cause. Mr. Pardee was also a close friend of Lorin B. Tousley, "the children's minister," so that, aside from his own, he had the added interest of these two families to increase his zeal and devotion.

Besides being a prosperous merchant Mr. Pardee was an intelligent and interested grower of small fruits, a writer for *The Culturist*, and author of a widely circulated work on strawberry culture. By his business ability and popularity he soon acquired a fair competency which enabled him to devote time and energy to lay preaching and Sunday-school work. The same system, acuteness, and diligence which he had shown in his business he brought into religious work. He was early in great demand in the organization and conduct of Sunday-school conventions and assemblies where methods of Bible study and Christian work were considered. His encyclopædic knowledge, gathered from wide observation, gave him such prominence that he was invited to take charge of the work of the New York Sunday-School Union.

The writer well recalls his tact and methodical business ways, for the first public experience in mission work was under his instruction. His wise management of that work commended itself to the leading Christians and churches of the city and gave the Sunday-School Union there a wide reputation for usefulness.

His diligent study of the problems confronting teachers and

[1] See article in *The Sunday-School World* for 1912, and his *Life*, by Philip E. Howard, 1905.

Bible school workers of that day, his keen discernment of the solution of difficult problems, and the practical observation which he carefully preserved in note-books from time to time, caused him to be regarded as one of the most sagacious leaders of his time.

After ten or a dozen years of service in the city he resigned his position to enter upon a wider work as lecturer on Bible study before theological schools and Sunday-school conventions and institutes throughout the country. For many years he was the most successful leader of teachers' training classes and institutes for Sunday-schools in his day. No man held an intelligent body of Sunday-school teachers with closer attention and greater profit in the Middle West than did this plain, apparently unlearned layman.

Professor John S. Hart, a competent critic, says of Mr. Pardee: "He was neither brilliant, nor learned, nor eloquent, nor original, nor profound. . . . Yet he accomplished, single handed, results not often vouched to those who have all these qualities and advantages combined." He has a graphic description of his first meeting with Mr. Pardee when, "after some pretty tall talking by sundry speakers, the little, wiry, unpretending man from New York came forward. . . . His appearance certainly was not commanding nor his voice musical. His movements were stiff and angular; he had none of the graces of rhetoric, and he was not very amenable to the laws of grammar, yet he held that audience—rather a fastidious one—spellbound. . . . We forgot the man in the absorbing interest of the thoughts which he gave us."

Mr. Pardee always had a pencil and a note-book, and carefully put down any thought, suggestion, illustration, or fact which he thought would be helpful to others. In this way he accumulated a mass of information and, with a good memory and a systematic mind, he could call any part of it up at will. This wonderful power gave him readiness of knowledge in all his practical addresses.

Mr. Ralph Wells testifies that Mr. Pardee was also a man of prayer. They often traveled together, and Mr. Wells states that "Many a night I have known him to get out of bed and spend half the night in prayer—and wonderful prayers they were." He was a frequent contributor to *The Sunday-*

School Times, and was the author of *The Sunday-School Worker's Manual* and *The Sabbath-School Index*.

He is said to have visited every state in the Union except California. It was well said of him that his life was a lesson to his generation of how to seek out a sphere where all one's power can be used to the best advantage in the service of Christ and be centered upon one work.

George Starr Scofield (1810–1887).

For the long period of about sixty years George S. Scofield served the Union as a lad, a salesman, depository agent in Philadelphia to 1854, and then in New York until his death in 1887. He was born in Stamford, Connecticut, June 11, 1810. When a boy, his father, a graduate of Yale who studied law and was a teacher of languages, moved to Philadelphia. His grandfather was an officer in the Revolutionary Army and for a time on Washington's staff. Young Scofield was ambitious to enter college, but impaired health did not permit it. He entered the store of the American Sunday-School Union as an errand boy about 1826. The store was then at 29 North Fourth Street. He delighted to tell how he aided in moving the Society's stock to the new store on Chestnut Street, near Sixth, in a wheelbarrow! His ability, good judgment, industry, and integrity were appreciated by the Society, and he was steadily advanced from one position of trust to another, until he became superintendent of the home depository when comparatively a young man.

He gave up his cherished plan to complete his college education, believing the Lord set before him an "open door" to make and distribute Christian literature. His great aim was to put the best and purest religious publications in attractive form and so cheap that the working classes and the poor could be provided with them. By his enthusiasm he persuaded author, editor, printer, and binder to aid in his scheme. He always regarded as his greatest business achievement the successful issue and circulation of "Ten Dollar Libraries," each having a hundred volumes of from seventy-two to two hundred and fifty-two pages per volume. His zeal surmounted almost endless difficulties then in the way of the scheme. He overcame one after another, finding a special way for the binder to do his

AUTHORS

Grace Livingston Hill Lutz.

Mrs. S. K. Reeves.

Lucy Ellen Guernsey.

Julia MacNair Wright

Edith Ferguson Black.

work, so as to furnish the hundred volumes for ten dollars. His success astonished all his doubters and even himself. In a year 40,000,000 pages of the first set were issued, and in less than twenty years 10,000,000 volumes of these remarkable libraries were distributed to schools and mission stations in America and throughout the world. He aided in manufacturing the *Union Questions*, reducing the price to six and one-fourth cents, so that millions of copies were sold.

For years Mr. Scofield devoted his best thought to the making of other good cheap literature for "settlers" and working classes to use in Bible study. Millions of souls will have reason to bless God for his efforts. His benevolence was nation-wide. He was also active in his own Protestant Episcopal Church for a generation as an officer and in charge of the Sunday-school. He was a Christian gentleman of the olden type, moving in social circles including such marked men as the elder Appleton, Aspinwalls, Townsends and others. Though welcomed in the social circle of wealth and refinement, he had the warmest sympathy for those in humbler walks of life, and was ever planning to reach them with the gospel of Christ. Few men have contributed so largely as he to the manufacture and distribution of religious literature for the young.

John W. Dulles.

Rev. John Welsh Dulles, D.D., son of Joseph H. Dulles, was a missionary of the American Board in Southern India, but was compelled by illness and loss of voice to relinquish that service. On the recovery of his health in October, 1853, he was placed in charge of the missionary correspondence of the American Sunday-School Union, and served the Society efficiently for three years, until October, 1856, when he resigned to become editorial secretary of the Presbyterian Publication Committee (new school).

He was modest and retiring in disposition, a man of polished and pleasant address, and an indefatigable worker. He prepared the interesting work, *Life in India*, for the Society, which had a wide circulation, running through several editions.

SECTION VI

An era of great civic and religious ferment preceded the origin of the Sunday-School Union, 1817 to 1824. People in all parts of Christendom were awakening to their privileges in religion, and demanding their rights in the governments of which they were a part and which they supported. The American republic was a government by the people. The French demanded a similar form of government, and the Greeks caught the inspiration and revived their ancient republican system. The new countries of South America were absorbing republican ideas and, in the world of religion, revivals of a national character were changing society under the preaching of the Wesleys, Whitfield, and Edwards. Modern missionary and Bible societies were organized. Christianity was manifesting itself in new and aggressive measures for the conquest of the world. Laymen were awaking to leadership.

Laymen Recognized.—The founders of the Sunday-School Union were doubtless influenced by a knowledge of these movements and caught a vision of the splendid service which might be rendered through the wider diffusion and study of the great Christian textbook—the Bible. They had, however, a discriminating sense of the conditions of their time, which is clearly expressed in the first part of the constitution.

Note the way in which the objects of the Society are stated: (1) To secure unity of effort, federation and co-operation of all friends of religious instruction in all sections of the country; (2) to give information by circulating "moral and religious publications in every part of the land," and, having secured these; (3) "to endeavor to plant a Sunday-school wherever there is a population."

Their records show that they proceeded in this order to accomplish their great purpose, putting first things first; that

188

is, unity, then information and instruction, then organized extension of the institution of Sunday-schools. It would have been impossible for them to have reversed this order with success. They must first prepare the way and prosecute a campaign of education. Only so could they overcome opposition and prejudice and win general favor for the great work they had in view. Moreover, the popular impression in regard to the institution of Sunday-schools then was that the work should be voluntary. If teachers gave their services, why should not managers and superintendents and others give their services also? It was thought that this voluntary principle could be applied successfully to the establishment of Sunday-schools in places where there were none, and no desire for them. This view overlooked the fact that into every such community someone must go to prepare the way by informing the people concerning the value of the institution, and to create some taste for it by showing how it would benefit each family and give religious education to the young.

Work by Auxiliaries.—Some conceived that this might be done by multiplying local auxiliary unions in every habitable section, and by disseminating circulars and pamphlets telling of the advantages of Sunday-schools, how to form them as well as how to conduct them, and the good results which had followed from their successful maintenance in other places. This preparatory work and these educational campaigns were exceedingly useful so far as they went, but so indifferent—not to say hostile—is the human mind naturally to the things of God that these agencies, however useful in their sphere, were found to be insufficient successfully to spread the institution in new communities, and often unavailable even in the corners of parishes where churches existed.

Because of the need of this preparatory work and the lack of funds, the Union tried various experiments to supplement their efforts for extension of Sunday-schools. Thus in 1819 they joined with the Bible Society in providing a traveling agent (Samuel Bacon) who should explain their plan and purpose, while at the same time he distributed circulars and literature and urged local auxiliaries to make vigorous efforts to plant new Sunday-schools wherever they were needed. This was followed, as already stated, by the appointment of

Rev. William C. Blair as a Sunday-school missionary in 1821. He gave his entire time to the special work of organizing and strengthening Sunday-schools in various states, in which work he was soon after joined by President Alden of Allegheny College and others and, as the work grew, the Board of Managers of the Union placed it under the charge of a Committee on Missions.

It therefore seems wise to present the history of the work in the order in which the founders planned and carried forward the magnificent enterprise which they had in mind.

Specialized Service.—While the managers of the Union were clear in their purpose to do first things first, they also speedily saw the complex ways of working required to make their plan successful. It was not yet the age of specialization as we see it. But, with a vision in advance of their age, they assigned branches of their work to special persons among themselves, designated as committees; having not less than seven such groups—the most important being the Committees of Publication, of Depositories, of Ways and Means, and of Missions. The Committee of Missions was instructed to communicate with clergymen and laymen of all denominations and in different parts of the country, awaken a higher sense of the importance of Sunday-schools, and stimulate them to vigorous exertions for promoting the institution. They were to seek out and appoint persons well qualified to be Sunday-school missionaries who should visit and establish Sunday-schools and organize Sunday-school unions. These missionaries were not to roam wildly over the country, but were to be assigned fields of labor and be instructed in their duties. Concerning this service the Committee was to report every month the number of missionaries appointed, their names, field of labor, and the whole number employed, with such other information as the managers might require.[1]

Beholding the wide-spread enthusiasm in Sunday-school work today, we can hardly credit the apathy, indifference and even opposition to the cause in the first part of the nineteenth century. Large-hearted and prominent Christians warmly advocated the movement, but they were in the minority. The bulk of even professing Christians looked upon it either

[1] *By-Laws*, 1825 to 1828.

as a marked innovation or as springing out of a religious enthusiasm fraught with dangerous tendencies. So they stood aloof, deeming it prudent to watch lest this new movement should overturn or in some manner harm the ark of the Lord. Strong, bold measures were required to overcome this general apathy.

Again, the general adoption of voluntary instead of paid teachers in Sunday-schools suggested, naturally enough, that the extension of these schools might be carried forward by like voluntary means. The employment of Sunday-school missionaries, giving their entire time as specialists to this work, did not meet with popular favor, and funds were hard to secure for their support.

Thus the proceedings of the early anniversaries of the Society and the speeches show that the Society tried to promote extension of Sunday-schools largely through the distribution of its literature through auxiliaries and by voluntary workers. In previous sections of the history the various kinds of literature and the diligence of the Society in distributing it have been pointed out. To give this literature greater effect the Society encouraged the formation of conventions and unions organized in different states. It enlisted some of the foremost persons in different denominations in presenting the importance and value of such auxiliary institutions, and of giving information upon the best way of organizing and conducting them in the work of extending the Sunday-school. Thus, as before stated, the Rev. Gardiner Spring, D.D., of New York attended a convention of Sunday-school teachers and workers in the state of New Hampshire in September, 1824, which resulted in forming the first recorded state Sunday-school union in America. Dr. Lyman Beecher, D.D., of Boston also was a voluntary delegate to another section of New England. And Dr. E. D. Griffin, president of Williams College; Dr. Francis Wayland, president of Brown University; Theodore Frelinghuysen of New Jersey; Dr. Archibald Alexander; Dr. John H. Rice of Virginia; Dr. Stephen H. Tyng; Thomas S. Grimke of South Carolina, and many others of national reputation and of different denominations responded to the call of the Society and rendered splendid service in giving its plan and work wide publicity. Besides these eminent volunteer advocates the Society employed for temporary periods, and at different times, young but trained educators to do a similar service in different parts of the country.

General Agents.—These general agents also gave a portion of their time to the direct missionary work of organizing Sunday-schools in towns and villages where they had not yet been introduced. They were also required to form auxiliary unions, to collect funds for promoting the general cause, and in every way—through distribution of circulars and literature as well as by public addresses—to give information and to stimulate activity in all forms of Sunday-school work. They were especially to point out the feasibility and the advantage of co-operation and concentration of interest and energy, and to group together those of different denominations for the common end of making more widely known the fundamental principles of our common Christianity. This could best be done by organizing Sunday services and Bible schools for the study of the Word of God. In this service were enlisted those who later were known as veterans in the work, as A. W. Corey, Rev. Howard Malcolm, D.D., Rev. George Boyd, Rev. Robert Baird, D.D., and a host of others too numerous to name. They gave their best thought and ability to the solution of the great problems of religious education and to creating an interest therein, and winning popular favor for the movement.

Voluntary Effort Insufficient.—However, a comparatively brief experience was sufficient to convince not only the Society but its supporters that Sunday-schools could not be efficiently organized and sustained where most needed merely by auxiliary unions and volunteer efforts. A more vigorous and trained agency was needed effectively to organize schools and even to distribute its literature. Therefore, in 1825 a permanent Committee on Missions was formed, which employed for short terms thirty-one missionaries as supplementary to its other methods of Sunday-school extension. But the Society was compelled to state its reasons for the employment of paid missionaries by affirming that they were required "by the necessity for arousing Christians," "by the ignorance of your plans which too widely prevails, and by the need of reviving some schools now languishing," declaring that missionaries "seem well-nigh indispensable, whether we consider the prosperity of schools now existing, or the necessity of their further extension."

Hence literature, depositories, auxiliaries, paid missionaries and volunteer workers were all combined in the effort of the Society to extend the Sunday-school movement. Thus in 1827–28, thirty-five missionaries from eight denominations were employed, including four volunteers without pay. Moreover, a general agent and twelve other agents were also engaged in upward of sixteen different states, stimulating auxiliaries, collecting funds, awakening an interest in the cause, and introducing the Select or Uniform System of Instruction and improved methods of conducting Sunday-schools.

Public Meetings.—The funds to support these agents and missionaries were secured with difficulty, and usually the contributions were inadequate. The dues from auxiliaries and from life and annual members were appropriated to the missionary fund, in addition to the direct gifts for that purpose, and still there was a yearly deficit. Appeals were made to churches and Sunday-schools and to individuals to support this laudable enterprise. The necessity for larger support of its benevolent work was made the theme of successive anniversaries held in May. The meetings of these May anniversaries brought together large audiences. Thus in May, 1826, it is reported: "Every arrangement was made for the accommodation of the audience which the spacious house could afford, but many hundreds who came to the doors were unable to obtain seats.[1] A similar throng attended the anniversary of 1827, when an original hymn written by W. B. Tappan for the occasion was sung, "with much spirit and effect by the children who thronged the galleries."

Delegated Conferences.—During the anniversaries delegates also appeared from auxiliary societies in different states, representing their respective unions, and often met with the managers to consider questions and measures of a national interest and to propose plans for promoting the cause throughout the country. Although benevolent contributions were slowly increasing from year to year, yet they were found wholly insufficient. While the Christian citizens of Philadelphia had

[1] *Report*, 1826, p. xxii.

loyally supported and royally given to purchase a lot and provide a building that should be suitable headquarters for the business of the Society, the very success of the institution had aroused the envy and opposition of others who assailed it "under a feigned regard for religious liberty." The objects of the Society became a "favorite subject of untiring misrepresentation and abuse." "Charges the most absurd and incongruous," said the managers, "have been alleged; the belief of which would suppose a degree of credulity little flattering to that public on whom they have designed to impose."[1]

Over against these misrepresentations the managers affirmed their object was "to extend to every town and hamlet of our extensive country, the blessings of early instruction in virtue and knowledge—to circulate as widely as possible a class of publications designed to illustrate by example and to enforce by precept those plain and simple gospel truths which are peculiar to no sect, but of vital importance to all."[2]

Partly in consequence of this opposition the Union found itself embarrassed in its benevolent work, and in May, 1828, there were two meetings of delegates; one with the managers, and another held by the delegates, specially to confer upon the state of the Union, and devise increased means of promoting its interests. At this meeting there were delegates present from fourteen states. It was presided over by Robert Cathcart of York, Pennsylvania, and Elias W. Crane of Jamaica, Long Island, was secretary. These delegates made a minute and careful investigation of the affairs of the Society, and, after due deliberation, expressed deep regret that it should be embarrassed for want of funds; recommended measures for its relief, and called upon Christian communities to enable it greatly to enlarge its operations "by the publication of suitable books for the Sunday-schools of our country; to establish more extensively Sabbath-schools among our German population, and to commence the translation of their publications into the German language; to establish Sabbath-schools among our seamen and other classes of people, who are not yet brought under the influence of the Sabbath-school system; and to employ an increased number of energetic

[1] *Report*, 1828, p. x.   [2] *Report*, 1826, p. xi.

agents, with a view to raise the necessary funds, and accomplish these measures."[1]

Referring to the opposition to the Society's application for a charter, this delegated assembly declared: "After having possessed and employed the most ample means of investigating the proceedings of the American Sunday-School Union, this meeting does cordially and unanimously approve of the open and undisguised manner in which its affairs have been conducted and hereby express their high commendation of the zeal, discretion, self-denial and diligence of its Board of Managers."[2]

At a subsequent meeting of the delegates it was stated that the Society began under its present name with a capital contributed by the citizens of Philadelphia of less than $5,000. At the close of 1827 the capital was about $25,000, exclusive of the buildings. Of this sum, $20,000 had been contributed by the citizens of Philadelphia, besides $15,000 for the Society's buildings. Loans had been secured to the amount of $35,000, while there was due from auxiliary societies and individuals, for literature about $20,000.

At this meeting in Philadelphia new subscriptions were received amounting to $4,760—a sum sufficient to encourage the Society to enlarge its operations and to consider new measures for the advancement of the cause throughout the nation.

Mississippi Valley Enterprise.—Out of the Union's experience and the information it had gathered during several years under the auxiliary and general agency system, and the earlier seven years' experience as the Sunday and Adult School Union, a wide interest was created for extending Sunday-schools over the whole United States. Several persons of ability and large experience were employed to gather and report information respecting the "western country," and particularly from the Valley of the Mississippi, upon the need of more vigorous and liberal measures for the establishment of Sunday-schools. As a result of this survey the managers of the Union were convinced that the Christian public was ready to sustain them in a movement the magnitude of which would have appalled less courageous souls. In Novem-

---

[1] *Report*, 1828, p. xviii.   [2] *Ibid.*, p. xix.

ber, 1829, they decided it was the duty of the American Sunday-School Union, if funds were furnished for the purpose, to establish Sunday-schools in all parts of the United States, "especially in the destitute regions of the West."

This action became known to philanthropists and business men in different parts of the country. It brought encouraging responses from various quarters, among them a proposition from a prominent business man of New York, Mr. Arthur Tappan. Writing early in May, 1830, he proposed that the Society undertake to form a Sabbath-school within two years in every town in the Valley of the Mississippi. "The adoption of such a resolution as I have stated," writes he, "would thrill through the Christian community and secure you the prayers and offerings of every Christian and philanthropist in the land." He estimated that it might require $100,000 to carry out his plan, and pledged himself to give $2,000 and also a similar sum of $2,000, "to be paid in sums of five dollars, to Sabbath-schools in the Valley that shall raise the same amount and remit it to the treasurer; the ten dollars to be laid out in books for a library."

This letter resulted in a tentative action of the Union to undertake the work proposed, provided it should be approved at the coming anniversary of the Society in May. Meanwhile the boldness and magnitude of the proposition amazed the public and won friends in its support. Such was the interest excited that at the anniversary, which was attended by over 2,000 people, this action was adopted by a unanimous rising vote of the whole congregation:

> Resolved that the American Sunday-School Union, in reliance upon divine aid, will, within two years, establish a Sunday-school in every destitute place where it is practicable throughout the Valley of the Mississippi.

Among the able advocates for it were the Rev. Thomas McAuley, D.D., LL.D., the Rev. Lyman Beecher, D.D., of Massachusetts, and the Rev. Stephen H. Tyng, D.D.—leading members of three different denominations. They regarded it as more important in its consequences than any previous act of the Union.

It was a "stupendous missionary enterprise," for a strong

society, and seemed presumptuous for the young Union, whose yearly mission funds were less than $1,000, to propose to cover a territory now occupied by over twenty states. The "Valley of the Mississippi" meant "all the country west of the Alleghenies to the Rocky Mountains, and from Michigan to Louisiana—an area then estimated at about 1,300,000 square miles—and included the nine states of Ohio, Indiana, Illinois, Kentucky, Tennessee, Alabama, Louisiana, Mississippi, and Missouri, and also parts of Pennsylvania and Virginia, and the 'Northwest territory' and the 'Territories of Missouri and of Arkansas'." The population was estimated at 4,000,000, of which 400,000 were believed to be children and youth. This immense section of the country was rapidly filling through immigration. So vast was this region that it was then predicted, "The population (in this valley) will soon give laws to our country."

The immense enthusiasm for this scheme did not "turn the heads" of the managers. They did not permit their zeal or enthusiasm to outrun their judgment, nor did it lead them to expend their energies in impulsive efforts. From a survey of the entire territory, they computed the number of Sunday-schools of every description in it at about 1,500, including those that were supported by Methodists, Baptists, and other denominations independent of those in connection with the Union.

They did not propose to establish a Sunday-school wherever there was none, but only in those destitute places where circumstances would make it practicable to do so. They stated, for example, that "if there is a place inhabited by six families, living three or four miles from each other and in different directions, and neither family having children over six years old, we should think the impracticability of establishing a Sunday-school there abundantly obvious." Then, too, it was stated that in some cases where no teacher could be found, no place of meeting obtained, and each family, distinct from the other five, having prejudices in favor of a different denomination from the others, what would be impracticable would become, under such circumstances, next to impossible. But in places where the number of the inhabitants and their relative location and circumstances rendered it practicable to a discreet and sensible person, there it was proposed to establish a Sunday-school. It was computed that not less than $30,000 would be required the first year to start the enterprise, and, if measurably successful, $60,000 or upward for the second year.[1]

The enthusiasm of the congregation of 2,000 in Philadelphia when the scheme was proposed became contagious. It spread through the city and won the admiration of the delegates from auxiliary societies of different denominations who were attending the National Religious Assemblies. Three successive mass meetings were held in Philadelphia. Men of national fame commended the action, and liberal subscriptions were received amounting to $17,000, besides an offer to form "one hundred and fifty schools," and further "to supply thirty-two counties" with schools, estimated to call for about $5,000 in addition to cash subscriptions. Similar meetings were held in New York, where hundreds who came could not get admission to the building. Vigorous speeches were made and $15,229 more pledged. The enthusiasm extended to Boston, Washington, Charleston, and other cities where like meetings were crowded with people who desired to learn more of the character and magnitude of this enterprise.

In Boston a forcible address was made by Dr. Lyman Beecher, who believed that "the crisis of the nation and of the world is at hand; the heart of the rising generation of the West will throb with benevolence or beat with iniquity and death."[2]

Another speaker declared that the freedom, righteousness and peace of the country would depend largely upon the character of the future people in the Mississippi Valley.

A National Meeting.—The meeting in Washington was even more remarkable for its national character. It was presided over by a United States senator, and the clerk of the House of Representatives acted as secretary. Among those who addressed the meeting in behalf of the enterprise were seven senators and congressmen, including Daniel Webster and Francis Scott Key. The magnitude of the Valley proposition appealed to their patriotism, and it was commended in the strongest terms as best adapted to put the stamp of a Chris-

[1] *Sunday-School Magazine*, 1830, p. 222.
[2] See *Report, Proceedings in Boston*, p. 20.

tian civilization upon the West and to promote the stability of the republic. The meeting was reported in the press of that period as "one of the most important ever held in this country."

The Hon. William Wirt, then Attorney General of the United States, sent a liberal donation and a letter regretting his inability to be present to aid in advancing this "great, Heaven-directed cause." He declared: "It is not in the nature of things that a popular government can long subsist except among an enlightened and virtuous people. Public virtue has no solid basis but in religion. I mean by public virtue," he added, "that which impels the man in all his public acts to look solely to the good of his country without any view of personal aggrandizement." In a note of warning he declared, "Private vice always keeps pace with public immorality. . . . One distinguished man is able to corrupt the neighborhood by his example and machinations; and the sphere of his pernicious influence becomes enlarged, in proportion to the eminence to which he has risen. . . . Mere human virtue is a cheat—a scintillation at best, which we see continually extinguished by temptation. . . . Nothing less than the living conviction of an ever-present God, before whom we are acting and thinking and speaking, . . . can impose a moment's restraint on the indulgence of human passion."

Senator Freylinghuysen, in a statesmanlike address, said, among other things, "Let us ponder with deep reflection, and cease not to repeat and reiterate the interesting truth, that our boasted liberties will not long survive the wreck of our public morals."

The Hon. Daniel Webster, senator of the United States, gave the significant testimony, that if we were sure of any thing, we were sure of this, that the knowledge of their Creator, their duty and their destiny is good to men; and that, whatever, therefore, draws the attention of the young to the consideration of these objects, and enables them to feel their importance, must be advantageous to human happiness in the highest degree and in all worlds. In civilized times, and in a Christian land the means of this knowledge were to be supplied to the young by parental care, by public provision, or by Christian benevolence. They were now assembled to supply, or aid in supplying the elements of knowledge, religious, moral and literary, to the children throughout a most interesting and important portion of the country.

Laymen's Mission.—Among other similar enthusiastic meetings in promotion of this measure to establish Sunday-schools in the Mississippi Valley, was a large meeting of the citizens of Charleston, South Carolina. Thomas S. Grimke, who was then widely known as an "eloquent and distinguished advocate of Christian education," made the principal address, in which, among other things, he declared: "An intelligent laity is the only pure, natural, living fountain of an intelligent clergy. Neither can exist durably, usefully, or honorably without the other. They must arise and advance, hand in hand and step by step." He asked why a great majority of statesmen, writers, philosophers, and scholars of Europe had done so little for religion, and declared that it was due to the fact that *the Bible had never entered into their scheme of mental culture.* But he noted that the Bible commanded the attention of giant minds like Bacon, Newton and Locke, as well as the more ordinary minds of Addison, Lyttleton and West. Referring to the establishment of Sunday-schools in the Valley of the Mississippi, he exclaimed: "What eloquence can magnify too much the dignity and importance of the enterprise! What poetry can paint, in adequate colors, a charity so enlightened, pure and beautiful!"[1]

Mission Plans and Results.—The region known as the Mississippi Valley was divided into districts and into fields by the Society, and agents and missionaries were assigned to these several sections where immigration was forming the greatest number of new settlements. As indicating the growth of the population, the state census of Illinois in 1825 was about 75,000; by 1830 it had added 86,000—showing that it had more than doubled in the five years.

In a short time, from $60,000 to $75,000 were actually contributed and expended in this unparalleled scheme of Sunday-school extension; and it was computed that over one-half of the 8,000 to 10,000 new settlements in that great valley were supplied with new Sunday-schools. Marvelous as this work was for that day, it did not proceed as rapidly as its friends had

[1] *Grimke's Address*, pp. 3, 8, 10.

hoped. This was due to various obstacles and the difficulty of organizing schools in sparsely settled districts and with a heterogeneous population. About eighty to one hundred missionaries were employed in the service and a library costing ten dollars or more was furnished to every school that raised five dollars or more itself, or through its friends, for this purpose. Thus, besides forming the new Sunday-schools, it was computed that about 1,000,000 volumes were put in circulation through libraries in these various districts.

Moreover, the reformatory and spiritual results of the enterprise were wonderfully fruitful. It had not been long in progress before the Society reported 20,000 teachers and 30,000 scholars in its Sunday-schools that had confessed their faith in Christ. The number in a single year was reported to be over 17,000. When it is recalled that this work was done while the foundations of society were being laid in these large communities of the Middle West, the educational value of such service in thousands of neighborhoods cannot be easily estimated.

Observing citizens in those times were ready to acknowledge the great contribution which the American Sunday-School Union made to general education and to the splendid system of public schools which now exist in the states of the great Middle West. The distribution of its literature which created a taste for good reading and increased the desire for an education in the young, adding students to schools and colleges, was noted by leading educators and journals. It increased Christian patriotism throughout the whole valley. The enthusiasm thus aroused in behalf of good reading and of education is believed to have stimulated legislatures in those great states to make early and munificent provision for free public instruction, and to give public schools better equipment and support in their respective commonwealths than anywhere else in the country.

Possibly this influence may have been slightly overestimated by some, yet none can know at this period how wide-reaching this service was in prompting the pioneer statesmen of this great valley to make splendid provision for free public schools in those twenty or more states now occupying that valley. It was a wise, patriotic, and religious movement that concentrated such efforts upon this great region at this formative period in its history. Though the state could not have an established religion, yet through physical and intellectual education it could prepare the way for it. Broad-minded statesmen and philanthropists invite and welcome a great educational work based upon the principles of our common Christianity, like that of the American Sunday-School Union to supplement, and in some measure to crown, public education with efficient instruction in morals and religion. Only so can strength, virtue, fidelity and perpetuity, with prosperity, be secured to a great people—a Bible-loving people—and only so can they maintain a foremost rank among the nations of the world.

The Southern Enterprise.—The apparent brilliant success of the Mississippi Valley scheme renewed the call from the South for a similar campaign, known as the "Southern Enterprise."

The Rev. Dr. William S. Plumer, then of Virginia, representing the many friends of the cause in that region, stated their desire for, and the importance of, Sunday-schools in the South to the managers of the Union early in 1833. Inspired by his southern eloquence, the managers agreed to undertake a similar mission, if the Society at its annual meeting should approve of the plan, and funds could be provided for it. It appeared from loud and pressing calls coming from various quarters in the southern part of the country, that the friends there were prepared for a vigorous and general effort for the extension of Sunday-schools, and desired the American Sunday-School Union to lead. Thus it came to pass that at the May anniversary in 1834 the following action was adopted:

> Resolved, that the American Sunday-School Union will endeavor, in reliance upon the aid and blessing of Almighty God, to plant and for five years sustain Sabbath-schools in every neighborhood (where such schools may be desired by the people and where in other respects it may be practical) within the bounds of the states of Maryland, Virginia, North Carolina, South Carolina, Georgia, Alabama, the District of Columbia, and the territory of Florida.

The area of this field was computed at 330,000 square miles and its population was about 4,000,000, about 800,000 of which were children and youth of a suitable age to attend such

chools, and 500,000 of them were white. One of the strong
easons for undertaking the work was that "the common
chools, provided at public expense, were not sufficient for the
opulation." The school funds of these Southern States were
omparatively small. The provisions for instruction were so
nadequate that it was stated a large number of white adults
n this great district could not read, and many children were
rowing up in ignorance. While this was not equally true of
ll those states, nor of every part of any one state, it was a
act in many places, according to the testimony of competent
itizens.

By the establishment of Sunday-schools it was computed
hat this deficiency in education might be in part supplied,
nteresting and profitable books distributed, and encourage-
nent given to a system of general education. Another reason
ssigned for this campaign in the Southern States was that a
areful survey of existing schools and conditions showed that
here were less than 75,000 members in all the Sunday-schools
f that entire region. While Maryland, which had a state
unday-school union, had been at work under a resolution for
ve years to establish Sunday-schools in that state, and a
imilar effort had been made in South Carolina, yet neither
tate, it was said, could complete the work without aid. More-
ver, it was added as a strong reason for this new campaign,
hat immigration was drifting from the South into the Valley
f the Mississippi, and that by efficiently prosecuting Sunday-
chool work in the South—which was counted one of the
radles of the West—the Society would thus be contributing
oward the solution of the problem of planting schools in the
Mississippi Valley.

It will be noticed that these two schemes partially over-
apped each other, Alabama being counted in both areas, but
his state was later classed with the southern rather than with
he Mississippi Valley group.

The southern people entered with alacrity upon this cam-
aign. It created an enthusiasm which swept over the
ountry, second only in magnitude to that aroused by the
arger Mississippi enterprise. Crowded meetings were held
n support of it at Richmond, Petersburg. Charleston, Savan-
ah, Columbia, and elsewhere in the South.

A number of widely known representative ministers and educators from the South were present at the anniversary in Philadelphia when the enterprise was proposed, and an enthusiastic meeting was held at which more than forty gentlemen arose in succession and gave pledges of what they would do in support of this campaign. About $5,000 were definitely subscribed, besides a large number of other pledges indefinite as to their amounts. Similar enthusiastic meetings were held in New York, New Haven, Hartford, Providence and Boston and from each of these places, as well as from the South liberal subscriptions were made and strong pledges given of increased support of the Union in carrying forward this southern campaign. By a few liberal gentlemen in Boston over $1,000 were subscribed, and about half as much in Providence. Over $1,200 were pledged in a single meeting in Hartford and upward of $800 in New Haven, and smaller sums in a number of places throughout New England and the North.

It is interesting at this date to note what stirred the zeal for it in the New England States, as voiced by Professor Goodrich of Yale College, who pointed out "the influence that this effort is going to exert in calming the political and sectional animosities which have too much alienated the South and the North." Although the Society had already accumulated a debt by the Mississippi Valley scheme, it entered upon this southern campaign with great vigor and prosecuted it with a large measure of success. It was partly handicapped by the fear of arousing antagonism between the races of the South, and partly by the difficulty of securing competent workers. The Union's purpose, there as elsewhere, was to secure agents and missionaries from the states in which the work was to be done. But properly qualified persons willing to engage in it were hard to obtain in sufficient numbers, and buildings in which to hold the schools were not easily found because of the limited number of public schools then in the South.

Moreover, the volunteer workers always associated with paid missionaries in prosecuting these enterprises, both in the Mississippi Valley and in the South, were not so easily secured nor so abundant in the South as in other sections of the country. Yet in the face of these obstacles the results of the work gratified the Christian people of those states. They noted many churches strengthened, and Bible study was widely increased. It led prominent Southern men also urgently to request the Union to supply libraries suitable for common schools in those states. In response to this 1,000 libraries, each of 120 volumes, carefully selected, were issued for this purpose.

Notwithstanding strong sentiment in favor of this scheme, it could not be carried out except in a modified form. The structure of our government does not admit of any union of church and state. It offers freedom of worship to all, and cannot, therefore, be partial to any one form of the Christian religion. Some statesmen and many politicians held that this scheme violated the spirit of our government; more broad-minded philanthropists dissented from this view. The larger number of these libraries, however, were purchased and distributed in private schools and families throughout that section. Thus modified, the original idea resulted in great good to a large number of communities.

Call for World-Wide Work.—Schemes of such immense magnitude as that for the Mississippi Valley and for the South Atlantic States seemed to have led the people to think that the Union could dare and do anything. Hardly had this Southern Enterprise been inaugurated before urgent appeals began to pour in upon the Society for increased aid in supplying publications to American mission stations in foreign lands and among the Indians. Donations of literature had been previously made to American missions in Burma, Syria, India, and the islands of the Pacific. It is recorded that in 1833, in response to "an irresistible appeal" in behalf of the youth of France made by a missionary there, $500 were appropriated to furnish publications of the Union and to aid in the translation of them into the French language. Similar urgent requests had come for publications in the Portuguese and Spanish languages to be used in Brazil and other countries in South America, and grants were made in response to them.

At the anniversary in 1834 Rev. Mr. Winslow, an eminent missionary from Ceylon, made an eloquent appeal for books

needed for the children of American missionaries and for those
of English residents in India, and also for native children, some
of whom understood the English language, in addition to
books and papers desired for translation. His request was
strongly endorsed by the American Board of Commissioners
for Foreign Missions at Boston. This strong appeal resulted
in a resolution of the Society to raise $12,000 "for the purpose
of supplying foreign missionary stations, sustained by Ameri
can churches, with sets of the Society's publications." With
three schemes of the magnitude of these already before the
Union it is not remarkable that the full sum for the last one
was not realized, although the Society did furnish complete
sets of its publications to many mission stations in Asia,
Africa, the Sandwich Islands and elsewhere.

The translation of Bible dictionaries and other biblical
helps into foreign languages was frequently encouraged by
liberal appropriations. Repeated appeals continued to come
for elementary works to be translated for use in all parts of
the world where American missionaries were proclaiming the
gospel. The Society again and again responded to these
appeals, having faith in the liberality of its friends to sustain
it in these benevolent measures.

The managers had a large outlook then, for in 1835 they
declared that the objects of the Society were "to assist in
carrying the Gospel to every family in the world, and to
ensure the religious instruction of every child, and the con
quest of the world for Christ."

Any one of the three great enterprises thus entered upon by
the Union within three years would, in those times, have been
sufficient to have appalled a much older and stronger organiza
tion. It need not surprise us that the projectors found the
realization of their plans far more difficult than they had at
first imagined. Looking back upon this history some years
later, and sobered by their experience, they stated the result
as marvelous, and yet as falling below their expectations.
They justified their hopes and acts by pointing to the small
facilities at hand and the great difficulties which confronted
their efforts. Thus they say, "We began without any plan
of instruction, without text-books, and in the face of dis
couragement and opposition." But they add:

We have a highly approved system of instruction now, adopted substantially in nineteen-twentieths of the Sunday-schools of the United States, embracing probably quite two millions of persons. . . . We began with no scheme of propogation; . . . we have now, on a reduced complement, seventy missionaries to explore the land, to seek out and supply the destitute. . . . We began without experience. It was a new thing among us and there was, therefore, no trained band of helpers and sympathizers on whom we could rely. . . . Now there are myriads of men and women, some of them occupying high positions in Church and State, whose warmest sympathies flow toward the Sunday-school. . . . We began when the Sunday-school interests of the country were almost entirely associated with one central organization. For many years the American Sunday-School Union was the only large publisher of books for Sunday-schools and formed the only national association for Sunday-school purposes. Now several large and powerful denominational societies have prolific presses and vast facilities for extending and strengthening the Sunday-schools connected with their various churches. . . . Moreover, other forms of service of great magnitude have sprung up in the churches and to some extent have overshadowed the agency of the Sunday-school which has been all the while preparing readers of the Bible . . . and training uncounted multitudes to habits of self-denial and benevolent exertions.

This fully answered the query why the Sunday-School Union had not accomplished even greater results up to that time.[1]

Women's Auxiliary.—Early in the organized Sunday-school movement in America the women had a large share, as already has been shown. They formed an early Sunday-school union in New York, and a society for promoting Sunday-schools in Philadelphia at the beginning of the nineteenth century. They do not appear to have been asked to aid in promoting the three great enterprises narrated above, except as they might be a part of any mixed assembly. It is, therefore, less remarkable that they were not conspicuous in forwarding an enterprise for the benefit of the children and the youth of the country. Yet unsolicited, not a few of them manifested a significant interest in promoting this cause on their own account. Thus a number of benevolent women of Boston and Roxbury, belonging to different religious denominations, voluntarily associated themselves together to devise a method for aiding the Society in establishing Sunday-schools in the Western States and territories. In transmitting the proceeds of a May Day Festival, they said: "Believing

[1] *Report*, 1849, pp. 12, 13, 18.

that the field of the West is fully known to the American Sunday-School Union, and understanding that many thousands of dollars could be employed by you in sending out libraries where they are urgently called for, we forward you $1,273.33, the avails of the May Day Festival." That sum provided libraries for more than a hundred different communities.

The grateful responses called forth from the communities receiving these libraries were published, and stirred up women elsewhere to provide further contributions to send libraries to other communities. Mrs. Sigourney wrote appropriate poetical lines commemorating the gift, and a floral procession of Sunday-schools was held in Philadelphia, which resulted in adding $500 toward Sunday-school libraries in the West, and later another festive season was observed, in which about $1,000 more was handed to the Union for a similar benevolent purpose.

> These floral processions were due to the skill and industry of a large number of ladies who kindly volunteered their valuable services for the occasion. Nearly two thousand baskets were made out of pasteboard in all the variety of form which fancy could suggest; and being covered with moss, were filled with beautiful bouquets, most of which were cheerfully contributed by the proprietors of public and private gardens in the city and vicinity. These baskets were borne by the children on light frames and, together with wreaths of flowers and tasteful banners, gave a beautiful appearance to the procession.

The assembly gathered in the open park on Washington Square, where appropriate music was furnished by an excellent band, whose services were generously tendered for the occasion. Hymns were sung, an address was made, and in the evening the flowers were arranged for exhibition and sale, which increased the funds for providing Sunday-school libraries for gratuitous circulation in the newer settlements of the West. This form of benevolence was unusual, and served to interest the givers and increase their desire for promoting the good cause, besides being of special blessing to thousands who received the gifts.[1]

Women were always abundant in labors as members of the teaching force in the Sunday-school. Indeed, without their

[1] *Report*, 1844, p. 81, ff.

SECRETARIES OF MISSIONS

M. A. Wurts, 1861–81.

L. Milton Marsh, 1881–83

J. M. Crowell, D. D., 1883–1908.

J. M. Andrews, 1908–10.

co-operation, it is doubtful whether the modern Sunday-school movement would not have proved a conspicuous failure. About three or four out of every five teachers in the Sunday-schools throughout the country were women. Besides the natural intuition of woman as a teacher of the young, many of these were trained, competent, and consecrated instructors. Pioneers engaged in the work of the extension of Bible schools in destitute places have repeatedly found that an experienced and earnest woman was the best leader in the community and made the best superintendent of the school. Moreover, having the care of the children at an early age in the home, women were quicker to see the need as well as the importance of religious training of the child, and, therefore, more heartily welcomed the coming of a Sunday-school missionary or other Christian worker to found and to foster a school in their neglected neighborhood. In simple justice, therefore, the large share which women have had in the success of this movement should receive generous recognition.

Women as Authors.—As successful authors and writers of juvenile literature, women have shown a marked aptitude in the preparation of literature suitable to start and to foster the religious education of the young. From the early days of this movement they were among the foremost authors of children's books. Many of them achieved distinction, and some won national fame thereby. In the field of juvenile religious literature, women were more numerous and more versatile in America during the early part of the last century than were their masculine associates. They were successful in presenting truth in simple terms and attractive forms, with apt illustrations suited to childhood and youth.

In view of the prominent service which women rendered to this movement in its teaching force and in contributing so largely to the preparation of its literature, it seems remarkable that they did not become more conspicuous in some organized capacity in the work of extending and improving Sunday-schools. Possibly it may have been because woman's day had not yet arrived. In most of the churches it was not popular for women to speak in public or to attempt to interpret the sacred Word. The learned interpretation of it was left to clergymen, theologians, and college professors. Women accepted the humbler but no less important sphere of instructing the race in its formative period and giving the young some knowledge of the rudiments of religion, laying a foundation upon which the church could safely build. It would seem a distinct loss, however, that the American Sunday-School Union should miss the opportunity of fostering and encouraging an organization of women in the work in which they might have become such valuable auxiliaries.

SKETCHES OF PROMINENT WORKERS

A. W. Corey (1803–1880).

At the large and enthusiastic meeting held in New York in 1830, to encourage the American Sunday-School Union in planting new Sunday-schools in the Valley of the Mississippi, a young man was present from its New York Depository. The next morning a superintendent of one of the largest Sunday-schools in the city called at the New York office of the Society and offered the services of himself and his wife for two years as missionaries, to aid in carrying out the resolution which was the theme of the previous evening's meeting. The offer was accepted, and the same young man of the office had the pleasure of fitting them out with a horse and a small wagon and other necessaries for the journey, which required about a month. They spent two years traveling in a similar way up and down the Mississippi Valley, in fulfilment of their mission. The missionaries were B. J. Seward and his wife, and the young man who helped them to start on their journey was A. W. Corey.

Mr. Corey was efficient in promoting the extension of Sunday-schools in the same valley for upward of fifty years. He was born in Orange County, New York, April, 1803, and was a schoolmate of Hon. William H. Seward, who became his lifelong friend. Giving up the study of medicine, he began to prepare for the ministry. Failing health forced him to suspend those studies and seek medical advice in Philadelphia. While in that city he aided in raising some of the earlier gifts to the American Sunday-School Union. Recovering his health, he entered the service of the Society in the New York Depository, 140 Nassau Street. He was one of the founders of *The New York Evangelist*, and later, in 1831, was with a religious paper in Cincinnati, and afterward secretary and editor for the Illinois State Temperance Society. His former services and his familiarity with the character of the people in the Mississippi Valley led to his re-entering the service of the American Sunday-School Union, and finally having charge of its missionary operations in that Valley. Under his supervision the missionary work was organized upon a system better adapted to the vastness of the territory, to the tide of immigration, and to the fostering of weak schools, which required months and sometimes years of oversight to give them stability and strength.

He was well qualified by his previous experience and training to master the wants of this vast district, grasp the work, organize forces at the command of the Society, appeal for funds, secure workers, direct their labors, and insure the largest results. He kept himself in close touch with all the missionaries and their schools not only by personal visitation, but by a voluminous correspondence, and was well informed of the conditions of the many communities scattered over the valley, and of their varied wants and of the practical ways to meet them.

He had a singular gift and perseverance in enlisting people of means to sustain the Society's work. Besides the sums which he aided in securing in New York, a Sunday-school teacher of St. Louis, Missouri, known to the public as "O. B.," gave many thousand dollars to the Society, through Mr. Corey, to aid it in furnishing its literature to new and needy Sunday-schools in the West. To the first two new Sunday-schools organized in any year in any county west of the Mississippi River he offered to give one-half of a Sunday-school library, costing either ten or twenty dollars, according to the size of the school, provided the school or its friends would furnish the other half. This offer cost him over $1,000 every year for more than eighteen years.[1]

Mr. Corey was a writer of force and ability. He prepared numerous pamphlets and tracts upon temperance, and many of the printed statements and appeals advocating the progress of Sunday-schools in the West were from his pen. He pre-

---

[1] Corey's *MS*. Narrative, p. 89.

pared an extended account of his labors near the close of his life and sent the manuscript to the Society. It is carefully kept in its archives, but has never been published.

Elsewhere is given a summary of Mr. Corey's work and that of his associates, in the great Valley of the Mississippi, taken from this unpublished manuscript. When age and infirmity began to interfere with his work he proposed to resign, but the Society declined to accept his resignation, believing that his long and faithful and efficient service in the Union deserved recognition and a continuance of his commission to the end of his life, which came soon after—May 18, 1880.

From his wide observation and intimate acquaintance with the progress of the work in that valley for over fifty years, it was Mr. Corey's opinion that beyond all doubt four-fifths of the Sunday-schools planted in the Valley of the Mississippi during his lifetime were due to the work of the American Sunday-School Union, and that the strong Sunday-school sentiment which pervaded the whole region was started in the Society's famous resolution of 1830.

John Adams, LL.D. (1772–1863), **Missionary** (1842–1853).

Near the close of his life Mr. Adams said, "In my epitaph do not put LL.D. nor any title after my name, but plain 'John Adams; a lover of children, a guide of youth, a sinner saved by grace.' " This request is an index of the man's character.

John Adams was of the same ancestry as the two presidents, John and John Quincy Adams. He was born in 1772, a graduate of Yale in 1795, a distinguished teacher, a foremost scholar, a profound, earnest, and sympathetic religious character. It was said that he directed more young men to college and into the Christian ministry than any other educator of his time. With his fellow educators—Drs. Noah Porter, Leonard Woods, Moses Stuart, and others—he aided in forming the famous weekly "Monday Evening Meeting" for "devising plans of doing good and advancing the Redeemer's Kingdom at home and abroad." In that little assembly some of the notable national institutions were first conceived, such as the American Tract Society, the American Education Society, the American Temperance Society, and the Sabbath Association.

Retiring from his work as principal of Phillips Academy,

Andover, Massachusetts, in 1833, he went to Jacksonville, Illinois. His habits of activity impelled him to seek some systematic work. He had good health and a good constitution. In looking for useful service, he was impressed with the missionary operations of the American Sunday-School Union, and, as an educator, studied its principles and methods. He was so strongly impressed therewith that he entered its service as a missionary in Central Illinois in 1842. His study of the conditions in that region at that early day forced him to look for the best agency for the salvation of new western communities which were soon to control the destiny of the country. "Something systematic and effectual must be done and that very soon, or it will be too late," was his belief. He found destitute neighborhoods where there were no day schools, no schoolhouses, no churches, no meeting-houses, no ministers; the Sabbath was spent in labor, trading, visiting, hunting, fishing, or sports. He gathered the people of each new community for Bible study, stimulated them to build a schoolhouse, form a library, and in the course of two or three years a church was organized. A few at first, for the sake of unity and strength, merged their individual preferences. He says, "The house of worship built and paid for and a minister secured, society was improved, virtue promoted, and reformation commenced at the right point." Out of his experience he could instruct teachers, showing them by example how to teach.

"Father" Adams, as he was familiarly called in the West, discovered Stephen Paxson on this wise: B. J. Seward had the oversight of the Mississippi Valley work, and found and employed Rev. John M. Peck as a missionary of the Union in that valley. Mr. Peck organized a Union Sunday-school at Winchester, Illinois. There was so much division and so little religious strength in the place that the school soon declined. Father Adams, a born educator, revived and reorganized the school. It was into this school that Stephen Paxson was brought by his daughter Mary, and there he was discovered by Dr. Adams, as a person of rare native gifts suited to mission work. Dr. Adams recommended him to A. W. Corey, then superintendent of the work in St. Louis. The future achievements of this stammering man proved the sagacity of Dr.

Adams in discerning a rare Christian worker, where multitudes of others would have overlooked him.

Closing his labors, Dr. Adams made a visit to his son, the Rev. William Adams, D.D., LL.D., then pastor of a large church in New York City. There he wrote out his experience and testimony: "Children need something more than occasional sermons, which are often few and far between and not adapted to their capacity. They and the families need to be taught not only to read the Bible, but to understand it. It is evident," he added, "that neither the home missionary nor the devoted colporteur alone can do this work, and the Sunday-school can do it effectually. This I know from my observation. In prosecuting my labors in the central part of Illinois, through twenty counties in about eleven years, I have gathered and organized 322 new Sunday-schools, embracing 2,500 teachers and more than 16,000 scholars. I have distributed among these and other schools about 50,000 volumes published by the American Sunday-School Union, besides Bibles, Testaments, and tracts."

The schools were organized in communities such as have been already described. He closes his testimony by saying, "For myself, now retiring from my field of labor, from my own observation of the necessity and benefits of Sunday-schools I do not hesitate to say that if I could bequeath $100,000 to the various benevolent societies in our land, I would give one-half of it to the Society that takes care of the children—the American Sunday-School Union."

Hon. John McLean, Second President of the American Sunday-School Union (1848–1861).

The Hon. John McLean, second president of the American Sunday-School Union, was a member of the Methodist Episcopal Church, loyal to its historic spirit and yet placing loyalty to Jesus Christ as the first principle of Christian service. This is well illustrated by the story of how he began family worship. He had been skeptical in early life, but was convinced of the truth of the Christian religion and accepted Christ as his Saviour. It is said he went home and was hardly within the doors before he said, "We are to have family prayers. Let us go to the drawing-room and pray together."

"But," his wife answered, "there are four lawyers there. They have come to attend court. We do not want to go there; let us go to the kitchen and have prayers." He is said to have replied, "It is the first time I ever invited the Lord to my house, and I do not propose to invite him to the kitchen. If I am a Christian I am to have family prayer." He then went in and said to the lawyers, "My friends, I have been convinced of the truth of Christianity. I have found that Jesus died for me. I have given myself to him. I am now to make my first prayer in my own house. You may, however, do as you please, stay or go." The lawyers said they would like very much to stay, and stay they did. This is the man who for his inflexible integrity and Christian fidelity was chosen the second president of the American Sunday-School Union. He was Justice of the Supreme Court of the United States at that time, and had been vice-president of the Union since 1829.

Judge McLean was born in Morris County, New Jersey, March 11, 1785. His parents removed to Ohio in his early childhood. There he studied and practiced law. He was a member of Congress, judge of the supreme court in Ohio, and Postmaster General under two administrations—Madison and John Quincy Adams—and Justice of the Supreme Court until his death, April 4, 1861. He was distinguished for eloquence and ability as an advocate, and for the sanity and wisdom of his decisions as judge. His dissenting opinion in the Dred Scott case, when he opposed the decree of Chief Justice Taney and a majority of the court, is celebrated in history. His patriotism was shown by his hatred of the spoils system, leading him to refuse to continue as Postmaster General under Andrew Jackson because it might require him to appoint some to public office for political service.

On the death of Alexander Henry, he was unanimously elected president of the American Sunday-School Union. He first declined the honor, fearing that his active duties in the government would not allow him to take as responsible a part in the Society's work as he would wish. However, he had such confidence in the principles of the Society's organization and in its adaptation to the religious and moral needs of the country, that he was willing to give it whatever influence and time his duties might allow. He stated his views upon religious education very forcibly and fully in a letter to the Union, and a year later in an address to the Society, when he presided at its anniversary in 1850. He expressed his belief as follows:

> Sabbath-schools must be relied on as a principal agent in this great work: to save our beloved institutions from a 'yawning chasm,' since free government can rest on no other basis than moral power. . . . A government founded upon the basis of universal suffrage must, in the nature of things, encounter popular excitement. . . . There can be no free government which does not rest upon a moral basis. Destroy this foundation, and anarchy or despotism necessarily follows. Men can be restrained from outrage and injustice only by moral and physical power. . . . Make it strong in moral power, and its glorious principles will be perpetuated. Therefore we commend this enterprise of the American Sunday-School Union to every friend of morality and to everyone who loves his country and desires to perpetuate our free institutions.

Judge McLean thus advocated the spirit and the work of the Society with that ardent love for Christ and with the patriotism which he exhibited so conspicuously in other public duties, illustrating the power of Christian principle to guide and direct in the discharge of public affairs.

John A. Brown (1788–1872), **Third President of the American Sunday-School Union** (1861–1872); **Merchant, Banker and Philanthropist.**

John A. Brown was born in Ballymena, Ireland, May 21, 1788. Owing to political agitation he emigrated with his father, a man of ample fortune, to Baltimore at the beginning of the last century. After receiving a fair education and a training in business with his father he became a successful merchant and banker in Philadelphia, being chosen a director in the old United States Bank under the great financier Nicholas Biddle, and was one of the founders of the banking house of Brown Brothers, of Baltimore, Philadelphia, New York, and London.

He was unanimously chosen president of the American Sunday-School Union in 1861, to succeed the Hon. John McLean. His eminence as a man of affairs, his probity, his sound judgment, his reputation in banking qualified him to

MISSIONARIES

John Adams, LL. D.

B. W. Chidlaw, D. D.

John McCullagh.

Stephen Paxson.

Henry Clay Trumbull.

Frederick G. Ensign.

guide the Society prudently through the exciting period of the Civil War. Indeed, the Society was passing through serious internal differences in regard to its polity which, added to the stringency caused by the war, crippled all branches of its work and even threatened its existence. Mr. Brown's leadership inspired confidence and courage among managers and friends of the Society. Like an experienced pilot he was able to steer it amid conflicting projects, bitter animosity and divided counsels which endangered its life.

Under his administration as president, the Society came safely through the greatest crisis in the history of the country. Its affairs were extricated from confusion without jarring the harmony which had been restored between its management and friends and the Christian public. Confidence in the value and efficiency of the Society's religious and educational work was fostered and increased under his prudent guidance.

He passed into the life beyond at the ripe age of eighty-four December 31, 1872, leaving to the Society $10,000 and to the world the legacy of an eminently Christian example, pointing to a wise use of wealth and talent for the good of humanity and the advancement of the cause of Christ.

Lorin B. Tousley (1804–1864).

Of the many persons noted for their exceptional ability in addressing children in America and abroad, Mr. Tousley stands in the forefront. He was one of the few speakers who could cause his audience of little people to forget the man and fix their attention upon what he said. More than a decade before the middle of the last century he came, a stranger, to old Johnstown, New York, and held the close attention of from 1,000 to 2,000 children (of which the writer was one) in the open air for more than an hour by his wonderfully graphic and terse presentation of gospel truth, illustrated with great dramatic power by incident and anecdote which alternately moved his audience of little people to laughter and to tears.

Mr. Tousley was born in Sharon, Vermont, July 17, 1804. His father moved to western New York during the childhood of the son. At the age of twelve the boy earnestly desired to join the church, but the then conservative views respecting church membership of children prevented his reception. This fact is said to have intensified his sympathy with children and to have given him zeal in his subsequent work for them. He had a common school education and for the rest of his training he humorously declared that he "was graduated from Jessup's tan-yard," as he learned that trade with Palmer and Jessup, who were tanners. His public religious career began by establishing a Sunday-school which ultimately grew into a Congregational Church. His aptitude for this work became so apparent that he was appointed city missionary for Buffalo. His intense zeal and energies here had full scope. It is said that "In Dr. Lord's church a large congregation of little folks hung on his lips, Sabbath after Sabbath, at the afternoon services, as with burning natural eloquence he preached unto them Jesus." It was clear that he was called of God and his services were in wide demand. At revivals, temperance and Sunday-school meetings, and at all services where children were assembled he was the favorite speaker. His addresses abounded in illustrations, anecdotes and arguments, now pathetic, now humorous, until tears and laughter swept the audience at his will.

For more than a score of years after 1840 he was missionary of the American Sunday-School Union for western New York, having his headquarters at Canandaigua. Thousands of persons in mature life and even in old age recalled his earnest words, his dramatic eloquence, and the fire and enthusiasm with which he pleaded with them to live the Christian life. His public career was brought to a sudden close by an accident, a falling timber of a building injuring his back and paralyzing his limbs. He lingered for several years, suffering much more from anxiety to recover that he might continue his work than from his accident. He is still remembered widely as an advocate of Sunday-schools, the loving friend of youth, and the children's "minister."

SECTION VII

IT takes time to gain experience, secure funds and form a satisfactory working system in any mission work. At first the American Sunday-School Union, like all new organizations, had neither the funds nor the knowledge sufficient to put its mission work on other than a tentative business basis. Rev. William C. Blair, Rev. Timothy Alden, President of Allegheny College, Mr. M. A. Remley, Dr. Howard Malcolm, and others had been employed to make surveys of the conditions and religious needs of the country from 1821 to 1825.

Systematic Surveys.—Another systematic survey was made in 1828, and again after 1830 by general agents, such as Rev. Robert Baird and others. The results of these surveys were widely and forcibly presented to the people, to persuade them to provide funds adequate to the magnitude of the work. Even the best theoretical system required testing to see whether it would fit the complex conditions of the country. Thus after years of experience could the managers of the Union formulate a system approximately satisfactory for its mission work.

Then, too, the constantly changing character of immigration, the difference in the nature of the various sections of the country to be settled, and the different occupations of the people called for changes, and hence great elasticity in any system that should be adopted.

Early in the missionary work of the Society the whole country was roughly grouped in three great divisions: First, New England and the eastern Middle States, that is, the country east of the Alleghenies; second, the Mississippi Valley, covering the states west of the Alleghenies to the territory of Wisconsin on the north and Kentucky, Arkansas, Tennessee, Louisiana, Mississippi and Alabama; and third, the Southern States, Virginia, North and South Carolina,

219

Georgia, and the territory of Florida. Later Alabama was transferred to the southern district.

For efficiency in prosecuting the Mississippi Valley Enterprise the first year was spent largely in exploration and survey of the conditions of this vast territory. An agent was assigned to each state, who was to become acquainted with each section, as far as possible, and secure additional means for prosecuting the work in the shortest time and with the least expense. The Society was responsible for the official acts of this agent. He had no authority, however, to appoint or dismiss missionaries. Forty-nine missionaries and agents were employed in the Valley of the Mississippi alone in the year 1830–31.[1] Following a survey they found that the tract of country to be supplied under this resolution embraced the present states of Ohio, Indiana, Illinois, Kentucky, Tennessee, Alabama, Louisiana, Mississippi, Missouri, the territory of Arkansas, territories north of Illinois and northwest of Missouri, western Pennsylvania, western Virginia, and a small section of the state of New York.[2] In this territory they found, from surveys, between 400 to 500 organized counties, subdivided into 8,000 to 10,000 villages and neighborhoods.[3]

Excluding so much of that region as might be already covered or would be reached by other benevolent efforts, independent of the Union, the managers said, "The object still retains enough of its magnitude to excite the most enterprising and to attract the most aspiring devotion."

The perplexity of the problem before them can be imagined when, in the employment of persons, every circumstance respecting a missionary or agent—his age, character, health, prudence, temper, spirit, knowledge of this particular business, knowledge of the world and, more than all, knowledge of himself, the compensation, the terms, the place of service, the difficulties, discouragements and opportunities of the field—must all be considered. Multiply this by fifty or one hundred —the number of persons who were immediately to be employed—and it gives some idea of the magnitude of their problem. Then, too, they wished to employ voluntary or gratuitous agents not only to increase their efficiency, but to lessen the expense. A score or more of voluntary missionaries

[1] *Report*, 1831, p. 34.   [2] *Report*, 1832, p. 26.   [3] *Report*, 1831, p. 33.

were employed, who offered gratuitously to supply a certain number of counties with schools without any expense to the parent Society except for equipment.

Then, too, owing to the dearth of suitable reading, the Society provided libraries in connection with each school, for these were found to be of incomparable advantage. The Society said, "We could fill our report with well authenticated facts to show what a single month's use of a good library has done to disabuse and interest the public mind. It wins its way very successfully to the kind hearts and sober judgment of all who use it."[1] In a single year they made donations of literature to 799 schools, amounting to $3,917.48; and inside of three years they distributed in that Valley over $30,000 worth of books.[2] In less than eighteen months the Society had received reports of 2,867 schools established and 1,121 visited and revived. In less than half of the schools established the number of scholars exceeded 60,000.

After a comparatively brief experience the Society found its missionary work was so complex as to require a careful reorganization not only in conducting its business through the Board, but also on the field. The reports of each committee became so voluminous as to take too much of the time of the meetings of the Board, and efficiency was lessened for want of some power that could keep in view all the departments of its operations. It was therefore decided in 1835 to confide the general control to an Exective Committee of seven members. Then, for greater efficiency in the missionary work, it was proposed to divide the United States and territories into five districts or chief agencies: first, the New England States, except Connecticut; second, Connecticut, New York and northern New Jersey; third, Pennsylvania, Delaware, Maryland and southern New Jersey; fourth, the Valley of the Mississippi; fifth, the Southern States. In each of these districts, it was proposed to appoint a person for the general supervision of the Society's operations, the establishing and assisting of schools, supplying of books, collecting funds, and promoting universal Christian education.[3]

By this plan the Society hoped to secure increased funds, interest the Christian public, and thus bring the whole country

[1] *Report*, 1831, p. 36.   [2] *Report*, 1832, p. 36.   [3] *Report*, 1836, p. 18.

and its wants within its knowledge and reach. Earlier than this it had employed the Rev. Robert Baird, D.D., as a field secretary, who gave the results of his investigation early in 1834.[1]

In introducing this new grouping and system the Society intended better to adapt its work to changing conditions, and to secure the greatest efficiency and the largest results for the least expenditure of time and money.

A few years later the entire country was further divided into seven or eight great districts, and a supervising agent appointed in each who was to have close personal oversight of the progress of the work, subject to the approval of the home Board. Collecting agents were also employed whose duties were not merely to solicit funds for the support of the work, but to stir enthusiasm respecting the need, importance, and methods pursued in the Sunday-school extension movement, tell the story of its achievements from time to time, and enlist the sympathy of the Christian public in all parts of the country.

A. W. Corey's Record.—Great care was taken by these general agents to collect and preserve the more important facts and results reported by the missionaries. Thus A. W. Corey, having for many years the oversight of the work in the Mississippi Valley, affirms: "I have kept a continuous register of all the schools organized, visited, and aided by all the missionaries and by myself. This register gives the name of the school, the town, county, and state where located, when organized, the number of teachers and scholars then enrolled, the amount of literature sold and donated, the number of copies of Scriptures furnished, and the name and post-office address of the superintendent." All these items he had reported for twenty-five years, month by month and year by year, to the home office at Philadelphia. The aggregate of schools visited and aided for twenty-five years was 24,451; teachers, 177,935; scholars, 1,260,847; literature distributed, $206,502.39, of which $150,175.80 was by sale and $56,326.59 by donation. [This was the number of teachers and scholars at the time of the organization of the respective schools.] He declares that every school was supplied with Bibles and records and no question was ever raised as to what denomination, if any,

[1] *Report*, 1834, p. 15.

the schools belonged or were likely to belong. The register he kept did not give an account of the common schools, the prayer-meetings, the temperance organizations, religious awakenings, conversions, or churches growing out of the schools. Mr. Corey computed that in these schools during the twenty-five years more than 3,000,000 children had received religious instruction and over 300,000 teachers had been engaged in giving it. In face of the fact that owing to the drifting of immigration, some of these schools were discontinued or consolidated with others in their neighborhood, the mortality among them has not been greater than the percentage of mortality in frontier churches under control of the various denominations.

Students as Missionaries.—The popular enthusiasm aroused by the Mississippi Valley Enterprise naturally began to wane in a few years. Funds for its support were more difficult to secure. Bountiful as were the gifts, amounting to $120,000 and upward, the Society expended several thousand dollars in excess of that sum (and of all contributions) in carrying out its resolution. To continue the work as economically as possible and to respond to calls for like missionary work in other fields, the Society decided to employ students of about a dozen different denominations from about thirty colleges and institutions of learning. These were employed during their vacation, which occurred chiefly in the summer time and when the season was most favorable for the work of organizing new schools on the frontier. Some students from Gambier College, Ohio, were employed as early as 1833.[1]

For a time this plan aroused new enthusiasm. The churches perceived that the students gained a valuable experience and training for future work, usually as pastors and evangelists. Therefore what was begun as an experiment was continued, from time to time, not only before our Civil War, but after it, when students were employed during vacations to aid and supplement the work of the permanent missionary.

Thus in 1854 the whole number of missionaries employed by the Society for the year was 322, of whom 237 were theological or academic students who devoted their vacations to this work. The next year the Society reported 324 mission-

[1] *Report*, 1852, p. 42.

aries in service, of whom 256 were students in a course of preparation for the gospel ministry. They devoted their vacations of from one to four months to this work at a season of the year most favorable for Sunday-school missionary effort. The following two years about 300 missionaries were employed in twenty-five different states and territories, the greater part of whom were students.

These theological and college students were employed as missionaries partly for economic reasons, as already stated. The Union was further influenced to continue the experiment because of the educational advantages to Christian young men. It urged the friends of the Society to welcome their services and to overlook any inexperience in the workers because of the advantage it would be in training them for their life work. The student missionary combined the various duties of exploring destitute neighborhoods, organizing new schools, visiting schools already in existence but needing to be encouraged and strengthened, providing Sunday-school libraries and helps to teachers where none were at hand, and giving information to the people generally on the principles and benefits of the Sunday-school as an institution. These zealous young workers discovered many sights and scenes strange to them, and their reports presented a checkered picture of the moral condition of communities which were alike interesting and, sometimes, humiliating to read. The students themselves reported positive results of their labors in the reflex influence exerted upon themselves while they were thus preparing in body, mind, and spirit for the responsibilities of the sacred ministry.

Eminent professors of theology commended in the strongest terms this kind of service as a preparation for the future usefulness of their students. The thorough business methods and careful preparation required for the work, the tact in visiting from house to house, the meeting of persons in various conditions in life, and with all sorts of prejudices in religion called for the largest practical common-sense, godliness, business accuracy, and ability to sway the public mind. It tended to cultivate these qualities in the student. They said: "The young student who goes into the mountains of Virginia and takes a hand-spike and heaves with the log rollers in order that he may talk Sunday-school with them, or plies a hoe beside the farmer on the Aroostook [Maine] for the same purpose (and this was actually done) will know something besides books. He must study the raw material, the stuff of which churches and congregations are made, and must deal with men as a student fresh from the schools cannot do." Some distinguished professors, eminent alike for learning and intellectual powers, told their students that such a service would be worth to them as much as a year of study.

Moreover, this experience did more than prepare them to deal with practical common-sense men; it also fitted them for more successful work with the young. It is little wonder, therefore, that the Union and its friends continued this form of service from time to time for many years. It had its drawbacks, however. Not the least of them was the fact that these young students, in their inexperience, made many mistakes which were sometimes fatal to the success of a Bible school. Then, too, their work was temporary, lasting only for a month or two, and in a field where often there was no permanent missionary and no nearby pastor to oversee the feeble schools thus started after the student left his field. Therefore the popular enthusiasm for this form of Sunday-school extension began to wane in spite of obvious advantages to the student.

Another reason for the decrease of this form of service was the revival of voluntary missionaries, which was made possible and practicable in consequence of the organization of state and county Sunday-school conventions and unions. Through better organization a more comprehensive system of extension of Sunday-schools became possible. The permanent missionary could thus find a larger number of persons who were so situated that they could give a part of their time besides Sunday to this service, and thus aid him in organizing and improving Sunday-schools in the country.

A significant illustration of the value of this student service is the experience of Jackson G. Coffing. In 1849 he was a student in Oberlin College, earning his way by teaching a country district school in Colerain, Hamilton County, Ohio. He also had organized and sustained a Sunday-school there for an autumn and winter, when he was found by Superintendent Chidlaw and employed during his vacations as a student missionary at a dollar a day and expenses. He worked in Ohio, and later in Indiana, founding twenty-five schools and distributing five hundred dollars' worth of literature, besides Bibles and Testaments, in communities where there was a meager supply. He completed a college course at Marietta, at the same time laboring as a student missionary in the Muskingum Valley. Again, while in Union Theological Seminary, New York, he continued to earn his schooling by labors in Sunday-school missions in that city, where he discovered and rescued an orphan waif in the slums of Baxter Street, New York. The waif was a little girl selling candy on the streets, having a home with an aged and poor woman in a cheerless garret. The girl was placed in a good school, as well as in Sunday-school, educated, and finally returned to her lost kindred in England a lovely, intelligent and religious young woman. The story of her rescue was published by the Union—a charming biography, entitled *Maria Cheeseman, the Candy Girl*—showing the value of missionary labors among the outcast and friendless.

The inspiration of his student mission work led Mr. Coffing to become a foreign missionary in Syria under the American Board, where he had a large and flourishing church at Aintab and a Sunday-school of over 500 scholars. While on his way to a missionary meeting in Mt. Lebanon he was mistaken for an English tourist, against whom a bandit had a grudge, and was instantly killed.[1]

Scores of these student missionaries afterward became successful workers for the Master in other fields as pastors, teachers and educators.

Student missionaries had an important influence in extending Sunday-schools in the Mississippi Valley and elsewhere. Many of their schools yielded splendid results. Thus of fifteen schools started by student missionaries from Gambier College, Ohio, in 1833, several grew into churches. In a neighborhood only eight miles from the college a student missionary formed a school in a very primitive and rough neighborhood, established a prayer-meeting, and began a Bible study service, out of which grew a church organiza-

[1] B. W. Chidlaw, *Story of My Life*, pp. 146-149.

tion. A house of worship was erected in the woods, but in the center of the settlement. Twenty years later, the same student officiated as minister in the church and reported that preaching had been continued from the first founding of the school.[1]

Again, thirty-four missionaries, mostly students, formed 158 new schools in Virginia in 1854, with 989 teachers, 5,536 pupils, and aided 171 other schools with 6,000 members, and put in circulation, by gift and sale, some 30,000 religious books, which reached thousands of families, in many of which religious reading was scarcely before known.[2]

Another of these student missionaries found the people "log-rolling." To win them, he took off his coat and vest and took a hand-spike and worked with them all day. As a result he founded a Sunday-school which was supplied with eighteen dollars' worth of books for a library, and he soon after succeeded in establishing five other new Sunday-schools in as many destitute settlements in that region.

During one year 156 students were employed, the time given by them equalling twenty-two years, two hundred and two days. They organized 909 Sunday-schools where none had existed, and supplied 1,545 other schools. They secured 6,688 teachers and 36,917 pupils to enter the new schools, and supplied more than 2,000 schools with an average of 110 volumes each, at an average cost to the Society of only $3.35 to each school formed or visited.[3] Another year the student missionaries organized nearly 800 new schools and placed in circulation, by sale and gift, over 150,000 volumes of religious literature.

When the work of the Society became more extended and was put upon a stricter system, it appeared to many communities that while it might be a profitable educational experience for the students to enter into this temporary missionary work in the frontier fields, it was not as satisfactory to the people. The permanent missionary often found that he could not properly care for so many new organizations beyond those that he would himself form, and the new schools often languished or were closed from lack of this oversight. The people were discouraged, lost heart, and it was much

[1] *Report*, 1852, p. 42.   [2] *Report*, 1855, p. 54.   [3] *Ibid.*, p. 15.

more difficult to revive such schools than it was to start them at first. Hence it was not deemed wise to continue the employment of student missionaries, except in special cases.

Overcoming Difficulties.—But to return to the history of the progress of the Mississippi Valley and other enterprises. The financial crisis of 1837 well-nigh suspended all mission operations on a large scale and left the Union heavily in debt, as before noted. No matter how forcible or frantic its appeals for increase of funds, the financial condition of the country was such as to preclude large returns. This is treated under the financial features of the Society's work.

The lack of facilities for transportation was another hindrance to the rapid progress of Sunday-school extension in the West and South at this period. Canals, steamboat lines and railways in the new West and in the South were not abundant as now. Thus the Rev. Robert Baird, exploring the field for the Union in 1833 and 1834, required many months to make a single tour of observation and inquiry through a few states in the Valley of the Mississippi and in the South. He traveled by steamboat and stage—mostly the latter—sometimes by private conveyance. A similar tour could now easily be made in less than as many weeks, and with much greater comfort. Wagon roads were rough, when there were any. Often the missionary had to travel on foot or horseback, following trails or bridle-paths. This made the work of establishing new schools in new communities arduous and very slow.

The work was further retarded by the difficulty of finding competent persons for missionaries. The aim was to secure them on the field where the work was to be done, believing that they would be best acquainted with the conditions, habits and speech of the people, and most likely to succeed in winning them to these new enterprises. But this was often found impossible; the men who were competent were not there, or, if they were there, they were unable to devote their lives to this service. It was almost equally difficult to find a sufficient number in other parts of the country who were properly qualified and willing to give themselves to this benevolent service, at any compensation, especially at the small one the Society could afford.

There was a further hindrance to the progress of the work, due to these pioneer settlers penetrating into sections remote from the few lines of public travel and transportation to be found in these new states and territories.

All these difficulties were added to the obvious one of the diversity of each community or settlement, in nationality, speech, religion and education.   In the same community or settlement were families so diverse in habits of life and training that no two would be alike.   There might not be two families with religious prejudices of the same kind.   Not a few of them were found to have drifted away from older civilization and religious influences to escape the restraints of religion. Adventurers, the lawless and the outlaw, and all classes of persons who desired to escape from the restraints of civilization—these must be brought into co-operation with each other and persuaded to unite in Bible service and in the study of righteous conduct and morals, as taught in the Holy Scriptures.   It meant a revolution in the lives of many of those to whom the messengers were sent.   The wonder is not that the progress was so slow, but that so great progress was made in this immense task.   But Christianity was compelled to tackle the question, or to confess its system a failure.   The American Sunday-School Union offered the most reasonable, as well as practical, basis and promise of success.   It is on this account that so many philanthropists and Christian people rallied to its support in carrying out these three magnificent enterprises; in the Valley of the Mississippi, in the South, and for the world-wide conquest of the nations.

In the face of these formidable difficulties, it is not remarkable that the progress of the Society was at varying speed. At one time it would seem to go forward with leaps and bounds, as at the beginning of the Mississippi Valley Enterprise. Again it seemed to be at a standstill, or almost going backward, as in the crises of 1837, 1857 and during the Civil War. As a great river, whose current, in the face of eddies and bends, really is flowing majestically on to the ocean, so the progress of the missionary work of the Union went steadily forward in the face of many financial bends and denominational eddies.

It may be easier for the reader clearly to grasp this onward progress when it is divided, say, into five great periods of twenty years each.

First Period.—The first twenty years was foundation work. The repeated surveys of conditions in the first decade suggested or shaped the principles upon which the Society was to be founded and conducted, and the methods to be pursued. In the second decade less dependence was placed than in the first, upon voluntary effort to extend Sunday-schools in destitute places. Not until the second decade was it clearly seen by the friends of the Society that a paid missionary force was necessary even to make such voluntary service efficient. This became the more obvious when the Society saw the magnitude of the Mississippi Valley Enterprise— the planting of Sunday-schools in ten thousand of its new settlements. It has seemed necessary, therefore, to treat this portion of the history of the Society more fully than the succeeding periods. For eight or ten years that enterprise, with others, was vigorously prosecuted, as has been already described.

Second Period.—In the second period of twenty years, the Society found its missionary funds inadequate to meet its demands. The whole country was financially crippled by the crisis of 1837. Furthermore, the managers also learned from experience that the transient visit of a missionary to start a school was not adequate for its maintenance; that the field of each missionary must be limited so that he could have constant oversight of the schools in his district. This called for increased expenditure at a time when funds were diminished. Thus for the year 1837, the contributions to the Valley Fund, which were the largest missionary gifts, were $10,744, while the contributions to the General Fund were $15,832. But this latter fund was for the general benevolent objects of the Society, and not specially for its missionary work. The managers, however, felt compelled to appropriate sums from this General Fund to sustain its missionaries. This decrease in contributions for mission work continued for several succeeding years, so that for nine or ten years following 1830 the average receipts for the Valley mission work were about $13,000 a year, or, in round numbers, $120,000, one-half of which had been received in the first two years. However, this condition did not discourage the Society. The managers had a large vision which may be fairly indicated by this very remarkable prophecy made as early as 1839:

> Nor is there anything extravagant in the anticipation that at no distant day an uninterrupted line of communication, by steamboat and railroad, will be established over this bright sunset land between the eastern and western world, by way of Australia, Polynesia and the Indian Archipelago; that our news from the Celestial Empire will be borne to us upon the western waters, and thus the whole earth will be encompassed by a settled channel of civilized, peaceful, Christian intercourse.

They had a vision of cataclysms, for they added:

> Revolutions in public sentiment and political institutions, many and mighty, may occur. The Church of the redeemed may be rent, and broken, and tumbled down. If the Lord will, let it be so. . . . To the Bible, as the fountain of truth, a guilty world must still come for light, for peace, for hope.

Other evidence of the realization of their vision was based upon the fundamental principles which had guided the Society, and these they repeatedly restated to be:

> *First*, unity of Christian forces; *Second*, increasing efficiency in religious instruction; *Third*, diffusion of knowledge; *Fourth*, the circulation of moral and religious publications; *Fifth*, a Sunday-school wherever there is a needy population.

During the years of this financial depression the Society was storing up wisdom and strength relating to its mission work for a decided advance as soon as the Lord should open the way. This is fairly indicated by the clear and full statement of the needs of the work and of the country as they saw them in 1843.[1] This was further emphasized by a restatement in 1844 of the origin and original purpose and objects of the Society.[2]

The financial depression decreased the support of all forms of religious effort, and drew attention to the possible overlapping of much of that work, inducing laymen to hint that such overlapping ought to be reduced to a minimum. This

---

[1] *Report*, 1843, p. 5, ff.   [2] *Report*, 1844, pp. 11, 12.

again led the denominational leaders to inquire whether funds were not going from members of their churches to objects not directly in support of the work of their respective denominations.

As the American Sunday-School Union did not form churches, the emphasis in its work was laid upon the broad, evangelical truths of Christianity. The Society avoided presenting the doctrines which divided Christians, teaching mainly those upon which they were united. This course was criticized from the first by certain ecclesiastical leaders. The financial crises and consequent diminishing income simply increased the volume and sharpness of this criticism against the Union. It was even insinuated by some that it was not altogether sound or evangelical in the conduct of its mission work.

In view of these repeated charges against the Society, the Board strongly, clearly and vigorously restated the evangelical basis upon which it was founded and conducted:[1]

> As Christian laymen, belonging to various denominations, we have associated for the purpose of endeavoring to establish Sunday-schools wherever there is a destitute population. . . . We can unite to teach *the truth that Christ taught, and as plainly as he taught it.* For, be it always remembered, that if we differ respecting the true construction of some of "the gracious words that proceeded out of his mouth," we say only just what he said, leaving those who read or hear to judge of his meaning. . . .
> In the doctrines of the supremacy of the inspired Scriptures, as the rule of faith and duty—the lost state of man by nature, and his exposure to endless punishment in a future world—his recovery only by the free, sovereign and sustaining grace of God, through the atonement and merits of a divine Redeemer, and by the influence of the Holy Spirit—the necessity of faith, repentance and holy living, with an open confession of the Saviour before men, and the duty of complying with his ordinances of Baptism and the Lord's Supper—in these doctrines we find the essential and leading truths of the Christian system; in the reception of these doctrines we agree, and with God's help, we endeavour to teach and inculcate them on all whom we properly reach.

This they stated as their guide in all their missionary, as well as other work.

The Society as an Educator.—In financial crises supporters of benevolent schemes inquire more rigidly into how much of

[1] *Report*, 1844, pp. 56, 57.

their gifts go to the direct work intended, and how much to collecting, administration and supervision. The collecting agencies of the Union did not escape criticism in this regard. It was not a new point to the managers of the Society. They had carefully taken it into account many times before attention was called to it by outside parties. The general agents whom they employed as collectors were given broader duties than simply to get money. This they pointed out distinctly by saying that the general agent properly fitted for his work "has favorable opportunities to enforce the great principles of religious training in all its branches and departments, and to urge motives and sanctions which are of universal interest and application." The amount he collected, therefore, was not a just test of his value. If he failed in the broader work assigned to him as an educator, he did not fulfil the design nor the desire of the Board in commissioning him.[1] The objection to this method had been felt nearly a score of years earlier at a meeting of delegates from auxiliaries, held in 1828. A thorough examination of the methods pursued by the Society was made by the delegates, who declared their "approval of the open and undisguised manner in which its affairs had been conducted." Dr. Lyman Beecher, at a large public meeting that year, also stated that the Society's work was "eminently adapted to promote the intellectual and moral culture of the nation—to perpetuate our republican and religious institutions; and to reconcile eminent national prosperity with moral purity and future blessedness."[2]

Literature as an Aid to Missions.—From the first, the Society saw the necessity of combining the equipment of schools with suitable literature and the employment of missionaries. Repeatedly the managers emphasized the necessity of these two kindred means—"building up schools and supplying them with books"—either gratuitously or at reduced rates, in order to make the work efficient.[3] They called attention to the increasing number of places where neither churches nor ministers could be sustained, and stated that in order to supply such places it required a distinct and separate agency, like paid missionaries; and that, to be successful and efficient, the work must be upon the principle of Christian

[1] *Report*, 1845, p. 25.   [2] *Report*, 1846, p. 12.   [3] *Report*, 1848, p. 32.

unity, and to be lasting, it must form the forces in each community into a compact and effective organization like a Sunday-school.[1]

In several closing years of this period (to 1857) the Society emphasized the need of more and better teachers, calling attention also to the development of child life, the rich incidental results of religious instruction, and of beginning that work with the first founding of communities. St. Louis, Chicago, and Cleveland were cited as illustrations of the excellent results of mission work. One year the student missionaries alone organized over 900 new schools in destitute places, and another year nearly 800. They put in circulation in one year 150,000 volumes. Their employment enabled the Society to do a much larger work with a diminished income. When the secretary of the student work resigned in 1856, it was temporarily merged into the regular and permanent missionary service.

The financial stress also hindered the Society in carrying out its supervision of the great districts into which the country had been divided. Moreover, the Society pointed out that the public schools were not keeping pace with the demands of the country, for more than a million of adult freemen in the United States were found to be unable to read or write, and this number was annually increasing. Nor was this ignorance wholly due to foreign immigration. Nearly three-fourths of the number of illiterates were American born and over twenty years of age.[2] This condition increased the difficulty in its mission work.

Missionary Conferences.—To unify the field operations of the Society and give greater efficiency to its missionary service, a convention of the secretaries and missionaries was held in Cincinnati late in 1855. Workers from twelve states and some territories were present to collate and compare their experiences gained on widely separated fields of labor. A number of topics connected with Sunday-school missionary work was discussed, giving new dignity, importance and interest to it. The missionaries themselves found that they were a part of a great system for the evangelization of the youth of our country. This gave them fresh courage and increased confidence, and greater intelligence in pursuing their work. The

---

[1] *Report*, 1848, pp. 49–51.   [2] *Report*, 1855, p. 24.

issionaries were surprised that they belonged to six or more different denominations—a fact which was discovered not by their views of the work, in which all seemed to be in perfect accord, but by a "register" of the various representatives at the convention.

As an indirect result of this convention, the Society was confirmed in a view which it had long entertained respecting one phase of its work: "We have found it better to have one man for the whole year than to have six men for two months each. The expenditure for traveling expenses, stock of books, freight, postage, etc., is much less."[1] As they closed this second period of twenty years the managers, looking back over the Society's history, marked the marvelous increase of territory added to the country—seven sovereign states with 787,000 square miles—and an equally marvelous increase of population, nearly three-fold.[2] No wonder they could not supply Sunday-schools fast enough to keep pace with such a marvelous increase in territory and population! They note also a deluge of poor books and worse literature flooding the country at that date, vastly increasing the obstacles in the way of better results.

This twenty-year period was rich in the development of many hundred faithful, humble, and efficient missionaries. Their names and their achievements fill many volumes of the records of the Society, but their greatest achievements will be known only when the "books are opened" and the awards made by the Great Judge. From among these workers there emerged some Sunday-school leaders of national fame, whose names became a household word; such men as A. W. Corey in the Valley of the Mississippi, B. W. Chidlaw in Ohio, John McCullagh of Kentucky and the South, and Stephen Paxson of Illinois. Nor can the less conspicuous but not less important work of a trained educator—John Adams, LL.D.—be omitted. He devoted nearly ten years of the ripest part of his life to establishing and maintaining Union Sunday-schools in the then needy portion of the state of Illinois. His biographer says that as an educator he had had under his care and inspired over 4,000 students.[3] As a missionary of the American

---

[1] *Report*, 1857, p. 45.   [2] *Ibid.*, p. 8.
[3] Dr. Adams was principal of Phillips Academy, Andover, Massachusetts, for many years and was the father of the Rev. Dr. William Adams of New York.

Sunday-School Union he organized 322 Sunday-schools, havir 2,519 teachers and 16,083 scholars. His presence was a ben diction. He was known and revered over the whole state "Father" Adams. Wherever he went children and grown pe ple crowded round him to look up into his reverent face, hear his simple anecdotes, and receive the books and pape which his old buggy always contained. He was a never-failir source of helpfulness and inspiration to younger missionarie He had a keen eye for character underneath a rough exterio and discovered Stephen Paxson and recommended him as missionary to the American Sunday-School Union.

Another remarkable leader, of a different type, was Lor B. Tousley, "The Children's Orator," whose work is noted another section.

Thus this period of mission work developed men of visic on the field as well as men of vision among the founders an managers of the Society.

Methods of Administration.—The managers of the Unio early perceived that to accomplish the objects they had in vie would require many and varied forms of effort, so many and varied that some division of labor was absolutely necessar Therefore, to secure efficiency, economy, and success som managers were given special oversight of the production an publishing of books, papers, tracts, and literature requisit for Sunday-schools. Other managers studied and mature better methods for organizing, conducting and teaching suc schools and for promoting their formation in villages and com munities throughout the country. Another group of mar agers considered special ways for securing funds in th benevolent work and in the distribution of literature, keepin account of the Society's widening operations.

Thus were developed various special and standing com mittees on publication, business, missions, finance, etc., repre senting some of the principal branches of the operations of th Society. The methods of administration necessarily varie with the changing conditions of the country and with th varied experiences the managers themselves gained in th progress of the work. Effectively to concentrate the effort of Christians upon the promotion of Bible study in our Bib schools required the cultivation of Christian unity and charity

Nor could a Sunday-school be efficient without proper literature. Here, then, was their first work.

Starting with the best equipment they could obtain, they next sought to extend the Sunday-school movement by voluntary effort, by local unions, by circulars, tracts and pamphlets setting forth the advantages of Bible study, and, later, by appointing experienced persons to present the value, objects and methods of Sunday-schools to Christian assemblies in all parts of the country.

The multiplied calls for information from all sides on the methods of forming and conducting Sunday-schools satisfied the managers that trained persons must be secured to give efficiency, even to those workers who were willing to volunteer to organize schools, but knew not how to do it. When such persons were found, they could not give their entire time to this service without support. This led to the employment of agents and missionaries, in some sense experts, who were paid for that service. The experiment began in 1821, but not until March, 1825, did the Board of Managers assign the special oversight of the extension work to a Committee on Missions, as they had already assigned a similar special service to a Committee on Publication.

In 1826 the Board of Officers and Managers appointed a standing Committee on Missions to "seek out persons well qualified for Sunday-school missionaries, whose duty it shall be to visit and establish Sunday-schools, organize Sunday-school unions, and promote the objects of this institution." This committee was to make plain to the missionaries the objects of their appointment, instruct them in their duties, fix their compensation, designate their fields of labor, and report monthly to the Board.[1]

In 1830 the title of this committee was changed to Committee on Missions and Agencies, with five members, and in addition to the duties before recited they were further required "to devise plans and, as far as practicable, execute them with the consent of the Board, for increasing the funds of the Society." They were also to direct "the labors of the General Agent, and appoint all subordinate agents, whose special duty it shall be to raise funds for the benefit of the

[1] *Minutes of the Board*, June, 1826, pp. 82–93. *By-Laws*, 1826 to 1830.

Union. They shall also instruct them in their duties, designate their fields of labor, fix their compensation, and have charge of this department of business."[1]

In 1835 the Committee on Missions and Agencies was discontinued, and its duties were distributed to other committees or transferred to an Executive Committee. This "Executive Committee shall have the control of every department of the Society's business not delegated to any other committee. . . . All letters received and copies of all letters written during the recess [of the Board] shall be laid before the Executive Committee at each meeting, together with the Minute Books papers, etc., of all the standing committees."[2]

In large districts of the country, from 1835 for a time, the missionaries and agents were under some special direction of a local board or agency in those respective districts. Thus there was a Western Agency of the Society at Cincinnati, another in New York, and some elsewhere. A committee of the New York Agency had "in charge all the agents and missionaries appointed by the American Sunday-School Union for this region. They shall superintend the correspondence with them and report to the Board in a condensed form all important and interesting facts which it contains. It shall be their steady aim to procure the establishment of a Sunday school in every common school district within our bounds, and to bring the friends of Zion to a constant and perpetual support of the Sunday-school cause."[3]

But from June, 1835 until 1840 *nominations* of agents and missionaries were made by or through the Executive Committee to the Board, and differences relating to their management and conduct were adjusted in a similar way, when approved by the Board.

The general correspondence of the Society on missions, as on its other affairs, was conducted by the corresponding secretary from the Home Office, aided by Mr. John Hall, who was for a time recording secretary of the Executive Committee and also engaged in revising and editing question books and lessons for the Union.

In 1840 marked changes were made affecting the admin-

[1] *Constitution and By-Laws*, 1830, p. 6.   [2] *Minutes and By-Laws*, June, 1835.
[3] *By-Laws, New York Board of Agency of the American Sunday-School Union*, 1835, p. 9.

stration in mission work. The Executive Committee was discontinued; the two standing committees being then the Committee of Publication and the Committee on Accounts. For ten years or more, from 1840, student and permanent missionaries and agents were nominated to the Society in various ways. Sometimes they appear to have come from a board of agencies in one of the districts where there was such an advisory board in connection with the Union, as in New York, Cincinnati, and elsewhere. Nominations also came through the corresponding secretary in Philadelphia and through the Committee on Publication. Special donations of publications were also made through the same committee until 1844, when a special Committee on Donations was appointed and that became a standing committee in 1846. This committee acted upon all applications for donations of books and reported to the Board. It does not appear to have been charged with nominating or recommending missionaries or agents or directing their labors in any special way other than in the matter of gratuitously distributing publications of the Society.

Early in 1855 the existing division of duties among the managers came up for consideration, and out of a lengthy discussion, continuing through some months, emerged a new adjustment of the administration in mission work. The Committee on Donations was discontinued and a Committee on Missions and Agencies, similar to that appointed in 1835, was revived. It was instructed to "supervise and direct the missionaries and [field] agents," nominate them for appointment and designate their duties and compensation. It was also to make grants of books to Sunday-schools to a limited amount, and to have "the services of two secretaries," viz., "the Corresponding Secretary who shall be ex-officio a member of the Committee, and a Secretary of Missions to be appointed by the Board of Managers."[1]

But in 1858 a fresh examination into collections and expenses of collecting agents induced the managers to abandon "the collecting system *as such*." In consequence of this action, therefore, the title of the committee was changed to "Committee on Missions" early in 1859. The book of in-

[1] *Minutes of the Board*, February to June, 1855.

structions to missionaries was revised as early as July, 185? because of these changes.

But the crushing debt of the Society, elsewhere described (se Finances, p. 320), necessarily hampered and seriously modifie the management in mission work. All the operations of th Society were for some time subject to the sanction of a com mittee of its creditors and a special committee of the Society These committees were in sympathy with the mission wor and endeavored to avoid serious interference with its prosecu tion. Moreover, the diverging views existing among th managers led to criticisms upon the conduct of the missio work, yet all favored its maintenance.

During the struggles, controversies and financial troubles the management in mission work underwent many change in common with all other operations of the Union. Th secretary of missions, the treasurer, editor of periodicals, anc some managers resigned, and new officers and managers wer elected in their places. These changes in the administra tion brought harmony in the Society's councils and increase the confidence of the public in its work.

The division of labor among the managers was readjusted The Committee on Missions was required to "nominate tc the Board all persons who are to be employed in the Mis sionary Department except the secretary of missions," tc designate "their duties and compensations, and direct anc control their labors." The secretary of missions "shall unde the direction of the Committee conduct the correspondenc and superintend all matters relating to the collection o funds for the missionary work of the Society and the labors o all persons employed by the Missionary Department at home and abroad."

The work of the Committee on Missions was supplemented by a special Committee on Finance which later became a standing committee. The duties of this Committee were "to devise and report to the Board such new plans and measures for increasing the Society's funds for missionary purposes as they shall deem expedient and execute and carry out such as the Board may adopt."[1]

The Committee on Missions aimed to conduct the mission

[1] *By-Laws*, 1861, pp. 7, 8; 1867, pp. 7, 8.

ork in accord with what was now clearly the sense of the
anagers—not of necessity to do a bigger work, but to do a
ood work by better methods and with the greatest economy
onsistent with efficiency. In promoting this end they were
ortunate in securing the services, as secretary, of a business
an who had charge also of a successful mission Sunday-
hool. But the breaking out of the Civil War seriously inter-
red not only with the prosecution of the mission work, but
ore seriously with obtaining adequate support for it. Under
iese circumstances the work was maintained only by a con-
ant struggle, and even then there was a succession of disap-
ointments resulting from a yearly excess of expenditures.
he Committee on Missions, with their best efforts, failed to
omply with the requirements of the Board, that "each depart-
ent of work should pay its own expenses."

But this dark and stormy period of the history was not
ithout some sunshine, as will elsewhere appear. The wish
f the managers to have more full information, so as to give
ore intelligent direction to its mission and to other branches
f its operations, was carried out, and culminated in 1880, in
supreme effort to remove the entire indebtedness, and secure
dequate capital for the Society. An Executive Committee,
onsisting of the executive heads of the three branches of its
ork—the editorial secretary (Edwin W. Rice), the treasurer
Richard Ashhurst), and the secretary of missions (Maurice
. Wurts and later Dr. J. M. Crowell)—was placed in charge
f all the business of the Society, which modified in some
spects the administration in mission work, materially in-
reasing and enlarging it. For that committee, in its plan
o remove the debt and increase the capital, proposed a re-
renchment in publications, but no retrenchment or inter-
erence with the current mission work. It further suggested
he full enforcement of the "no debt" policy which had been
epeatedly approved, but never carried out. The Society
herefore authorized the statement that "in receiving funds
o liquidate the debt it was under a pledge hereafter not to
ncur indebtedness." Of course this pledge applied to its
iission work as to all other forms of its work. How the ex-
enses in the mission work could be properly forecasted a year
head had already been pointed out by the chairman of this

Executive Committee (as stated in another section of the history).

"No debt" Policy.—Some feared that the announcement of the "no debt" policy would increase the difficulty of getting contributions to the mission work—a fear which proved to be without foundation. In fact, so far from a decrease, there followed a decided increase of the gifts for this purpose. The records show that in the ten years following the announcement of the "no debt" policy during which the efforts to remove the debt continued and were successful, the contributions to the current mission work more than doubled.

Moreover, the measures proposed by the Executive Committee had the hearty concurrence of Dr. Samuel Ashhurst, chairman of the Committee on Missions for twenty-five years. He declared, "The managers have uniformly held that the work of the Union is one, and that all its operations, whether publication, financial or missionary, were integral parts of one organism, working heartily for a common purpose." This statement was approved by the Society. He further said that it was in harmony with this view that the Executive Committee, consisting of the representative officer from each of the three branches of the Society's operations, was appointed, and added, "The numerous special gifts, amounting within the past ten or fifteen years to the munificent sum of $250,000 or more, have all come from friends in Philadelphia, New York and vicinity, in addition to their gifts to current benevolent work; and these gifts were made after a pledge or clear understanding that the Society would avoid running into debt."[1] The then secretary of missions, Rev. James M. Crowell, D.D., was equally emphatic in his advocacy of these measures.

The work of the Executive Committee from 1880 to 1908 was so important and helpful that the Board decided to add to its standing committees an Executive Committeee consisting of the chairmen of the Committees on Publication, Missions, and Finance, and two managers from the Board. The powers of this Committee were broad: "They shall have, unless otherwise provided, general management and direction of all the Society's affairs, subject to the approval of the Board,

[1] *Report*, 1896, pp. 8, 9.

. . . suggest ways and means whereby its work and usefulness may be increased and developed, . . . require a monthly report from the Committee on Publication, the Committee on Missions, the Committee on Finance, the treasurer, and such other employees as they may deem advisable."[1]

Thus it will be seen that this Executive Committee with its broader scope was charged with the duty of increasing and developing the Society's efficiency in all its operations. The evident purpose of this action is in harmony with the views of the managers uniformly held as before stated, that in all its operations the work of the Union is one.

The tendency of the administration in the present century, in view of the changed conditions of the field and of the character of the Society's work, has been to increase the number of districts into which the United States has been divided, with a superintendent in each district, as more likely to secure greater efficiency and closer supervision. It provides also the means for more definite information with regard to the needs of each district and the progress made in meeting those needs.

Secretary of Missions.—Previous to 1853 the Union had no officer with this title. The missionary correspondence appears to have been in charge of the corresponding secretary, shared for a brief period of the early Executive Committee (1835 to 1840) by John Hall, the secretary of that committee, who acted with the corresponding secretary.

Student missionaries also were employed by a special field or traveling secretary, a position held by the Rev. Wm. E. Boardman and by the Rev. R. B. Westbrook. The Committee of Publication had suggested in 1851 the appointment of a secretary for the Missionary Department—a suggestion which does not appear to have been finally adopted until 1853, when the Rev. J. W. Dulles, D.D., was placed in charge of the missionary correspondence, the corresponding secretary still noting the receipts and expenditures of the Society.[2]

In 1856 the Rev. R. B. Westbrook, D.D., who had served the Society in student and field work, was appointed secretary of missions, which office he held until January, 1861, when he

---

[1] *By-Laws*, 1909, 1910, 1913.
[2] *Minutes*, October, 1851, 1853; *Report*, 1854, p. 23.

was succeeded by Maurice A. Wurts. Since that date the secretary of missions has been ex-officio secretary of the Committee on Missions and under its direction has charge of the correspondence with the missionaries and all matters relating to the labors of persons employed by the Missionary Department. Of course, all such acts are subject to the approval of the Board.

Mr. Wurts continued as secretary until 1881, aided by the Rev. Edwin W. Rice, who was assistant secretary of missions from 1871 for upward of twenty-five years. From 1881, owing to the protracted illness of Secretary Wurts, L. Milton Marsh was acting secretary until after the death of Mr. Wurts in 1883, when the Society chose the Rev. James M. Crowell, D.D., secretary of missions. Dr. Crowell rendered faithful and efficient service for twenty-five years. Jefferson M. Andrews followed in 1908 for a brief period, until his sudden death, and he, in turn, was succeeded (in 1911) by the Rev. George P. Williams, D.D. Thus the Society has been served by six secretaries of missions during the period from 1855 to 1917; the longest service so far rendered being that of the genial Dr. Crowell.

The invested funds of the Union for mission and benevolent work are under the special supervision of the Committee on Finance, which "shall also devise and report to the Board such new plans and measures for increasing the Society's funds as they shall deem expedient, and execute and carry out such as the Board may adopt."[1]

For the decade from 1850 to 1860 it is proper to note that student missionaries often received their commissions from the field or traveling secretary and made their reports to the district agent for the region where they labored. They had little or no correspondence with the home or central office at Philadelphia. The writer of this history well remembers that this was the case in 1854 when he served the Society as student missionary in upper Canada, and also in 1856 when his field of labor was in Wisconsin.

Third Period (1857–1877).—The third twenty-year period (1857 to 1877) was the stormiest in the Society's history. It began in a moral earthquake due to the unfaithfulness of

[1] *By-Laws*, 1913.

a leading and long-trusted secretary. The whole country, also, was swept by a financial tornado threatening the ruin of business and benevolent enterprises, and wrecking the personal plans and hopes of multitudes who were forced to seek ways to extricate themselves. A great temptation came to the secretary, as his personal investments were in peril. "For a third of a century this officer had been entrusted with the general oversight of the Society's business, including its money transactions." [Brief Statement, p. 3.] In this capacity he had charge of the Society's credit. In its earlier years all his transactions were made on a cash basis. "In the course of time," the managers say, "and chiefly on account of the *advances made for the support of missionaries and the gratuitous distribution of books*, it was found necessary to obtain credit."[1] Drafts were drawn on the Union by parties furnishing materials or doing work, which were accepted by this officer, and these drafts were negotiated in the market, the proceeds being returned to the secretary, whose duty it was to turn them over to the treasurer. In the embarrassed condition of his personal affairs here was his temptation. He caused drafts to be issued and no record made of them on the books of the Society, so the proceeds were appropriated to his personal use. "Unqualified confidence was reposed in his integrity" for thirty years, but distrust of his faithfulness was awakened by the maturity of one or two drafts or acceptances in 1857 which did not appear upon the Society's books.[2] An investigation revealed that he had used the Society's credit for private purposes to a very large extent (about $88,000).[3] Although he confessed his wrong and made restitution so far as he was able (about $15,691), yet this did not prevent a partial undermining of confidence in the Society by the public. Fortunately it was not believed to involve the loss of any contributions made to the Society's missionary work. For, in fact, the large sum amounting to over $76,000, which had been already expended in missionary and benevolent work in excess of what had been received from all sources for its support, was the money in peril. To provide for this excess in mission and benevolent work the advances already noted were made, and that, in turn, required the Society to secure credit by the

---

[1] *Report*, 1858, p. 10.   [2] *Report*, 1861, p. 2.   [3] *Report*, 1858, p. 62.

issue of drafts and notes. Thus the managers were enabled to say that, so far as was known, no contributions made by the public for missionary operations, but only the borrowed money to meet the excess, had been lost or perverted. That the institution itself might not seriously suffer, the managers and a few friends "personally assumed the whole of the [supposed] loss ($35,000)[1] which these fraudulent transactions involved."[2] (See further facts under Finances, p. 319.)

The embarrassment to the missionary work was increased by a falling off in benevolent receipts, as compared with the previous year, of over $12,000. The managers expressed great thankfulness that the decrease was no larger, considering the extraordinary derangement of the financial affairs of the country.[3] Less than half of the receipts for the year came from churches, about one-third from individuals, and the remainder from Sunday-schools and the mission fields.

Thus the missionary work of that year was prosecuted "as extensively as the very limited means would justify." The Board proposed to expend in the support of missionaries and in the gratuitous distribution of books "as much money as may be received or pledged for these objects, and no more."[4] In reducing expenses the Union decided to abandon collecting agencies. Serious doubts had arisen respecting the wisdom of this form of securing its funds. "Careful analysis of facts and figures and an obviously increasing dissatisfaction with this plan of raising money for benevolent purposes, led the Society to resolve upon its total abandonment." In taking this action the Board stated that it would be difficult, if not impossible, to secure a more efficient corps of laborers, and the decision had been reached from the conviction that the amount of money received through these agencies would not justify the large discount for expenses.[5]

---

[1] $35,000 was the net actual loss, as *estimated;* thus:

Total spurious obligations		$88,042.27
Taken up by others	$ 4,177.15	
Secured by real estate (McDowell)	33,173.98	
Restitution by Porter	15,691.14	53,042.27
Leaving the actual estimated loss		$35,000.00

The real estate taken as security at $33,173.98 was subsequently sold for $16,908.28. Dissatisfaction in the Board caused some of the subscribers to the $35,000 to be released, so that the Society did not realize the whole amount. Later, these losses were made up in other ways.

[2] *Report,* 1858, p. 12.   [3] *Ibid.,* p. 14.
[4] *Ibid.,* p. 21.   [5] *Report,* 1860, p. 28.

The Society reserved to itself the propriety of employing its secretaries, superintendents, and missionaries to make collections when consistent with their other duties, but this collecting work on their part would be entirely incidental and in addition to their chief duties, so that they were not properly to be regarded as mere collecting agents.[1] This view, however, was not general. *The New York Evangelist* voiced the opinion of some of the people in saying, "The stream of benevolence will not continue to flow without somebody to watch its secret springs. Much of the clamor against agents has been raised by mere selfishness and parsimony. Many who are misers at heart have made an excuse not to give because so much of their contributions would go to agents." But the managers, after carefully considering the matter, put confidence in the Christian public and decided to throw the claims of the Union and its support upon the generosity of the people.

To impress its claims more forcibly at this time it called attention anew to the value of Union Sunday-schools to the churches. It claimed that the Sunday-school was the pioneer of the church, and printed a tract collating evidences in proof of this statement. Thus one minister, a missionary of the Society for twenty years, gave a list of fifty churches that had grown out of Union Sunday-schools organized by himself or his associates. Another reported forty churches following the Union Sunday-schools in his field. And still a third, well qualified to judge from his records, gave it as his opinion that eight-tenths of the churches in the Valley of the Mississippi, organized in the previous fifteen years, had grown out of Sunday-schools first established upon the union principle.

But even if some of the Union schools did not grow into churches, would not the fact of bringing thousands of children under Sunday-school instruction, and leading them to the belief and practice of the duties of religion as held by evangelical denominations be helpful to all denominations and be a great gain to the cause of Christ?[2]

Moreover, in printing these appeals for missionary funds, the Union had repeatedly emphasized the need of money for distributing its literature; for it said, "The missionary and the

[1] *Report*, 1858, p. 19.   *Report*, 1846, p. 24.

living teacher would avail little without the silent teaching of the printed page. The sound of the living voice impresses strongly while it lasts; but it soon dies away on the air. The printed page remains in the house after the missionary and the teacher have gone. . . . It is there to teach, not for an hour on Sunday merely, but all the week through."[1] Impressed with the value of this combined agency, the Society now issued the *Sunday-School Times*, a folio weekly teachers' journal and family paper, similar to *The Sunday-School Journal* of 1831.

The Civil War.—The financial stringency throughout the country forced the Society to study the greatest economy in its missionary and benevolent work and in theory to adopt the policy of "no debt"—a theory which it was not able, unfortunately, at that time to put into practice, but which was done later, as already stated. Among the many obstacles to maintaining a "no debt" policy, besides the temporarily divided views of the managers of the Society itself, was the tense anxiety and bitter feeling between the North and the South arising out of the existence of slavery. So wide was the difference, and so tense was this strain, that several of the Southern States seceded from the Union and formed the Confederacy. This brought on the terrible and bloody Civil War between the North and the South. All communication between the two sections (the states that remained in the Union and the states that formed the Confederacy) was suspended or destroyed, the Society's missionaries were cut off from the home office, and their work rendered impossible in the South. Havoc, if not impending ruin, also threatened all the Society's activities in the North. It called for wisdom, patience, and great self-sacrifice to readjust the mission work, even throughout the Northern states, under the devastating and destructive war spirit which swept over the whole country.

It was obvious at once that the homes throughout the country from which the stalwart young men had gone, leaving women, and children, and dependents behind, would need the support and consolations of the gospel more than ever before. The little churches throughout the country were sadly crippled and often compelled to intermit services.

[1] *Report*, 1859, p. 48.

Thus immense responsibilities were thrown upon the missionaries of the American Sunday-School Union. The calls for their services to keep alive and encourage these little centers of religious life throughout the country were multiplied many fold. Not a few of these missionaries were Christian patriots and felt constrained to respond to the call of the North to save the Union, and in the South to defend the Confederacy as citizens of that section All the resources of the country were strained to meet the demands and emergencies created by the war. Contributions which had been counted as certain for the support of mission work suddenly ceased, or were greatly diminished. The Society could not appoint new missionaries; it could not pay those already in commission. The managers trembled as pay-day approached.

Self-Denial of Workers.—But tense as was their strain, their abiding faith in God supported them in the gigantic work of bringing the moral and religious forces to bear upon the problem before them. They said, "This grand principle must rule from the cradle to the grave." Their hopefulness was well expressed in this sentence, "Had we been assured at the beginning of the fiscal year [1862] that our sales and contributions would be half what they were in the preceding year, we should have been relieved of much anxiety, but we have done far better than that—the diminution of our sales being only about thirty per cent. and of our contributions twenty-three per cent." They ascribed this result to the inherent vigor of the institution, to the depth and extent of the good will of the public, and to their implicit trust in God that he would put it into the hearts of his people to supply their wants. They did not minimize the obstacles. These came in a three-fold form: (1) A large diminution of the accustomed receipts; (2) an embarrassment from inability to meet the wants of destitute neighborhoods; (3) both these embarrassments grew largely out of the unhappy strife desolating the land. In two states alone, where the Society had 3,000 to ,000 schools, contending armies swept hither and thither, dissipating many and destroying their libraries.

The call for missionary service was so urgent that the missionaries would not allow the Society for a moment to entertain the idea of abandoning the fields. They said, "The work must go forward"; "We will bear each other's burdens"; "If a further reduction becomes absolutely necessary, make it"; "We will go without tea, coffee and other luxuries."

The Society appealed to Sunday-schools and had particular gratification in the generous sympathy and the liberal donations from them, as well as from societies, churches and individuals. Equally gratifying was the development of new workers on the field. The war had depopulated many of the rural districts of their male inhabitants. One missionary from Wisconsin wrote, "In a large number of the schools visited there was not a male officer or teacher—all having gone to serve their country. Devoted women have engaged to supply their places. Indeed, you rarely pass a farm where noble women are not engaged both indoors and out in supplying the place of men who have gone to the war."[1]

In the face of these terrible and bloody struggles, the managers of the Society and its workers had an abiding trust in Almighty God, as expressed in these terms:

"Clouds and darkness have at times surrounded us, but now, as we review the way wherein he has led us, we can truly say, 'Hitherto hath the Lord helped us.' "[2] The managers and friends of the Society were encouraged by the cheering reports which came from the soldiers' camps—from the Confederate warriors in grey, as well as from the Union soldiers in blue. In numberless cases, before the battle, the soldiers in these two opposing armies turned their thoughts toward the faith which they had learned in the little country Sunday-schools. Missionary Childlaw, who became a chaplain, testified:

> This experience afforded me a new standpoint to observe the value of early religious education, and the power of the Sunday-school with its divine textbook, its religious literature, and sound oral instruction in affording that education. . . . Nearly every Sunday-school in the loyal states has its representatives on the tented fields of our country. The religious element in the army is to a very great extent the exponent of Sunday-school labor and training. . . . The men that gather around the camp-fires at the close of the day and sing the songs of Zion were taught to sing in the Sunday-school; and the men who love the Bible, read, mark and learn its precious truths, had studied the heavenly tactics in the Bible school at home. The men who encourage and co-operate with the chaplain, . . . wait upon God in the camp prayer-meeting, and whose godly lives honor

[1] *Reports*, 1862, 1863, p. 5.   [2] *Report*, 1863, p. 23.

the glorious Gospel of the Son of God, have been blessed with early religious training, and most of them in the Sunday-school.[1]

Superintendent John McCullagh, whose home and head-quarters were in Kentucky, a border state swept alternately by Confederate and Union armies, tried to carry on his Sunday-school work "as though peace were reigning." The bitter hate and strife between the opposing parties was deadly; neighbors and even members of the same family, on opposite sides, suspected each other of being spies—and the spy received no mercy. McCullagh's tact and wisdom retained the goodwill of some in both armies. He was a personal friend of leading officers, Confederate as well as Union. This personal acquaintance saved him from several serious mishaps in passing through the lines of the contending armies.

A missionary was caught and carried under guard to General Morgan. There he was sharply questioned and his story of proposing to found a Sunday-school was not believed until he showed a letter, signed by the Society's secretary and countersigned by John McCullagh. Morgan recognized the signature as that of his friend McCullagh, but compelled the missionary to sing, which he did as best he could with officers and rough soldiers in groups leaning on their rifles itching to shoot him. But the singing convinced General Morgan, and he cried out, "This man is all right. Let him go." So marked was this experience during the Civil War, that on the border, Christian men on both sides regarded the American Sunday-School Union as a link binding the North and South.

Rehabilitation.—When the war closed the Southern States, impoverished and ruined, were in need of help of every kind. Conditions were sad enough in the North, but, following those dark days, it would be impossible to describe the state of things in the South. The freeing of 4,000,000 slaves added to the general desolate condition, while there was imperative need for the restoration of churches and schools destroyed by the war. The Society was called on to furnish literature by the 10,000 volumes to the people, many of whom were homeless, heart-sick, and hungry for the bread of life.

[1] *Report*, 1864, pp. 19, 20.

The Society responded as best it could to these calls. Its gratuitous distribution of literature for the five years immediately following the war amounted to over $71,000, besides gifts to auxiliaries of upward of $20,000, and these calls continued with scarcely any diminution for an entire decade (1865 to 1875). With the large amount previously overdrawn in its mission work, the reader will wonder how the Society was enabled to meet these demands. For just previous to the war it had been under a heavy strain to satisfy its creditors. Indirectly, the war was a blessing in disguise, for it brought about "the suspension of payments," so that all creditors deferred collecting their claims and were exceedingly patient with the debtor class. Moreover, the call for the Society's literature during the war to supply the soldiers in camps and hospitals was unexpectedly large, while the generosity of the people scarcely knew any bounds in providing comforts for the soldiers. Thus the sales for two years, ending with March, 1865, were nearly double those of the previous two years. A large proportion of these sales was evidently to supply the soldiers in camps and hospitals. This gave the Society more ready money, though the profits on the books were small. The Society thus found it possible to meet its obligations for large interest on its bonds and loans made because of the excessive expenditure before the war, amounting in four years to over $30,000. It was also able to make an appropriation of about $100,000 in literature through its auxiliaries, and to sustain its missionaries, although the entire sum donated in legacies for ten years (1855 to 1865) was but little more than $530,000, of which $100,000 was for life memberships subject to yearly grants of literature.

It is almost impossible to conceive of the disheartening and desolating conditions which war brings unless one has actually passed through the experience. Thousands of Sunday-schools, if not broken up, were weakened by the constant loss of superintendents and teachers. Thus a report says, "in many cases not a single male teacher has been left." Often a superintendent was elected to supply the place of one gone to the war, when, in a few weeks, the post was again vacant from the same cause. Then there was an insufficient supply of library books and literature, the books having been read and re-read until the scholars were tired of them. The want of papers and elementary books, with no means to procure them, broke all hope of further effort; then the missionary, coming with a donation of needed books and papers and words of encouragement, infused new life into the school. "Without this assistance many of these schools would not be in existence," and "this is a success for which we have reason devoutly to thank God."[1]

Chicago Conference.—One of the most inspiring events in the history of the Society during this period following the war, was the convention of missionaries and workers held by the authority of the Board of Managers in Chicago in November, 1866. Sixty missionaries from twenty-two states were present. The deliberations were characterized by great earnestness, for they came together to tell what they knew, what they had experienced, and what God had given them to see and to understand concerning the progress of the Kingdom and the blessings of the gospel in the country.

It was particularly helpful in promoting efficiency in the mission work and in cheering the workers as they considered the three-fold character of the operations of the Society— its work, its field, and its ways of working. They were profoundly impressed that its work was of God; that its field was the entire country. This impression was voiced by one of its oldest missionaries, "O God! write it in letters of light on our hearts that we may plant the Sabbath-school in every destitute neighborhood, and that all our children may be taught of the Lord."

Teacher Training.—Side by side with the reconstruction of Sunday-schools, North and South, after the war, sprang up also a new emphasis upon the training of teachers for giving more efficient instruction. There was a special need for this immediately after the war because of the lack of competent teachers, or any teachers at all. Thus Sunday-school institutes and normal classes had been started in various parts of the land, East and West, as elsewhere noted in this history. These temporary schools of instruction for teachers were widespread and very popular during the last half of this period (1867 to 1877).

[1] *Report*, 1863, pp. 6, 7.

Furthermore, workers in the field were also impressed with the necessity for carefully ascertaining the facts respecting their fields in order to plan and work more efficiently. This led to a simultaneous canvass or survey of fields in several districts by townships and counties, as in New England and Pennsylvania and in the Middle West. Each set of workers was inspired to this service without knowing that those in other fields were doing the same. Some remarkable discoveries were made by these careful surveys. Thus in New England, in four counties supposed to be fully supplied, three townships were found absolutely without any Sunday-school and twenty townships with only one in each. In one-third of all the towns there was a lack of religious instruction—two-thirds of the children not being in Sunday-school. In Pennsylvania, a survey of five counties revealed three-fifths of all those between five and twenty years of age out of Sunday-school all the year. In a survey in the Northwest, in eight counties, some of the best in Wisconsin and Minnesota, three townships having 4,000 population were found without any Sunday-school.[1]

This systematic and careful information respecting the conditions of the country produced immediate improvement in missionary work. The marked gains reported from year to year would have been much more hopeful had they included the number of conversions, churches grown out of schools, church buildings erected, and other influences for the betterment of communities, difficult to put into statistics.

Evidently the management was not frightened by the large increase of expenses in mission work, for, in addition to the indebtedness the Society was carrying on account of previous expenditures and to the interest it was paying on loans made therefor, a new excess of missionary expenditure was reported in 1868 of over $29,000, and in the following two years of over $21,000 more, expended in that branch of its service above what was received from the public.

Their unbounded faith was such that these overdrafts in benevolent work in addition to their great indebtedness, did not discourage them from fostering an agency for foreign work—that is, the planting of Sunday-schools in Europe—

Reports, 1864, pp. 35–38; 1866, pp. 9–11, 46; 1868, pp. 31–34.

through Vice-President Albert Woodruff.[1] Their chief purpose, however, was "to bring all the children of our country to Christianity by teaching them His Word." Indeed, they were sure that could they attain to this end, they would "accomplish various and important subordinate ends." They hoped to aid in making good citizens, but chiefly good Christians, that they may "glorify God and enjoy him forever."[2]

This pushing forward in the face of accumulated debt will not be so great a marvel when we recall how the managers believed the work was of God, that his grace was working in them and prompted them to labor for him, and that his Spirit imparted the wise and understanding heart. They were obeying the command, "Go, teach."[3]

Another important event in the history of missionary work in the latter part of this twenty-year period was a successful effort to bring the expenses in missionary work substantially within the Society's expected income year by year. Frequent but unavailing efforts to do this had been made before. The necessary enlargement of the mission work following the war increased the labors of the secretary of missions. These were further multiplied by the desire and real necessity for fuller information in respect to the results of the mission work, not only in a careful record of schools founded and aided, but also in other direct results, such as the number of Christian conversions in those schools, the number of churches growing out of them, and the families supplied with gospel and Christian literature.

A Trained Helper.—Properly to gather and classify this information and otherwise to aid in secretarial work in Philadelphia, it was deemed wise to look for some person having a practical missionary experience in the field, which had not fallen to the lot of the secretary. Moreover, the Society required an experienced and competent person as assistant in editing the periodicals, and here again it was thought that one with a practical knowledge of the mission field would be valuable. The choice fell upon one who had been in the Society's mission work in the Northwest for over ten years, and who had also been successively on an editorial committee, publish-

---

[1] *Reports*, 1870, p. 72; 1875, p. 30.   [2] *Report*, 1870, p. 75.   [3] *Report*, 1872, p. 4.

ing first a local denominational paper, and later a similar journal representing Sunday-school and Christian association work. This was the Rev. Edwin W. Rice, then superintendent of the Society's work in Wisconsin and Minnesota. He was called to Philadelphia in the double position of assistant secretary of missions and assistant editor of periodicals. Greatly to his surprise the first work assigned him, soon after reaching Philadelphia, was to solve the problem of why the Society had closed its work with a deficit, year by year, almost uniformly for the past sixty odd years. Some of those who were interested in gathering the funds for this work thought there must be "a large leak," but no leak was known or could be discovered.

It was said that only as many missionaries were reappointed at the beginning of each year as the pledges for the support of the missionary work would warrant. Whenever new gifts in excess of these pledges were made, new workers were appointed. Yet a yearly deficit occurred. From his experience in his own district along these lines the assistant secretary suspected that the deficit was probably due to the pledges never being fully redeemed in cash. A careful comparison of these pledges with the receipts thereon, year by year for five years, proved that from one cause or another only about 75 to 80 per cent. of these pledges were really paid, causing a deficit varying from $10,000 and upward a year. As it was found easier for those presenting the claims of the Society to gain money for new work rather than for making up a deficit, it was decided that hereafter missionaries should be appointed only up to about 80 per cent. of the pledges in each field.

As this was based on the expenditures and receipts, not for one year but for a series of years, indicating whether the trend was toward an increase or a decrease of funds, it was as safe a basis for projecting the work of any year as are the tables of life insurance companies. The plan was sharply discussed and disputed for a time, but was finally adopted, and worked to the entire satisfaction of the managers.

During this period greater care was taken to secure and preserve more accurate reports in regard to the mission work, in respect to the schools formed and aided, the families provided with the Scriptures and gospel literature, conversions, and churches resulting from the work.

Secretaries Wurts and Rice carefully computed some results of the mission work of the American Sunday-School Union for the half century from 1824 to 1874. Their computation was based upon the written, as well as the printed reports, so far as they were accessible. They found that for some years, from 1817 to 1824 and 1839 to 1845 inclusive, no accurate record of schools founded by the Union had been preserved. For the remaining forty-three years to March 1, 1844, there had been new schools organized, 57,799; with teachers, 386,242; and pupils, 2,545,787. Computing the seven years (1839–1845 inclusive) at the average of five hundred schools per annum, with six teachers and thirty scholars in each school—which was far below the average of the preceding and the following years—and adding this to the previous statistics, the total result to 1874 was: new schools organized, 61,299; teachers, 407,242; pupils, 2,650,787.[1] Besides this the records showed that the Society had accomplished a vast work by reviving and aiding schools with literature in 87,291 cases, with a membership of 647,959 teachers and 4,842,768 pupils. The amount expended in missionary operations from 1824 to 1874 was $2,133,264.13, of which about $517,000 was for literature to needy schools and families. The total value of the Society's literature circulated by sale and donation for those years was computed at about $6,000,000.

A Jubilee.—In 1874 the Society had a Jubilee Anniversary, it being the fiftieth year of its operations under its present name—the American Sunday-School Union. Besides the celebration in Philadelphia, a special Jubilee Missionary Meeting was held in New York, in the Broadway Tabernacle Church, at which Vice-President George H. Stuart presided, and some of the missionaries from the field gave thrilling accounts of the remarkable work which they had been enabled to do. Among them were Stephen Paxson, F. G. Ensign, John McCullagh, Martin B. Lewis and B. W. Chidlaw.

The chairman noted some personal incidents in presenting

[1] To this result must be added the records of schools from 1817 to 1824. The Sunday and Adult School Union reported, in connection with its auxiliaries, 723 schools, with 7,300 teachers and 46,619 "learners." It also reported fourteen schools in Philadelphia not in connection with the Union, containing 162 teachers and 1,230 "learners." (*Seventh Report*, Sunday and Adult School Union, pp. 72 and 91.)

these pioneer missionaries to the audience as illustrating the marvelous grace of God. Thus, Mr. Paxson was spoken of as a man of strong characteristics, a hatter, who earlier in life gave part of his time to the teaching of dancing in primitive Western neighborhoods. But, brought into Sunday-school by his daughter and accepting the Saviour, under divine grace, the way was opened to him for the great work of gathering thousands of children into Bible schools. Of Mr. Lewis it was announced that he was first awakened and finally converted to the truth through a lay sermon, the preacher of which was a vice-president, Hon. William E. Dodge, then on the platform and privileged to hear a good report from the convert. And Mr. McCullagh was spoken of as a pupil of Thomas Chalmers, and a veteran Scotch Sunday-school missionary from the South, who had uninterruptedly pursued his work even during the Civil War.

Thus it will be seen that the severe experiences of this stormy period (1857 to 1877) were not without compensating blessings. The storms helped to clear the air and gave opportunity for the reconstruction of the missionary work especially, upon an improved basis with more efficient methods. The struggles and the storms of this period were also a severe test of the sublime faith of the managers that the work was of God, and that he was leading them by a way they knew not. Confronted again and again by obstacles that to the business mind spelled ruin, and over which there seemed no way even to the large vision of the managers (except the way of faith), providential deliverances, marvelous even in their eyes, unexpectedly appeared, so that the Society came out into an open and larger field of service year by year.

National Leaders.—Among Sunday-school workers in the Society who attained national fame in this period was Henry Clay Trumbull. His varied activities began in revealing and supplying the need of Sunday-school mission work in the New England States. He was a self-sacrificing and successful bearer of the gospel as chaplain to the soldiers. He attained national and world-wide reputation as Normal Secretary by stimulating to great activity in teacher training, by contributing widely and efficiently to the success of the National

Sunday-School Conventions, and by advocating the Uniform Sunday-School Lesson system.

Three of the Society's representatives mentioned in the former period—B. W. Chidlaw, Stephen Paxson and John McCullagh—continued to be recognized as national representatives of the Society, and to guide in its counsels during this period with singular fidelity and success. Nor should the eminent services of Richard G. Pardee, representing the Society's largest auxiliary (the New York Sunday-School Union), be passed without mention of his recognized nation-wide service in Sunday-school institutes and teacher training. His labors extended over most of this period of the Society's history.

Fourth Period.—The fourth period of the Union's history (1877 to 1897) was remarkable for a successful struggle to pay its debts and provide an adequate capital. It was conspicuous for a steady and vigorous growth in its missionary work. Moreover, it was a period in which marvelous progress was made in promoting the spirit of co-operation among all Christians in extending the Kingdom of God.

The far-reaching influence of the International Uniform Lessons in producing this result amazed and delighted the Christian world. This system of uniform Bible study was wide-spread, general, and more thorough than any the world had ever seen. It put emphasis upon the fundamental truths of our common Christianity, and not upon its differences. It exalted the essentials rather than the non-essentials in Christian doctrine. Thus it led Christians to perceive the spirit of Christian unity and of brotherhood which should be possessed by Christ's disciples. Furthermore, this Bible study stimulated, if it did not create, a new era in biblical scholarship and criticism in which the foundations of Christian truth were submitted to searching examination. Never before in the history of Christianity had there been such a concentration of learning, scholarship, and criticism upon the Christian's great textbook, the Bible. The Bible was thrown into the crucible of criticism, to discover any possible particle or bit of alloy, and to separate it from what was thought to be pure divine revelation. Many of the faithful looked upon this criticism as exceedingly destructive, tending to undermine confidence in God's word. To others it seemed to reveal anew the strength, the purity, and the wisdom of God in that revelation

Of the remarkable popularity of the Uniform System of Bible Study of 1872 and later, and of its concentrating the scholarship of the world upon the Bible and promoting a spirit of Christianity, special mention is made in another section of this history. The two events that immediately concern the missionary work of the Society in this period are: (1) The struggle to pay its debts and provide a suitable capital; (2) the remarkable enlargement and vigorous growth of that work. To the record of these events we now address ourselves.

In consequence of the united researches and suggestions of Secretaries Wurts and Rice, the Society introduced improved methods of administration, and a more complete system of reporting and recording the results of missionary labors. For several years, a careful analysis of the resources, expenditures, and results of mission work had been made, year by year, so that the Society was enabled to forecast with reasonable certitude the probable amount of contributions to be expected, and to avoid excess of expenditures in that work, thus placing the Society upon a more healthful financial basis.[1]

While the burden of suggesting and executing the plan for extinguishing the debt and providing adequate capital fell chiefly upon Dr. Rice, as chairman of the Executive Committee, Dr. Crowell, the secretary of missions (after the death of Mr. Wurts), contributed in large measure to its success by his wisdom and efficient co-operation. His familiarity with the conduct of that work, combined with the field experience of the assistant secretary—who was now the editor and chairman of that committee—enabled the Society to carry out this financial campaign, not only without interfering with the current receipts for the support of its mission work, but in such a manner as even largely to increase them.

The way was providentially paved for this effort by a bequest of $100,000 from the John C. Green estate in 1877. The disposition of much of this estate was committed to legatees. They were induced to make this bequest to the

[1] *Report*, 1882, pp. 72, 73.

Union because of the improved system of administration of that work and a wider collation of its results which was presented to them through Robert Lenox Kennedy. In behalf of the legatees, he made this gift on condition that five-sixths of the income should be devoted to the support of missionaries and to the furnishing of the schools they should found, and one-sixth to aid in procuring Sunday-school literature of the highest order of merit germane to the objects of the American Sunday-School Union.

The effort to liquidate the indebtedness and provide capital continued for about fifteen years, as elsewhere narrated. That special appeals for this purpose had contributed toward the increase of current receipts for missionary work was evident, as those receipts more than doubled during that period. Large givers investigated the great work the Society was doing and decided that it was worthy of their largest gifts. Alexander Brown, the first contributor to the debt by a gift of $25,000, soon after added $15,000 more to found the "Raikes Fund," the income of which is used in missionary work.

Thus the splendid work the American Sunday-School Union was accomplishing in the religious education of those in the otherwise neglected districts of our country commanded the respect and support of large givers as never before. The further fact that the Society proposed to carry forward its work on the "no debt" policy also strongly appealed to Christian philanthropists who were interested in large financial enterprises.

The Union Sunday-School a Handmaid of the Church.— The managers stated anew the great purpose of the American Sunday-School Union. As the agent of all the churches, its primary aim was and is to proclaim salvation and to promote the betterment of the thousands of places in the country, unreached by the local church. Fresh surveys brought out needy fields of amazing magnitude in this work. Following the war, there were millions of freedmen, seventy per cent. of whom were illiterate, to be educated in morals and religion. An immense population of mountaineers or highlanders in the South was also discovered who had been hitherto neglected, and sadly needed the gospel. Vast regions once occupied by Indians were being opened for settlement at a rate before unknown. It was reckoned that 40,000 settlers entered Oklahoma in one day.[1] The calls from the Pacific Coast for a united effort to present the gospel to communities there were multiplied. Hundreds of settlers on islands and jutting lands along the Atlantic Coast were found absolutely without any religious services whatever, and to these a "Coast Island Mission" was maintained for several years.[2] The migrations from the older to the newer and more attractive regions of the West caused rural churches to be closed and abandoned—over 1,000 such churches were reported in New England, and a larger number in some of the states of the Middle West. This opened another large field for united effort by the American Sunday-School Union.

Meanwhile the nation's wealth was increasing by leaps and bounds. But religion occupied neither the foremost nor the middlemost, but the hindmost place. The conditions required an agency which expressed the united spirit and forces of all the churches to make an impression upon the materialism of the age, in its mad pursuit of wealth. Corporations and trusts for gain grew to giant proportions, but none looked for great, federated, religious trusts. The little company of Sunday-school missionaries was appalled, but not disheartened, by this piling up of vast fields of labor. They believed the work was of God, and that he would provide. Their singular faith and courage, and their hopefulness in efforts to concentrate all Christians and philanthropists upon their work, inspired a resolution by the managers, in 1884, "to establish and maintain a Sunday-school in every needy community in the vast territory from the eastern base of the Rocky Mountains to the Pacific."[3]

This large faith for an immense task commanded the attention of the secular press throughout the country. In the Middle West, *The Chicago Tribune* declared that the Union's successes were "a volume of argument for the unity of Christian work. The real results in the conflicts with the devil and his numerous and industrious agents must be accomplished by these union societies, which work outside the interests of any particular denomination."

The New York Tribune went further in declaring that "the

[1] *Report*, 1893, p. 11.　　[2] *Report*, 1882, p. 68.　　[3] *Report*, 1884, p. 7.

hearty work of the American Sunday-School Union for one year, in striving to train little children into a truthful manhood, into temperate devout servants of Christ, has accomplished more actual good in the world, and has helped the progress of mankind upward, higher than all the doctrinal squabbles or fires kindled against heresy since time began."[1]

From time to time other journals gave similar testimony, more weighty because they were located in the region where the largest work of the Society had been accomplished. Moreover, the Society was, in the main, successful in maintaining the "no debt" policy. Repeatedly its annual reports note a prospective shrinking in income because of the financial depression in the country, but also note corresponding economy or retrenchment in expenditures. While they continued to emphasize the value of reaching destitute settlements by new organizations, they attached great importance to sustaining and strengthening those that had already been formed.

Sunday-School Evangelism.—Another leading feature was increased activity in evangelistic campaigns in winter. A marked gain in this direction began early in this period.[2] Simultaneously with this, greater diligence was also given to searching out families in districts remote from churches and unreached by religious influences, and to providing them with tracts and religious literature. Thus the importance of this as a mission agency was strongly emphasized over and over again.[3] The missionary work of the Society grew, in this way, strongly *intensive* as well as *extensive*, looking to the efficiency of each existing school as well as to the organizing of new schools in communities.

This increased method of *intensive* work speedily bore rich fruit. The missionaries began to report hundreds and thousands of conversions, so that those actually reported were 5,000, 8,000, 10,000 a year, with mention of multitudes of places where those who confessed Christ were neither numbered nor reported, so that it is quite safe to say that from 10,000 to 20,000 a year were led to confess Christ in the rural communities where the Union schools were the chief agency

---

[1] *Report*, 1879, p. 3, cover.   [2] *Report*, 1878, p. 17.
[3] *Reports*, 1881, pp. 8–13; 1884, p. 58; 1890, p. 6; 1894, p. 6.

for proclaiming the gospel. As a natural result, likewise
churches of different denominations also began to be reported
following these evangelistic campaigns. (Appendix, p. 474.)

Bible Supply.—The United States Census of 1880 reported
about 10,000,000 families in the nation. From a wide survey by missionaries and others, it appeared that one family
in every thirty was without a Bible, four out of five being
without a library or without even half a dozen religious
books. This survey was one of the incentives for the adoption
of the resolution (1884) already given. The great number of
Christian women active as teachers in Sunday-schools, and
their deep interest in training the children, caused the managers to suggest also that to no other society would an auxiliary women's organization be more appropriate than to the
American Sunday-School Union.[1]

Story of Mag.—The serious consequence of neglecting one
little girl was strangely enough placed in the same report.
The story of "Mag, the Mother of Criminals," forcibly illustrates that "an ounce of prevention is better than a pound of
cure." Mag had no education, no home, but became the
mother of a long line of criminals and paupers. In seventy-
five years her descendants increased to the number of about
1,200, of whom 80 were paupers, 140 criminals, and the entire
family was submerged in pauperism, crime and insanity.
The neglect of that one little girl cost the state of New York
upward of $1,308,000—a sum then said to be sufficient to
establish about 65,000 Union Bible schools!

Pastoral Service.—The gain resulting from the increased attention to intensive mission work is further indicated by the
fact that while the number of missionaries employed was
scarcely doubled in this period (1877 to 1897), the number of
families reached by pastoral visits of the missionaries for religious influence was increased over six-fold. The average
number of families annually reached in the first five years of
this period was about 16,000, while in the last five years it
was about 95,000.

Moreover, during this period, special donations of the
Society's literature were made in particular fields not included in missionary reports. Students depending upon

[1] *Report*, 1883, p. 44.

their own earnings for their education in colleges and theological schools were granted over 20,000 volumes in one year during this period, and 28,000 volumes in another year; besides 38,000 volumes given to supply hospitals, prisons, United States life-saving stations, and forts.[1] Special evangelistic, winter campaigns were also conspicuous modes of missionary effort in this period. Communities unreached by the churches were found needing this form of effort, and multitudes of such places were visited with showers of blessing.[2]

In consequence of these evangelistic campaigns, the Society began to take *special* note of the churches of various denominations which followed its Sunday-school efforts. But, as in the reports of conversions, there were multitudes of instances unreported except in a very general way, and which could not be enrolled in any statistical table. Those that were reported were significant as indicating the increased efficiency of the religious work done by the Society. Thus in 1893, 186 churches were noted as following its schools; in 1894, 105 churches followed in one district; in 1895, 117 churches were reported; and in 1896, 117 churches. These reports show conclusively that all evangelical denominations were reaping the harvest sown by the American Sunday-School Union, although the Society did not specially undertake to organize churches of any denomination.

House-to-House Work.—Those whose homes are within the sound of the church bell which calls them to service four or five times a week can hardly realize what the pastoral visit of the Sunday-school missionary means to homes where the church bell is never heard, and church services are too far away to be attended. Some in these families rarely hear a sermon or attend a church service from one year's end to another and lose all desire for the comforts of the gospel except when sickness or death enters the home, and many children have never heard a prayer. To these isolated and secluded souls the Sunday-school missionary brings the message of the gospel and the sense of the nearness of God to them, and leaves an appropriate book or tract to remind them of his visit and his message after he has gone.

[1] *Reports*, 1884, p. 58; 1894, pp. 5, 6; 1891.   [2] *Reports*, 1878, p. 17; 1893, p. 5, etc.

To many such homes, far away from the regular services and influences of the church, such a missionary visit is a benediction, like the coming of an angel of the Lord. When w think that well-nigh 100,000 such homes were reached ever year in this period and nearly 200,000 yearly in the nex period, and that in each of these homes there were from two to ten souls, so that each year from 500,000 to 1,000,000 individuals received a *personal* message of the gospel and th *personal* call to God, the blessed influence of such a service can only be estimated by the recording angel above. If th Union Sunday-school missionaries performed no other service than this, it would be well worth the cost of their time and service.

Briefly, then, the special features characterizing the work o this period were:

(1) Paying the Union's debt of $266,000 and beginning to secure funds, the income of which might tide the Society's work over years of financial depression or other emergencies.

(2) The successful application of the "no debt" policy.

(3) Increased attention to intensive as well as extensive mission work, and carrying the personal message of the gospel to secluded homes.

(4) Increased evangelistic campaigns in winter, resulting in rich harvests of souls brought to Christ.

(5) A wider recognition of Union mission work by Christians of all faiths, their larger gifts, and their greater sympathy and prayers for its success.

SKETCHES OF PROMINENT WORKERS

Benjamin Williams Chidlaw, D.D. (1811–1892), **Missionary and Superintendent** (1836–1892).

Early in the last century a little Welsh boy with his father embarked on a sailing vessel for America, "The land o apples." The impulsive young lad was eager to make the journey, for one day his father had held a handkerchief to ar eastern breeze and said, "A fair wind now to take people to America, where there is no king, no tithes; where poor people can get farms, and apples abound." After forty-seven days on the ocean, they worked their way by sloop up the Hudson, westward by wagon, keel boat and steamboat to Ohio, settling in a log cabin in the wilderness. The father soon died from fever. The brave lad hewed out a home in the woods for his mother, and with his axe chopped his way in the backwoods to a college education, graduating at Miami University in 1833, then studying theology at Oxford (Ohio) under Dr. J. W. Scott, the father-in-law of President Benjamin Harrison.

He revisited his native land to perfect himself in the Welsh language and returned to enter upon evangelistic tours, preaching in both Welsh and English, besides having charge of a church near his home. In January, 1836, he spent a week among the Welsh of Cincinnati. Here he met B. J. Seward and A. W. Corey, who proposed that he give one-fourth of his time as a missionary to the American Sunday-School Union. His commission was signed by John Hall, later of Trenton. In 1844 he resigned the pastorate and gave his whole time thereafter to Sunday-school work, in the service of the Union, until his death.

His magnetism and Welsh fire kindled inspiration wherever he went. His name became a household word in the valley of the Ohio, and familiar to many Christian homes in America and England. His refined manners, his tender sensibilities, his quick perception, and his warm heart, added to his fervency in speech, made him an orator of unusual power. He discharged his well-rounded sentences with an electric force that thrilled his audience. His long and varied career gave him abundant illustrations, and his sincerity in the service of Christ led him not only to improve every opportunity to plead the cause of the Master, but to do it with energy, fervency and with a vigor which astonished his associates.

For years he traveled up and down the valleys of the Ohio and the Mississippi, gathering children for Bible study, preaching, calling at homes, and in every way persuading the scattered people in new communities to live the better life, loyal to Christ. Born of the Spirit and so far God-inspired, his swift soul-inspiring story of Christ and of salvation held his hearers spellbound and swayed his audiences with unwonted power. It mattered not whether he was speaking in his mother tongue to his countrymen from Wales, or in the acquired tongue of his adopted land, to backwoods' crowds or to cultured city audiences in the centers of wealth and refinement; all alike bowed before his persuasive pleading and his fervid eloquence.

He was always a popular and conspicuous speaker at Sunday-school celebrations and conventions in America and a welcome representative of the Union at the Raikes' Centenary in London, 1880, and at the World's Sunday-School Convention in 1889. During the Civil War he was not only missionary but chaplain in the army, rendering efficient service in the Sanitary and Christian Commissions. He often thrilled audiences or melted them to tears as he told of the tragic incidents of the battlefield.

Perhaps the greatest effort of his life was at the last annual meeting of the Christian Commission in Washington, 1866. Vice-President Colfax unexpectedly called upon him to speak of the work of the Commission in the South and West. Mr. Chidlaw made his way through the crowd to the speaker's platform, perplexed and surprised, as well as embarrassed. But gradually he recovered his self-possession, and his extempore oration ended in a spontaneous dramatic scene, which is well described by one who was present:

> Rev. B. W. Chidlaw carried off the palm for eloquence last night at the final annual celebration of the United States Christian Commission. His speech took the house by storm, and thoroughly aroused the vast assemblage, which became perfectly enthusiastic and gave the reverend gentleman round upon round of applause during the course of his remarks. He thrilled the vast audience with his eloquent illustrations of the noble work done. His allusions to the closing labors of the Commission were so affecting as to melt the audience to tears. He was unanimously dubbed the orator—par excellence—of the occasion.

Dr. Chidlaw was a trustee of the Miami University, a commissioner of the Ohio Reform School, and interested in many other benevolent institutions, but gave his life chiefly to work for the young. Little children loved him; he always caught their ear and held them with rapt attention.

The end came while he was on a visit to his native Wales. His life went out like a flash. One moment he was in high spirits, laughing and joking with those about him, for it was his eighty-first birthday. Suddenly he threw his hands over his heart and retired to his room, and the next moment was found dead. There seems a beautiful fitness in the closing of his life near the Welsh village where it began and on his birthday. He was the last of a great trio of Union pioneer Sunday-school missionaries—Stephen Paxson, John McCullagh and Benjamin W. Chidlaw—long to be remembered for their successful work in connection with the Society which they delighted to honor, and thus serve the Master.

In *The Story of My Life* Chidlaw has recorded with singular simplicity and graphic power, as well as modesty, the remarkable experiences through which the Lord led him. See *The Story of My Life* and *Sunset and Evening Star* for further account of Dr. Chidlaw's life and work.

John McCullagh (1811–1888), **Missionary and Superintendent** (1841–1881).

John McCullagh, a Scotch lad born in 1811 near Glasgow, became a scholar in Dr. Thomas Chalmer's Sunday-school. His father dying when he was young, his education broken by poor health, he studied engineering and some theology at the University of Glasgow. The death of his mother and the loss of his fortune by signing notes for a friend, led him to sail for America in 1834. In New York he learned of the American Sunday-School Union through Robert Carter, the publisher. Mr. McCullagh became a teacher at Monticello and did voluntary Sunday-school work in that region, and then engaged in surveying in Illinois, where he met Abraham Lincoln. In 1840 he founded the Eclectic Institute at Henderson, Kentucky, and a Union Sunday-school. His Sunday-school mission work attracted the attention of the Rev. J. H. Huber, agent of the American Sunday-School Union at Louisville, who engaged Mr. McCullagh as a missionary of the Society in 1841, a work in which he had signal success for forty-seven years.

For many years he had charge of the extension of Sunday-schools in the entire South (1852–1884).

Mr. McCullagh was of medium height, broad shouldered, with prominent features and a marked Scotch mental temperament. His versatile talents, tactful and shrewd manner, fitted him to win men in fields where churches were unknown, and religion and Bible study at a discount. He was facile at bringing together diverse characters and persons of widely varying prejudices and nationality, making him a successful pioneer missionary. He made the Sunday-school center upon the Bible, but regarded the circulation of religious books as one of the most important features of his mission. His genius is illustrated by capturing "bark-peelers" through a snowstorm, and, while a civil engineer surveying railways, he succeeded in organizing Sunday-schools among the pioneer people. The first Sunday-school he founded in Henderson, Kentucky, was followed by no less than twelve churches and fifteen Sunday-schools there, and in the vicinity. His industry and success is indicated by his having started in one year (1850) over ninety new Sunday-schools. His numerous missionary experiences, like those at the "Travelers' Rest," "Two Books in a Furrow," "Rebecca Thomas' Ring" (which brought $14,000 to the Society's work), "Emma Hill's Dollar" (which brought the Society $17,000), and "Noah's Carpenters," were often repeated by him with thrilling effect.

In 1880 an appeal was made for a missionary in Virginia, and was answered by one who signed himself "Unknown Friend." The missionary was unwittingly located in the town where this friend resided, but neither Mr. McCullagh nor the missionary knew who the unknown friend was, nor where he lived. The friend was a Methodist layman who often met the missionary and accompanied him in his work and never gave a hint of who he was. But the friend was so well pleased with the investment that he soon gave enough to employ another worker. From this it will be seen how successful he was in reaching the hearts and purses of the people.

He was one of the few persons who, during the Civil War, could pass between the contending armies without serious question. The commanders on both sides knew him and trusted him as the "Sunday-school man." He received a cordial welcome at "Liberty Hall," the home of Hon. Alexander H. Stephens. Mr. Stephens was a Sunday-school lad in the old Power Creek log schoolhouse near what became his home, and declares that it was a great epoch in his life when he entered that school. Reading the Sunday-school books of

he Union at night by a pine-knot light inspired Mr. Stephens
o seek an education and he became one of the foremost statesmen of the South.

Mr. McCullagh is credited with having organized (as a
volunteer and commissioned missionary) 1,000 Sunday-
schools, containing 66,200 members. A goodly number of the
schools have grown into churches.

He passed to the larger life August 19, 1888. The president of a leading railroad wrote to the son, "I have often said
I would rather have your father's crown in glory than any
man's I have ever known."[1]

Stephen Paxson (1808–1881); **Missionary** (1848–1868); **Agent**
(1868–1881).

"You will find a broad belt of light through Central Illinois
and Northern Missouri caused by the labors of a pioneer
Sunday-school missionary." This was the happy way in
which Prof. P. G. Gillett, LL.D., presented the missionary,
Stephen Paxson, to the National Sunday-School Convention
at Indianapolis, in 1872. As he intimated, Paxson needed no
"introduction"; he was probably better known to the delegates than President Gillett himself.

Mr. Paxson was regarded as peculiarly a representative
product of pioneer Sunday-schools of America, because of
his efficient service of from twenty to thirty years and of his
remarkable career. Few men start with so many handicaps as
he did. He was nicknamed "Stuttering Stephen," from an
impediment in his speech; he was a crippled boy and, though he
partially recovered, was lame for life. He had no schooling,
but learned his letters from signs on the shops.

Paxson was born in Ohio in 1808, of English ancestry.
When he was a child, his father died and he found a home
among strangers. He served apprenticeship in the hatter's
trade, walked to the Ohio River, worked his passage down to
Tennessee, and had a romantic marriage. Wishing to cross
a stream, he saw a girl in a skiff on the opposite side and beck-
oned her to row him over. She complied, he gallantly taking
the oars. But he was inexperienced in rowing and the boat

---

[1] See also *Sunday-School Man of the South*, a graphic sketch of John McCullagh's
life and labors by his son, the Rev. Joseph H. McCullagh, with an introduction by
Edwin W. Rice, Phila., 1889.

was caught in the current and whirled round and round
The young girl resumed the oars and safely landed the boat.
Her blue eyes and curls and quiet manner captured the
stranger. His commanding personality, black eyes and black
hair in like manner attracted the girl, and, after a few months
it ended in a marriage, to the displeasure of the girl's father
portly Squire Pryor. He moved successively to Virginia
Alabama, and Illinois, plying his trade by day and entertaining dancing parties at night by his skilful playing of the violin
and his proficiency as a master of the dancing art.

Rev. J. M. Peck, one of the missionaries of the American
Sunday-School Union engaged in the Mississippi Valley
Enterprise, formed a school in Illinois near where Stephen
Paxson then lived. The school soon declined, but later was
reorganized and revived by Dr. John Adams, another missionary of the Society. Into this school Paxson's little
daughter Mary, brought her father. He became a faithful
member for four years, confessed Christ, and united with the
church not far away, along with his wife who had been a
member for some time. Paxson showed the sincerity of his
new life by voluntary work, organizing schools in new places.
Dr. Adams, a born teacher and keen in his judgment of character, perceived that Paxson had the qualifications for a missionary evangelist and recommended him to the Society.
With true western energy, Paxson accepted and, for economy,
moved from the village into the forest at Hickory Hill, built
a rude log cabin for his family in which blankets were hung
for the windows and doorway and for dividing the room, and
started out upon his mission, achieving remarkable success for
twenty years.

Mr. Paxson possessed those native qualities of tact, common sense and keen perception which fitted him to be a successful pioneer in Sunday-school work. He was never
daunted by bad weather. A favorite expression with him was,
"A Sunday-school born in a snowstorm will never be scared
by a white frost." And in pleading his cause, whether argu-
ing for the establishment of a Sunday-school among the
backwoodsmen on the prairie, or telling of his work before cultured audiences in the East, he gave his experiences, for he
said, "Facts are God's arguments." Most of his pioneer work

was done on horseback or with horse and wagon. His horse, named Robert Raikes, was said to have carried him more than 100,000 miles. The horse "would never pass a child on the road, or a house, without stopping," sure that his master wished to speak to the child, or tell of his work at the home. When the horse was worn out, Ralph Wells of New York sent $100 to purchase "Robert Raikes, Jr."

After some years of experience as a pioneer, Mr. Paxson was frequently called East to awaken an interest and secure funds for the extension of the work to needy fields. His intensity of manner, homeliness of speech, and graphic sketches always deeply interested his audiences.

A city daily in New York reported, "Stephen Paxson made an address in which his aristocratic auditors were so deeply interested that they wept and smiled alternately, never heeding mistakes in grammar or rhetorical discrepancies." Similar reports were made of his addresses in Boston and other cities of New England, as well as in those in the Middle States.

In twenty years he reported organizing 1,314 new Sunday-schools with over 83,000 members. He was credited with reviving the series of Sunday-school conventions in the West and was always counted the leading speaker for inspiration and helpfulness in whatever assembly he entered.

He had business offers that were flattering, one in which a friend proposed to invest $50,000 in the purchase of land, Paxson to do the work and the two to share equally in the profits. Years afterward the two compared notes. His friend had doubled his $50,000. Paxson, from his memorandum, pointed to a record of 50,000 scholars gathered into Sunday-schools up to that time and said, "I would not alter the record nor change the investment."

When Paxson had grown weary and worn by incessant toil and travel, organizing schools in tobacco barns and crossing swollen creeks, the Society placed him in charge of the depository in St. Louis, which left him free to attend missionary conventions, meetings and institutes whenever he desired. After a dozen years of this experience, the old pioneer, free from pain and weariness and surrounded by his family, passed from earth, as the last rays of the setting sun fell upon his weary couch, April 22, 1881, in the seventy-third year of his age. The story of his life is sketched with filial sympathy by his daughter Belle, in a little volume entitled, *A Fruitful Life.*

The bronze bust of Paxson has just been presented to the Society by the Pilgrim Congregational Church, of St. Louis, Mo., of which he was a member.

William P. Paxson, D.D. (1837–1896), **Superintendent** (1868–1896).

Inheriting a love and catching an inspiration for mission work from his father, Stephen Paxson, Dr. William P. Paxson was early trained for Christian service. While only a lad of fifteen, he accompanied his father in missionary tours and, on completing his education, entered the missionary service, first in Arkansas and then as a voluntary Christian worker in Illinois, until 1865, when he was appointed missionary in Missouri. By energy and ability he won the position of superintendent of the Society's work in the Southwest, and directed it for over a quarter of a century. He inspired his co-laborers with the ambition to extend Sunday-schools, organizing as many as possible every year in destitute places. His enthusiasm and skill stimulated them to do their best in this line of the Society's work.

Dr. Paxson was a forcible and eloquent speaker, presenting the claims of the Society in a manner that carried conviction. He had a fine presence, thorough familiarity with his subject, an easy flow of language, a ready wit, and he marshalled his facts to sway and win his audience. His whole soul was in his work and he wished every speech to tell for it. His last service closed with a burst of eloquence—a fitting period to his useful life.

Rev. Dr. George S. Bishop, pastor of the church, said, "Paxson was remarkable for his knowledge of the Bible. . . . The prophecies were his favorite theme. After this great sermon in East Orange, New Jersey, he was suddenly stricken with paralysis. Just before it he exclaimed, 'Oh, if the Lord Jesus would but come just now! What rapture!' He loved his country—the Indian country—and was full of anecdotes concerning the West. He understood the mingled races, red, white, and black, and how to deal with each of them from its own level and standpoint. He was a many-sided man. He went as in a chariot."

Dr. Paxson was buried in the cemetery at St. Louis beside his father, Stephen Paxson, over whose grave stands a monument erected by voluntary contributions from Sunday-school people.

Maurice Alexander Wurts (1820–1881), Secretary of Missions (1861–1881).

Maurice A. Wurts had an enthusiastic love for the young. Thus in the Greenway Mission, Philadelphia, when the school had repeated the Fifth Commandment, he would exclaim, "Boys, you honor your mothers, of course you do. Don't I honor my mother? I would go on my hands and knees to serve her."

Born in Louisville, Kentucky, in 1820, he came to Philadelphia when young and entered the mercantile business, first with his uncle and later as a partner in the house. He became a warm personal, life-long friend of his pastor, the Rev. Henry A. Boardman, D.D. His delight was in mission work among the poor. He founded the Moyamensing Mission, out of which grew the Holland Memorial Presbyterian Church, and in 1858 took charge of the Greenway Mission, West Philadelphia, an undenominational Sunday-school then in an exceedingly destitute part of the city.

Mr. Wurts' business and mission experience led the managers to elect him secretary of missions and recording secretary of the American Sunday-School Union in February, 1861. It was a time that "tried men's souls." The society had a crushing debt, divided views over its management and the horrors of a national civil war. But the Lord blessed the Society in bringing comfort and consolation to multitudes of sick, wounded, and dying soldiers, and to stricken and sorrowing families. When peace came, the Union promptly resumed its suspended mission work in the desolated South. During the twenty years of Secretary Wurts' supervision of its mission work, many improved methods of conducting it were introduced, a more systematic plan of reporting and recording the results of missionaries' labors was adopted, and increasing emphasis was laid upon improving the schools and making more of them permanent. The resources and expenditures in mission work were also reorganized upon a more healthy financial basis.

His delicate sense of honor, his frankness and diligence, commanded the confidence of business men. When a speaker in Minnesota, in 1872, charged that the Union's missionaries interfered with denominational schools, Secretary Wurts was present, unknown to the speaker, and sprang to his feet to tell the audience that any missionary of the Union who had so far forgotten his instructions as to be guilty of the conduct charged would be instantly dismissed. He called on the speaker for the name of the school and the missionary, but the speaker, so unexpectedly challenged, had to confess that he was unable to name either the man or the school. It was said of Mr. Wurts that he was "educated in God's school" of experience, with Christian merchants, men of affairs, and by his long years of service in mission schools. The rarer graces were never better seen than when he was severely criticized. He kept his courteous manner, calm spirit, and his simple modesty and humility. Naturally nervous in temperament, the care of the missionary operations of the Society was a great strain; his health failed, and he died December 15, 1881. His co-workers placed on record many strong and loving tributes to his memory.[1]

Martin Brown Lewis (1820–1912), Missionary for Fifty-two Years.

Martin B. Lewis had a pioneer missionary career remarkable for length, earnestness, and efficiency of service in the field. His life illustrates what intelligent, consecrated laymen can do as Sunday-school evangelists. Born at Milo, New York, on the shores of the beautiful Seneca Lake, November, 1820, on completing his education, Mr. Lewis entered mercantile life in Penn Yan, New York. The health of his wife demanding a change of climate, he moved to Red Wing, Minnesota, and engaged in the commission business. He started there with large business prospects, but the financial crisis of 1857 and the recklessness of a partner forced the

---

[1] See Maurice A. Wurts, memorial volume, *An Unselfish Life*, 1882, *The Sunday-School World*, 1882.

house to suspend. Meanwhile Mr. Lewis had become a prominent worker in the church that had grown out of an Indian mission (Wah-coutah). In 1859 when the American Sunday-School Union requested its missionary, E. W. Rice, to secure another pioneer worker, he recommended Mr. Lewis, who with some hesitation accepted the call and began his pioneer Sunday-school work in April, 1860.

As a layman he had been trained and prepared of God for such a service. Genial in manner, warm of heart, fervent in his Christian life, ever ready to witness for the Master, he carried the gospel message for over half a century to the lonely homes over the western prairies and into the sparsely settled regions of the Mississippi Valley in Minnesota and Wisconsin. In this work Mrs. Lewis was a wise companion and a splendid helper, who by her discreet counsel and devout prayers cheered him in his arduous and often wearying labors in the new settlements then forming in that region.

Summing up his labors for the first thirty years, he recorded more than 800 new schools, reaching 30,000 members, and forming a nucleus for the organization of more than 150 churches of different denominations. Near the close of his life, as if in a vision of the world beyond, he seemed to hear voices of redeemed ones re-echoing through the years of shadow and of sunshine, and to see the pastors of churches, teachers in schools, and leaders of thought who had been won to the nobler life by his lay ministry.

Few Christian workers were so winning and successful in individual work for individual souls. He was remarkably successful in bringing the great question of personal religion home to the lonely settler in the new West, and was equally winning in narrating the simple story of his mission to persons of means and of fortune, whether in Chicago, New York, or elsewhere. Many large contributions from business men are in no small measure due to his interviews with them when he was called from his field to tell of his work.

The blessed influences of his life will long linger in all that region, as a benediction in many homes where he brought the light of the gospel, or its consolation, in days of sorrow.

The Society presented a loving-cup to Mr. and Mrs. Lewis in April, 1910, "In loving recognition of their fifty years of continuous and faithful missionary service." His fellow missionaries and the officers of the Northwest district also presented him with a silver bread plate as a testimonial of their esteem for him in his long service.

He passed to the other land March 30, 1912, and eleven days later a similar call came to his faithful and life-long companion, both rare spirits, unitedly consecrated in life, whose influence is felt far beyond the bounds of their personal acquaintance.

L. Milton Marsh (1820–1892), Missionary (1859–1892).

Mr. Marsh used playfully to say that the "Lord had set him aside to fill gaps." Born in New York in 1820, he became a teacher of vocal music in Wisconsin, and was in business for several years until the financial crisis of 1857 swept away his means. Thus the Lord prepared him for a call to Sunday-school missionary work which, with much diffidence, he accepted in September, 1859. His rare gift of song, his love for children, and his magnetic power over the young, gave him remarkable success in Sunday-school missionary work in Wisconsin, New England, Iowa, Kansas, and in other fields where he was successively called to labor. His tact, discretion, and winsome ways qualified him to win confidence and to be entrusted with responsible positions, as Superintendent of the work in the Rocky Mountains, as Acting Secretary of Missions in Philadelphia, and as Agent in New England, and later, District Secretary of the Society in New York.

One of the managers said of him, "He had a single eye for God's glory and the good of souls." He was slow in expressing an opinion, wishing to examine any plan in all its bearing before he came to a decision. When he did, it was hard to move him from it. He scattered gladness all about him, so that in the homes where he went parents were grateful for his interest in their children; the boys and girls loved him, and even the little ones would climb upon his knee and nestle in his arms.

He had a stalwart faith in God, and his work was the all-absorbing interest of his life. He was successful in persuading others to sustain the work—collecting thousands of dollars for the Society in New England—and persuaded friends in New York to enlarge their support of the work for upward of ten years, until his death in 1892.

F. G. Ensign (1837–1906), **Superintendent of Missions for the Northwest** (1870–1906).

For thirty-five years Frederick G. Ensign aided in promoting the missionary work of the American Sunday-School Union in the region of the Great Lakes and of the Mississippi Valley. Of indomitable perseverance, he acquired unusual skill and tact in securing competent men as missionaries, and funds toward their support.

Though born in Pennsylvania, he was of Puritan ancestry. His early life on the prairies of Illinois developed habits of industry and a vigorous constitution. He desired to obtain a good education, but was prevented through his limited means from taking a complete college course. His course of study in theology was also interrupted by the war in 1863, when he became an army missionary and entered the service of the Christian Commission. After completing his theological course in 1866, he became secretary of the American Christian Commission. These various experiences and services prepared him for entering upon the work of the American Sunday-School Union, at Chicago, in 1870, in charge of the "Northwest District," comprising five interior states. Hardly had he entered upon this new service when the great Chicago fire occurred, and D. L. Moody requested him to aid in securing funds for the rebuilding of the Young Men's Christian Association headquarters and in establishing the Moody Bible Institute. With Mr. Moody, he aided in raising a fund of $150,000 for the former, and $225,000 for the latter institution. Meanwhile the work of the American Sunday-School Union, which had been prosecuted in that region for over forty years, now called for special attention and funds to restore it to its wonted efficiency. It required great perseverance and intense earnestness to win the friendship and support of Chicago's busy, hustling business men. Friends in the East had poured vast amounts of money through the Union to found gospel institutions in the various states in the Mississippi Valley. Sooner or later Christian business men in that region were bound to recognize the important services which the Society had rendered in that formative period.

Mr. Ensign saw a great opportunity to present these facts to the grandchildren of those early settlers who had been aided in the founding of Christian schools throughout that vast region of the country. He could point to the hundreds of churches, to the thousands of ministers and Sunday-school teachers, and to the tens of thousands of conversions that had resulted from the earlier work of the Society in these states. Moreover, into portions of this vast territory were now again pouring immigrants from all nations of the world. Thus this territory offered a magnificent opporunity for still larger service of the Union in that section. Mr. Ensign, in common with others in the Society, had a clear foresight of what might be done under such conditions in shaping and molding the spiritual welfare of the Northwest to a greater degree than ten times the amount of such labor might accomplish a generation later. Christian business men, here and there, responded generously to the call. Mr. Ensign's zeal and enthusiasm and his commanding personality won many friends who aided in enlarging the work and in contributing funds for its support. The records indicate that over 16,700 new Sunday-schools were established, with 65,600 teachers and over 500,000 scholars, besides aid given to other schools, reaching more than 3,500,000 scholars and searching out homes into which 125,000 copies of the Scriptures were introduced, and more than 57,000 persons confessed Christ and upward of 1,400 churches were formed during the thirty-six years of his supervision in that district.

Philanthropists and Christian business men in that section have recorded their gratitude for the work the Union did and their estimate of what it can still do by enrolling themselves among the most generous of its contributors. This is due, in no small measure, to the magnetic appeals of F. G. Ensign. His valued services continued until his brief illness and sudden death in 1906, lamented by the friends of Sunday-schools not only in the Northwest, but in the entire country.

SECTION VIII

HOUSING THE INSTITUTION

Housing the Sunday-school.—The modern Sunday-school started in a small room, a kitchen, in a private house. The buildings in which it has generally found a home have never been wholly suitable, nor quite favorable for its best work. A room in some dwelling, shop, public hall, schoolhouse, or church basement, was the common place for it, until comparatively recent years. Only within the present generation has attention been given to the erection of buildings or churches adapted to modern Sunday-school ideals. As already indicated, the churches generally were not hospitable to the Sunday-school at the beginning of the movement. They either offered it no shelter, or suffered it to occupy a damp cellar or basement poorly lighted and ventilated. In rare cases, with great magnanimity it was allowed a secluded corner in the gallery or loft of the church. The writer well remembers his first introduction into the infant class of the Sunday-school, in the "thirties" (1835–1839) of the last century. It was in the rear basement room of the church, under the main audience room, and lighted by short upper windows; the entrance at the rear was nearly on a level with the sloping ground. The room was plastered and furnished with benches, and was regarded as a superior place at that time in the Eastern and Middle States.

Housing in Great Britain.—In Great Britain up to near the close of the nineteenth century, the Sunday-school was generally housed beneath the church auditorium, or in small siderooms, sometimes in galleries, and makeshift places. There were some notable exceptions, in London, Manchester, and a few other cities. The famous Stockport School was housed in a building in some measure suitable. The majority of British Church schools, however, were housed in the Gothic cathedrals and church buildings, erected to suit mediæval ideals.

281

Some Nonconformist churches have been constructed with a central auditorium and classrooms in the rear and sides, or with a gallery having classrooms, as in some places in America. The industrial regions of Britain have large Sunday-schools, where the demand for better housing has become more acute. Buildings with departmental rooms for Primary, Junior, and Senior classes, and cloak rooms—with separate entrances for each department—are being erected to meet the newer organized methods of these Sunday-schools.

Housing in America.—As in England, so in America, in the early era of the Sunday-school cause, the schools were held in private dwellings, in halls, schoolhouses, sheds, barns, and in shops, or groves, uniformly outside of church buildings.

In communities remote from churches, and on frontier settlements, the spirit of toleration and religious liberty long prevailed, so that the public schoolhouse was generally thrown open on Sundays for the Sunday-school. This is not so common now. Toleration is extended to all kinds of educational, civil and social meetings in the schoolhouse, except for religious worship or Bible instruction. In many sections of the country, meetings of the latter kind are no longer tolerated in the buildings set apart for the public education of the young!

When the institution was widely accepted by the churches, nearly a century ago, none of the church buildings had been erected in anticipation of housing a Sunday-school. The best that could be offered to this new movement was a temporary place, originally planned for an entirely different purpose, as a prayer meeting, a singing gallery, or a basement intended for a storeroom. As new church buildings were erected, improved accommodations were gradually provided for the school. About 1870 special study began to be directed to the structure of edifices, to suit combined church and school service. Lewis Miller, of Akron, Ohio, planned a type of edifice intended for both purposes. It was a parallelogram in shape, the desk or pulpit at one side, instead of at the end as was common. There were entrances at two of the corners, the auditorium having small rooms on three sides. The partitions were set so that the desk might be visible from every classroom, the main audience being seated in the large space, between the desk and classrooms. As the classrooms could be closed by glass folding-doors, this plan made it possible to have general exercises for the whole school, led by the pastor or superintendent at the desk, and also to have class instruction follow in the separate classrooms. Many modifications of this plan were designed. The same building with the auditorium was also available for church services. The Uniform System of lessons (1872) increased the popularity of buildings modeled after this design. It did not, however, always prove as satisfactory as some of its advocates predicted. The classes were in some measure still separate, and this marred the social effect desired in assembling together for worship.

When graded and departmental lessons began to be introduced into America and Great Britain, the dissatisfaction with existing buildings became wide-spread among the advocates of specially graded lessons. In part this condition was anticipated by George W. Kramer, an architect, who designed and exhibited a plan for separate rooms and separate departments of a Sunday-school at the World's Fair in 1893. He and many other architects have since designed similar buildings, providing for almost every variety of church and Sunday-school activities. They include such features as an auditorium, lecture room, dining room, parlors, gymnasium, kindergarten and mothers' rooms, library and reading rooms, class and departmental rooms, kitchen, superintendents', secretaries', and other officers' rooms, toilet, storage and cloakrooms, a swimming pool, lockers, bowling alley, and clubrooms, and, in some plans, a prayer room. The problem of a building satisfactory for the modern Sunday-school and modern church service also is a very complicated one. It awaits solution. Practically two buildings quite different in structure are indicated as the possible solution.

Housing Union Schools.—The largest proportion of American Sunday-schools started in the country for forty or fifty years following the enthusiasm awakened by the Mississippi Valley Enterprise, were upon the union plan. They were housed in whatever was available and the most convenient shelter. Usually it was the building used on week-days for the public school. Quite frequently, however, the Sunday-school was the pioneer educational and religious organization in frontier communities. Then it found a temporary shelter in a shack, an unfinished building, storehouse, hall or tent. Later it might be moved to a grange, or town hall, or a chapel might be erected for it and for other meetings, civil and social. The lack of a building rarely prevented the establishment of a Sunday-school in any rural community.

The American farmers are resourceful from necessity. Their women discover many mysterious ways of dividing a one- or two-roomed dwelling to meet emergencies. So the problem of making temporary classrooms in a hall, or in any one-roomed building, for the country Sunday-school departmental grades is a very simple one to them. They screen off one corner with quilt or sheet for the Primaries, another for the Juniors, and a third corner for an Adult Bible Class, leaving the center for the Main, or Intermediate Department. This is not an ideal housing, but in the formative period of a frontier community farmers' wives have long been better trained than their husbands to accept makeshifts good naturedly—though not content with them. They suffer many inconveniences cheerfully for the good of their children.

Mission Chapels.—In factory, industrial, and mining centers, outside the cities, where the workmen and their families, of diverse race, speech, and habits, are often crowded together in small houses, the Sunday-school shares its shelter with other welfare work. The buildings vary in shape, structure, and inside appointments, according to the idea of their owners and the demands of the people. Many of the large mining and industrial corporations are making liberal provision for welfare work, including Sunday-schools among their employees, and are paying the salaries of suitably trained persons to supervise this service.

Large mission schools in cities, and wherever there are congested populations, have been furnished with buildings intended to be specially adapted to their needs by Christian philanthropists. These have not always proved satisfactory. The conditions require to be more carefully studied in order to design a building fitted closer to particular needs. Each field has problems and conditions of its own to be considered, just as every child must be studied in successfully training him for the country and for God. Plans for Sunday-school buildings and rooms are varied and abundant, especially those adapted for housing large schools. Marion Lawrance, *Practical Study of Sunday-School Buildings;* C. W. Stoughton, *Housing the Church School;* G. W. Kramer, *Twentieth Century Church and Architecture* in *The Encyclopedia of Sunday-Schools,* give some later suggestive plans for better housing the institution.

Housing Sunday-School Societies.—The home of an institution, like that of a person, may reveal to us the circumstances, the ideals, the ambitions, and much of the character of the occupants. Thus the Sunday and Adult School Union was busy for two years (1817 and 1818) in sizing up the magnitude of the task it was to undertake, and in considering the housing which it would require or could command. Meanwhile the managers held their meetings, sometimes in Mr. Gartley's schoolroom, and at other times, in Mr. Van Pelt's schoolroom, or in the building at the northwest corner of Fourth and Arch Streets, Philadelphia.

Abraham Martin, who was recording secretary of the Union in 1824, from his recollection about fifty years later, stated that "the depository of the Sunday and Adult School Union was in a room ten feet square on Fourth Street, third house above Cherry Street."[1] This may have been a place of business some time during 1817 or 1818, but no definite statement of this fact in the printed or written records of the Union has been found.

The next year, late in 1819 or early in 1820, the room on Arch Street was found inadequate, and the entire floor at 29 N. Fourth street was leased. The depository and business of the Society centered here until the Sunday and Adult School Union changed to the American Sunday-School Union in 1824.

Under its new name the Union soon found the depository too small for its business, and on January 1, 1825, rented the entire dwelling No. 13 N. Fourth Street, which was found convenient for a depository and for necessary offices and also for meetings of the managers.[2]

The literature of the Union grew rapidly in public favor and

[1] *Report,* 1864, p. 3.   [2] *Report,* 1825, p. 6.

the business increased in volume, so that in 1826 the managers complained of the "straitness" of their accommodations. They believed that the citizens of Philadelphia would cheerfully provide this national Society with a suitable building, similar to one which New York had so generously furnished for the American Bible Society. Encouraged by the sympathy of the public, the Union purchased the lot and dwelling at 146 Chestnut Street in March, 1827, for $28,000. The alterations, additions, and the perpetual insurance of $18,000 brought the total cost to $42,654. "The buildings on Chestnut Street had been altered to suit the purposes of the Society and its various tenants." "In addition to the room used by the Society, and that rented to the Mercantile Library Company, Loud and Brothers, and J. B. Longacre," the premises were "occupied by printers, stereotype-founders, bookbinders, and engravers, each paying their separate rents, but holding no other connection with the Society than giving them the preference in the work to be done at the current rates in the city."[1]

The records of the Union indicate that nearly all the contributions toward the building (fully six-sevenths of them) came through the Committee of Publication, as the building was required for that purpose. The missionary work had not yet developed so as to require more than desk-room and a part of the time of Corresponding Secretary Porter, whose time was chiefly devoted to the preparation and distribution of publications. These contributions of 246 citizens of Philadelphia, like the subsequent contributions for the building, were to provide for the conduct and the maintenance of the publication work of the Union, and were specially given for this purpose.[2]

The appeal was made in the following terms:

" During the year a bindery for the Society's publications has been established under the same roof as the general depository. The necessity of having the whole business of the Board conducted under its immediate superintendence, and the increasing amount of that business render it indispensable in the view of your Board that some suitable building should be erected in this city for the accommodation of the Society. They are desirous of drawing the attention of the citizens of Philadelphia to this object, believing that they would will-

[1] *Report*, 1828, p. 3.   [2] *Ibid.*, p. 4.

ingly afford that aid to the only charitable Society strictly national, having its seat here, which the inhabitants of a neighboring city have so nobly furnished to two of our national societies located among them."[1]

By 1845 the Union again found the "buildings designed for a dwelling house" unsuitable and too straitened for business purposes. "Since that building was purchased," the managers said, "our publications and the weight of our stock have increased nearly five-fold, and of course the inconvenience and unsuitableness of our premises were proportionably aggravated." The entire premises were rebuilt and completed for occupation in December, 1845. Additional contributions were received from the citizens of Philadelphia to aid in this rebuilding, which cost about $20,000.[2]

Again in 1853 the Union found its buildings too limited and unsuitable for its work. The managers declared the demand for room to transact the business of the Society could not be met on the premises (146 Chestnut Street). The location was central and the front on Chestnut Street ample, but there was no access to the rear of the buildings and there was not sufficient available space for a suitable warehouse in the rear of the lot, and the surrounding buildings were so crowded and high as to make the place extra hazardous.[3] Accommodations which amply sufficed for 1817 were too narrow for 1827, and those which answered for 1827 were not adequate to the necessities of 1847.[4]

For these, among other reasons, the Union purchased a new site on Chestnut Street above Eleventh—316, later 1122, Chestnut Street—on which they erected a new building, ample and convenient for the various branches of the business, and which was occupied at the close of that year (1853). A special meeting of the Board of Officers and Managers, with the agents and missionaries nearby, was held February 2, 1854, in recognition of the entrance into this new building. They state that the exercises of the occasion were peculiarly impressive.

This new building occupied the entire lot between Eleventh and Twelfth streets—30 feet front on Chestnut Street by 229

[1] *Report*, 1826, p. viii.   [2] *Report*, 1846, pp. 10–15.
[3] *Report*, 1853, p. 35.   [4] *Report*, 1854, p. 67.

feet deep, extending back to George, now Sansom, Street. Many of the friends of the Union regarded this as a move "out into the country" at that time. The building was designed by a well-known architect, John McArthur, Jr., and was counted a fully up-to-date building for the operations of the Union. The cost of the lot and of the new buildings, including the furnishing, was $71,876.18. From the various records of the Society, it appears that the citizens of Philadelphia had contributed sums additional to those already mentioned for the buildings, the total amount being represented as $54,276.18, and the balance on this new building, in 1854, was secured by a mortgage of $17,600.[1]

The front of this new building on Chestnut Street was of Quincy granite; the salesroom being on the first floor and the rear part of the building being occupied as a shipping-room. The second and third stories front were divided into rooms for managers, committees, editors, secretary of missions and agents. The fourth floor front was appropriated to the storage of maps, charts, and special Sunday-school requisites issued by the Society. The rear portion of the building was a warehouse of five stories, in which was the principal stock of books and other publications of the Society, classified by titles, some in sheets and some in bound copies. On the Quincy granite front was engraved the corporate seal of the Society, consisting of two hands clasped in a wreath of olives.

This building continued to be the headquarters of the Union for more than half a century. Various alterations and additions were made to it during the period to meet the changing demands of the publication work. Chief among these was the addition of the "Teachers' Hall and Parlor," which was built in the second story between the offices and the warehouse. This provided a suitable place for holding teachers' meetings conducted by the Union, which were begun in January, 1878. The free use of this hall or assembly room when not required for the Society's business meetings was granted to various religious and benevolent organizations for meetings, such as the McAll Mission, Women's Bible Readers Society, Women's Union Missionary Society of America, Fe-

[1] *Reports*, 1854, p. 70; 1858, p. 62.

male Domestic Missionary Society. The hall was also used for meetings of ministers, teachers, Sunday-school organizations, and others interested in the moral and religious training of youth. It cost about $5,000, of which the late John R. Whitney obtained about three-fifths, and the balance was provided by the Society.

At the beginning of the twentieth century, the Union found its business had so changed as again to render the building, which was once well suited for its work, out of date and calling for expensive changes to adapt it to these new conditions. As the site had become valuable, the managers, after prolonged deliberation, were led to believe that a new site and a new building in a less expensive location would be an advantage, as it would enable them to make a building suitable for their purpose and also to have a general fund left from the proceeds of the sale of the old building to provide for the maintenance of the new one or for the larger prosecution of the publication work. In consequence of this belief, the Society sold the property at 1122 Chestnut Street for $325,000, purchased a lot and dwelling of about the same size at 1816 Chestnut Street, between Eighteenth and Nineteenth streets, for $125,000, and reluctantly left the place hallowed by many memories. On the rear of this new lot they built a new fireproof warehouse of reinforced concrete and altered the front building into offices adapted to the work of the Society in all its departments, at a total cost, for new buildings and alterations, including the furnishings, of about $185,000.

By this sale and removal in 1907, the Union saved a general fund of upward of $125,000, the income of which could be devoted to the maintenance of the new building and the prosecution of the publication work of the Society, in accord with the intent of the generous donors.

This new building, fronting on Chestnut Street, has the salesroom on the first floor, with offices for business superintendent and treasurer and a counting room. On the second floor is the assembly or teachers' hall, for the meetings of teachers and of the Society. The use of this hall is freely accorded also to other evangelical organizations for meetings for business and devotional purposes. The upper portions of the front building were made into offices for the use of those engaged in the editorial and missionary work of the Society, including a library and a historical museum. On the rear of the lot stands the new warehouse where supplies of publications of the Society are stored. The first floor is occupied as a shipping-room and the upper floor as a bindery and folding-room. In the basement is a large vault for holding the electrotypes and engravings of the Society. The printing and manufacturing for the Union has always been done by contract in the open market. It has never owned a printing house.

Around these buildings, especially the Quincy granite front building at 1122 Chestnut Street which was occupied for more than half a century, many memories clustered, making it hard for the older managers and workers to break away from these associations. These changes in its headquarters, however, plainly indicate that the Society does not intend to become "moss-grown," nor to stay in a rut, but is as eager now as it ever has been to increase its efficiency and to march in the front rank of progress for the religious education of this country.[1]

The London Sunday-School Union, formed in Surrey Chapel, erected a Jubilee Memorial Building, 56 Old Bailey, London, which was formally opened October, 1856. This gave an opportunity to concentrate the Society's work and to afford rooms for various local auxiliaries to hold conferences and committee meetings facilitating the growth of its work. In 1892 the trade and publication department was removed to 57 and 59 Ludgate Hill, to relieve the congested conditions in the Memorial Building and to accommodate the various training and normal classes for teachers and for special examinations conducted under the auspices of the London Union. The Union also aims to provide holiday homes for poor or sick children, rest homes for teachers and a convalescent home for scholars, by the seaside or in the country, all of which work is directed from the central building in London.

Housing Denominational Sunday-School Organizations.— In America the Sunday-school organizations of the leading denominations may not be ideally, but are comfortably, housed. Some of them occupy palatial buildings costing from $1,000,000

---

[1] For a further account of the laying of the cornerstone, see *The Sunday-School World*, 1907, pp. 157, 158.

upward.   Brief mention of a few will be sufficient to indicate the general character of the buildings without a detailed description.

The Sunday-school headquarters of the Northern Baptist Convention is in the handsome edifice of the American Baptist Publication Society, Chestnut and 17th Streets, Philadelphia, Pennsylvania. From this center go millions of copies of periodicals and aids for Baptist Sunday-schools, including "The Baptist Teacher," as prepared in the commodious offices occupied by the editorial force.   The circulation of their publications is said to be among the largest of their kind in the country, and are specially intended for Baptists.

The Sunday-school work of the Southern Baptist Convention centers in the modern imposing white-faced brick building in Nashville, Tennessee, having commodious rooms for those who aim to meet the demands of the Southern Baptist Sunday-schools.

The Publishing Board of the National Baptist Convention (Colored) has a large plant, not very new, in Nashville, but wishes to build a new modern structure for the housing of its Sunday-school publishing work for the colored Baptists of the South.

The Sunday-school and publishing work of the Brethren occupies a large modern and substantial brick edifice in Elgin, Illinois, where is prepared much of the literature for that denomination.

The Congregational Sunday-school and Publishing Society is housed within the commodious and well-known Congregational House on Beacon Street, Boston, Mass., which furnishes "The Pilgrim Teacher" and literature relative to all phases of modern Bible study, teacher training, and denominational activities characteristic of the modern Pilgrim and Congregational family.

The Sunday-school work of the Evangelical Association has its home with the other activities of the denomination in buildings not very modern in Cleveland, Ohio, which have been adapted to their purpose.

The Sunday-school work of the Lutheran General Council will occupy quarters in its new publishing house in Philadelphia, and the Bible work of the Lutheran General Synod is also in another building devoted to publications of that denomination in the same city.

The Bible study and the Sunday-school activities of the Methodist Episcopal Church occupy spacious rooms in several buildings in three great cities. The first may be found in the large and valuable edifice of the "Book Concern," on Fifth Avenue, New York City; the second, in a new and palatial structure in Chicago, Illinois; the third, in Cincinnati, Ohio. From these centers issue "The Sunday-School Journal" and the "Christian Advocates," and other literature to the large numbers of Methodist adherents throughout the Northern United States.

The Biblical literature for Methodist Sunday-schools and churches for the South centers in the imposing gray-stone building in Nashville, Tennessee, where commodious rooms are provided for the publication of its Sunday-school and other literature.

The Presbyterian Board of Publication and Sabbath-School Work occupies ample space in the palatial eleven-story Witherspoon Building in Philadelphia, which it shares with some other organizations of the same church, and furnishes "The Westminster Teacher," with an ample supply of literature for the denomination. The Home and Foreign Mission work of that church has headquarters in the magnificent building on Fifth Avenue, New York City.

The Sunday-school headquarters of the Presbyterian Church in the United States (South) is with the Publication Committee of that denomination in its building that is modern, homelike and commodious, in Richmond, Virginia.

The Sabbath-school work of the United Presbyterian Church finds a home with the Board of Publication of that denomination in its old but commodious building in Pittsburgh, Pennsylvania.

The Reformed Church in America (Dutch) has its Sunday-school quarters with its Board of Education in 22d Street, New York City. While the Reformed Church in the United States (German) has its Sunday-school home with its Board of Publication in a new, modern edifice in Philadelphia, Penna.

The Bible work of the United Brethren is cared for in their

Publication House in Dayton, Ohio, which is new, modern and commodious.

A number of the denominational Sunday-school organizations also have separate large manufacturing plants for printing their literature. The American Bible Society, which furnishes Bibles and Testaments for Sunday-schools, and for all people, possesses a large square on which is an old historic building and valuable premises, well known as the "Bible House," Astor Place, New York City.

Most of the other Sunday-school organizations of the Protestant denomination (thirty or more) are sheltered, if not commodiously housed, in buildings or edifices of their own, in different parts of the country, so located that they are accessible to the majority of their constituents. From this very brief sketch it will be inferred perhaps that the Sunday-school organizations are sometimes comparatively better housed than their individual or local schools. It may be further inferred that there is room for a large improvement in the structure and arrangement of the buildings now occupied. The plans of the more expensive edifices even have not been designed always with the view of adapting them to further the most efficient work of the occupants. Many need to be better equipped for promoting as they should the progress of all phases of the religious education of the people.

SECTION IX

Uniform and Graded

THE system of International Lessons did not spring up in a night, although its enthusiastic adoption was a surprise. The plan was the culmination of a long series of experiments with systems of biblical study. Roughly speaking, there were not less than five eras or stages leading up to the Uniform Lesson System of 1872. When the modern Sunday-school movement began, its curriculum of study did not rise above the prevailing theories of education. These were so confusing and even contradictory that Jean Paul Richter said of them that "they were a jumble equal to those produced by a harlequin on the stage who brought a bundle of orders under one arm, which he delivered, followed by a bundle of *counter*-orders under the other arm." But a few clear and definite principles of education were beginning to emerge.

Preparedness for Them.—1. The first stage was the reading and spelling era. The introduction of the free public school system in America soon rendered this form of Sunday-school work largely unnecessary.

2. The second was the memorizing era, when pupils received rewards and prizes for committing to memory the greatest number of verses from the Bible and from hymns. This was widely popular in Great Britain and in America.

3. This was followed in Great Britain by a "Lesson System," revised and exploited by James Gall of Edinburgh, Scotland. Its use was less general elsewhere.

4. The simultaneous instruction method of Robert Mimpriss had warm advocates and served a useful purpose, but was limited chiefly to lessons from the Gospels, and was not widely adopted in America.

294

5. The training system of David Stow likewise won many advocates, especially those interested in infant or beginners' classes.

Overlapping these later plans in England was the "Collective System" of lessons by the London Sunday-School Union. This was topical, but the Bible texts were too long for the younger classes, being suited chiefly to advanced Bible classes, and failed to provide a satisfactory knowledge of the entire Scriptures for all ages. These systems, overlapping one another, were more or less simultaneous in their use in different localities. Each was introduced into America, but, after gaining some local popularity, was laid aside—none of them attaining general adoption.

In America similar systems can be roughly indicated, though they overlapped each other here as abroad. Following the first two stages (1) of reading and (2) memorizing, there came in America (3) a story-telling or lecture stage, described in another section of this history. Succeeding this era of lecturing and of story-telling, which was neither so long in duration nor so widely popular in America as the memorizing era, came (4) The "Limited Uniform Lesson Plan" of 1825 and on. The origin of this plan is elsewhere noted. It was not based upon, but antedated Gall's "Lesson System" here, though Gall's work had some influence in shaping the helps upon the Limited Uniform Lesson System five years later, about 1830.

Nor was this uniform system based upon the memorizing a "verse a day" plan, prevalent among the Moravians. There was an unsuccessful attempt widely to introduce these seven verses as the topic of weekly study. The verses were selected consecutively from Scripture, but often ended in the middle of a topic or narrative, and were, for this and other reasons, counted unsatisfactory and unsuitable for a weekly lesson study in the Sunday-schools.

The Limited Uniform Lessons (1825), in general use for a generation, were followed, as elsewhere stated, by lessons putting special emphasis on denominational doctrines.

(5) The Independent Lesson plan or so-called "Babel Series." Each denomination and prominent Sunday-school publishing house put forth a scheme of lessons of its own, putting emphasis upon its creed, or planned to suit its constituency.

The era of this "Babel" series of lessons prevailed, rough[
for about twenty years (1850–1872). Dr. Sampey suppos
that it held sway for forty years.[1]   But the Limited Less(
scheme held sway through the *Union Questions*, endorsed [
the National Convention of 1833, and continued to be wide
used until after 1850.   The National Sunday-School Conve
tion so late as 1859 approved of the system in *Union Qu*
tions as one of the best extant for the use of many schola
in Sunday-schools.

Mimpriss's simultaneous instruction scheme, published
1838, and the two schemes of the London Sunday-Schc
Union in 1840–1842, pointed rather to the independent th:
to the uniform principle of lesson study.   The list of t[
London Union for 1842 suggested a uniform topic of study f
the different departments of schools using their series.   Th(
did not, however, contemplate a general uniform scheme
lessons like the International Lessons of 1872, nor did t[
system have so many features of uniformity as the Limit(
Uniform Lessons of 1825–1850 in America.   There was not
ing in the list of lessons prepared for Sabbath-schools in Sc(
land suggestive of the later or earlier Uniform Lesson schem(

In America the Civil War conspicuously emphasized t[
peril of division to society and religion.   Hence it did mu(
to lessen denominational prejudice.   Its influence, howeve
upon series of lessons for Sunday-school study was not imm
diate.   The "Babel" series continued to multiply.   Amor
them were "Lessons for every Sunday in the year," by Oran§
Judd, used widely in Methodist Episcopal churches (186:
1867); lessons in *The Chicago Sunday-School Teachers' Quarter*
(afterward *The National Sunday-School Teacher*), edited su
cessively by John H. Vincent, J. L. Hammond, C. R. Blacka
and Edward Eggleston.   The "Berean Series" of lessons, b
John H. Vincent (which superseded Judd's Lessons); Henr
C. McCook's "Westminster Series" used widely in the Pre
byterian Church, while the undenominational, rural, an
Union schools used the "Explanatory" and "Union Series" (
lessons, prepared by Dr. Richard Newton and Dr. S. Austi
Allibone, of the American Sunday-School Union (1868–1872

Another important influence preceding the Internation:

[1] *International Lesson System*, p. 32.

Uniform System of study was the Sunday-school institute movement. Dr. Simeon Gilbert thinks that uniform lessons would never have been practicable had it not been for "this institute movement which preceded it."[1] Horace Mann founded the normal school system of his state (1837–1848), and advocated reforms in teaching and improving teachers at conventions, through lectures, addresses and reports, which virtually revolutionized the common school system. Dr. Henry Barnard, among others, was active in conducting normal schools or institutes where, for a brief period, systematic instruction was given on methods of teaching and of instruction. This idea was conceived also by Sunday-school leaders and applied to their work. Among the foremost national workers in this line was Richard G. Pardee of New York. Others of prominence in the same work were Henry Clay Trumbull and Ralph Wells for the East, and John H. Vincent, D. L. Moody, J. V. Farwell in Chicago, and Alexander Tyng, Stephen Paxson, William G. Reynolds, B. W. Chidlaw and E. W. Rice, in the Middle West.

A uniform topic of study in the same school was warmly advocated in Sunday-school teachers' institutes held from 1862 to 1869. The agitation of this idea among teachers at institutes and conventions created a state of ferment out of which some remarkable changes were expected to emerge. The institute was the chief agency for crystallizing the new uniform idea. The convention exploited it with enthusiasm. Besides these, there were influences molding and developing the idea in small, deliberative companies of leaders, who discussed, from time to time, the best types of uniform study. Edward Eggleston voiced the sentiment of a large number:

> One lesson for the school—the same in the Bible classes, the main school and the infant class, but adapted by teachers to the capacities and wants of each, is . . . the foundation for all true advancement. It gives concentration, oneness, heart, life, success. . . . Without a uniform lesson there can be no teachers' meeting; general exercises are impossible; unity of thought in hymns and prayer is out of the question; the moral power of a large number studying the same passage is destroyed. There can be no such thing as an effective school without a uniform lesson of some kind.[2]

[1] *The Lesson System*, p. 22.
[2] *Eggleston's Manual*, pp. 10, 11, Chicago, 1869.

If such a system of study could be effective in one school, wh
not in all schools?

These views were considered in the National Sunday-Scho
Convention of 1869. Dr. Trumbull states:

> The wish was again and again expressed by individuals, period-
> icals, and local associations, that the same portion of Scripture
> should be studied week by week in all the land. Various un-
> successful attempts to unite the several publishing houses on a
> common series were made from year to year. At last the aid of
> the Executive Committee of the National Sunday-School Con-
> vention was earnestly sought for the furtherance of this plan.
> The movement for uniformity was *popular* rather than *personal*.
> B. F. Jacobs of Chicago became, in a measure, its representative
> leader, but his strength in it was chiefly due to the general and
> growing sentiment in its favor the country through. Apparently
> no publishing society or house was originally desirous of the
> experiment. Most of the prominent Sunday-school men of the
> nation doubted both its feasibility and its desirableness. It
> was the common people of the United States—the great mass of
> Bible students through the length and breadth of the land—
> who pressed for it, creating a public sentiment in its behalf not
> easily resisted.[1]

Committee Conferences.—Prominent Sunday-school leade
met in conference at Plainfield, New Jersey, with John I
Vincent. It was clear that several were decidedly opposed t
the Uniform Lesson idea. The subject was again brough
before the Executive Committee of the National Sunday
School Convention at New York, July 10, 1871. Of thi
committee, Edward Eggleston was chairman, and H. Cla
Trumbull, secretary. As a result of its deliberations, it wa
affirmed that "The Sunday-school cause in our countr
would be greatly promoted if the publishers of Sunday-schoo
lessons would unite on a uniform series of topics for th
lessons of 1872." To carry out this action, the Executiv
Committee appointed B. F. Jacobs, Alfred Taylor and J. S
Ostrander to convey this sentiment to the publishers and t
urge upon them such conference as may "lead to this co
operation." This committee recommended that a confer
ence be held in the Bible House, New York, August 8, 1871.

Twenty-nine representatives of Sunday-school publishin
societies and houses responded to this call and met in Nev
York to discuss the question of uniformity in Bible lessons

[1] *Report National Sunday-School Convention*, 1872, p. 20.

"Some," says Secretary Trumbull, "opposed it on theoretical grounds, others saw practical difficulties in its way. Some were decidedly in its favor if all would adopt their series of lessons. Others were quite willing to try the experiment, while doubtful of its success. A few advocated it warmly. Nearly all admitted the fact of a strong public sentiment in its favor."

Finally they agreed, by a vote of 26 to 3, to appoint a committee who should select a trial list of Uniform Lesson topics for Sunday-school study for the year 1872. It was understood that this would be an experimental list to test whether it was a workable plan. The committee consisted of Edward Eggleston of *The National Sunday-School Teacher;* Richard Newton, editor of the periodicals of the American Sunday-School Union; John H. Vincent of the Methodist Episcopal Sunday-School Union; Henry C. McCook of the Presbyterian Board of Publication; and B. F. Jacobs, Baptist, of Chicago. Three of the committee—Edward Eggleston, J. H. Vincent and Henry C. McCook—after consultation, decided it was impossible to agree upon a satisfactory scheme of lessons for 1872 and issued a public announcement to that effect. But the next morning, influenced by Mr. Jacobs, the decision was reversed and the committee selected a course of lessons for 1872 that the experiment of Uniform Lessons might be tried.[1]

One of the chief difficulties was to decide upon what principle or plan the lessons should be selected. This was a hard problem to solve. Different plans were proposed: (1) That doctrinal studies be made the basis of the plan; (2) that practical duties be the foundation; (3) that the plan follow the liturgical readings of the ecclesiastical year, recognizing Christmas, Easter, and other similar holy days. Each of these plans had strong advocates and the battle was on, as it was tersely described, for "doctrines, duties, or days," and at last a compromise was effected on the basis of a study of the Bible as a whole; that is, a scheme which would include a study of the entire Scriptures and therefore virtually would include all the features of the other three plans proposed.

But other obstacles confronted this plan. Several of the

[1] *Report National Sunday-School Convention,* 1872. Simeon Gilbert, *The Lesson System,* p. 48, ff.

editors and publishers had already outlined schemes of lessons for the year 1872, and naturally wanted their selection in whole or in part woven into the proposed lesson scheme. For the sake of peace, this was done. The new scheme was made up of three or four quite diverse selections of lessons already decided upon, chiefly by *The National Sunday-School Teacher* of Chicago, the Methodist Episcopal Book Concern of New York and one quarter's lessons chosen by the committee.

The plan of study for 1872 included twelve lessons upon "Jesus after His Ascension" (Acts, Hebrews and Revelation), and a review; twelve lessons upon Elisha and Israel, and a review; twelve lessons in the Epistles, and a review; and twelve lessons upon Daniel and his times, and a review.

It is remarkable that this imperfect, "patchwork" list of lessons should have satisfied the Sunday-schools of America, that a uniform system of study was workable and feasible, or that it should have led to the enthusiastic adoption of Uniform Lessons.

The System Approved by the American Sunday-School Union.—When this trial list of new Uniform Lessons was agreed upon, there were upward of fifteen publishing societies and houses, providing as many different series of lessons for the use of Sunday-schools in the United States. The most prominent of these were the series by *The National Sunday-School Teacher* of Chicago, the "Berean series," the "Westminster series," and the new "Explanatory series" of the Union. The Berean and Westminster series were denominational. The Explanatory series of the Union were intended for rural schools, embracing members of various denominations. The American Sunday-School Union was represented at this conference of publishers by its editor, Dr. Newton, who was made chairman of the sub-committee for the selection of the lessons for 1872, and by Henry Clay Trumbull, secretary of the National Executive Committee, proposing the movement, who was also New England secretary of the Union. The Union naturally favored the principle of uniform lessons, as it had issued a series of lessons on this uniform principle a generation earlier. Moreover, it had just called from the Middle West a missionary superintendent and institute worker, the Rev. Edwin W. Rice, to a responsible position on its editorial staff. He at once proposed to secure a foremost biblical scholar to prepare helps on the new Uniform Lessons to be issued by the Union. He suggested Rev. John Hall, D.D., of New York, as eminently fitted for this service by his experience in Sunday-school work and his high reputation as an expository preacher and biblical scholar. This proposal was heartily concurred in by Dr. Newton and unanimously approved by the managers of the Union.

The list of Uniform Sunday-School Lessons for 1872, as agreed upon by the committee of publishers, was issued by the American Sunday-School Union in *The Sunday-School World* October, 1871, with an announcement of its system of helps thereon. Each society or publishing house adopting the new Uniform Lessons was free to prepare its own explanations, analyses, questions, and other helps on the lessons for its constituency. The aim of the committee representing the publishers was to secure uniformity in the *Scripture subjects* only, and not a uniformity of the treatment of them, or of methods of instruction.

The Union announced its helps upon these lessons under the title of "The American Series." Dr. John Hall prepared the expositions; Dr. Newton furnished "Gleanings from the Holy Land"; Henry Clay Trumbull added "Suggestions on Methods of Teaching and on Normal Work"; Edwin W. Rice contributed illustrations and applications and records of progress out of his experience in the mission field and in conventions and institutes in the Middle West; John B. Smith supplied a weekly review of the lesson for the superintendent's desk; and Mrs. Alice W. Knox gave suggestions for teachers in primary and infant classes. This combination of specialists on the lessons for the use of teachers introduced a marked advance in methods of biblical study and was widely appreciated by schools throughout the country. As a result of these teaching helps, the circulation of *The Sunday-School World* increased four-fold or more within two years.

Graded Helps.—Graded lesson papers and a Handbook for scholars also attained even greater favor and much larger circulation. A system of graded lesson papers for scholars was issued in three grades: (1) For advanced or adult classes; (2) for intermediate classes; and (3) for primary classes. These lesson papers for scholars were different and distinctive in each grade, in their methods of presenting the same Bible text. They were prepared by the assistant editor (Rev. E. W. Rice) in harmony with the explanations furnished for teachers by Dr. Hall in *The Sunday-School World*. Studies for scholars had been hitherto chiefly a series of questions, but these studies were based on modern pedagogical principles, combining explanation, illustration, question and application, and were adapted to successive grades in the progress of child development.

In addition to these lesson papers, a *Scholars' Handbook on The International Lessons* was prepared upon a new plan by the Rev. Edwin W. Rice, and issued by the Society. "The Bible text was printed in paragraphs, while the verses were numbered in the margin. Besides the central truth, daily Bible readings and historical and geographical information, there were brief explanations of difficult and obscure texts and questions for the scholar to stimulate further study, together with illustrations, pictures, and blackboard outlines, with plans for a quarterly review." This was, in fact, a scholars' commentary on the Bible text. The editor of *The Sunday-School Times* said of it:

> Somehow the author is the only one who has thought of the scholars' need. All the helps which have come into our hands have been intended for teachers. It is a pleasure to find the children remembered and such an excellent provision made for their wants. The plan is new. . . . The best idea of all is the citation of an illustration which embodies and will impress the principal moral lesson under each subject.

Another editor stated:

> Do not complain that the scholars will not study until you have seen them refuse this valuable aid. It is the only book of its kind among all the so-called "helps" on the lessons. A teacher recently told us that a boy who seemed losing his interest in the class was wonderfully waked up by this *Handbook*, and knows something now when he comes to school.

The value of this *Scholars' Handbook* is also indicated by the fact that a close imitation of it in all its chief new features was soon after issued by one of the largest denominations in the United States, and another denomination issued an edition, adapting it to the church year.

The system of instruction and the plan of Bible study thus presented by the American Sunday-School Union for teachers and for scholars were recognized by Sabbath-school workers not only as an advance in methods of instruction, but as marking a new era based upon sound principles of instruction. Thus its analysis of the Bible text displaced the unsatisfactory "mechanical" and "verbal" and "parrot-like" question lessons, and the lecturing and story-telling which was discovered to be "amusing," rather than teaching. Thus the five "W's" (when, where, whom, what, why), and so-called "new system of Sunday-school study" with a mechanical plan of "four P's and four D's" (parallel passages, persons, places; dates, doings, doctrines and duties) were declared unsound by educators. In fact, they were an apparent imitation of a plan of "heads" in sermons, used by old divines of the seventeenth and eighteenth centuries to aid the memory of hearers. These, again, were an echo from the more ancient rabbinical plan of the four letters P R D S (פ ר ד ס) in the Hebrew word "paradise."

The studies in the Union helps were the plain common-sense method of emphasizing the truths and phases of truths taught in, and growing out of the Bible text itself. They did not hamper the mind nor load the memory with merely mechanical or verbal mnemonic devices. The "helps" compelled and concentrated the attention of the teacher and scholar upon the meaning and very heart of the Bible text. Moreover, to aid the superintendent in clinching some great truth, week by week a suggestive review on each lesson was given by an accomplished superintendent.

Primary Class System.—Furthermore, the unsatisfactory plan of conducting the infant or primary department as one large class was discarded. The little more than parrot reciting of certain verses, and amusing the children with stories, gave place to real teaching. Alice W. Knox, a successful primary worker, had applied the class system to the primary department for twenty years. This class plan at first was opposed as impossible or impracticable by many primary workers of that day. They even attempted to laugh or ridicule it "out of court." Erwin House, speaking for the old practice said, "With a separate room and suitable teacher, a hundred or a hundred and fifty are as easily taught as forty." In fact, he urges, "If you swell the one hundred to one thousand, brightness of eye and quickness of heart will be wonderfully intensified."[1]

Mrs. Knox declared: "It was easy to *amuse* the children with a story, but it was a difficult thing to *instruct* them so that they would not forget the truth taught." She forcefully showed that it was violating a primary principle of instruction to depend upon one teacher for the Primary Department, because there were many children of different ages, sizes, capacities and degrees of mental culture, calling for specific care in the instruction, and for different teachers successfully to give it. One teacher might interest and entertain children in the mass, but if they were divided into small classes, with a suitable teacher for each class, they could be *instructed*, and some effective work could be done. It may surprise Sunday-school workers now to be informed of the opposition to dividing the Primary Department into small classes, and that many favored the old style of herding the infants by hundreds into a small room to be taught by one teacher. It required more than a decade of argument and pleading by advocates like R. G. Pardee,[2] John S. Hart,[3] Ralph Wells and others who were enlisted with Mrs. Knox,[4] to bring about this reform in the face of much opposition and ridicule.

Convention of 1872.—The adoption and continuance of the Uniform Lesson System was the chief topic of interest before the National Sunday-School Convention held at Indianapolis in 1872. At this convention twenty-two states and one territory of the United States were represented by 254 delegates, and eighty-four others were enrolled as interested members, including persons from Canada, Great Britain and India. After prolonged and exciting discussions, the convention by an overwhelming majority (only ten voted nay) authorized the appointment of a lesson committee of ten persons from the leading denominations, with instructions to select a seven years' course of uniform lesson topics (1873–1879) for Sunday-school study. The resolution adopted reads:

[1] Erwin House, *Sunday-School Manual*, p. 42.
[2] R. G. Pardee, *Sunday-School Index*, p. 127.
[3] John S. Hart, *Thoughts on Sunday-Schools*, pp. 71–75.
[4] Mrs. Alice Knox, *Helps for Primary Teachers*, passim.

That this convention appoint a committee, to consist of five clergymen and five laymen, to select a course of Bible lessons for a series of years not exceeding seven, which shall, as far as they may decide possible, embrace a general study of the whole Bible, alternating between the Old and New Testaments, semi-annually or quarterly, as they shall deem best, and to publish a list of such lessons as fully as possible, and at least for the two years next ensuing as early as the first of August, 1872; and that this convention recommend their adoption by the Sunday-schools of the whole country; and that this committee have power to fill any vacancies that may occur in their number by reason of the inability of any member to serve.

The convention appointed the following as the first committee on Uniform Lessons:

Rev. John H. Vincent, D.D. (Methodist Episcopal), Rev. John Hall, D.D. (Presbyterian), Rev. Warren Randolph, D.D. (Baptist), Rev. Richard Newton, D.D. (Protestant Episcopal), Rev. A. L. Chapin, D.D. (Congregationalist), Philip G. Gillett, LL.D. (Methodist Episcopal), George H. Stuart (Presbyterian), B. F. Jacobs (Baptist), Alexander S. Tyng (Protestant Episcopal), Henry P. Haven (Congregationalist). Rev. J. Monro Gibson, D.D., and Mr. A. Macallum, from Canada, were afterward added to the committee.

Lesson Cycles (1873–1918).—By common consent the Sunday-school societies and publishers acquiesced in the appointment of this permanent lesson committee (for seven years) by the National Sunday-School Convention of 1872. They virtually approved the action by adopting the lessons proposed, each society or publisher issuing such explanations and helps as were suited to its own constituency. The first seven years' cycle of lessons was based upon selecting the more important passages in a general chronological order from the Old Testament, beginning with Genesis, and like passages from the New Testament, and devoting a half year (or less) first to one Testament, and then to the other Testament. Thus, in a fragmentary way, the entire Bible was covered in the seven years' cycle (1873–1879). Some years the alternation between the Old and the New Testaments was made every three months, but usually every six months. The lesson texts were commonly limited to from ten to twenty verses per lesson. Thus about 4,500 or 5,000 of the 31,173 verses (or about one-sixth of the entire Bible) were studied in the first seven years' cycle. The original intention was so to select the lessons as substantially to go over the entire Bible in each course, for the purpose of historical, biographical and doctrinal study, in order to gain a general knowledge of the contents of the Scriptures every seven—and later every six—years. This intention was not fully realized, as we shall see. Forty-eight lessons were selected for a year's study, the last Sunday in every three months being reserved for a review or a lesson selected by the school. In 1878 the last Sunday of every quarter was used as a review of the lessons of the quarter, or as a missionary, temperance, or other special lesson selected by the school

The second seven years' cycle (1880 to 1886) was upon a similar plan except that the cycle began with the Gospel according to Matthew, and alternated between the Old and New Testaments as before. A special feature of this cycle was the consecutive study of the entire Gospel according to Mark in 1882. For the first two years of this cycle, only forty-four regular lessons were selected for each year. The review was transferred to the last Sunday but one in the quarter and the last Sunday was left open for a lesson chosen by the school or for a missionary lesson during two quarters and a temperance lesson for the other two quarters of the year. In the third seven years' cycle (1887 to 1893) some changes in details were made, such as a year of continuous studies in the Gospel of Luke (1890). Attention was called to missionary and temperance topics. The fourth cycle of lessons was limited to six years (1894 to 1899) and more proportionate time was given to studies in the New Testament than to those in the Old Testament. The fifth cycle of lessons (1900 to 1905) was selected by a new committee of fifteen members, most of them being clergymen, and many of them new members. They again co-operated with the British section of the Lesson Committee which consisted of eight members. In this cycle, prominence was given to scripture selections of a biographical nature, just as in a previous cycle prominence had been given to material of a historical character. The aim in introducing the biographical element was "to bring forward the persons in the Scriptures whose lives illustrated the presence and will of God among men, supreme over all, the Word made flesh, the only begotten Son of God." The further thought was to suit the whole cycle of lessons better to those least able to select a course of lessons for themselves. This principle of selection was not, however, uniformly kept in view throughout the later selections in this cycle of the lessons.

The sixth cycle of lessons (1906–1911) was selected by a committee of fifteen (twelve clergymen and three laymen). They were instructed to select one Uniform Lesson for all grades of the Sunday-school and authorized to issue an optional Beginners' Course for scholars under six years of age. During the same cycle, two years' advance courses of lessons were recommended, but were not widely adopted.

The seventh cycle of lessons was selected by the same number of members in the American section, while the British section of the Committee was increased to eighteen members. During this period, several optional courses of lessons were proposed; one on the ethical teachings of Jesus, an advanced course of lessons for Bible classes, and a graded course of lessons was also suggested.[1]

Moreover, some radical changes were made in the mode of appointment of members of the Lesson Committee. An unwritten law or custom of the National Sunday-School Convention was that the American section of the International Lesson Committee should be appointed by the delegates openly in convention; that no Sunday-school publishing society or house in America should appoint a delegate to that convention, nor elect a member on the Lesson Committee. The denominational houses were permitted, however, to *suggest* members, though they did not elect them. Previous to this, the convention or Association had become an incorporated body and under the charter the management of its business affairs was placed in the hands of a certain number of persons, who could legally appoint the Lesson Committee, as well as transact other business. None of these acts required the approval of the Convention to confer validity. At the convention in San Francisco, 1911, the Lesson Committee changes were made not by the delegates to the convention, but by the *trustees* of the convention (now incorporated as an "association") and

[1] See *Graded Lessons*, p. 294.

simply reported to the convention. This radical change was at variance with the original custom of appointing the lesson committee by representatives in open convention. Meanwhile the Editorial Sunday-School Association, composed of members of denominational and undenominational Sunday-school societies and publishing houses combined, which had prospered for several years, had been superseded by a "Sunday-School Council" exclusively denominational in membership.

This Council was composed of representatives of denominational Sunday-school publishing societies who voluntarily associated themselves together—from twenty to thirty different denominations in America—to form this new organization. This denominational council claimed the right to control the selection of all lessons to be issued by the Lesson Committee. This gave rise to a serious conflict of authority. After a number of conferences, a compromise was finally reached on the appointment and structure of the Committee. It was agreed that thereafter eight members of the future Lesson Committee only be elected by the International Sunday-School Association in convention; eight others by the Sunday-School Council of Evangelical Denominations, and that each denomination now having, or that may have, a special committee on lessons may appoint at least one added representative on the general Lesson Committee. As there were upward of twenty denominations having a special lesson committee, this action increased the number on the International Lesson Committee to nearly forty, of which all but eight would be exclusively representatives of denominational organizations. Thus the denominations, as ecclesiastical bodies, secured a preponderating influence in all the acts of the International Lesson Committee. Moreover, it excluded any direct representation from organizations like the American Sunday-School Union, and the independent Sunday-school publishing houses. Even the International Sunday-School Association did not recognize any delegates to their convention from the American Sunday-School Union or from independent publishing houses.

Lesson Committee, British and American Sections.—The British section of the Lesson Committee was likewise changed in its structure, part of its members being appointed by the

ondon Sunday-School Union, and all the officers of that
Union also became ex-officio members of the British section of
the Lesson Committee. Besides these, there were, on the
British section, other members chosen by eight or more denominational bodies, all of them Nonconformists. Three
corresponding members represented Ireland and India—in all,
thirty-two members of the British section. There was no
representation from the Church of England, the Established
Church of Scotland, nor did there appear any direct representation from the churches of Australia. The Church of
England, comprising one-half of the Sunday-school membership of England, did not adopt the International Lessons in
any form, nor did the Established Church of Scotland. In
Great Britain there were two or three sets or courses of
lessons even among some Nonconformists.

Thus the American and the British sections were practically free to solve their own problems in their own way;
neither was bound to adopt the selection of the other for their
schools. The new American Lesson Committee continued
the Uniform Lessons, with some improvements and changes,
in cycles of eight years, beginning with 1918; the lessons for
each year being on historical or biographical lines for nine
months and three months of each year to consist of topical
lessons.

Estimates of Lesson Systems.—The "International Uniform
Lesson System," since 1872, notwithstanding its wide-spread
popularity, has called forth sharp criticism. It has obvious
demerits, as well as merits. Among the objections made to it
were: (1) That it was not in accord with the best theories of
education; (2) that it did not give satisfactory opportunity for
denominational instruction; (3) that it was too fragmentary. It was dubbed a "Kangaroo, hop, skip and jump
method"; "An erratic work of careless shears and paste-pot";
"A mere skimming of the Bible."

To this last criticism, its advocates wittily answered that
"the users had great thanksgivings over the remarkably rich
cream that they had skimmed from it!" Further they
asserted that educators in the classics in universities did not
read everything in the classics, even of works such as Homer,
Virgil, Horace and Juvenal. And finally, that the advantages

far outweighed the defects of the system, for it was claimed that those who adopted the Uniform Lessons gained a more comprehensive knowledge of the Bible; that instruction was made vastly easier; teachers' meetings were possible; unity of instruction was promoted; a mass of fresh biblical literature of great value was developed by it; and, best of all, that the wide use of Uniform Lessons was a great object lesson and argument for the unity of Christianity, besides widening and deepening its spirituality and power.

Graded Lesson Systems.—But a large school of modern educators continued to attack Uniform Lessons as violating sound principles of education. It is, however, a misconception that Graded Lessons are something new. The principle has been recognized in Sunday-schools for more than a century. There are two kinds of grading: one is grading in the teaching and in the themes; the other, grading in the statement of the themes and the texts upon which the lessons are based. Where Scripture texts are not used as a basis, the grading is of the olden type and relates chiefly to the subjects of the lessons. Thus at the Convention in 1914 a prominent speaker, Dr. Benjamin S. Winchester,[1] advocating that a new emphasis be placed upon the educational aspects of the Sunday-school, presented a list of ten different courses of lessons which were considered by the Sunday-School Council of Evangelical Denominations. None of these courses was stated to be based upon the Bible, although some of them might include Scripture texts. Each of these courses was to be adapted to the successive stages of development of the pupils and was supposed to be denominated Graded Lessons *par excellence*.

Grading of the lessons prevailed early in the history of the modern Sunday-school movement, especially in schools existing in communities where some adults had not yet learned to read. These graded lessons were vigorously attacked in those days because they were not exclusively upon the Scriptures and were frequently forced out of the schools for this reason. Even the Uniform Lesson material is always graded in teaching and often graded also in themes. This was the case in the early Uniform Lessons of 1826, as also to some extent in the *cycles* of the Uniform Lessons of 1872 and on. The editors

[1] *Organized Sunday-School Work in America*, p. 401.

and writers on those lessons further graded themes growing out of the Bible texts and adapted them to several grades and departments in the Sunday-school. Thus the germ of recent departmental grades was in the thought of the workers and of those who prepared the lessons for Sunday-schools for more than a generation.

The Uniform Lesson idea therefore embraces both graded teaching and graded lessons. The new graded lessons, however, are practically opposed to uniformity or unity of instruction in different grades. Carried out logically, the new graded lessons have a theme adapted to each grade and each theme must be based upon a different text also adapted or graded. Some educators declared that the proposed new graded lessons were unsound on the question of the new birth; that the Scriptures were wrested from their natural meaning to provide a basis for some of the lessons; and that the Lesson Committee are, through the structure of the graded lessons, *interpreting* the Scriptures for Sunday-schools—a work contrary to the spirit of their appointment. Moreover, it was further charged that the new graded lessons did not provide for, nor meet, all the elements in the problem of religious education and, therefore, must be upon unsound principles of pedagogy or they would provide for all the fundamental elements of the problem.[1]

Agitation for new graded lessons reached a crisis when a tentative course of lessons for primary scholars was proposed in connection with the Uniform Lessons. Similar courses for Beginners were issued in 1901 and 1902. In 1903 an optional advanced course of lessons was proposed. In 1905 an advanced or senior course of lessons was also recommended in connection with the Uniform Lessons. In 1908 there was outlined a new series of graded lessons which extended to about seventeen grades, each grade having a different lesson. Some of these lessons were extra-biblical and, on this account, were rejected by some of the leading Sunday-school societies of America. In place of these rejected lessons, an optional list of biblical lessons was substituted later. These courses of lessons were denominated the Extra-biblical Series, and The

[1] Discussions at Boston, Philadelphia, New Orleans and Chicago Conferences, 1908–1915.

Biblical Series of lessons, respectively. It is proper to add that these new series of graded lessons were the outcome of a number of conferences of prominent Sunday-school workers at London, England, and at Boston, Massachusetts, and elsewhere in America, for nearly a decade previous to their final adoption. Moreover, these new graded lessons are subject to constant changes and are not fixed or permanent. It was at first supposed that the course of lessons for the same grades could be used over and over again, and thus the expense to the schools would be less than for the Uniform Lessons. This did not prove to be the fact, as the lessons were constantly being so changed that new editions required to be purchased. Thus the expense was far greater for the New Graded Lessons than for the Graded Uniform Lessons.[1]

Early in 1915 the American section of the International Lesson Committee proposed to improve the Uniform Series of Lessons by a more careful observance of the adaptation of the lesson material to the needs of the pupil. To this end the Committee selected "a given portion of Scripture, usually including a story or narrative, which shall serve as a common source of material for study in the different departments of the school." It designated "appropriate portions of this common Scripture for study in the several departments of the school," specifying "a suitable sub-title and memory verses, and references to other Scripture material specially suited to any given department, in addition to the regular assigned portions for the day." Furthermore, the Committee aimed to "keep in mind the devotional needs of the school, and when deemed advisable, to suggest an additional passage to meet these needs."

It was further agreed at a joint meeting of these Sunday-school organizations that in the preparation of lesson courses this foremost basal principle must be maintained, "Unity of lesson courses with denominational freedom for any desired modifications." Thus the door was open for each denominational Sunday-school board to make any changes in the Uniform Series of lessons, or any other series, which the special lesson committee of that denomination or of that organization might choose to make. It is natural that any

[1] See *British Graded Lessons*, p. 314.

denominational committee might magnify its office with the result that uniformity in lessons would be liable to be reduced quite to the vanishing point.   The chief bar to this practical destruction of Uniform Lessons would be the wide-spread sentiment in favor of Christian unity among the many Protestant sects.

Even this concession to denominational pressure did not satisfy the ecclesiastics. Later, still another step was taken, in which it was demanded that the Lesson Committee submit its lesson courses "to the various denominations, subject to such revision and modification as each denomination may desire to make, in order to adapt the courses to its denominational needs."[1]   This was recognized as a step backward toward the old "Babel Series" of lessons, in which every denomination and every publishing house had its own.   It would be unfair to charge that the denominational leaders who aimed at intensity of denominational culture deliberately intended to break up the real principle of Uniform Lessons, but the whole drift of these successive acts lay in that direction.

A course of lesson study universally satisfactory is yet to be developed.   It appears to lie in the direction of unity of theme of study with diversity of adaptation.   Whether real unity can thus be secured depends upon the amount of grace and love for the larger things and the fundamentals of Christianity existing in Christ's disciples.

The dream of a world-wide international series of lessons has been realized only in name—not in reality.   In 1915 even the British Nonconformists found they had reached the "parting of the ways."   The British and the American sections of the International Lesson Committee abandoned joint work.   The term "international" at first meant only the United States and Canada, but with the association of some British workers it was hoped it would become world-wide. The British section was only in advisory relation to the American Lesson Committee for several years.   The cycles of lessons were planned and worked out in detail in America and submitted to the British section for criticism and adaptation. Later a further adjustment or co-operation was attained,

[1] *Organized Sunday-School Work*, 1914, p. 62.

which gave the two sections, British and American, equal status in the selection of the lesson cycles.

This plan speedily aroused discontent in America and it was not wholly satisfactory to the British section. The differences in Sunday-school development in America and Britain, it was urged, required different lesson systems. A discussion of these principles resulted in convincing most of the leaders that independence of action would enable each to render better service to its own constituency. Therefore it was announced that "The British Committee has been reluctantly compelled to break the fellowship of past years and to face the necessity of independent action." This was done in the best spirit and good feeling. The secretary of the British Committee wrote to the American section:

> It is with genuine regret that we . . . sever for the time being our present co-operation. . . . We hope and pray that the independent action on both sides may work for the ultimate good of Sunday-schools the world over. Whatever severance there may be in action, there is none in our regard for you, nor in the sympathy and friendship which time has enriched with many gracious memories. . . . Our growth is not one into any fancied superiority, but only one, like that of our American kinsmen, into a desire for the freedom which will enable us to serve best the Sunday-schools we represent. We cannot fetter them. They do not wish to fetter us. The break is but on the surface and for the purpose of better serving the Kingdom of God. At heart we are one.[1]

Behind these general decisions expressed by prominent editors and leaders were many earnest and progressive workers, some advanced and some conservative in their attitude. What were the wishes and views of the majority of the more quiet but equally faithful friends of the cause? The great body of the Sunday-school forces in Christendom will eventually make themselves felt, and will, by their acts, give the supreme decision respecting the character and general form of the lessons for Bible study in Sunday-schools. What will it be? History indicates that experience and time are required for the final answer to this question.

British Graded Lessons.—The courses of Sunday-school Lessons current in Great Britain, both Graded and Uniform, are quite as many and as diverse as in America. The two sec-

[1] *Sunday-School Chronicle and Christian Outlook*, May 13, 1915, pp. 313, 314.

tions, American and British, of the International Lesson Committee each sought to have "harmonious co-operation with their colleagues," and at the same time provide courses of lessons suited to the needs of their respective constituencies, in America and Great Britain.

Experience of a few years proved the conditions of the two countries were too widely different to make this plan satisfactory or even practicable.

The cleavage began to appear early in the International Uniform Lessons, where the American section conceded to a pressure for four temperance lessons in each annual series. The British section considered "such provision unnecessarily frequent and ethically out of proportion."[1]

Many other differences arose that could not be satisfactorily adjusted because of diverse conditions that could not be changed. Similar difficulties arose in respect to graded lessons. The "elaborate system" issued in America was rejected in favor of a "simpler one" in Great Britain, extending to five departmental grades as against seventeen and upward in the American system. Both systems are, however, in a formative stage, the British tending toward closer grading, the American calling a halt, if not inclined to a less number of grades. British and American graded lessons agree in starting with "nature talks," or "lessons," though the British regard their "nature talks" for the wee ones as supplementary and really not a part of their plan of graded lessons. The two also agree that all or a large majority of lesson subjects "shall be taken from the Holy Scriptures." Hence a prominent British writer (W. H. Groser) declares that "complexity and competition must give way to simplicity and unity." Whether that would satisfactorily open the way for one system or world-course of lessons for America or Europe remains to be proved. The conditions remaining diverse, surely many very serious obstacles would also remain to be overcome.

The British Graded Courses are prepared "by interdenominational counsel and co-operation," which includes most of the Nonconformists. The Church of England, the Friends, the Calvanistic Methodists of Wales, and the Episcopal

[1] W. H. Groser in *The Encyclopedia of Sunday-Schools*, p. 614.

Church of Scotland, however, each maintain a system of graded lessons of their own.

The Standard Graded Courses outlined by the British section of the International Lesson Committee covered nine years (for pupils from the age of nine to eighteen) in three or more grades.

Graded Courses for those below nine years of age were arranged for Beginners and for Primaries. The Junior (nine to eleven), Intermediate (twelve to fourteen), and the Senior (sixteen to eighteen) followed the lower grades. Each grade of a school was assigned, so far as possible, the same great division of Scriptures for study. But this principle could not be consistently applied in all grades.

The American Graded Series called for seventeen or more grades, viz.: Beginners (four to five years of age), two grades; Primary (six to eight), three grades; Junior (nine to twelve), four; Intermediate (thirteen to sixteen), four; Senior (seventeen to twenty), four; also Bible classes of mature and older persons, for which further provision is required according to the conditions and character of the communities and classes.

In Great Britain a strong minority of workers is in favor of Graded Lessons, "though fine grading is distrusted," for the majority of Nonconformists still hold to the Uniform Lessons, believing that the system can be constructed from the standpoint of child development "in a way that would meet all the evangelical needs of the average school."

Among British graded courses are those by the British International Lesson Committee, the Friends' First Day Association, and the Church of England. Each course or system agrees on the general principles of grading, but differs in the point of view and in the details of the system. Thus the so-called international scheme begins in "nature talks" for those four years old; stories of Jesus and creation stories for those five years old; two years with Jesus for Primaries (six to eight); biography and teachings of Jesus for Juniors (eight to twelve); ministry of Jesus and early Old Testament history for Intermediates (twelve to fourteen); Synoptic Gospels and Genesis to Judges for Seniors (sixteen to eighteen).

The Friends' Course of Graded Lessons is less minute, with apparently closer study of Scripture history and themes.

The Church of England's graded courses adhere closely to the church year, and have three departmental divisions—Kindergarten, Middle and Upper School—with five main grades, viz., for those four to five years of age; six to eight years; eight to ten years; ten to thirteen years; and for those thirteen years and upward.

Thus it is evident that both British and American graded leaders feel that they have not yet attained or laid hold of the ideal system. Apparently they are "forgetting the things that are behind" and are "stretching forward to the things that are before." Graded systems of lessons are, therefore, predestined to undergo many and frequent changes for a long time to come.

SECTION X

The support of Sunday-schools has been as phenomenal as their growth. The world was amazed to see millions of persons—many educated and cultured—giving their time and talents to the instruction not merely of neighbors and friends, but of strangers, of outcasts, and of the neglected—and doing it without hope or expectation of pay. This fact is an evidence of divine approval. The various ways of supporting and financing local schools are indicated in the history of the movement.

Working by Faith.—The financial experience of the American Sunday-School Union is a story of successive plunges into borrowing, into debts, and of unexpected and surprising deliverances from financial perils, and it illustrates the financial history of many Sunday-school societies. It began in 1817, with neither gold nor silver. Its chief capital was a cry—the cry of the children. The first money in its treasury was borrowed from friends. With this borrowed money it bought a little stock of publications, poorly adapted to its purpose, and promptly began the preparation and issue of works better suited to its service.

Missionaries were not then employed. Sunday-schools were organized and promoted by voluntary workers, by circulation of literature, and by auxiliary societies. The latter sought to create enthusiasm for mission work through local conventions. In similar meetings appeals were made to a generous public for voluntary contributions from friends of the cause. Funds were received from the sale of publications, but scarcely enough to pay for the cost of production. The object was not commercial profit, but promotion of the cause. It was a gigantic work then to unite Christians of different denominations, to convince them of the importance of founding Sunday-schools, and to provide them with suitable literature.

318

This the friends of the movement aimed to do in America, and to some extent throughout the world.

The Union did a large work with limited means in those formative years before its name was changed to the American Sunday-School Union in 1824. Then its funds amounted to $590.52 cash, and its publications and material were reckoned at a nominal value of about $5,000, against which there were debts and loans of upward of $1,300. It enrolled about 321 auxiliaries, with 1,150 schools and a membership of 93,992, and with its small capital proposed to furnish all the Sunday-schools in the United States with literature at the lowest prices, and also "to place the means of learning to read and understand the sacred Scriptures within the reach of every individual in our country." [1]

General Fund and Mission Fund.—The Missionary Fund in 1824 amounted to $330, including $245 in a savings bank from previous years. The General Fund was the largest fund in the early years of the Union's work. Six missionaries were employed for a short period that year and sustained by borrowing $1,400. About a million copies of publications, besides periodicals, were issued within the year, yet these were found too limited in range and quantity to supply the demand from schools. The Union made forceful appeals concerning the need of cheap Bibles, Testaments, and other publications for the promotion of the Sunday-school cause in the country, and received quite generous responses. Although its receipts from this small beginning soon increased by leaps and bounds, year by year, there seemed to be no end to the large demands from communities wide-spread over the land. It expended about $5,000 in 1823 and in 1824, but in 1829 its expenditures leaped to $75,000. About one-third of its receipts consisted in borrowed money. The managers had faith that friends would approve of these large outlays, in view of the crying demand for schools, and would sustain them in so new and noble a work. So urgent and multiplied were the calls upon the Union for literature and for help in sustaining Sunday-schools, that the managers found it impossible to keep their expenditures within their receipts. (Appendix, p. 467, for Henry Ward Beecher's Appeal and Apology for the West in 1848.) This

---

[1] *Report*, 1825; *Appendix*, p. 31.

effort grew hopeless in 1830, during the period when the unprecedented wave of enthusiasm swept over the country for establishing Sunday-schools in the Mississippi Valley. Though the contributions to the Union's *mission* fund made the amazing leap in one year from $1,000 to $25,000, the calls upon that fund soon exceeded this unprecedented increase. At the end of two years, notwithstanding this hitherto unknown liberality, the receipts fell short of expenditures by $5,000, and the money borrowed by the Union was increased to $74,000.

Increased Overdrafts.—A like wave of enthusiasm for Sunday-school extension in the South sprang up spontaneously in 1832–33. The opposition of a few to the Sunday-school movement served rather to swell than to lessen this enthusiasm. Thousands of dollars were pledged for this new southern movement. The pressure upon the Union for enlarged work was too strong to resist. The Valley Fund was largely overdrawn, the Southern Fund was also speedily exhausted, leaving the Union to carry the burden of increased debt as best it might. Further to embarrass the Society, appeals poured in upon it from foreign mission workers for gratuitous supplies of Union publications, and for money to translate them; to aid mission fields in distant parts of the world where American missionaries were carrying the gospel. Under this added pressure the Union proposed to appropriate special gifts up to $12,000 for this object in foreign fields. It is little wonder that these enterprises, magnanimous and noble as they were, not only exhausted the Union's resources but well-nigh exhausted its credit also. To save the latter, its stock of publications was reduced thousands of dollars and sold at large loss. The Rev. Robert Baird and the Rev. Howard Malcolm and others were engaged to solicit funds, and friends were urged to make loans to tide the Society over the crisis. These strenuous efforts and drastic measures brought temporary relief, enabling the Union to continue its missionary work, though the publications suffered by the serious retrenchment.

The financial crisis of 1837 came, embarrassing creditors, debtors and contributors alike, and seriously diminishing the contributions to its work, so that the debt again increased to $82,000, including a mortgage on its building. In this emergency the Union further curtailed one branch of its extension work—that of furnishing stocks of publications on credit to auxiliaries. This liberal advance of publications to auxiliaries had been made in order to aid them in founding and fostering Sunday-schools in their respective districts. As there were from 350 to 400 auxiliaries, the capital required was large, making the plan too expensive for securing the comparatively small amount of mission work reported by the auxiliaries. A limited number of supply depots was substituted as a temporary measure, to prevent any serious discouragement to mission work. Owing to the financial stringency in the country, these changes gave but partial relief.

The embarrassment returned in 1841 and was so serious that the Society decided to discontinue most of its supply depots and declined longer to sell on credit or commission, proposing to sell for cash only. But as the publications were sold so near to, and sometimes below, the actual cost of production, this measure did not give relief. Then too the pressure for increasing its work in the Mississippi Valley and the West was renewed, due to a fresh, inrolling tide of immigration, and an alarming increase of religious destitution. Large outlays were demanded in response to this irresistible call. By 1849 the advances made in this extension work were so great as again to cripple the issue of publications, periodicals, books, and lesson material, but that was deemed necessary "to save the missionary service from disaster." [1]

Working under the heavy debt and with borrowed capital, somehow the "commission" and "credit" system again crept in; the borrowing went on and held sway for several years. In consequence of these conditions the financial panic of 1857 found the Union already staggering under a crushing debt. This debt included $76,677.21, resulting from excess of expenditures in missionary work, and required the Society to issue obligations for an equal amount for paper, printing, and binding. Besides this, loans had been made to the Society by different parties amounting to $20,750.29, and open accounts of $16,745.36, making the liabilities $114,172.86 (exclusive of mortgages and temporary loans amounting to $44,000 more).

Debt and Porter Loss.—This indebtedness, which appalled

[1] *Report*, 1849, p. 54.

the managers in the financial crisis of 1857, was as nothing compared with the amazement which confronted them in the same year, owing to spurious obligations issued by Corresponding Secretary Porter in whom the greatest confidence had been placed for over thirty years. The character of these spurious obligations was fully reported. The amount of the obligations issued by Mr. Porter without the knowledge of the Society was $88,042.27. Measures were immediately taken to secure the Society from loss. Mr. Porter handed over to the Society all his personal property, and other parties indirectly involved gave notes and mortgages toward making up the loss, so that it was supposed that the net loss to the Society would be only about $35,000, and this amount was promptly subscribed by managers and friends.

The financial depression, however, was changing values rapidly; $37,351.13 of these spurious obligations, which were issued for the benefit of other parties, were replaced by notes secured by a mortgage on real estate as collateral. Owing to the failure of Joseph McDowell, the Society later was compelled to sell the collateral securities, realizing only about 50 per cent. of the amount due.

All the creditors of the Society were anxious for payment and held a meeting at which they appointed a committee to inquire into the Union's financial condition. The Society appointed Lewis R. Ashhurst, H. J. Williams, and the assistant treasurer, W. J. Cheney, as a committee "with full and final powers to arrange with the creditors of the Society."

The liabilities of the Union were reported to be $246,275.59, $198,892.62 of this bearing interest. The available assets were stated at $168,000. The Society's committee proposed payment of the liabilities by instalments, to be completed in ten years. This proposition did not satisfy the creditors, and it was finally agreed that the Society should issue bonds to an amount not to exceed $200,000, and make payments of the same at the rate of 10 per cent. of the principal every six months, with interest on amount due, so that the indebtedness would be paid in five, or five and a half years. This proposition was accepted by the Society as the best that could be obtained from the creditors, but with a distinct understanding that it could not make these payments unless large sums were

SOME PROMINENT SUPPORTERS OF THE SOCIETY

Francis Scott Key.

Elliott Cresson.

Thomas Murdoch.

John Crerar.

S. B. Schieffelin.

contributed by its friends, and that the success of the whole plan would be dependent upon such outside financial aid. The creditors agreed to accept the bonds of the Society in lieu of the notes, acceptances, and obligations which they held, surrendering them to the Society and taking bonds therefor.[1]

It is not surprising that these financial conditions should lead to a division of views and even dissension among the managers themselves. Provision must be made for the payment of the bonds to the creditors, not only by appeals to the friends of the Society for funds, but also by such an efficient and economic management of its operations as would promise some margin toward meeting these obligations.

Expansion or Retrenchment.—Two ways were proposed: one of decided retrenchment in all branches of its operations; the other of a bold and unprecedented advance, the Society throwing itself upon the generosity of the Christian public for relief. After prolonged discussion, the latter course was adopted by a small majority. The entire operations of the Society, publication and missionary, were projected upon a large scale. A weekly Sunday-school and family paper of large size (*The Sunday-School Times*), similar to *The Sunday-School Journal* of 1831, conducted in the spirit and taste of modern journalism, was projected and begun. New illustrated papers—one weekly and the other monthly—displaced the *Penny Gazette*, and the issue of a Sunday-school book every week was decided upon, and a vastly enlarged policy in its missionary work. The announcement of their plans arrested public attention and created some zeal in many quarters. New parties were found temporarily to grant fresh credit, and the Cresson bequest of $50,000 (net $47,500 which was finally used to clear the Society's building) aided in launching the new plans and made them appear feasible.

This expansion system brought a large increase in nominal sales of publications computed at list prices. The discounts granted on these sales and the cost of copyrights and plates were such, however, that the profits did not avail to reduce the debt. Legacies given for the general purposes were either unavailable or proved insufficient to do more than change the

---

[1] *Minutes of the Board for October and November,* 1857; Report of Lewis R. Ashhurst, February 19, 1861, *Minutes of the Board,* 1861.

form of the Society's liabilities.   While the credit of the Union was temporarily improved, the new plan produced fresh embarrassment by its large expenditures, forcing an appeal for more funds.

In the midst of these perplexing conditions the measures proposed for relief gave rise to further dissension among the managers, culminating in a formal protest from twelve of the older members against the course of policy pursued in the management, followed by a decision formally to resign—an action which they were urged to postpone, in the hope that differences might be adjusted.

These managers were constrained to take this action because the Board declined to make each department—missionary, periodical, and book—bear its own charges and expenses, and were influenced also by the temporary suspension of the work of the Committee on Publication.   A few months later the work of the Committee on Publication was resumed, but those members of the Board who had protested against the course stood aloof the greater part of the year from participation in the management of the Society.

In December, 1860, the managers were informed of "another financial crisis in the affairs of the Society," and a special meeting was convened to secure a new loan of several thousand dollars, which was needed, it was said, to save the Society from bankruptcy.[1]   Later this was approved.

Financial Perils.—The expansion plan had not proved successful.   The older and more experienced managers who had dissented from it were requested to return and save the Society from disaster.   They accepted the task on certain conditions, and provided from $60,000 to $90,000 in loans, and adjusted an added issue of bonds.

As in former crises, the burden of retrenchment again fell upon the publications.   *The Sunday-School Times* which had been started in 1858–59 was transferred to private parties, the other periodicals were consolidated, fewer new books were issued, and the accumulated stock was sacrificed at greatly reduced prices to furnish ready money to pacify the creditors. Owing to the depressed financial condition in the whole country it was impossible to realize the amounts expected upon the

[1] Report of Lewis R. Ashhurst, February, 1861.

roperty and assets turned over to secure the Society against
·sses by Mr. Porter. Contributions diminished, and were
·ry hard to secure. A new issue of bonds was authorized
·te in 1861, partly to replace the old ones and to provide for
·le large interest ($12,000 a year) and for other payments on
·count of the debt. One series of bonds amounting to $50,150
·as issued in November, 1861, and another series of eight and
·velve-year bonds, to an amount not exceeding $140,000, was
·thorized early in 1863.

Moreover, the great struggle in the country—the Civil War—
·using the suspension of specie payments and the breaking
·p of business and benevolent operations alike, seems to have
·en a gracious interposition of Providence indirectly favorable
· the Society. While the Civil War suspended the Union's
·issions and destroyed its business in the entire South and
·riously crippled its resources in the North, yet friends again
·llied to its support in this crisis and some large contributions
·ere made for its relief. A large demand came for publica-
·ons of the Society suited for distribution in the camps and
·ospitals of the armies in the Civil War, and these sales, al-
·lough almost at cost, put ready cash in the Union's treasury.
·loreover "war prices" soon prevailed, greatly inflating the
·ominal value of its stock, which enabled the Society to show a
·arked increase of available assets.

The Civil War of 1861–65, which forced a suspension of
·ecie payments as stated, produced other radical changes in
·le country's finances and business. Drastic measures for
·le collection of debts and obligations were impracticable.
·ll creditors, including those of the Society, became more
·nient and deemed it wise to be generous in granting exten-
·on of time for payment.

Among the efforts made toward reducing the liabilities of
·le Society was the formation of a "Book Fund." The plan
·as to secure a fund of $100,000, the interest of which was to
·e used in distributing the Society's publications to needy and
·ruggling schools and kindred objects. About $40,100 were
·bscribed, $8,400 only in cash and $31,700 in the Society's
·onds, which were surrendered for this purpose. But as
·le Society had already expended in benevolent work the full
·nount of the principal of these bonds, besides paying interest

thereon, which was two-fold more than the $8,400 cash, t▮
gain was nominal rather than real.   The "Wurts Fund"
$10,000 was likewise created by giving up bonds of the Societ▮
The interest of this fund (5 per cent.) was used in mission se
vice.   But again this entire sum (in the Wurts fund) had ▮
ready been expended by the society in benevolent work, so
merely changed the form of the indebtedness.

The inflated prices of its publications during the war *appc
ently* increased the assets and induced the managers to a▮
propriate $10,000 of these apparent assets toward relief of t▮
mission work.   A $10,000 bequest by John A. Brown w▮
also applied to reducing the mission debt.   A reduction
40 per cent. on the value of the stock in the hands of t▮
missionaries was also made, in anticipation of a shrinkage
the normal prices which prevailed before the war.   All the
efforts brought no reduction, but rather an increase of t▮
financial burdens upon the Society.

Near the close of the war another effort was made to remo▮
the debt and provide capital for the Union, but this, like t▮
previous efforts of 1830, 1846, 1854 and 1858, was only pa▮
tially successful.   In 1866 about $30,000 were contributed ▮
friends in Philadelphia, specially to supply "depots" of t▮
Society with its publications for distribution in the Midd
West, but this sum too was absorbed in benevolent disti
bution of literature in mission fields.

New Measures.—The embarrassed condition of the countr▮
coupled with the vastly increasing demands for missiona▮
work at the close of the war, virtually forced the Society aga▮
to increase its missions beyond the amount it received the▮
for, so that in 1873, $35,000 more were added to the Society
missionary liabilities.   This $35,000, however (except the i▮
terest), was provided for later out of the discounts allow▮
on sales of the Society's publications through its missionarie
Some indirect gain also came from the previous efforts to r▮
move the debt; for the assistant secretary of missions (Re▮
E. W. Rice), at the request of the managers, ascertained th▮
one cause of the excess of expenditures in missionary wo▮
was due to rating mission pledges made at the beginning of t▮
year at their face value, whereas it appeared from the recor▮
of the Society for years that only about 80 per cent. of tho▮

edges had been redeemed in cash. If allowance had been
made at the beginning of each year for this shrinkage, the
receipts would have covered the expenditures in benevolent
work. This plan was finally adopted and proved satisfactory.
In the decade 1870 to 1880, the receipts for current expenses gradually increased. The John C. Green Fund of
100,000 was created by the legatees of that estate in 1877,
the income to be used for two specified objects. However, the
liabilities steadily increased by accruing interest and still
weighed heavily on the Society.

New Executive Committee.—To provide for the bonds becoming due and for this interest, a new issue of bonds for
125,000 was authorized by the Union early in 1877. Besides
this amount, over $100,000 had been borrowed from trust
funds to provide for the payment of excess of expenditures in
missionary and benevolent work, and there was a floating
business indebtedness of over $20,000.

After careful consideration of the debt and measures for
relief, in 1879 the treasurer and chairman of the Finance
Committee resigned, as unwilling to grapple with the financial
situation. A new Executive Committee was created which,
with the Committee on Finance, as reconstructed, formed a
plan for paying the debt and for providing the Society with an
adequate capital, without interfering with the support of its
mission work. This Executive Committee comprised the
editor (Rice), treasurer (Ashhurst), and secretary of missions
(Wurts and, on his death, Dr. Crowell), the heads of the three
branches of the Society's activities at that time. The Executive Committee (through its chairman) presented a sketch of
the growth of the debt and of the efforts which had been
unsuccessfully made for relief, with some of the probable
causes of the failures.

The liabilities of the Society in 1880 amounted to
266,978.78. The causes of the debt were stated to be chiefly
two: (1) furnishing the publications to the public for many
years at less than the cost of production; (2) expending more in
benevolent distribution of literature and in missionary work
than was contributed for those purposes. To insure the success of the plan, an inquiry was made in regard to the necessity for Union schools and for publications issued on the

Union principle, which extended to every state in the natic
The replies were reported to be uniformly emphatic that su
schools were more widely needed than ever and that such ١
ligious literature was an absolute necessity. Further to insu
the success of the plan, without diverting contributions frc
current missionary work, it was decided not to make a *pub*
appeal. Moreover, it was unanimously agreed that the "٢
debt" policy, which had been repeatedly approved but nev
enforced, should now be faithfully carried out. As a conditi٠
upon which funds were to be solicited, the Society placed its٠
under a pledge not hereafter to incur debt.

The Executive Committee further adopted measures f
eliminating waste in labor, time, and in unproductive detai
putting the business on a strictly cash basis, buying and se
ing for cash and discounting all bills. This resulted not on
in bringing the business expenditures within its receipts, b٠
in providing means for paying the floating indebtedness whi٠
amounted to several thousand dollars.

While there was no *public* appeal, as already stated, t٢
Society's work and some results were presented privatel٢
personally, and by correspondence. Besides adhering to t٢
"no debt" policy, it was agreed that hereafter the expenc
tures in *each branch* of the Society's operations should be pa
out of the receipts for that branch.[1]

Funds to be Increased.—After many months of caref
study of the Union's history, and successive seasons of pray٠
by the managers, the plan was matured and approved. Tl
first contribution of $25,000 was volunteered by Alexand٠
Brown, Chairman of the Finance Committee. He afterwaı
added $15,000 to form the "Raikes' Fund"; the income of tl
latter to be used in mission work. Meanwhile, by a provisic
of the John C. Green Income Fund of $100,000, $20,000 of tl
Society's bonds in that fund were to be retired. The princip٠
of the Green Fund was to be kept intact by gradually r٠
placing this amount from the income. J. W. C. Leveridge, tl
Society's attorney in New York, at Dr. Rice's suggestion, iı
fluenced a special bequest of $20,000 for the same object, ٤
that before 1900 the indebtedness of over $266,000, with tl
interest, was entirely canceled.

[1] *Reports*, 1861, p. 12; 1882, pp. 10–12; 1900, pp. 7–9; 1909, pp, 7–9.

Moreover, while these efforts to remove the debt and increase the capital were being made, the current receipts of the Society for mission work were more than doubled. The Union thus had its building, stock of publications, and plates free from incumbrance, and had also gained over half a million of income-bearing funds, the income to be used for missionary and other forms of its benevolent work.

The benevolent gifts and bequests to the Society for the first forty or more years came from many individuals and organizations widely scattered over the country. Large gifts from one party were rare, and large gifts from one place were also quite infrequent. Thus among the first large gifts to the Society were $15,000 and upward contributed in 1828 by the citizens of Philadelphia for the buildings to be used as headquarters of the Union.

The enthusiastic appeals for planting Sunday-schools in the Mississippi Valley brought returns in seven years (1831 to 1837) of $102,078. The contributions to the general work or General Fund of the Society (not missionary), for which there was no special enthusiasm during the same seven years, amounted to $74,540. While this was not given for missionary purposes, the Society was compelled to appropriate a large proportion of these gifts to meet the excess in mission expenses incurred in planting schools in the Mississippi Valley and in the South, expecting that these sums would be returned to the General Fund for which they were designed by the donors.

There were many small bequests and legacies left to the Society during the early part of this period, but the first one on record of $5,000 or over came from Mary Fassett of Philadelphia in 1853–54. The next year, 1855, a bequest from Jabez Godell of Buffalo, New York, paid in instalments during five years thereafter, amounted to over $25,000. A year or two later came the $50,000 (less inheritance tax of $2,500) from Elliot Cresson of Philadelphia, and $10,000 from Seth Grosvenor of New York.

In the period from 1857 to 1877 there followed numerous legacies and gifts intended or used for meeting the special demands upon the Society during the Civil War, or for reducing the heavy debt and maintaining the credit of the Society, as heretofore stated.

Churches Founded.—The chief support of the Society's work during sixty years was derived from a wide circle of living contributors. A large proportion of schools formed by the missionaries of the American Sunday-School Union on the frontier opened the way for founding churches of various evangelical denominations. This was the intention and expectation of the Society in maintaining its pioneer work. In each of these communities the Union sowed the gospel seed and developed a few Christian disciples who could be used as the nucleus of a church. The kind and character of the church were determined, not by the Union, but by the majority of the people in each community. Because of this pioneer work, the stronger Sunday-schools and churches in the older part of the country cheerfully aided in sustaining the Union's operations, believing it an effective way of promoting the growth of their respective denominations in the newer parts of the country. It was not uncommon for two or more church Sunday-schools in that period to unite in support of a Union missionary on the frontier.

Later, when the denominations, through their ecclesiastical organizations, began Sunday-school missionary work, the schools aided their respective denominations, as was natural, and their contributions to Union work gradually diminished. It was providential that the success of the plan for extinguishing the debt and providing an adequate capital for the Union led to a more careful cultivation of individual givers and the developing of a wider circle of supporting friends.

Plan for Capital.—In working this plan the first effort was to retire the $125,000 outstanding bonds and the interest. At the same time the stock of publications was reduced and the whole business put upon a cash basis by reduction of expenses to such an extent that it provided for the liquidation of the floating indebtedness of over $20,000. The second step in the plan was to provide for the payment of upward of $100,000 borrowed from the trust funds. Part of this sum had gone into bonds for the formation of a so-called book fund, as before stated. When this fact was explained to those who gave the bonds, the majority of them cheerfully made the same an absolute gift to the Society, to the amount of over $30,000. The remaining sums temporarily borrowed from the trust funds were repaid by individual contributions to meet the general indebtedness and provide capital for the Society.

Literature at Cost.—Clearly to understand the financial history of the Society it must not be forgotten that over and over again its friends and the public were informed that it was believed to be necessary to furnish its literature at, and often below, cost as a part of its early benevolent work. This was done, as already stated, to encourage the forming of schools in new communities unable to provide wholly for their own equipment. This deficiency was intended to be provided by contributions given with this distinct understanding, that they were for the "General Fund." But the heavy and, to some extent, the unwarrantable drafts made upon that fund from time to time to pay missionaries had been one great cause of the accumulated indebtedness. Churches, schools, and individuals had made gifts to these several objects, sometimes to one and sometimes to the other, as the reasons therefore appealed to them.

When the Society not merely adopted, but finally decided to adhere to, a "no debt and cash policy," and many of the churches and schools that had hitherto been contributors turned the larger portion of their gifts to support their own denominational work, the wisdom of enlisting a large number of individual givers in the support of the Union work was more apparent. Several of those who were prominent in its management and direction had long perceived the advantage of giving greater prominence to the cultivation of individual donors, and were ready to follow up efforts along the same line that had been pursued in the plan for removing the indebtedness and providing an adequate capital for the Society.

Bequests and Gifts.—It is not necessary to weary the reader by going into any detailed account of this phase in the development of benevolent Sunday-school missionary finances. Suffice it to say, that those sections of the country which had been most benefited by the early work of the Union and where the greatest number of pioneer Sunday-schools had been established—as, for example, in the Mississippi Valley and the Middle West—enrolled the largest number of generous individual supporters. In fact, the managers were greatly surprised to find so large a list of supporting friends in nearly every section of the United States.

It will be obvious to those experienced in benevolent work that the sums received by bequests or legacies are often due to influences which have been set in motion many years before the bequests are received.

The Christian and philanthropic people of the New England States, famed for their conscientious and liberal giving, had their attention turned to the benevolent work of the Society very early in its history. The earnest advocacy of its efficient pioneer work in the newer sections of the country, as presented by Francis Wayland, Henry Clay Trumbull, Nelson Kingsbury, Addison P. Foster, W. L. Carver, and many others equally worthy, has brought to the Society from the New England States, in addition to thousands from living givers for current work, many legacies and bequests. A few may be noted: the Harris bequest, $31,000; the Camps legacy, $8,000; the Chase, $5,000; Charles Cobb, $6,000; the Cook, $5,000; the Beach gifts, $12,000; the Colby, $15,000; the Graves, $3,000; the S. Mead bequest, $39,000; the Billings, $15,000; the Consecration Fund, $4,000; the Kendall bequest, $5,000; the Kimbell, $10,000; the Botsford gift, $3,000; and many others.

Similar personal work in New York by S. B. S. Bissell, J. H. Burtis, F. H. Wisewell, L. Milton Marsh, E. P. Bancroft, and others, wonderfully aided and supplemented by officers and managers of the Society resident in the city, and by such pastors as the late Dr. John Hall, increased its resources by these among other notable gifts and bequests: Dr. Silliman, $50,000; the Andrews gifts, $22,000; the Elys, $75,000; S. B. Hill, $30,000; Peter Lott, $18,000; the Stuarts gifts, $80,000; the Neefus, $15,000; Webster, $4,000; Strong, $13,000; Stone, $61,000; the Jesups gifts, $150,000; the Schieffelin Bros., $40,000, and many like generous givers, who were interested in some particular form of service rendered by Sunday-school agencies.

Most of the large sums, named above and below, were intended for some special form of work or were limited to some special district, so that neither the principal nor income could be used for the Society's general work. For the support of Sunday-

Schools and Bible instruction in all its branches, throughout the country, these specific gifts have greatly increased the necessity for a large increase of contributions for the general work. These individual givers and gifts must continue to multiply in order to sustain the ordinary work not only, but are needful to enable the Society wisely to use the special funds.

The officers and managers in Philadelphia and vicinity during the last thirty years became specially interested in making personal gifts and in influencing others to add to the Society's resources. Besides the several gifts and bequests, which have been noted in previous pages, the Cresson, Green, Wurts, and Raikes funds and other sums given to liquidate the indebtedness and to relieve the embarrassment of the Society, the following, among others, may be mentioned: S. C. Brace, $15,000; A. M. Powers, $14,000; Samuel Ashhurst, $7,000; H. S. Benson, $25,000; Brunot, $4,000; Detwiler, $6,000; J. L. Erringer, $5,000; C. W. Henry, $5,000; Lowry, $110,000 (less $5,000 tax); Troutman, $5,000; and several who requested that their names and gifts should not be made public.

In the central section of Ohio, Indiana, and Michigan, Chidlaw with his Welsh eloquence, W. A. Hillis with his magnetic personality, Thomas Wright, Geo. F. Henderson, and others, have awakened an interest among the people of that region that was really nation-wide and brought numerous gifts and bequests bearing the ear-marks of personality. These, among others, will be recalled by residents of that district: S. Houston, $25,000; Davis, $5,000; and the Yandes Brothers, $67,000.

As might be expected, there was a splendid development of individual donors in the Middle Northwest, with Chicago as a center. It was in this region of the Great Lakes and the Mississippi Valley that the first great pioneer work in planting Sunday-schools was accomplished. When the people of that region who became the spiritual inheritors of that work began to amass wealth, it was Christian and natural that their gratitude should be expressed in generosity toward the organization that had been prominent in fostering the pioneer religious work of that region. It is significant also that many of the leaders were laymen. There were A. W. Corey, Stephen Paxson, D. L. Moody, and, conspicuously, F. G. Ensign, with his associate E. B. Stevenson, and others. Mr. Ensign was especially happy in his appeals to business men. "Let us not be deceived," he said, "unsanctified wealth and unsanctified, though cultured, brains have elements of weakness in a republic like ours. To spend a million of dollars a day in building railroads, and $350 a day to give the 11,000,000 children and youth the Sunday-school, is like building a palatial ocean steamer, furnished with every modern appliance, and then to add a ten-dollar rudder made of tin."

With his great zeal and his commanding presence, he was successful in enlisting the business men of Chicago and the Middle West to a remarkable extent in the support of the Society which he served. The gifts and bequests from this region represent much self-denial; the multitude of small amounts being quite as noble as the more princely sums. Among them were the fund of the three Adamses, $39,000; Barney, $9,000; Crerar, $50,000; Curtis, $7,000; Drake, $21,000; J. N. Field, $45,000; L. Gould, $11,000; H. A. Jones, $10,000; Murdock, $700,000 (less $50,000 tax); S. Reid, $5,000; Sprague, $19,000; G. and R. Scott, $33,000; K. S. Isham, $20,000; E. French, $17,000; Hinckley, $4,000; Keith, $5,000. Nearly all these sums were for special work in the Middle West, and were and are not available for the promotion of Sunday-schools in other great and very needy sections of the country.

The South, Southwest, and the Pacific Coast have been so absorbed in caring for their own local work that they have not yet responded by as many large gifts toward the accumulated resources of the Society. There are not wanting, however, many indications that the people of these sections are interested, and as material prosperity increases their characteristic generosity will be manifested side by side with that which has been recorded of those in the North. We note these bequests among those: G. S. Jones, $7,000; J. T. Clark, $10,000; besides those from many givers yet living.

Funds Yet Needed.—Lest the reader should infer from these generous bequests that the American Sunday-School Union does not need large gifts, let him be advised that no small portion of these gifts were promptly used in support of benevolent work—the Society distributing the same over one or more decades to avoid undue expansion and contraction in its service. Other of these gifts were designated for specific and special fields in which the donors were particularly interested during their lifetime, and the income of which cannot be used for any other purpose. Thus the Society is required to expend the income from many of the largest bequests in what was known at the time they were executed as the Northwest District, and cannot use them elsewhere. The very fact that these bequests enabled the Society to do so large a work in the Northwest created a demand for a similar service in other sections which the Union had no funds to meet. It has an imperative need for $100,000 to aid in sustaining mission schools in the rural South, and an equal sum for the Southwest. Another larger sum will be required to provide Bible schools for many sections remote from churches in the growing Pacific Coast region.

The demands for elementary teacher training everywhere, in the Union schools remote from churches and from centers where such advantages are available, are so numerous, and the means of the people needing to be reached so limited, that more than $200,000 are required efficiently to maintain this Union teacher-training work. The multiplied calls also for better equipment of rural schools, for improved appliances and to introduce the improved modern methods of instruction, are so pressing that the workers in their desire to meet these imperative needs are overtaxing the resources of the Society year by year. The Union should have an income of $250,000 to apply to the equipment and improvement of schools that cannot be well cared for by the country churches, and for many that are yet beyond the reach of any church.

And lastly, although not least, a campaign of education and information for the moral and spiritual betterment of rural communities where the churches are weak would immensely strengthen the influence of the weak churches and increase the power of Christian churches throughout the rural sections of the country. The Society ought to have at least another $100,000, the income of which might be applied for this splendid work.

Finances of Conventions and Associations.—The expenses of the National Sunday-School Conventions of 1832, 1833 and 1859 appear to have been provided by voluntary contributions from a few leaders and friends. The delegates to these conventions provided their own traveling and other expenses, or they were paid in some cases by the local organizations and schools which they represented.

At the meetings of the National and International Sunday-School Conventions of 1872 and on, appeals were made to the delegates in session for funds to carry forward the work for the triennium succeeding each convention. A change in name from National to International Sunday-School Convention was made in 1875, and it met thereafter (as it had from 1869) once in three years. The method pursued at the International Convention in 1899 will indicate its general plan for securing funds during the past generation. At the Convention of 1899, B. F. Jacobs, acting for the Executive Committee, outlined the plans of the Convention for the coming three years, and said to carry them out would require not less than $12,000 per annum, or a total of $36,000 for the triennum. He said:

> We have at least two ways of getting this offering and securing this money. The first is to have the money pledged by the state association or provincial or territorial association directly for the support of the work. The best plan as I believe is that a Sunday-school shall not be called upon to make but one offering for international, state and county Sunday-school work; that the boy who gives one cent knows that he is giving a part of that cent to his county work, to his state work, and to the international work; and I hope the time will come when he will give a part of it to the work in the world outside of that. As an illustration of his plan, Mr. Jacobs added, Our expenses reach about $10,000 per annum in Illinois and we do not know what it is to suffer for money. It all comes in this way, and there is not a company of a few rich men who stand back and make up deficiencies. Pledges were called for from the delegates, and it was said, Understand, it is not a legal obligation when you make a pledge, you will be forgiven if you are unable to pay it. But it will have to be forgiveness and not excuse. We want the money. We will have the cards passed. Understand the amount pledged is so much per annum for three years.[1]

The pledges were then made by states and provinces amounting to nearly $30,000. The pledges were to be paid one-third each year in advance. Similar methods had been pursued at several previous conventions and were continued at the convention meetings of the International Sunday-School Association into the present century. When the International

[1] *Report*, Organized Sunday-School Work in America, 1899, pp. 131–133.

unday-School Convention was incorporated as the Inter-
ational Sunday-School Association in 1907, the funds were
rovided in part by life memberships of $1000 each, in addi-
ion to the pledges made by delegates at the convention.
Among the leaders conspicuous in making this change were W.
N. Hartshorn, Marion Lawrance, E. K. Warren, George W.
Bailey, H. J. Heinz, Fred. A. Wells, J. J. Maclaren, W. A.
Cudaly and others, who became trustees by the charter.

Since the act of incorporation, this Board of Trustees is
"charged with the financial affairs of the Association, includ-
ng the raising and disbursing of all money and the auditing
of all bills."

State Sunday-School Unions.—As early as 1825 and before,
he Sunday-school workers in each state began to form organ-
zations which were then called "State Sunday-School Unions,"
which were usually auxiliary to the American Sunday-School
Union.   Their finances were provided by voluntary gifts and
pledges in part, supplemented by appropriations in cash, or
n publications or services furnished by the parent Union.
Similar appropriations were made also to local unions in large
cities like Philadelphia, New York and Cincinnati.   Thus
the reports of the American Sunday-School Union show that
appropriations were made to the New York Sunday-School
Union Society for ten years (1848–1857) exceeding $36,000,
and in the next ten years (1858–1867) similar appropriations
were made to several auxiliaries, including New York, amounting to upward of $45,000.   The appropriations made by the
parent Society to local Unions previous to 1873 amount to
over $130,000, not including those previous to 1844, of which
no detailed accounts have been found.   The financial efforts
of these State Sunday-School Unions and of the local Unions
from 1825 to 1870 prepared the way for raising the funds required by the later State Sunday-School Conventions which
were formed in that period and have continued for about
half a century.   Most of these state conventions or associations are incorporated in their respective states and are independent of one another, while they co-operate more or less
efficiently with the International Sunday-School Association.
They solicit funds for their own work, and several of them
have been accustomed to appropriate a certain amount toward

the support of the International Association. Many of th
states raise their finances in a manner similar to that pursue
by the International Association as described above.

The denominational Sunday-school organizations provid
their finances by direct appeal to the churches and Sunday
schools of their order, and to their friends. While these ar
also voluntary gifts, the members recognize an obligation t
sustain these and other phases of their special church work.

Finances of Local Schools.—The methods pursued by th
local schools to provide for their respective expenses var
widely according to conditions and customs and ideas of th
people of the community where the school is located. Th
answers to the question asked by the first National Sunday-
school Convention, "What is your method of raising funds for
the support of the school?" reveal the methods of schools then.
The replies, for the most part, stated that they raised funds by
voluntary subscription, by contributions and by collections.
In some cases the church was expected to support its school,
but the answers from many quarters indicate that this expectation was not realized.

Some remarked that it was a disgrace to the church that in
so many schools the teachers are often left to bear the greater
part of the expenses.[1] In other cases some committees or
persons were appointed to obtain the funds. In a few cases a
regular tax was levied on teachers and on individuals to support the local school. In other cases a number of persons
voluntarily joined together, to make an annual subscription
and contribution, sufficient to pay the expenses of the local
school. Collections for this object were often made at the
Monthly Concert of Prayer, at meetings of the local association, or of the teachers, and at stated seasons collections were
sometimes made at the church service, after hearing an annual
sermon relating to Sunday-school work.

In many places the churches have adopted modern business
methods for providing these local expenses. Churches place
the expenses of the Sunday-school in with the general budget of
annual church expenses, just as it should be whenever practicable. It is a lamentable fact, however, that in many communities the teachers and friends, who give the time and at-

---

[1] On Value of Sunday-School Teachers' services.

ention to the conducting of the school, are also left to defray
he expenses or to secure funds therefor, as best they may
rom their friends. When all of the followers of the Master
ecognize their obligation in full, then the expenses of the local
schools, like all other funds required for carrying on religious
work, will be furnished according to the Apostle's general rule:
'Upon the first day of the week let every one of you lay by him
in store, as God hath prospered him." "Every man as he
hath purposed in his heart, so let him give; not grudgingly,
nor of necessity: for God loveth a cheerful giver" (1 Cor. 16 :
2; 2 Cor. 9 : 7).

SKETCHES OF PROMINENT WORKERS

Jay Cooke (1821–1905); **Manager** (1854–1861); **Vice-President**
(1870–1905).

Jay Cooke attained world-wide fame as a financier. He
became a manager of the American Sunday-School Union in
1854, serving on important financial and special committees,
and aided in persuading the creditors of the Society to grant it
an extension and permit it to continue its work, though very
heavily in debt. Pressed by raising finances for the government during the Civil War, Mr. Cooke felt constrained to
withdraw from the Society's service for a time. In 1870 he
accepted the position of vice-president, giving the Society
counsel, time, and contributions until his death in 1905.

Mr. Cooke was not only a great financier, he was a noble
patriot and a sincere Christian. His sagacity, enthusiasm,
and patriotism successfully floated great war loans in 1861–65
and inspired the people to take government bonds to the
amount of $2,500,000,000, when great bankers declared
$50,000,000 would be the utmost that could be expected.

He was born in Sandusky, Ohio, 1821, and trained as a
banker in Philadelphia. His firm, Jay Cooke & Co., maintained the nation's imperilled credit. Some years later, when
forced to suspend, and start comparatively a poor man in
business life, he succeeded in making a fortune and in paying
all his creditors in full, with interest. During his entire career
he practiced a systematic plan of benevolence, putting aside a
definite part of his income for charity. But his gifts were al-

ways without display, and often without the giver being known. His large gifts were usually made without solicitation.

He had a sunny disposition and spread brightness and happiness around him through his long and useful life. He was a generous friend of the American Sunday-School Union, using many hundreds of dollars' worth of literature, which he distributed regularly to those unable or unwilling to purchase it, making gifts to its mission work, besides sharing in its counsels and financial management.

With characteristic fidelity, he examined anew into the economy and efficiency of the management of the American Sunday-School Union before responding to the personal appeal of its Committee for Special Contributions to liquidate its debt and provide it with adequate capital. The writer recalls Mr. Cooke's searching questions, demanding a knowledge of authentic documents and the financial records of the Society to answer. When satisfied by his investigations, with his usual quietness Mr. Cooke gave a check for several thousands of dollars, remarking, "Do not publish nor tell any one of this contribution." "How then shall it be acknowledged by the Society's treasurer?" he was asked. "Oh, just say 'From a friend.'" It was a happy illustration of what the Master said about giving (Matt. 6 : 3).

George Hay Stuart (1816–1890), 1848–1883.

Of mercurial temper, with flashing blue eyes and an energetic personality, Mr. Stuart was a conspicuous person in any assembly, and was happy in presiding over large meetings. He delighted to speak of all the great men of his day as special friends. Cosmopolitan in his views, probably he will be longest remembered for his service during the Civil War (1861–65) as chairman of the Christian Commission. For more than thirty years he was the superintendent of the Sunday-school in his own church and was unanimously chosen president of the third National Sunday-School Convention, Newark, New Jersey, 1869. He had then been a manager of the American Sunday-School Union since 1848 and continued to be an officer of the Society until 1883.

The youngest of three children, he was born in Ireland in

1816 of a well-to-do family, members of the Irish Presbyterian Church. He came to America when young, finding a home with his uncle, William H. Scott of Philadelphia, in 1831. He was active and ardent in many forms of religious work.

His interest in the American Sunday-School Union led him frequently to entertain three of its old and faithful missionaries, John McCullagh, B. W. Chidlaw, and Stephen Paxson, when they came to the East to tell the story of their work. He was a great admirer of Stephen Paxson and counted him "a man of a thousand." Paxson's racy humor and inexhaustible fund of anecdotes delighted Mr. Stuart. His sketches of frontier experience brought vividly before his host a life fascinating through its contrasts with that in the East, so that he declared, "Few men living have occupied a warmer place in my heart." Mr. Stuart was apt to spring questions upon the Society and carry them through by sudden excitement. In the trying period of 1857 to 1861, when the Society was heavily in debt—the impending war cutting off its resources so that its friends were discouraged if not almost in despair—two courses were open: severe retrenchment, or wild plunging ahead, meeting all calls, however large, and trusting to the boldness of the movement to bring increased support and income. Conservative managers favored retrenchment and placing all the Society's operations on a cash or "no debt" basis. But the enthusiasm of Mr. Stuart in favor of inflation temporarily prevailed. Among other things, it was determined to publish a new book each week, start *The Sunday-School Times* weekly, for teachers, and undertake corresponding expansions in mission work. Unfortunately for this view, the public mind was too busy with the coming storm of Civil War to give attention to these dashing plans or to respond to the call for funds to support them.

Mr. Stuart chafed under these conditions. He was restless as a caged lion. His own firm going into liquidation, he had only counsel and advice to give. His enthusiasm made him a prominent leader, though not always a prudent one where economy as well as efficiency was required. But at times he appreciated the less spectacular side of every good work. Thus he declared at one of the Union's anniversaries,

> This Society has not been making a great noise, but it has been doing a great work. . . . It goes before all the churches as the breaker-up of the way. It goes into the wilderness and waste places, preparing the way of the Lord. It organizes Union Sabbath-schools that afterward become churches. They may be Episcopal, Baptist, Methodist, Reformed, Lutheran, or Presbyterian, or any one of the various names, but the Union goes before them all, preparing a way for them.

His characteristic breeziness of manner made everybody give attention when he appeared on the scene, whether it was a public assembly, or a deliberative meeting of managers, or a conference with the officers of the Union. He was often laid aside by distressing attacks of asthma, but when he appeared afterward it would seem that he wanted to make up for lost time, for he would dash into the Society's building like a cyclone, asking questions and calling for information that would take the time of a dozen workers for weeks to furnish. Later his disagreement with the majority of the managers became more pronounced and his health more uncertain, so that, his term of office expiring, his connection with the Union came to an end in 1883. Having such a man in an institution made stagnation impossible.[1]

Robert Lenox Kennedy (1822–1887), Fourth President of the American Sunday-School Union (1873–1882).

Among men of large administrative abilities, Robert Lenox Kennedy was esteemed for his integrity, his far-sighted business wisdom, and his singularly retiring disposition. He was born in New York, November 24, 1822, and graduated at Columbia College. He studied law, but never entered the profession. He chose business and banking, and rose to eminence, for over ten years being president of the Bank of Commerce, then one of the largest banks in New York. He filled many positions of honor and trust in benevolent institutions, among them the Lenox Library, founded by his uncle, Robert Lenox. His attention was drawn to the work of the American Sunday-School Union by a daughter of one of its managers, whom he married.

After serving as manager for upward of a dozen years, he was unanimously elected president of the Society, May, 1873,

[1] See also *Biography of George H. Stuart*, edited by Prof. Robert Ellis Thompson.

to succeed John A. Brown. He applied the same ability, discrimination, and judgment in grasping its work that he had shown in business. Its objects and methods had a firm place in his confidence. He became interested in the faithful service of "Father" Martin, and showed his appreciation of it by a gift of $10,000, creating the "Wurts Fund," in memory of his first wife, requesting that the income be applied toward the support of Mr. Martin during his lifetime. Mr. Kennedy was the trusted friend and advisor of John C. Green and, on behalf of Mrs. Green and the other residuary legatees, he conveyed in trust to the American Sunday-School Union $100,000 from the Green Estate, to promote the Union's work. With the cordial concurrence of Mrs. Green, the trust directs that five-sixths of the income of this fund be applied to the support of the Society's missionary work, and one-sixth of it be set aside to aid the Union "in securing a Sunday-school literature of the highest order of merit." This may be done either by procuring works upon a given subject germane to the objects of the Society, to be written or compiled by authors of established reputation or known ability, or by offering premiums for manuscripts for publication by the Union, in accordance with the objects of the institution. Many valuable works have been issued under the provisions of this fund. (Appendix, p. 479, List of Green Fund Books.)

His frequent absences abroad and his many business and benevolent interests so absorbed his strength that Mr. Kennedy positively declined re-election to the presidency in 1882. He passed to the other life while returning from Europe, September 14, 1887, leaving the world an example of Christian integrity and noble service.

Lewis R. Ashhurst.

For thirty-five years Lewis R. Ashhurst was regarded as foremost among the managers of the American Sunday-School Union. Indeed, so influential was he in its councils that it became a facetious remark among some of his close friends, "Mr. Ashhurst carries the American Sunday-School Union in his breast pocket." The records and correspondence of the Society during the stormy period of 1860 and 1861 impress one with the general truth of this humorous remark. Mr. Ashhurst shunned anything spectacular, and never "played to the galleries." His repeated reports upon the finances and missionary and general work of the Society show that he had gained a comprehensive and exact knowledge of the purpose, history, and polity of the Society at first hand. He was familiar with every important measure adopted or proposed for a generation. His services were manifold and important, as the writer has abundant reason, personally, to know. His influence was foremost and powerful in securing the adoption of the Uniform Lesson scheme of 1872. His strong convictions and sense of justice made him a strong friend of Dr. F. A. Packard, and his wisest and most efficient supporter. To him, as much as to any other person, is the Society indebted for its deliverance from the long and distracting dissensions which preceded the Civil War.

James Bayard, his life associate, voiced the esteem in which Mr. Ashhurst was held:

> As a practical man of business and of excellent judgment, he made himself familiar with all the workings of the Society and was invaluable as a manager. A steady friend in all circumstances of adversity as well as prosperity, he stood firm in times of greatest peril and contributed largely and efficiently by his counsels and his means for the support of the Society. As chairman of the Committee on Missions, and member of the Committee on Publication, he exerted a constant influence on all the operations of the Society.

His associates declared that his removal by death deprived them of a wise counsellor, an efficient manager, and a highly esteemed friend. It was due to his patient investigation of its obligations, and his financial wisdom, that the Union succeeded in satisfying the pressing demands of a committee of its creditors for immediate payment. His presentation of the services of the Society in promoting the betterment of the country, and of its record and conditions, was so lucid and strong that the creditors cordially granted extension of time and proposed to aid the Union to continue the good work in which it had achieved so much. They appreciated the beneficent spirit which led the managers of the Society to respond so liberally to the calls for aid in frontier and forming communities, and which was the chief cause of the financial embarrassment. They recognized, also, that with men like Mr. Ashhurst, Jay Cooke, John A. Brown, and James Bayard the Society would surely and honorably discharge every obligation, and that they, as creditors, would be acting discreetly to win its friends as customers. In all phases of this delicate and difficult situation Lewis R. Ashhurst proved the man for the hour, raised up of God for this important service.

Levi Knowles (1813–1898). Manager. Treasurer and Vice-President (1842–1898).

For the long period of fifty-six years Mr. Knowles served the American Sunday-School Union as manager and officer. Successful as a flour merchant, diligent in business, yet he gave large portions of his time, money, and abilities to benevolent and philanthropic work. Bountiful in his service to his own church (Baptist), he was abundant in labors in undenominational organizations; having, at one time or another, been the treasurer of no less than fifteen benevolent societies and a prominent officer in six other similar institutions.

He became a manager of the American Sunday-School Union in 1842, treasurer in 1861, and vice-president from 1875 until his death. He outlived all his associates in service, continuing vigorous in mind, active in body, and young in heart. He counted his service in the Union as the best of his life. He was earnest, never impulsive; prudent, yet progressive; patient, never in haste, yet thinking and acting with dispatch and precision. His high sense of honor, conscientiousness, and sterling integrity commanded the confidence of his associates, so that he was urged to remain in the Board even when an expansive policy was adopted (1859–1861) contrary to his best judgment, and was soon elected treasurer and aided in carrying the Union through a financial crisis in its history. As treasurer, he humorously said he "received no compensation, not even a postage stamp," but he did receive the esteem and gratitude of all his co-laborers. Calm and courteous in manner, sound in judgment, clear in his grasp of affairs, his patient examination into every phase of great questions, his prudent counsel, his firm adherence to convictions, his self-denial for others, and his generous gifts, won a high place in the esteem of all his associates and inspired them with thankfulness to

God for the blessed fellowship they had so long with him in the work of the Lord.[1]

Hon. William Strong, LL.D. (1808–1895), Fifth President of the American Sunday-School Union (1883–1895).

Judge Strong came to the leadership of the Society at a time when there was a call for a deliverer—some one able to point the way to a marked advanced movement. For nearly a quarter of a century he had been one of its officers. For more than fifty years the Union had responded to pressing calls for missionary and benevolent services, even when its treasury was empty and it was already burdened with a heavy debt. Spasmodic efforts had periodically been made to reduce or remove the debt, but without much success. One of the results of these spasmodic appeals was a tendency to lessen regular gifts. It was evident that the debt must be wiped out or the Society crippled and possibly crushed. Judge Strong's long familiarity with the Society's work, his learning, and his distinguished reputation as a Justice of the Supreme Court of the United States, qualified him to lead the Society in a plan for liquidating this debt and in providing adequate capital. Vigorous in mind and earnest in purpose, he gave the Society the benefit of his valuable legal knowledge in completing the measure which resulted in the removal of every dollar of indebtedness of the Society, clearing the Society's buildings, and providing a reasonably adequate capital to tide it over critical periods in the country's finances. He was deeply interested in, and highly valued, its literature as an evangelizing agency, and forcibly expressed his view of its great usefulness at an anniversary held by his request in Washington in 1892. (See *Sunday-School World*, 1892, p. 266.)

He was honored by three colleges with the degree of Doctor of Laws. He reached the ripe age of eighty-seven, vigorous in his mental faculties, "His eye was not dimmed nor his natural force abated." He passed to his reward August 19, 1895, having led the American Sunday-School Union through a great crisis and successfully inaugurated one of the most important eras in its history.

[1] See *Levi Knowles—In Memoriam;* also *Sunday-School World*, 1898, p. 84.

Alexander Brown (1815–1893,.

Among the prominent managers of the American Sunday-School Union in critical periods of its history, Alexander Brown stands easily in the front rank. Born near Baltimore, July 13, 1815, graduated at Rutger's College, associated with his father, John A. Brown, in business, he devoted his life, aside from banking, to philanthropic and Christian benevolence. He served the Society as manager and was an active member of each of its standing committees, being chairman of the Committee on Publication for nearly thirty years and of the Committee on Finance for twelve years. In a bustling age he ever possessed quiet poise of judgment, broad wisdom, and great generosity; giving time and money to large benevolent operations. With characteristic modesty he firmly declined the position of president of the Society which was tendered him, but accepted an almost equally responsible, but less public position at the head of its finances. At that period the Society was struggling with a heavy debt which had grown to such proportions as to threaten its life. Under his direction the writer of this history drew up a plan for liquidating the debt and providing adequate capital and funds for its work. When the plan was perfected and approved by Mr. Brown and his committee, he called one day with the remark that he had a "small contribution" to start the plan, and placed $25,000 on the table before us. A little later he gave an additional $15,000, forming the "Raikes Fund"; the income to be used in benevolent work. His wisdom, augmented by his generosity, marked a new era in the Society's history.

Mr. Brown did not favor impulsive appeals, either by letter, telegram, or other devices, which tended to secure hasty action. He desired to have every appeal carefully scrutinized, and approved only after thoughtful deliberation. His reputation, his rare judgment, and his tact brought success to the Union's financial plans. He counted it better to get a thousand persons to give $100 each, than to have one person give $100,000. In every measure he sought accurate information and hesitated to endorse any plan until it had the unanimous support of the managers and the best friends of the Society.

Mr. Brown also had a singularly clear faith and abiding confidence in God. Before the plans for providing larger funds for the Union were undertaken, he proposed that the managers should seek divine wisdom. Following this suggestion, a half-hour preceding each monthly meeting of the Board of Managers was spent in earnest prayer for divine guidance in forming plans for an enlarged income for the Society. When, after ten years of struggle and labor, it was announced that their efforts were crowned with success far beyond the expectations of any of the managers, the great debt paid and half a million in invested funds secured, his joy was shown by proposing that they spend a half-hour again of their stated meetings in devout thanksgivings to Almighty God for his signal blessing upon the American Sunday-School Union.

The estimation in which he was held by his associates was voiced by Justice Strong, who knew him intimately for many years, "He was so gentle, so unostentatious, so steadfast in his convictions of Christian duty, and so uniformly charitable that he commanded the love and respect of those who knew him well."

Samuel Ashhurst, M.D.

For thirty years Dr. Samuel Ashhurst was the faithful advisor of the American Sunday-School Union, as his father had been before him. Endowed with many abilities similar to his father's, and through him becoming familiar with the Society's history, he had a clear conception of how every measure had worked and of its results. Hence Dr. Ashhurst's counsel was of the highest value when measures apparently new were under consideration, for he often showed that what seemed to other workers and managers to be new measures, were, in fact, old ones that had already been tried and were reappearing under some new form or from a new quarter. He was a man of positive convictions, and firm and courageous in avowing them. Hearty and vigorous in support of reasonable and progressive measures, he was strong in opposing everything smacking of display or sham, or "smart and tricky" ways of the world, in advancing the cause of religious education. He was quick to detect anything base or dishonorable, or tending to pride or worldly ambition. The father and the two sons rendered unselfish and invaluable service to the Society for sixty-five years, aiding it in forming Bible schools in needy places and furnishing evangelical literature, believing that the latter was essential to secure the permanence of the schools.

Dr. Ashhurst was specially strenuous for an evangelical gospel. He wanted every publication to contain something which would point the reader to the way of salvation. When exigencies arose he would, like his father, often give hours of a busy day to master some new plan under consideration and to satisfy himself in respect to its probable wisdom and efficiency. He persuaded his brother, Richard Ashhurst, to become treasurer, because of his familiarity with finance and business, was foremost in urging a "no debt" policy for the Society, and was exceedingly hopeful that the measure proposed for paying the Society's debt and securing adequate capital would succeed, when others were quite hopeless because of the magnitude of the task. He proposed the appointment of an Executive Committee to formulate and carry out the measure, and persuaded the editor, as chairman of the Committee, to undertake this added task. The success of the plan was, in no small way, due to Dr. Ashhurst's hearty and persevering advocacy of it. The sincerity of his faith was as transparent as his convictions were positive.

The American Sunday-School Union owes much of its present prosperity to the humble but wise advice and earnest support of friends like the Ashhursts and Alexander Brown, and should gratefully keep them ever green in its memory.

John H. Converse, LL. D. (1894–1910).

John H. Converse was the son of a Congregational minister of Vermont, and was born in Burlington, December 2, 1840, graduated at the University of Vermont and soon afterward moved to Philadelphia. He attained nation-wide reputation by his varied and large business interests as a man of affairs and for his deep interest in benevolent and religious organizations. He supported a missionary of the American Sunday-School Union for many years and was vice-president of the Society, serving on the finance committee for fifteen years, being its chairman from 1901 to his death May 3, 1910. His counsel in the affairs of the Society was deliberate and wise, and his influence encouraging and helpful to those associated with him. In his church he was a valued and honored member and officer, his catholic spirit rising above denominational limitations, and in matters of beneficence he was at the front with open hand and warm heart, responding cheerfully to calls for service that came from the Master.   He aided many young men to gain an education that better qualified them for Christian usefulness.   No call for service was too small to be accepted and no summons for work or responsibility was so great as to daunt him.   His candid and balanced judgment made him efficient and helpful in every field of effort in which he became interested.   The wisdom derived from his rare business and financial experience was freely at the service of the Society and highly valued by the members of the Union.

SECTION XI

CONVENTIONS, ASSOCIATIONS, INSTITUTES, ASSEMBLIES AND
ORGANIZED DENOMINATIONAL SUNDAY-SCHOOL WORK

CONVENTIONS or conferences to consider questions relating
to doctrines, worship, polity, and the progress of religion are
as old as Christianity. The first recorded convention was held
in Jerusalem about A. D. 50, to adjust certain questions
respecting Gentile disciples. Similar assemblies were held
during the early period, up to the noted first Council at Nice
in A. D. 325, which undertook to clarify the doctrine of the
divinity or deity of Christ. Councils or assemblies of a general character were held for four or five centuries, followed by
like ones in the Greek and in the Latin church and during the
Reformation era.

Early Conventions.—In the nineteenth century in America
conventions, conferences, and commissions became the
"fashion." They are a conspicuous feature in American life.
Other peoples are amazed at what they are pleased to count
the American craze for organization. They humorously say,
if an orphan child is to be fed, a poor family to be provided
with a bucket of coal, or a dog or cat to be rescued, an American immediately calls a convention and forms a society to do
the work. This is a caricature which our neighbors make of
us, but it indicates that the convention is a spectacular feature
in our social work.

The modern Sunday-school is no exception. American
Sunday-school workers held local conferences and conventions
early in the last century in regard to their work. From 1820
to 1825 numerous local conventions were held in the Eastern
and Middle States, and in the South Atlantic section, either
to form local Sunday-school unions or to consider various
phases in the conduct of Sunday-schools. Thus the first
recorded state convention in 1824 was held in New Hampshire,

to form a State Sunday-School Union. This was followed by similar conventions, organizing state unions in nearly all the then existing states, all these becoming auxiliary to the national society, which then had taken the name of the American Sunday-School Union.

Preliminary National Sunday-School Convention.—Conferences or conventions of a broader type, comprising representatives from the auxiliary societies in different states, were also held as in connection with the anniversaries of the American Sunday-School Union, May, 1824, 1826, 1828 and 1830. Thus, in 1826, there were representatives from about a dozen auxiliary societies besides similar representatives from a number of other schools of the country, who took part in the discussion of questions and voted for the five conclusions which were reached at that meeting, May, 1826.

Again in 1828 a similar conference or convention was held on three different days, comprising representatives from about twenty auxiliary societies and Sunday-School Unions in different parts of the country, who considered the reports and information laid before them from the various sections of the country and recommended an enlargement of the Union's operations in the publishing of suitable books, the establishment of Sunday-schools among seamen and other classes of people, and also suggested that the Society offer premiums for securing suitable books along special lines adapted to the Sunday-school and, finally, that the Society should take immediate measures to establish or cause to be organized Sabbath-schools in every state of the United States or its territories where there is a sufficient population. Among the representatives present at that convention were Dr. Lyman Beecher, F. A. Packard of Springfield, Massachusetts, Dr. Ezra Fiske of New York, Dr. Samuel Miller and Robert Baird of New Jersey, Dr. Robert Cathcart of Pennsylvania, Joel Parker of New York, Dr. G. T. Bedell of Philadelphia, and many others then prominent in different denominations.

At the meeting or convention of representatives in 1830, after a noted sermon by Francis Wayland of Brown University, the representatives considered the question of establishing a Sunday-school in every destitute place in the Valley of the Mississippi, which was moved by Thomas McAuley, D. D.,

LL. D., and advocated by Dr. Lyman Beecher. The matter was discussed by Dr. Stephen H. Tyng, the Rev. Dr. Fiske, and further advocated by Dr. William A. McDowell of South Carolina, Dr. James W. Alexander of New Jersey, and Dr. Rice of Virginia, and a number of prominent laymen.

At these conferences or conventions the Society placed before the representatives the results of surveys and inquiries which had been repeatedly made by their auxiliaries, and conditions reported in response to forty-two interrogatories sent out inquiring into the religious condition of the communities and churches in different sections of the country.

A convention of a different type was inaugurated by the managers of the American Sunday-School Union in 1832. At a stated meeting of the Society held April 10, 1832, a national Sunday-school convention was proposed and definitely recommended in the following terms:

> In view of the signal tokens of God's favor toward the Sunday-school [institution] in the United States, especially during the last year; and considering the importance of reducing to some simple and general principles a system of religious education so necessary—so well fitted to the character and institutions of our country, [and] promising such vast results; considering, also, the advantages which flow from mutual confidence and sympathy, and how much this confidence and sympathy are increased by a personal interchange of feelings and views;
>
> *Resolved*, That it be recommended to the superintendents and teachers of Sunday-schools in the United States to convene at some suitable time and place for the purpose of considering the principles of the institution; the duties and obligations which attach to the several officers of Sunday-schools; the best plans of organizing, instructing and managing a Sunday-school in its various departments, and such other topics as may pertain to the general objects of the convention;
>
> *Resolved*, That it be further recommended to the superintendents and teachers of auxiliary Sunday-schools, from different parts of the country, who can make it convenient, to hold a meeting in Philadelphia, on the 23d day of May next (the day succeeding the approaching anniversary of the American Sunday-School Union), for the purpose of considering the foregoing resolution; and if approved, that such measures be taken as shall be deemed necessary respecting time, place and arrangements (for the proposed convention) to secure the accomplishment of the desired object.

In taking this action, the managers not only suggested the time and place of meeting, but also indicated the kind of as-

sembly which should be brought together to consider these
questions.

"It is desirable," they said, "that all who are *actually engaged*
as superintendents, teachers, or active officers of Sunday-
schools should attend the proposed preliminary meeting, and
such only are invited."

The purpose of the meeting was definitely set forth in
The Sunday-School Journal of the Union, May 9, 1832:

> It is obvious that at present there is no definite system of
> organizing and instructing Sunday-schools. Hundreds of thou-
> sands are engaged in them as teachers or pupils, and it is pre-
> sumed that there are not two schools among the whole which
> are taught or superintended alike. Some have one superin-
> tendent and some two, or more. Some are attended in the
> morning, some during the interval between morning and after-
> noon service, some in the afternoon, and some in the evening.
> The time of instruction varies from one to five hours. Some
> schools are opened with prayer, singing and reading the Scrip-
> tures; others with two of these exercises, and others with only
> one. The character, size, etc., of Sunday-school books and the
> manner of distributing them are almost as various as the features
> of the human face. The discipline of a school; the form, order,
> and arrangement of classes; the order of business; the subjects
> and modes of instruction; the duties of teachers in school and
> out of school; the use, place, and organization of adult, infant
> and Bible classes; the disposal of children during church service
> —these and a multitude of topics which need not be particu-
> larly suggested, and which probably have often occupied the
> thoughts of reflecting teachers, are to be considered by the
> convention. And the proposed meeting on the 23d inst. is
> called to consider: 1. The expediency of holding such a con-
> vention. 2. Where and when it shall be held. 3. What subjects
> shall be presented for its consideration. 4. How shall they be
> presented.
>
> A general attendance of 'teachers and superintendents from
> various sections of the country is very desirable.

The plan for the meeting was also clearly outlined:

> There should be a simple, intelligent and well-adjusted plan
> capable of all necessary modifications to suit various circum-
> stances, but in its main principles fixed and settled.
>
> Such a plan should be formed after a full investigation of
> the history of Sunday-schools, a diligent study of the lessons of
> experience which are furnished by those engaged in them, and
> an accurate survey of their present character and prospects.
>
> The proposed convention is designed to afford such advantages
> for devising some general system of proceeding not TOUCHING
> IN ANY POINT THE RIGHTS OR PRIVILEGES OF ANY
> SCHOOL, NOR THE THINGS TO BE TAUGHT, but simply

the external organization, and such circumstances depending on this as may be thought susceptible of general regulation; and here there can be no design to dictate or control, but to recommend and suggest.

The course now proposed for the teachers of Sunday-schools has been adopted some time since by common school teachers, and with a promise of very useful results. We hope it will be fairly tried, and we have no doubt it will promise as much for us.

Called by American Sunday-School Union.—In response to this call of the American Sunday-School Union, a preliminary meeting of teachers and superintendents was held in Philadelphia May 23, 1832. It was attended by superintendents, teachers and delegates from Sunday-schools from thirteen states of the then twenty-four states, and two of the four territories, and enrolled ninety-one members. Only those who were enrolled as members took part in the discussions. The plans proposed for the first National Sunday-school Convention were carefully completed and, after prolonged deliberation, it was decided to recommend

to the superintendents and teachers of Sunday-schools in the United States to convene at some suitable time and place for the purpose of considering the principles of the Sunday-school institution; the duties and obligations which attach to the several officers of Sunday-schools; the best plans of organizing, instructing, and managing a Sunday-school in its various departments, and such other topics as may pertain to the general objects of the convention. Also, That a series of interrogatories be prepared, embracing topics connected with the subjects specified in the foregoing resolution which shall be circulated as extensively as possible among the superintendents, teachers and other friends of Sunday-schools in the United States or elsewhere; and that a committee of five be appointed to receive replies to the same, and condense the information, to be used in such manner as shall be directed by this meeting.

Several places were proposed for holding the convention, but after much discussion it was decided to call it in the city of New York, "on the first Wednesday in October next" (October 3, 1832).

The mode of representation was also considered, and after some discussion it was unanimously agreed that

Every Sunday-school union or association, or any association that may be formed for that purpose, shall be entitled to be represented by one or more delegates at the proposed convention, the number and mode of appointment being referred to said unions and associations respectively; and that every Sunday-school not connected with any union or association shall be entitled to be represented by one delegate in said convention, the delegates in every case to be superintendents, teachers, conductors, or otherwise actually engaged in Sunday-schools; provided, however, that in every case where the schools connected with a union or association prefer to be represented independently and shall elect delegates accordingly, such schools shall be entitled to be represented by one delegate each, as aforesaid. For the Call and Seventy-eight Interrogatories, see Appendix, pp. 469–474.

The mode of representation in the convention of 1832–33 was identical, but at the convention in 1859 this was changed, so that, "each evangelical Sunday-school in the Union [or nation] is invited to send at least one delegate; and ministerial brethren are affectionately invited to share in the deliberations and exercises of the convention."

In suggesting the convention of 1832, the managers of the American Sunday-School Union sought to secure the widest experience and the freest expression of opinion from all classes of Sunday-school workers. Moreover, they desired to have it entirely free from that professional air which it might seem to have in the eyes of some people if it were controlled in any manner by officers of even a national organization. Therefore, while *proposing* the national convention, they aimed to keep it entirely free from official or any other connection with the Society, though they themselves, as individuals, had a deep interest in its proceedings and in its results, and as they say in *The Sunday-School Journal* they anticipated great good from it and hoped to share the benefit with the multitude of the brethren from all sections of the country.[1]

It is noteworthy that a majority of the leaders and active members in that first convention were in one way or another connected with the American Sunday-School Union, their relations to both the Union and the convention being as individuals and as workers in Sunday-schools.

First National Sunday-School Convention.—The first National Sunday-School Convention met at New York October 3, 1832, attended by about 220 delegates, among whom were leading laymen and clergymen, representing organizations in fourteen states and territories out of the twenty-four

[1] *The Sunday-School Journal*, 1832, pp. 78 and 155.

states and four territories then in the United States.[1] In view of the limited facilities for traveling (there were less than 300 miles of railway in the country) and of the scourge of Asiatic cholera that visited New York and other cities that year, this was a large attendance.

Hon. Theodore Frelinghuysen was elected president, William A. Tomlinson and Gen. William Williams vice-presidents, and Dr. D. M. Reese and James B. Brinsmade secretaries. The Committee on Interrogatories prepared a carefully digested series of seventy-eight questions, grouped under thirteen general heads, intended to cover the field of Sunday-school activities as then pursued. Three thousand of these "Questionnaires" were printed, with a circular explaining them, and requesting replies. They were printed on eight pages, full-sized letter paper, spaces being left for answers to each question. The circular was signed by John Hall, then one of the editorial secretaries of the American Sunday-School Union. These circulars were sent out to schools and persons in all parts of the United States.

Answers were received from 142 unions and schools (only 138 at the convention) and from twenty states. The answers were referred to a committee of five (four only serving, namely, Joseph H. Dulles, F. W. Porter, John Wiegand, and John Hall), who were to collate these answers and present a report to the convention. The committee collated the information under topics, and their report fills five closely printed 20-inch long columns in *The Sunday-School Journal* of the Union, and extracts from 142 replies were afterward published week by week, filling twenty more columns in the same *Journal* for 1832 and 1833. These original replies in manuscript were gathered into a quarto volume of about 1,150 pages and are preserved in the archives of the American Sunday-School Union.

In explanation of the character of their report on these interrogatories the committee say, repeating the assertion made in the commencement that no analysis of the contents of the returns to the circulars can do justice to their value, they would again express the hope that some means may be taken to preserve them in a form in which they may be universally accessible. With respect to the great objects before this body, they

[1] It is significant that the number of states represented was only one more than were represented at the preliminary convention.

would adopt the suggestion of an able superintendent in refer ence to our meeting:

> We must not forget the great variety of circumstances that prevail in our schools. What is most suitable in one place, would be improper in another. Teachers become discontented when they find their schools not exactly modeled as some others which are recommended. One grand object of the system should be to adapt it as far as possible to all circumstances and all situations. This cannot be done if a precise system is insisted on or too strenuously urged.[1]

This committee with their digest of the answers presented to the convention, recommended the following topics for consideration:

> (1) Frequency and length of sessions of Sunday-schools; (2) Importance, modes and results of visiting; (3) Teachers' prayer meetings; (4) Teachers' preparations for the duties of the school; (5) Training scholars to become teachers and methods of doing it; (6) Influence of personal habits of teachers on the scholars; (7) Influence of the superintendent on the character and prosperity of the school. A special report on modes of instruction was made by James W. Weir, and widely circulated as a tract for teachers.

Some of these topics would now be regarded as unimportant, yet at that time they created much excitement, as these among others:

> Should a publishing society take a copyright for a book or a publication?—it being thought that such copyright would limit its circulation and usefulness. Attention was also directed to a declaration that "after fifty years Sunday-schools are mostly carried on independent of the church." Large place was given to exploiting a monthly concert of prayer for Sunday-schools as an evangelizing agency. Some schools, it was said, had sessions of from four to six hours in length, and it was suggested that no session should exceed two hours without intermission. Other themes were considered similar to those which have engaged Sunday-school thinkers for two generations since. Thus this First National Convention discussed the value of uniform Bible classes for the whole land, and it was declared that the world should be regarded as a series of Sunday-schools. Nor did the convention overlook the peculiar nomenclature or terms in use. It proposed that the word "pupils" displace the word "children" in all reports of the convention where practicable. They advised a careful classification of scholars, from the youngest in the infant department in a room by themselves, to a normal class having advanced lessons in Scriptures

[1] *The Sunday-School Journal*, October 10, 1832.

and receiving instruction upon evidences of religion, sacred geography, biblical antiquities, and the like.

The value of study classes in methods of instruction, to train scholars to become teachers, the formation of teachers' libraries, the systematic visitation of parishes to interest parents, improvement in schoolroom furniture, better ventilation of rooms, reviews of lessons by the whole school—sometimes by the pastor and before the whole congregation, systematic giving, weekly meetings of teachers for study, and teachers' prayer meeting before school sessions and children's week-day prayer meetings, improved methods of conducting the general exercises of the school, plans for advanced Sunday-school institutes, and many other similar topics were considered by this first convention, indicating that the members were progressive workers and thinkers—far in advance of their day.

So important and varied were the topics before this convention that many of them were not sufficiently discussed to reach a conclusion, and others were barely mentioned. Indeed, the delegates at the convention very early in their sessions declared that it would be impossible to conclude the work they had in hand at that convention, and at once proposed to have another national convention in Philadelphia.

The committee on interrogatories recommended that special committees be appointed to report in full upon many of the subjects named to a *future* convention. So general was the impression upon the importance of a more careful and prolonged consideration of these topics that it was resolved to call another convention to meet in Philadelphia May 22, 1833, the representation to be the same as already established for this convention, and the committee on interrogatories to make arrangements for it, collecting further information and preparing the business to come before the convention. Finally, at the suggestion of this committee, *nine special committees* were appointed to prepare reports on as many different phases of the Sunday-school work to come before the Philadelphia convention. The various reports and suggestions of the committees made to this first convention were printed in *The Sunday-School Journal* of the Union in successive weekly issues, and formed the basis for the discussion of the various topics at the next year's meeting.

Second National Convention.—The second national convention met in the Cherry Street lecture room, Philadelphia, May 22, 1833. Hon. Willard Hall of Delaware was president,

Matthew L. Bevan of Pennsylvania and Gerrit Smith of New York vice-presidents, and Louis G. C. Elmer of New Jersey and M. B. Denman of Pennsylvania secretaries. This convention was not as largely attended by delegates from various schools, societies and unions as the first one, though there were delegates from nine states, of whom it was said, "Among the members were some of the most distinguished and enlightened friends of Sunday-schools which our country furnishes." [1] At this distance, it seems to us rash to have called a second national convention within eight months after the first, particularly when we consider the limitations of transportation and travel in those days. But evidently the pressure was strong to thresh out the important questions which had been raised at the first meeting, and which were placed in the hands of the special and regular committees—about fifteen in all—who were to prepare and submit papers or reports upon as many important phases of Sunday-school work of that day.

Each of these committees consisted of five and sometimes six workers, who had gained more than a local reputation. They were given time to study conditions, gather and arrange facts, and agree upon some recommendation or deliverance on the respective subjects under consideration. Among the questions referred to them by the New York Convention were the following:

> (1) Infant schools; (2) organization and discipline of schools; (3) plans of instruction; (4) libraries; (5) best means of qualifying scholars for teachers; (6) establishing schools in prisons and almshouses; (7) teachers' meetings; (8) temperance societies and Sunday-schools; (9) duties of superintendents and teachers.
> Papers were also read from committees on other subjects, as (1) private Sunday-schools, meaning schools sustained by persons in private houses, (2) on interesting ministers and officers of the church in Sunday-schools, (3) on organizing missionary and other benevolent societies in the schools. These papers reveal a breadth of experience and a careful study of conditions. They were comprehensive and explicit, evidently not exploiting visionary theories, but based on a profound practical experience. The papers occupied about fourteen columns in *The Sunday-School Journal* for 1833.

Among important measures commended was a proposition to make a general simultaneous effort on the "Fourth of July

[1] *The Sunday-School Journal*, June 5, 1833.

next to invite all persons to attend some place of Bible instruction." This proposition was suggested by the managers of
the American Sunday-School Union for reasons which they
stated thus:

> The inquiry is natural, why the influence of such an associa-
> tion, or of the Sunday-school institution generally, instead of ex-
> erting a very partial influence over 600,000 or 800,000 children
> between five and fifteen years of age, does not extend its benefits
> over the entire population of the country and the world, in
> forms suited to the various circumstances of the inhabitants.
> The true answer is, *It has never been attempted.*
>
> So far as our own country is concerned, there has never yet
> been a general simultaneous effort to ascertain to what extent
> subjects of Sunday-school instruction can be collected. It is
> high time such an effort was made; and as some particular day
> must be assigned for the purpose, in order that it may be simul-
> taneous, . . . the *Fourth of July next* is proposed.

The resolution was first presented at the Anniversary of the
American Sunday-School Union May 21, 1833, by Gerrit
Smith, Esq., of New York, thus:

> That the proposed general simultaneous effort on the fourth
> day of July next, to visit and invite all suitable subjects of
> Sunday-school instruction to attend at some appointed place
> on the succeeding Sunday (July 7th) be commended to the min-
> isters of the gospel, and the superintendents, teachers, and
> other officers and friends of Sunday-schools, and Sunday-school
> societies of every denomination, for prompt and complete
> execution.

The convention, in approving this proposition, recommended
officers and friends of Sunday-schools "to district the territory
which it belongs to them to explore, and to assign to each individual his or her section; and that a report of the result of
each person's labor be made to the proper officers, and by them
to some union or other association, so that the information may
reach the various Sunday-schools as soon as practicable."
This, in fact, was the germ of the modern systematic plan of
house-to-house visitation, clearly conceived and defined in the
last century.

The recommendation upon private Sunday-schools; that is,
schools under the direction and at the expense of private individuals in their own homes, was discussed and reported upon
at length, and their advantages urged as follows:

(1) Wild and wandering children are more willing to enter a room which has not the appearance of formality and display. There is nothing appalling in a small apartment and there is more in the circumstance to attach them to their instructors.

(2) There are no prejudices on the part ·of parents against any particular sect to encounter. It is an individual enterprise, coming necessarily under no denomination.

(3) These are not confined exclusively to the destitute.

(4) There is a favorable opportunity for the united operations of Christians of different denominations.

(5) Opportunity is afforded for private Christians to consecrate their houses to God.

(6) It gives an opportunity to every Christian to become a working Christian.

These two early national conventions did not wholly meet the expectations of the workers of that day. *The Sunday-School Journal* voiced public sentiment on the first convention thus:

> We have been somewhat disappointed in the results of this meeting. Our expectation was that the convention would adopt some active measures, the influence of which would at once have been felt in all the schools.[1] The distribution of thousands of copies of the Interrogatories adopted has, of itself, had a beneficial effect. The attention of teachers has been drawn to subjects which had not before engaged their thought. . . . In several places the teachers of a school, or of several schools united for the purpose, have met to discuss the questions and to propose replies, and they acknowledge the advantage of the employment.[2]

Again, referring to the "three Sunday-school conventions" (the *Journal* counted the preliminary meeting, May, 1832, as one), it concludes its own and the public opinion of the meetings thus:

> Few questions of practical interest are likely to come up at any time which have not been considered with more or less particularity at one or more of these conventions. So completely is the object of the convention already accomplished that no question of education in this country or any other presents a like degree of order, uniformity, and consistency of principles, and the application of them, as the investigation just closed shows the Sunday-school system to possess.[3]

It is evident that the chief thought and discussions were concentrated upon the fundamental purposes of the institution.

[1] *The Sunday-School Journal*, October 17, 1832.
[2] *Ibid.*, October 8, 1832.
[3] *Ibid.*, June 5, 1833.

In the application of principles, the widest scope and the largest freedom of method were allowed.   New conditions constantly springing up among the rapidly developing American peoples could not be anticipated.   The questions they raised would best be solved by further experience

State Unions and Conventions.—The conventions of 1832 and 1833 threshed out fundamental questions relating to the organization and conduct of Sunday-schools, and did it so thoroughly and so much in advance of their age that no desire for a subsequent gathering of this kind came into prominence for twenty-seven years.   Meanwhile all the states had Sunday-school unions, holding annual or other conventions to consider their local interests in biblical instruction; these unions being generally auxiliary to the national Society, the American Sunday-School Union.   They were largely fostered by the latter Union in the hope that they would be efficient in promoting the extension of Sunday-schools and the improvement of the same throughout the country, thus relieving the national Society in some measure of the employment of so many Sunday-school missionaries.   This expectation was not realized. The national Society found these state unions, though often well organized, a heavy drain upon the treasury for administrative and other expenses, much of their energy being exhausted in machinery, leaving little force for really effective field work. The interest in them, therefore, languished.

Sunday-school workers in these various states had discovered, however, the benefits of getting together and comparing their various methods, and soon longed for something similar, which resulted in the calling of voluntary state conventions at irregular intervals.   These conventions at first had no close relation one to the other.   In 1846 a Sunday-school convention met in the territory of Wisconsin, largely due to the influence of J. W. Vail, an agent of the American Sunday-School Union, supported by William H. Byron, a member of the first National Convention of 1832.   Conventions were also held in that territory after it became a state, but at irregular intervals, being twice revived by the agents and missionaries of the national Society.   A similar convention was held in 1855 in Massachusetts, and a year or so later in New York and Connecticut, these conventions being very similar in their voluntary character and structure, and meeting chiefly for inspiration and diffusion of information.

Interdenominational Convention.—The nation-wide religious revival of 1857 gave a new impetus to the Sunday-school convention movement. The workers in New York, such as R. G. Pardee, Lucius Hart, Albert Woodruff, Ralph Wells, and A. A. Smith, suggested the calling of a national convention of Sunday-school teachers at Philadelphia under the supposition that they had a new idea and that no such gathering had ever before been held. The call was issued by Drs. Thomas Brainerd, Richard Newton, W. T. Brantley, W. J. R. Taylor, and by Messrs. George H. Stuart, Jay Cooke, John S. Hart, Matthew W. Baldwin, and Abraham Martin, for a convention to be held in Philadelphia, February 22, 1859, requesting each evangelical Sabbath-school in the union to send at least one delegate. The clergymen of the schools or churches were included in the call in view of their office and work.

John S. Hart, LL. D., editor of *The Sunday-School Times*, then published by the American Sunday-School Union, was temporary chairman of the convention. Ex-Governor James Pollock of Pennsylvania was chosen president, and H. Clay Trumbull of Connecticut and George Baughman of Virginia were secretaries. On the Committee on Arrangements were Louis Chapin, Nelson Kingsbury and James W. Weir. Nearly all these persons were officers or workers connected with the American Sunday-School Union. Among the representatives at this convention were several who were prominent in the previous conventions twenty-seven years before, as Amos Tappan of Massachusetts, Jeremiah H. Taylor of Connecticut, James W. Weir of Pennsylvania, and William H. Campbell from Washington. Scotland was represented by Peter Sinclair. It was noteworthy that Mr. Weir, who was prominent in the first and second conventions, drafted the resolutions which were adopted as the platform of the third convention. In fact, the chief aim and effect of this convention was inspiration rather than instruction.

The discussions and proceedings of the convention were reported by I. Newton Baker, then assistant to Editor Hart, and were published in *The Sunday-School Times* then issued by the American Sunday-School Union. Mr. Baker had shown himself a skilled and successful reporter, and afterward proved to be an able and influential Sunday-school editor.

Ten years elapsed before another national convention was called. The delay was due to the turbulent condition of the country from the Civil War of 1861 to 1865. The war had wrought so many changes that in a great measure the remembrance of the convention of 1859 passed out of the minds of a large portion of the Sunday-school workers of the country. A few workers in attendance at a convention of Young Men's Christian Associations in Detroit, Michigan, decided to call a Sunday-school convention of two delegates from each congressional district in the United States and twenty-five delegates from Canada. They soon learned that a committee appointed by the convention of ten years previous was in existence, which they do not appear to have known before, and the two committees finally issued a call for another national convention to be held in Newark, New Jersey, April 28, 1869.

This convention was attended by 526 delegates, from twenty-eight states and one territory, besides some representatives from Canada, England, Ireland, Scotland, Egypt, and South Africa. But seven-tenths of these delegates were from the immediate vicinity of New York and New Jersey, while eighteen of the twenty-eight states represented had only twenty-five delegates present. Much enthusiasm was created by the crowded houses and the stirring speeches, and information was diffused through the consulting of representative workers in "six sections," meeting in different churches to consider various departments of Sunday-school work; the chief subject was the promotion of teacher training through institutes and normal classes. The convention disapproved of the idea that the Sunday-school was in any sense a substitute for family or pulpit instruction, or that it was to be regarded as independent of the church.

The president was George H. Stuart, and the secretaries, H. Clay Trumbull, John H. Vincent, and B. F. Jacobs, while the chairman of the Executive Committee was Edward Eggleston of Illinois.

The fifth National Convention met at Indianapolis, April 16, 1872, attended by 254 delegates from twenty-two states and one territory, and eighty-four visiting representatives from

Canada, Great Britain and elsewhere.   Philip G. Gillett, of
Illinois, was president, and Rev. George A. Peltz, of Pennsylvania, secretary.

This marked an important event in the history of Sunday-
schools—the adoption of a system of uniform lessons and the
appointment of a lesson committee to make the selections for
the following seven years.[1]

First International Convention.—The sixth *National* became the first *International* Sunday-School Convention, and
was held at Baltimore, Maryland, May, 1875.   Upward of
300 delegates were present from twenty-seven states, the
District of Columbia, and Canada.   Rev. George A. Peltz
of New Jersey was president; Rev. Edwin W. Rice of Pennsylvania, Rev. M. B. Dewitt of Tennessee, Rev. Alfred Andrews,
E. C. Chapin and Eben Shute, were secretaries.   The special
feature of this convention was a statistical report of Sunday-
schools for North America, showing the membership to be
about 6,500,000 in the United States and 300,000 in Canada.

International Sunday-School Conventions were held once
every three years from 1875 until 1914, when a change was
made to quadrennial meetings.

The second International Sunday-School Convention was
held at Atlanta, Georgia, April, 1878; the third at Toronto,
Canada, June, 1881; the fourth at Louisville, Kentucky, June,
1884; the fifth at Chicago, Illinois, June, 1887; the sixth at
Pittsburgh, Pennsylvania, June, 1890, with a report from its
paid superintendent, William Reynolds; the seventh at St. Louis,
Missouri, August, 1893; the eighth at Boston, Massachusetts,
June, 1896; the ninth at Atlanta, Georgia, April, 1899, characterized by sessions of the Field Workers' Association; the tenth
at Denver, Colorado, June, 1902, when Secretary Marion
Lawrance made his first triennial report; the eleventh in Toronto,
Canada, June, 1905, marked by an exhibition of historical publications illustrating the history of Sunday-schools; the twelfth at
Louisville, Kentucky, June, 1908, at which the charter granted
in 1907 by Congress was reported; the thirteenth at San Francisco, California, June, 1911, registering its change of name from
Convention to *Association*, and reporting a new lesson committee appointed by the trustees instead of by the convention
as hitherto; and the fourteenth convention at Chicago, June,
1914, reporting that the dissension arising out of the incorporation of the association and its appointment of the lesson committee by trustees had been adjusted, an agreement being made
with the Sunday-School Council of Evangelical Denominations
creating a joint international lesson committee, eight members

[1] See section on *International Uniform Lessons.*

only being chosen by the convention, eight by the Council, and one by each of the denominations having a lesson committee.[1] The president of this convention was Dr. H. M. Hamill of Tennessee.

The fifteenth convention is appointed at New York in 1918.

World Sunday-School Conventions.—Meetings looking to a world-wide view of the work were held at irregular intervals on and before the Jubilee of the founding of modern Sunday-schools in 1830, observed in 1831. The first *formal* conference or general Sunday-school convention of this type, however, was held in London, in connection with the International Industrial Exhibition, September, 1862. Delegates were present from all parts of Great Britain, from America, European countries, and Australia. Carefully prepared historical papers were presented by leaders of high repute upon the growth and influence of Sunday-schools in England, Ireland, Wales and Scotland, and discussions were had by prominent workers upon the objects, classification, etc., of Sunday-schools, and of the state and prospects of the work abroad.

Suggestions for a world-wide conference had been made repeatedly by workers in the American Sunday-school Union, but a definite proposition was made to call a convention of this kind at a meeting held in Chautauqua, New York, in 1886. This so-called first World's Convention met in London in 1889, attended by 242 delegates from the United States.

The joint general secretary, Frank L. Brown, furnished the following statement:

> The World's Sunday-School Association was organized at the World's Convention at Rome in 1907. Conventions were held successively at London, 1889; St. Louis, 1893; London, 1898; Jerusalem, 1904; Rome, 1907; Washington, 1910; and Zurich, 1913. At the Zurich convention 2609 delegates were present, representing fifty-eight countries and about seventy-five denominations.
>
> The Executive Committee of the Association is composed of fifty-seven members, exclusive of the officers. The world-field, for purposes of administration, was assigned to American and British sections of the Executive Committee, the American section taking Japan, Korea, the Philippines, South America, and the Moslem fields. To the British section was assigned China, India, South Africa and Europe. The purpose and policy of the Association stated by the Rome Convention were:

[1] See section on *International Uniform Lessons.*

(1) That this Association shall hold conventions and gather information concerning the conditions of Sunday-schools throughout the world by correspondence, visitation, and other methods.

(2) That it shall seek to extend the work and increase the efficiency of Sunday-schools by co-operation with Sunday-school and missionary organizations and otherwise, especially in those regions of the world most in need of help.

(3) That it shall seek to improve as far as possible the methods of organization and instruction in the Sunday-schools, and promote the formation of Sunday-school unions and associations.

The Association was incorporated in America in 1916. The budget of the American section of the Committee is about $40,000 annually. Salaried secretaries are under appointment in Korea, Japan, China, the Philippines, India, Moslem fields, South America, and some of the countries of Europe. These secretaries develop literature, promote conventions and institutes, and train a Sunday-school leadership. The membership of the British section includes representatives of the Mission Boards. One-half of the American section of the Executive Committee is composed of representatives of the Mission and Sunday-school boards of America.

The Association reported, at Zurich, the world Sunday-school membership as 30,015,037, with 310,057 Sunday-schools and 2,669,630 officers and teachers.

The officers of the Association of 1916 are H. J. Heinz, Pittsburgh, Pennsylvania, Chairman of the Executive Committee; Rev. Carey Bonner, London, England, and Frank L. Brown, New York City, General Secretaries; Rt. Hon. T. R. Ferens, M. P., London, England, and Arthur M. Harris, New York City, General Treasurers; E. K. Warren, Three Oaks, Michigan, Chairman of the Central Committee.

The conspicuous methods taken by the World Association to promote its objects has been the sending of deputations to visit the various countries round the world, including Australia, India, South America, Japan, China, Korea, the Philippines, and South America, under the leadership of H. J. Heinz, E. K. Warren, George W. Bailey,[1] Fred A. Wells, Marion Lawrance, Carey Bonner, Sir Robert Laidlaw,[1] Rev. F. B. Meyer, Frank L. Brown, W. N. Hartshorn, and others.

Conventions or Associations.—The history of the Sunday-school convention movement indicates the tendency of these gathering to change from a mass meeting, composed of representatives from individual schools, to a permanent association with legislative functions. The leaders who proposed the first National Sunday-School Convention aimed to secure a meeting which would give the widest freedom of expression to representatives direct from the school, each convention to be self-

[1] Deceased.

controlled and self-managed in its arrangements and proceed-ings, and when the same was concluded its authority should cease or should not extend beyond the suggesting of a call for a future similar assembly.

The functions of the convention were to be limited to the gathering and collating of information in respect to the pres-ent condition of Sunday-schools, advising improvements that could be made in view of the experience of the past, and arousing greater enthusiasm for the cause.

In the course of time new leaders came to the front who proposed to change the conventions to a permanently organ-ized body to be called "association." This tendency was stoutly opposed by early leaders, who declared that the useful-ness of the convention would be seriously impaired by this course. They opposed the drift toward a permanently organ-ized body, or the assumption of any legislative powers, believ-ing that while there might be a gain in stability of organiza-tion, there would be a loss of its real purpose: the representa-tion from the individual schools would disappear, and a free expression of views by the ordinary workers would be lost—conditions very desirable to retain.

Whether this impression was correct or not, it is a fact that the change of the convention to "The International Sunday-School Association," governed by trustees instead of by dele-gates, created dissension, resulting in the Association losing the authority to choose the majority of the Lesson Committee, and in a diminished enthusiasm and interest in its plans within the rank and file of some active Christian workers.

In the International Convention, moreover, the appoint-ment of delegates, when made by the state and provincial associations, left the individual schools often without special representation, a condition prevailing in many of the state and provincial associations themselves—and a condition which the originators of conventions definitely planned to prevent.

In the county conventions there was some definite effort to preserve special representation from the individual schools and to have a greater freedom of popular expression from the or-dinary workers. The larger schools, however, in this case natu-rally absorbed much of the time and attention of the conventions; the smaller schools gained less benefit than from the meetings of earlier conventions.

Superintendents and missionaries of the American Sunday-School Union say that the influence of the Sunday-School Association work does not reach more than 15 to 20 per cent. of the Union schools in the country. The Master teaches us to be helpful not alone to the strongest but also to the weakest, and to give inspiration and a helping hand to those who are struggling in feebleness and in ignorance to become strong.

Institutes.—As early as 1824 the American Sunday-School Union recognized the importance of trained teachers, and started *The American Sunday-School Magazine*, "to place within the reach of every Sunday-school teacher the improvements in the system and information on subjects which may render their labors easy and efficient." [1]

Two years later it published with approval a plan proposed by its auxiliary in New York, "to open a school for teachers on some week-day or Sabbath evening for the purpose of instruction in the practical duties of a Sunday-school teacher," giving "a thorough acquaintance with the best plan of teaching a class and a uniform system of instruction."[2]

In 1836–37 the Legislature of Massachusetts created a Board of Education, with Horace Mann, who had been a member of the legislature, as secretary. The object of that board was to develop and discuss principles and collect information on education for the improvement of teachers in public schools. This board issued an address to the public inviting the friends of education "to assemble in convention in their respective counties," and instructed its secretary, Horace Mann, to be present, to obtain information in regard to the condition of schools, and to explain to the public what was the motive and object of the board. These conventions, which were really institutes, were held for several years, and the *Lectures on Education*, presented by Mr. Mann, were published.

From this movement emerged the later institutes for public and Sunday-school teachers. In 1839 a well-known educator, Henry Barnard, LL.D., held meetings, known as "Teachers' Institutes," in Connecticut. In 1843 the Church of England

---

[1] *Address to Friends of Sunday-Schools in the United States,* 1824.
[2] *Report,* 1827, p. 47.

Sunday-School Institute was formed in London, one of its objects being to supply teachers with aids in the instruction and management of its classes. But the term "institute" seems to have designated an organization of more general character than the specialized Sunday-school teachers' institute of America.

The plan of the New York Sunday-School Union of 1827 was carried out to a limited extent in different cities. When institutes for public-school teachers gained some popularity, a similar plan for Sunday-school teachers was revived. Dr. D. P. Kidder, in 1847, suggested voluntary organizations to instruct teachers, similar to those then common in New York and other states for public-school teachers, but the next year expressed the fear that the day for the coming of such institutions was far distant. The need, however, was widely felt and suggestions and efforts appeared spontaneously in various sections of the country, calling for some movement to train teachers and make them more competent for their work. For it was said that conventions—local and general—were useful in gathering information and in suggesting improvements, but that the best conventions still left an important work undone. Inexperienced persons and young teachers required special training and instruction to make them competent and efficient and this could be done better by an organization limited specially to giving instruction in principles of education and methods of teaching. It was not to displace or supercede conventions, which were excellent for inspiration, but to supplement them by meetings which would be devoted more exclusively to instruction.

Out of the conferences of teachers upon the miscellaneous and general topics relating to their work, gradually emerged a system of instruction more closely resembling a real school for teachers. These conferences and lectures began in the West as early as 1861, by John H. Vincent, followed by Edward Eggleston and others. The idea was heartily approved by Dr. John S. Hart, an educator and editor with the American Sunday-School Union, and was adopted by R. G. Pardee, Ralph Wells, Henry Clay Trumbull and many others.

Thus American Sunday-School Union workers were quick to adopt and develop Sunday-school institutes as a means of improving teachers in Union schools. The course of instruction became orderly and systematic, being grouped under three chief heads: the subject taught, the learner, and the teacher. In the early sixties a chain of these institutes was held in Wisconsin and Minnesota, in which this system of instruction was introduced by Edwin W. Rice and his colaborers. A report of this work was commended by the Society in these terms:

> The Board cannot withhold the expression of their gratification in the evidence of the system, thoroughness, and energy with which these missionary labors have been prosecuted, under Mr. Rice's direction, by the missionaries associated with him; and they are specially interested in the efforts made and proposed to elevate the character of Sunday-school instruction on their fields by means of normal classes for training teachers . . . and similar improvements.[1]

The plan and course of preparation for teachers commended by the Union gave special attention to the development of the child mind, and suggested ways of adapting instruction to the several stages of mind growth. Most of the institute work up to 1872 overlooked these successive steps in the development of young and mature minds, as the programs of that period indicate.

The normal department of the Northwestern Female College issued a plan of study in 1866, covering 40 sessions, and noted five books for study, to wit: Pardee's *Sunday-School Worker*, Hart's *Thoughts on Teaching*, Packard's *Teacher Taught* and *Teacher Training*, and Alfred Taylor's *Sunday-School Photographs*.

But none of these excellent treatises points out the marked changes in mental development, or emphasizes the importance of adapting instruction to these changes, as the course of instruction used in Wisconsin attempted to do in 1865 and 1866.

So rapidly did this plan of training teachers gain in the Union's work that by 1871 it appointed Henry Clay Trumbull, who had been conspicuously successful in this form of labor, as Normal Secretary. In making this appointment, the Society announced: "While the position of Normal Secretary of this Society is a new one, the duties attached to it are by no means

[1] *Report*, 1866, p. 49.

novel. The prime object of the Society has ever been as well the improvement of Sunday-schools generally as the forming of new schools in needy districts. . . . The progress of the Sunday-school cause of late years increased the demand on all sides for special laborers to train teachers for and in their work and to exhibit before them approved modes and appliances of Sunday-school instruction."

While the Sunday-School Teachers' Institute was intended to instruct teachers in the principles and methods of teaching, it did not hold continuous sessions. It was flexible also in its size and the field represented. Sometimes representatives in a small district, or a whole county or a whole state, would be gathered into such a meeting. Nor was there a stereotyped program or order of procedure. Often they took a wide scope, dealing in miscellaneous and general matters relating to the school as well as to specific instruction and training of the teacher. While not a permanent institution, institutes continued for many years to be very useful in promoting higher ideals and a better knowledge of the best methods of reaching or developing child mind, as well as adults.

Assemblies and Schools of Methods.—Among the many modern movements in religious education which have been the outgrowth from the early and ancient councils and conferences, the summer assemblies call for a brief notice.

Following the appointment of H. Clay Trumbull as Normal Secretary of the American Sunday-School Union in 1871, and his activities, came the Chautauqua movement started by John H. Vincent and Lewis Miller in 1874. They instituted the Chautauqua Sunday-School Assembly with a course of normal study which they said was "in substantial agreement with that adopted by the normal departments of the Baptist, Presbyterian, and American Sunday-School Union Boards."

The Chautauqua movement very soon expanded, taking in broad educational schemes, literary and scientific circles, and the correspondence schools. It was incorporated, and owns upward of 300 acres of land on Chautauqua Lake, New York, with assets amounting to about $1,000,000, with liabilities approximating $400,000. Its early vision along Sunday-school lines was not realized. Normal Sunday-school work became an incident only in its educational and other schemes. Though under the control of the Methodist Episcopal denomination, Chautauqua invited leaders in other denominations to have organized "assemblies," allotting to them space on their grounds and privileges for holding separate denominational meetings.

In the twentieth century, summer assemblies have become numerous, many being held in each of the states and provinces of America, Some of them have become regularly organized bodies, under the control of some denominational or inter-denominational organization, and meet at such times and places as may be determined by the controlling body.

Comparatively few of these summer assemblies relate exclusively to the work of the Sunday-school. Nearly every conceivable form of mental and religious activity is represented or attempted to be promoted by them. Even those that are formed for the Sunday-school take up different phases of that movement, specialize in adult classes, training secretaries and field workers in forms of Bible study, and various other activities allied to the Sunday-school movement. Thus the summer assemblies at East Northfield center about Bible study, while the one at Lake Geneva, Wisconsin, centers about training of secretaries.

The drift of these summer assemblies away from the Sunday-school is illustrated by a brief sketch of the Chautauqua movement under the leadership of Dr. Vincent and Mr. Miller. The Rev. E. Morris Fergusson, who was interested in these assemblies as State Sunday-School Secretary of New Jersey, and later in denominational educational movements, has expressed his views in regard to these movements substantially as follows:

John H. Vincent and Lewis Miller, in the woods on the shores of Chautauqua Lake, had an inspiration to bring out there a great tent-colony of Sunday-school teachers and so solve the normal problem of the Sunday-school. But they were never able to make it an economic, self-supporting reality. The normal class feature took second place to the vacation feature. Good came through the working out of standard forms of normal lessons by the leaders, Dr. Jesse Lyman Hurlbut and others. Other courses of study soon threw the Sunday-school courses quite into the shade. There were five distinct movements: the Sunday-school course, the vacation opportunity, the auditorium platform, the professional courses, and the general meetings. From the second of these came a sixth, real estate proposition, for cottagers to "buy a lot and put up a bungalow." Efforts to keep the commercial feature out did not always avail. And the seventh feature followed, of a four year course of study on educational problems—a feature which has given Chautauqua its distinction and its fame.

An effort to hold these assemblies to the Sunday-school problem was made in other places, as at Monteagle, Tennessee, under the direction of Dr. and Mrs. H. M. Hamill.

The denominational summer assemblies have drifted, so that Sunday-school features are not the most prominent, but rather incidental, as they have become at Chautauqua.

In view of this failure to hold Chautauqua and other assemblies to the Sunday-school idea, Mr. Fergusson says:

> I proposed a different policy. Abandoning the effort to benefit Sunday-school teachers in general, who could not be brought to a summer resort for a course of study, I determined on a short course for primary teachers only, which was began at Asbury Park in 1894. [In Mr. Fergusson's view, this type did persist without the need of support from any adjunct features.] At Winona a modified form of the summer school feature was grafted on a summer assembly and continued for some time. The young peoples', and student, and general conferences now held there are not directly in the interest of Sunday-schools, but generate an atmosphere of their own.[1]

Out of this drift has come "the school of principles and methods," held at different places under the direction of denominational and interdenominational associations. A list shows twenty-eight such schools of methods in fifteen states, and three British provinces in America are under *interdenominational leadership*. Twenty-two such schools in thirteen states are known to be held with some regularity under denominational leadership. Both denominational and interdenominational schools of this character are held in Ohio. Thus we have one or more of these schools in twenty-seven of the forty-eight states in the country.

No doubt these schools prove of great advantage to the comparatively few who can avail themselves of their privileges. The workers in Union schools in the rural districts are seldom reached by these methods of improvement, since distance and the time and expense put them out of reach of the great mass of those in the farming districts of our country.

Some elastic method of offering a teacher-training course of study and improvement to these isolated workers must be

[1] Letters of Rev. E. Morris Fergusson to Edwin Wilbur Rice, April, 1916.

provided if we are to attain efficient teachers and a constant improvement and advance in religious education in the rural districts of the nation.

Teacher Training.—Teacher training merits a full treatment, but it must be passed in review, and the reader referred to special works for full information. From the beginning of the modern Sunday-school movement the proper equipment of the teacher has been held essential to its life. The teacher must inform, inspire, and train his scholars. To do so he himself must first be informed, inspired, and trained. He must possess the fundamental elements of character, not pretend to have them. To this should be added sincerity, sympathy, experience, knowledge, and mental training—points that have been persistingly urged, in many ways, for a century. Training classes, model schools, normal schools and departments, child-development study courses, studies in art, laws, principles, methods, and ideals of teaching, and talks on pedagogy, have been presented in forms and in volumes innumerable, reasonable and unreasonable, light, humorous, stilted, wise and otherwise. To the ordinary teacher much of this display of wisdom was as bewildering as a dense forest, crowded with a denser, impenetrable growth of underbrush, would be to a lost hunter. Early in the twentieth century many attempts were made to clear up this confusion and reach some common standard of attainment in teacher training.

The International Sunday-School Association, with upward of 3,500 classes and over 40,000 students, set up a tentative standard for all teachers who wished to gain its diplomas. Several of the state associations also had "standard courses" for teachers, and granted diplomas.

The Sunday-School Council of Evangelical Denominations in 1910 found various courses extant, and decided to revise teacher-training standards for its constituents. The Religious Education Association also investigated the teacher-training standards, and reported its views in 1912. The general discontent with the standardizing of teacher-training courses thus far attained was expressed by the Committee on Education at the International Convention in Chicago, June, 1914, under eight specifications: (1) The results are inadequate, compared with the time and energy expended; (2) 51 per cent. of the enrollment fail to complete the course; (3) the reading habit has not been created and libraries not encouraged; (4) a sense of self-sufficiency has been created.   The remaining specifications state, among other things, that the first standard course of text-books have not proved an incentive to advanced study, and that a "higher type" of work is desirable.

The Sunday-School Council of Evangelical Denominations in 1915 reached similar conclusions, and recommended that denominations "plan to issue only one teacher-training diploma and that not less than 120 lesson periods be requisite for the recognition."   The particular features in the plan were detailed in thirteen added specifications.

Many other plans of instruction have been projected and are available for Sunday-school teacher training.   The training class in the local Sunday-school, courses of lectures and of study in some colleges, seminaries, and universities, special summer courses, conferences, and correspondence school studies are among the many types of training open to teachers. In schools using the "uniform lessons" teachers' meetings are widely useful and still successfully maintained.

Union Sunday-schools in rural districts may be greatly aided by the training courses specially adapted to their conditions and prepared by the Rev. James McConaughy, Litt. D., Editor of the publications of the American Sunday-School Union.[1]

Trained Leadership.—The demand for trained leadership has become imperative.   The development of this sorely needed class of workers has begun in many places, but in rural and smaller Sunday-schools it has been undervalued or overlooked.   No matter how well trained the teachers or officers are, however, other qualities are required for an efficient leadership.   The position calls for great resourcefulness, quick initiative, open-minded views, wide knowledge of methods, a strong magnetic personality, and deep spirituality.   A competent leader will put new life into any school or group of schools.   The grouping of rural Union schools that has been adopted in many sections offers a wide field of usefulness and has created a greater demand for trained leadership.   The

[1] See *Reports of the American Sunday-School Union*, 1826–1917, *passim;* also of the *International Sunday-School Association*, 1914; *Sunday-School Council*, 1915; and Dr. B. S. Winchester, on *Teacher Training* in *The Encyclopædia of Sunday-Schools*.

best leaders, others things being equal, will be developed in the communities and groups of Sunday-schools where their services are most needed. An "imported" leader is handicapped from the first by want of knowledge of habits, education, and conditions of the people, and must stumble along in the dark until that knowledge is gained. Adequately trained leadership is the crying need of the institution, especially in the rural schools where churches and pastors have not arrived. Even where there is a good country Sunday-school and church, a specially trained leader is essential to make the rural church or the school the center of influence for the betterment of the community—such a center and power as it may and ought to become to fulfil its rightful mission. It will be a great forward step in the usefulness and progress of religious education in country districts when the rural Sunday-school earnestly enters upon the development of a trained Christian leadership.

Organized Denominational Sunday-School Work.—Organized Sunday-school work by separate denominations was a natural development in the modern Sunday-school movement. The religious instruction of the young in the churches was committed to the clergy, the officers, and heads of families. This method of teaching chiefly by catechisms and oral instruction, which prevailed long before Raikes began his work in Gloucester, was preferred or generally promoted by churches of all denominations for some time after his day. Thus, distinctive denominational Sunday-school organizations followed those of the union type in America, though not until a generation later, and, after nearly two generations of organized union Sunday-school efforts, in Great Britain.

Early in the last century the doctrines that divided religious bodies were more ardently proclaimed and more zealously held to be essential to salvation than in this generation. When Sunday-schools were widely introduced into the churches for the religious instruction of the children of the church as well as for those in families outside its pale; the denominations, one after another, deemed it necessary to organize a "department" or "society" for promoting Sunday-school work in accord with its peculiar creedal belief.

The Methodist Episcopal Church was foremost to insist upon having text-books and catechisms in its Sunday-schools that gave prominence to the distinctive doctrines of Methodism. In 1827 the Methodist Episcopal Sunday-School Union was formed (according to some of its secretaries) as a protest against the aim and ideal presented by the founders of the modern Sunday-school movement expressed in the various unions, such as the London Sunday-School Union, and the American Sunday-School Union. It has been reorganized several times, as in 1828 and 1840. It was consolidated with the Board of Education in 1904, dissolved, and succeeded by the Board of Sunday-Schools in 1908. It issued *The Sunday-School Advocate* bi-weekly, in 1841, and weekly in 1872. It now publishes *The Sunday-School Journal* monthly, with periodical lesson helps on the Uniform and on the Graded Series of Lessons, besides library books, manuals for teachers and workers, hymn books, and a full line of publications for the equipment of its schools. This literature has been developed and its use promoted by such leaders, among others, as Dr. D. P. Kidder, Dr. Daniel Wise, Dr. John H. Vincent, Dr. J. L. Hurlbut, Dr. J. T. McFarland, and Dr. H. H. Meyer, aided by a large corps of associates. Its Sunday-school work is now carried on through six departments, in charge of a special committee of the Board, composed of twenty-nine lay and clerical members appointed by the quadrennial General Conference, and with the general office in Chicago, and an editorial office in Cincinnati, Ohio. It reports about 3,900,000 under all forms of Sunday-school instruction.

The Methodist Episcopal Church (South) was organized as a separate body in 1844–45, and continued Sunday-school work through a committee. It began *The Visitor* about 1850. In 1854 the committee said, "we must look for sound conversions more as a blessed sequence of a system of thorough religious education than as a result of those sudden and overwhelming conversions which characterized those times when such training was impossible." Later a "Sunday-School Society" was formed with a board of sixty-eight managers. The Society is said to have broken with its own weight, and was superseded, in 1870, by a general Sunday-school secretary, who was placed in charge of that department of its church work. Rev. Dr. A. G. Haygood filled this position with great efficiency, followed by Dr. W. G. E. Cunnyngham and others, and now

(1917) by Dr. E. B. Chappell, as editor, aided by a Board consisting of a bishop, ten preachers and ten laymen, with a corps of assistants and field workers. It reports a Sunday-school membership of 1,692,275.

There are fourteen other Methodist bodies, white and colored, in America that enroll about 1,000,000 or more members in Sunday-school, the *largest* of them being the colored Methodist Episcopal, with about 360,000 teachers and scholars.

The Baptist group of churches also comprises fifteen or more different bodies, each with some form of organized Sunday-school work. Chief among these are the Northern Convention, having over 1,000,000 membership in its Sunday-schools, the Southern Convention with nearly 1,500,000 enrolled in its schools, and the National Convention, colored, with 1,000,000 total school membership. The New England Baptists early co-operated with the Congregationalist, Methodist, and Episcopal workers in forming the Massachusetts Sunday-School Union in 1825, but it dissolved in 1832, the Baptists and Congregationalists each forming a denominational society of their own. Later the "Baptist Tract Society" was followed by the "American Baptist Publication Society."

The government of Baptist churches is of the democratic or congregational type, and all their Sunday-school organizations are purely voluntary, not exercising any judicial or ecclesiastical authority. The Baptist Publication Society has long been recognized as in the front rank of Sunday-school methods and work, providing a full series of helps on the Uniform Lessons, and also a special Graded Series. It early issued twenty different question books. Prominent among workers in this department, past and present, are Drs. Howard Malcolm, P. S. Henson, C. R. Blackall, A. J. Rowland, Mr. B. F. Jacobs, Dr. George T. Webb and W. E. Raffety, Ph. D. The Society inaugurated a Teacher Training Institute with a special director and has enrolled about 30,000 students.

The Southern Baptist Convention has its center of Sunday-school work at Nashville, Tennessee. It maintains a large publishing society, issuing helps in great variety for its schools. Its teacher-training work is conducted chiefly in large classes, basing the instruction on manuals, presenting six chief topics: history, organization, methods, child study, Bible study, and doctrines.   The Southern Baptists have a field Sunday-school work in each of the fifteen states of the South, which is under direction of their state Mission Boards, and all the workers are united in a Field Workers' Association to promote the general cause.   Dr. I. J. Van Ness, Dr. J. M. Frost and Prof. J. R. Sampey have achieved a national reputation by their services in Bible educational work.

The Baptists of Great Britain, with the Independents, were active in the London Sunday-School Union.   The Metropolitan Tabernacle (formerly Spurgeon's), London, has the largest Sunday-school in the denomination, enrolling, with its fifteen mission schools, over 6,800 pupils.   Of the 416,000 members of Baptist churches in Great Britain, about one-fourth are teachers or senior pupils.   The total Baptist Sunday-school membership in Great Britain is 612,900 in over 3,000 schools. They have produced Bible educators of world-wide reputation, among whom are Joseph Angus, Charles Waters, of the Bible Reading Association, Carey Bonner of the London Union, and F. B. Meyer, well known around the world.

The Congregationalists have always been conspicuous for the emphasis they placed upon religious education and a scientific study of the Scriptures.   Upon the division of the Massachusetts Sunday-School Union in 1832 the Congregationalists formed the Massachusetts Sabbath School Society, and secured the Rev. Asa Bullard of the Maine Sunday-School Union as general agent, who continued in this important work for fifty years.   It retained an auxiliary relation to the American Sunday-School Union until 1839.   In 1854 the Doctrinal Tract Society and the Evangelical Society were merged, forming the Congregational Board of Publication, and the Sabbath School Society was consolidated with it also in 1868, and changed to the Congregational Sunday-School and Publishing Society.   Its plans were enlarged and modified in 1880 and 1883, and the Rev. D. A. E. Dunning chosen secretary (1881). In 1892 the control by life and annual members was changed, and state associations or conferences given a distinct representation in the management.

The Sabbath-School Treasury, issued by the Massachusetts Union from 1825 to 1832, became Congregational, and its name changed to the *Visitor.   The Wellspring* for the young people was begun in 1844 (soon after the *Penny Gazette* in Philadelphia). Question books of various types were issued from 1835 on, and hundreds of volumes for Sunday-school libraries published. *The Pilgrim Teacher*, started in 1885, with *The Congregationalist* are among its leading religious journals. Among its well-known Sunday-school workers, besides those already mentioned, are M. C. Hazard, Ph.D., Prof. Amos R. Wells, Frank K. Sanders, Ph.D., B. S. Winchester, D.D., Dr. George M. Boynton, Dr. William Ewing, Erastus Blakeslee, Dr. F. N. Peloubet, Dr. Josiah Strong, Dr. H. A. Bridgman, Prof. W. Douglas Mackenzie, and others. It sustains a missionary and extension work, employing about forty field workers, having organized over 12,000 Sunday-schools since 1884, from which have developed 1,559 Congregational churches in twenty-nine years. The enrolment in Congregational Sunday-schools of the United States is stated at about 758,000 in 6,000 schools.

The Lutherans inherit from Luther a strong desire for the religious instruction of their children. They are divided into about twenty-one bodies, or denominations, with a total church membership of nearly 2,500,000, enrolling about 1,000,000 in the Sunday-schools of all these bodies. The largest Sunday-school membership is in the General Synod and the General Council churches. Many in the latter do not use the English language, and many of the smaller bodies of Lutherans in this country speak German, Finnish, Danish, or some Scandinavian dialect.

The general Lutheran view is that the church and the Sunday-school are identical. The religious teaching of the young was under the direction of the pastor from the start, and the schools or *Kindergärten* for elementary, classical, or biblical learning were in the churches, or under their control. Jacob Spener, August Francke, and Pastors Stuber and Oberlin conducted the training of youth along these lines, which influenced the methods of H. M. Muhlenberg in America. Dr. Chas. S. Albert, Dr. Charles P. Wiles, Dr. T. E. Schmauk, Prof. Geo. Mezger, Dr. Edwin Heyl Delk, and others are among leaders aiding in prosecuting the religious training of Lutheran youth.

The Presbyterian family of churches comprises twelve bodies or denominations. Of these, the Northern, the Southern, and the United Presbyterian, respectively, have the largest Sunday-school membership. The General Assembly (Old School) in 1838 formed the Presbyterian Board of Publication, which began to publish periodical Sunday-school literature in 1851, issuing *The Sabbath School Visitor.* The General Assembly (New School) in 1837 also organized a Committee on Publications to issue works of a doctrinal type and those for Sunday-school use, until the two bodies (Old and New School) were reunited in 1870. Special denominational Sunday-school work was then enlarged under a general superintendent in 1871, J. Bennet Tyler being called to the position from a like work in the American Sunday-School Union, and he was succeeded by the Rev. James A. Worden. About this time it discontinued its extensive colporteur work and followed it by Sunday-school missionaries and field workers. In 1873 the special lesson helps of the Board were followed by the Uniform Lessons, treated in the *Presbyterian at Work* (changed to *The Westminster Teacher* in 1879), and by lesson leaves, quarterlies, question books, and other requisites for its schools, in English and in several foreign languages. Among the well-known people prominent in this Board may be mentioned Dr. John W. Dulles, Dr. James A. Worden, Dr. E. R. Craven, Dr. Alexander Henry, Dr. J. R. Miller, Dr. E. Morris Fergusson and Dr. John T. Faris. The Northern Presbyterians (Presbyterian Church in the United States of America) enroll over 1,300,000 in Sunday-schools. The Bethany Presbyterian Sunday-school in Philadelphia, founded and conducted by John Wanamaker, is reputed to be among the largest and the most widely known of the world's Sunday-schools.

The Presbyterian Church in the United States (South) began organized Sunday-school work under "Committees" in 1861, which was more fully organized soon after the Civil War (1865). It furnishes lessons, Uniform and Graded, textbooks, training courses, and full equipment for its schools. Dr. A. L. Phillips, R. E. Magill, and Dr. Robert A. Lapsley have proved efficient and wise workers in this cause. The enrolment in its Sunday-schools is about 278,000.

The United Presbyterian Church of North America has always given great care to the religious training of its young people. This was long done through committees of the various Synods or Presbyteries. In 1880 it organized a Board of Publication which was required to prepare suitable literature for its Sabbath-schools. It issues helps on the Uniform Lessons and a series of Graded Lessons also. The Rev. Dr. W. B. Smiley and Dr. R. J. Miller have been prominent in developing and promoting the cause in that church. Its Sabbath-schools enroll upward of 160,000 members.

The Presbyterian Church in Canada organized a separate department for Sunday-schools in 1898, with Rev. Dr. R. D. Frazer as editor and manager, which provides a complete series of lessons for the young in the church. It issued a teacher-training course in 1902, and later secured the Rev. J. C. Robertson to develop this work. It reports upward of 3,500 schools, with about 275,000 members.

The Presbyterian Church of England has a committee on the instruction of youth, with the well-known Dr. Oswald Dykes, Richard Roberts, and Dr. Monro Gibson as leading members. Its schools are using chiefly the British Standard Graded Lessons, elsewhere described. Its membership in Sunday-schools is upward of 80,000.

The United Free Church of Scotland conducts its Sabbath-school work through a Committee of Sixty, which approves of, or suggests, courses of studies and reports to the assembly on its 2,300 Sabbath-schools and the instruction of about 233,000 pupils.

The Protestant Episcopal Church in the United States is the child of the Church of England, and continued similar modes of instruction here for the youth of the church. In 1788 Bishop William White returned from England to Philadelphia, impressed with the Raikes movement, and, though opposed by some of his vestry, cordially joined with laymen of non-liturgical views in forming the First Day, or Sunday-School Society, of which he became president. This was to give instruction to those outside the church. When it was proposed to form the "Sunday and Adult School Union" in 1817, for the instruction of all, whether in or out of the church, the good bishop declined to join it, though some of his parishioners favored the project. He, however, decidedly preferred a separate denominational organization for general work, such as the Philadelphia Protestant Episcopal Sunday-School

Society, which preceded the Protestant Episcopal Sunday-School Union of 1826. Bishop Whittingham, later of Maryland, was the active leader in promoting this denominational religious institution, followed by Bishops Alonzo Potter, G. W. Doane, and by Drs. Stephen H. Tyng and Gregory T. Bedell. From 1835 until after the Civil War various discussions accentuated the divided views upon the principles and methods of religious education in the church, checking the progress of any united Sunday-school movement. After the Civil War George C. Thomas was active in promoting a local Sunday-school Society, which grew into the American Church Sunday-School Institute in 1875, enlarged in 1884. Of this society Rev. Dr. H. L. Duhring became the efficient secretary and leader, with the co-operation of the Rev. Dr. Richard Newton, Rev. Wm. Thomas, and others. It began to issue a Sunday-school magazine in 1885, and a complete system of Diocesan Lessons for its schools.

The New York Sunday-School Commission was begun in 1898, under Bishop Henry C. Potter, followed by other Diocesan appointments, and in 1904 by a "Joint Commission" on Sunday-school instruction which led to the organization of a General Board of Religious Education in 1910. This board is composed of bishops, clergymen and laymen—seven each—and of sixteen other members, representing a Sunday-school commission; the object being the unification and development of religious instruction under the auspices of the church. It has instituted a standard course of teacher training, and a correspondence school for teachers, and set forth a standard curriculum not confined, however, to Sunday-schools. Among those active in developing these movements in the church board were the Rev. W. W. Smith, the Rev. William S. Gardner, Rev. Lester Bradner, Ph.D., Rev. Stanley Kilbourne, the Rev. Dr. Walker Gwyne, Bishop Beckwith, and Dr. Hayes. They prepared and edited several courses of lessons based on the Prayer Book and the Creed, and also a Graded Series adapted to four principal departments: Primary, Junior, Senior, and Graduate studies. This church reports upward of 500,000 membership in its Sunday-schools.

The Reformed Church in America (Dutch) claims to be the oldest body of the Presbyterian type in America, founded in

1623–26. It formed a Sabbath School Union, independent of the American Sunday-School Union (with which it co-operated) in 1828, which was changed to a Board in 1839, and merged into the Board of Publication in 1863. It issues lessons and literature for its 800 Sunday-schools, enrolling about 124,000 members.

The Reformed Church in the United States (German) in 1834, by "overture," requested the American Sunday-School Union to propose a "Sunday-school agent to assist in extending that work in her churches." A Sabbath School Committee was formed in the denomination in 1841, followed by an association in 1863, and a distinct Sunday-school board in 1887. In 1893 Dr. Rufus W. Miller was chosen secretary, with able members of the church co-operating to prosecute religious education in church schools. This began a new era of systematic, effective service in every phase of religious education of the youth of the church. The important lines of work are educational and missionary and the editing of suitable literature. At present (1917) they are providing a building to be used as the church's headquarters, known as the "Schaff Building," in Philadelphia. The Rev. Drs. C. Clever, C. A. Hauser, and J. H. Bomberger are among the widely recognized workers in this church.

The Denominational Council.—About thirty or more of the various denominations, through representative workers, formed a voluntary organization in 1910, known as the "Sunday-school Council of Evangelical Denominations," which seeks to promote organized denominational Sunday-school work among all the bodies participating in it; each denomination, however, reserving the right to modify or change any approved general plans that may be deemed suitable to the needs and conditions of the respective denominations.

The Sunday-School Council of Evangelical Denominations aims to advance the Sunday-school interests of the co-operating denominations in three ways: by conferring together, by giving expression to common views, and by co-operative action along educational, missionary, editorial and publishing lines. It is composed of representatives from about thirty denominations. It gives attention to the preparation of standard courses of study for teachers, but leaves the preparation of the material for these courses to each denomination; supervises the selection of lessons for Sunday-school study, and seeks to correlate the entire work, so as to avoid overlapping, yet leaving each denomination absolutely free in the conduct of its own work.[1]

A Commission on Religious Education under the "Federal Council of the Churches of Christ in America" is also pursuing a similar work, with nearly the same scope and purpose. If continued along the lines projected they are likely to overlap unless they are consolidated. These agencies are also urging upon colleges and universities special departments for the training of Sunday-school teachers and workers. We may reasonably expect, in the near future, a great advance in religious education through these competing and co-operating denominational activities.

Meanwhile, the many schools, widely scattered through the outlying country districts, where the people speak different dialects and where not more than two or three families hold the same religious creeds, and no church is practicable to be sustained among them, and often none is near, or strong enough to attract and help them, this multitude of schools must be encouraged, their teachers trained, and leaders developed, until they become a moral and religious force, for the betterment of the secluded communities of which they are the natural center, and a power for the spiritual growth of the people, as servants and disciples of the Lord Jesus Christ.

[1] See *statement of Dr. Webb*, Secretary, June, 1916.

SECTION XII

WHAT is the religious condition of our rural communities in the twentieth century? What are the material, social, educational and religious demands of these communities? How can they be properly met? How can higher social, moral and religious ideals be successfully introduced into rural life? What influence does rural have on city life, morally and religiously? Numerous commissions and organizations—governmental, federated, interdenominational and denominational—have been and are busy in "surveys" to aid in giving answers to these questions.

Rural Conditions.—Since the opening of this century and during a period of twenty years (1897 to 1917) the American Sunday-School Union asked these questions. It further asked how it could concentrate the religious forces in any given community so as to bring rural life nearer to Christian ideals. The Society enrolled, among its managers and supporters, some who stood in the front rank of Christian men of affairs and some who were also eminent for their scholarship and high Christian ideals. Among its officers were Morris K. Jesup, its president; Jay Cooke, William E. Dodge, Homer Merriam, Levi Z. Leiter, Gen. O. O. Howard, Louis Klopsch, John H. Converse, Horace B. Silliman, B. B. Comegys, Thomas Murdock, William H. Wanamaker, and scores of others of nationwide renown as Christian citizens and patriots. Under their leadership the managers undertook, in 1900 and on, a prolonged and painstaking re-examination of the field, the basis, the polity and the methods of Sunday-school service, with a view to discover, if possible, how it could be more closely adapted to existing conditions throughout the country. Their purpose was to secure the highest efficiency in bringing about the betterment of rural life; producing not only better citizenship, but a high type of Christianity.

388

Out of this investigation came a reaffirmation of the general principles outlined by the founders of the Society and a resolution for an aggressive campaign to increase the distribution of the literature and to enlarge all the activities of the American Sunday-School Union. In the view of President Jesup and of other officers familiar with the polity of religious and benevolent institutions, it was announced that appeals for funds for the Union should be made to include all branches of its work. They declared the aim should be to secure general funds that could be applied broadly to promote the best interests of the great cause of Sunday-schools.

In support of this view they were of the opinion that the time might come when it would be found that large funds limited or restricted to special fields and to special work could not be as wisely expended as now to promote the best interests and the greatest efficiency in religious education.[1] It is noteworthy also that the Society had already found the income of two small funds thus limited could not be expended wisely according to the letter stipulated by the givers. They might be used in accord with the spirit or interest *implied* by the givers. Missionaries were to be employed as heretofore, the Board declared, but in doing this appeals for other important operations of the Society were to be no longer sidetracked, as they had of necessity been during the debt-paying period. Henceforward the Society was to emphasize the broader outlook of the founders. This the managers reaffirmed:

> We believe the origin and objects of the American Sunday-School Union were to disseminate useful information, circulate moral and religious publications in every part of the land, *and* endeavor to plant a Sunday-school wherever needed.

Furthermore, they directed that "appeals be made in our publications and through our missionaries and other agents for contributions to enable the Society to distribute its literature in larger amounts and at lower rates to the needy."

It was made clear to the board from this inquiry that the basis upon which the Society was founded was evangelical, and that its charter was broad enough to justify its past, present, and any probable future activities. And the polity which

[1] See unpublished letters to the Editorial Secretary, 1900–1905.

had grown out of many experiments and long experience was believed to represent the sense of the great body of its life members and supporters.

The managers were made well aware that the literature and educational work which had been happily termed the "left arm" of the Society and which had been largely sacrificed to save the life of the body, ought in equity and business prudence to be restored by a fresh campaign in its behalf. The publication work, having never been conducted upon a money-making or commercial but upon a benevolent basis, as truly as the missionary work, should be put in a position to do its share in promoting the greatest efficiency in Union schools. This was in perfect harmony with the earlier purpose of the Society's founders. Its literature was never distributed to the public by its missionaries or otherwise at a profit, but often at or below the actual cost of manufacture; the difference being specially provided for out of a general fund.

While the literature was to be issued on a benevolent basis, it was the Society's polity through all its history to have the receipts from sales and for the distribution of literature equal to the expense of issuing it; as a rule calling on the public only for such contributions as were required to pay for the portion that was distributed as a gift to the needy. To aid in this it was a part of the Society's polity for years to keep the manufacturing expenses at the lowest point. The paper, printing, and binding were secured by competitive bids from responsible houses, required to furnish a standard quality at the lowest terms. Further to maintain this polity, the catalogs of the Society's literature had been rigidly scanned from time to time to bring the stock on hand within the lowest market values. But as often noted heretofore extension made it impossible always to maintain its polity, or fitly to carry out its rules and words.

New channels and methods of circulation had been sought. The best ways of supplying American colonies had been considered. Ways and means for increasing the Society's general fund, including the distribution of literature to those unable to purchase, had been sought and adopted, so that this action of the opening century was only a repetition of the real purpose of the managers, although not always heretofore realized.

BUILDINGS OF THE SOCIETY

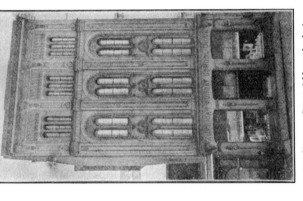

316 Chestnut Street (old numbering)
1122 Chestnut Street (new numbering)
1853–1907.

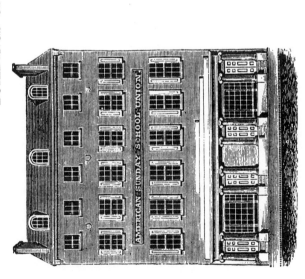

146 Chestnut Street
(above Sixth Street)
1827–1853.

In accordance with these views and this action, among other measures it was suggested that a competent and foremost financial representative, recognized as a leader in this broad educational service, be looked for; one who could command the attention of philanthropists and educators, as well as of large audiences throughout the country by a presentation of the broad purpose of the American Sunday-school and of religious education, indicating its relation to other great religious institutions, while pointing out the special field for which God in his providence had seemed to raise up this Society.   A Christian educator of such talents, it was quite clear, would not be easily found, and when found would doubtless have a dozen calls in other directions.   But it was believed that the immense field for such service and the importance of it would appeal to someone whose training and education had qualified him for such a nation-wide work.

Evangelical Literature.—A glimpse at the conditions of rural Christianity in America and elsewhere at the beginning of the century revealed the importance of these measures. To note a single feature—the distribution of evangelical literature—in the last decade of the last century the total distribution of the Union's publications from Philadelphia, exclusive of New York, had resulted in a margin of gains eight years out of the ten; the net gain for the ten years being about $33,000, which was expended in the improvement of its literature.   This was a decided financial improvement in the business over previous decades for fifty years.   But the improvement in usefulness was not so apparent, for the volume or bulk of literature issued by the Union was steadily decreasing in face of constantly lower prices.   A similar fluctuation was shown by other leading religious societies, notably by the Religious Tract Society of London, whose output of evangelical literature is the largest of its kind in the world.   During the same closing decade of the last century its sales fell off fully one-third in amount; in 1889 being 163,000 pounds and in 1899, 109,000 pounds.   In like manner the volume of its distribution of publications decreased in the last seven years of that period from 50,000,000 copies annually to 39,000,000 copies.   The reasons assigned for this fluctuation were various, among them the fact that the people did not want to hear of sin and salvation. They might *need* to know it, but they wanted not evangelism, but "culturism." They might be persuaded to read such literature if it were attractive and furnished to them at a nominal price.

Referring to the broader view of the Society's work, the managers in their report for 1904 took note of the change of name of the Society in 1824 from the Sunday and Adult School Union to the American Sunday-School Union. The earlier name, they say, indicated that the founders were chiefly in Philadelphia and vicinity; yet the field of operations was never so limited, but quickly extended to all the states of the Union. The new name "American" implied that it was a combination of supporters throughout the nation, but it was not intended to restrict the work of the Society to America. While it was natural that the work should begin at home, it was not the idea of the founders that it should be confined to the United States. This is clear from the earlier reports which give a view of the progress of the work not merely in every state of the Union, but in British America, South America, the West Indies, Europe, Asia, Africa, and the islands of the sea. Repeatedly the Society extended a helping hand to workers in different parts of the world diffusing religious instruction. In the middle of the last century it maintained missionaries in upper and lower Canada and in other portions of the British dominions in America, and later it aided in establishing schools on the continent of Europe.

In view of this drift and these measures the Union stated in 1901 that it should have $20,000 a year to meet ordinary calls for literature and $50,000 for properly supplying rural districts.[1] The next year the Society stated that the rural population wanted free libraries and other literature; that it had received through Editorial Secretary Rice a gift of $27,000 for this purpose, in addition to $20,000 received through the same channel shortly before. Moreover, upward of $30,000 more were added to funds for permanent investment that year.[2] And the following year upward of $100,000 were received from eight or ten donors for similar permanent investments, in addition to what was given for current work.[3] So that in five years from this announcement (1901–1906) upward of $240,000

[1] *Report*, 1901, p. 10.   [2] *Report*, 1902, pp. 8, 9.   [3] *Report*, 1903, pp. 14, 15.

were received (besides contributions for current work), to be added to the invested funds of the Society. Soon after the Lowry bequest of $110,000 was received, due largely to the tactful information and courtesy of a faithful saleswoman (Sarah Andrews) in the Union's bookshop. This proved that the friends of the Society were ready to sustain it in the broader work which it proposed as fast as it showed the ability to perform it. Many other generous bequests were received, as noted in the section on Finances.

United States Commission.—Some sidelight was thrown upon the moral and religious conditions existing in the rural communities of the country at the opening of the century by a governmental country life commission. While the chief inquiries of this commission related to the economic and financial conditions of farm life in the United States, some glimpses at the moral and religious conditions were reported. The attitude of the Commission was friendly and favorable to the promotion of the highest spiritual interest of the people, as the following extracts will amply show.

In a special message transmitting the report President Roosevelt, in 1909, clearly indicated its character and scope. To gain this information the Commission held thirty public hearings attended by farmers and farmers' wives from forty states and territories. One hundred and twenty thousand answers to questions sent out by the Commission were also collated.

Of the conditions, deficiencies and remedies relating to the great problem of betterment of country life, including education, the Commission had much to say. On the moral and religious problem of spiritual forces the Commission declared:

> We miss the heart of the problem if we neglect to foster personal character and neighborhood righteousness. The best way to preserve ideals for private conduct and public life is to build up the institutions of religion. . . . The whole people should understand that it is vitally important to stand behind the rural church and to help it to become a great power in developing concrete country life ideals.

The Commission recommended conferences on rural progress

> designed to unite the interests of education, organization, and religion into one forward movement for the rebuilding of

country life. Rural teachers, librarians, clergymen, editors, physicians, and others may well unite with farmers in studying and discussing the rural question in all its aspects. We must, in some way, unite all institutions, all organizations, all individuals having any interest in country life into one great campaign for rural progress.

The difficulties in the moral and religious part of the problem the Commission thus describes:

We have farmers from every European nation, and with every phase of religious belief often grouped in large communities, naturally drawn together by a common language and a common faith, and yielding but slowly to the dominating and controlling forces of American farm life. To this diversity in language and religion must be added the peculiar character which the farmer develops in himself. The training of generations has made him a strong individualist, and he has been obliged to rely mainly on himself. Self-reliance being the essence of his nature, he does not at once feel the need of cooperation for business purposes or of close association for social objects. . . . He does not, as a rule, dream of a rural organization that can supply as completely as the city the four great requirements of man—health, education, occupation, society.

On the other hand, it is said, "the centralized agencies should be stimulative and directive, rather than mandatory and formal. Every effort must be made to develop native resources, not only of material things but also of people."

Of public education in the rural districts the Commission affirmed:

The schools are held to be largely responsible for ineffective farming, lack of ideals, and the drift to town. This is not because the rural schools, as a whole, are declining, but because they are in a state of arrested development and have not yet put themselves in consonance with all the recently changed conditions of life. . . . The most necessary thing now to be done for public-school education in terms of country life is to arouse all the people to the necessity of such education, to co-ordinate the forces that are beginning to operate, and to project the work beyond the schools for youth into continuation schools for adults.

In reconstructive work the Commission urges:

It is of the greatest consequence that the people of the open country should learn to work together. This is applied to economic conditions of buying and selling, of good roads, better homes, transportation, rural delivery, telephones, betterment in household appliances, running water, and whatever makes not only for the physical comfort of the rural community and home, but also whatever will be helpful to progress in knowledge, in morals, and in religion, for the whole community.

The rural church must take a larger leadership, both as an institution and through its pastors, in the social reorganization of rural life.

Here the Commission was confronted with almost insuperable special obstacles which it points out:

> As a rule, the country people are conservative. Ordinarily the financial support is inadequate. Often there are too many churches in a given community. Sectarian ideas divide unduly and unfortunately. . . . Few of the churches in the open country are provided with resident pastors. . . . Most of the gatherings are designed for the church people themselves rather than for the community. The range of social influence is therefore generally restricted to the families particularly related to the special church organization, and there is likely to be no sense of social responsibility for the entire community. . . .
>
> It hardly seems necessary to urge that the spirit of co-operation among churches, the diminution of sectarian strife, the attempt to reach the entire community, must become the guiding principles everywhere if the rural church is long to retain its hold.

The Commission recognized that to apply any remedy successfully and to secure adequate leadership the voluntary principle, which underlies the Sunday-school movement, must be introduced and adopted. Thus the Commission affirms: "Everything resolves itself at the end into a question of personality. Society or government cannot do much for country life unless there is a *voluntary response* in the personal ideals of those who live in the country.

As a forerunner and pioneer of the churches, and as representing the great body of the Christian people of the country, the Union Sunday-school has been an economic and effective scouting organization—a pioneer and leader preparing the way for the larger coming of the Kingdom. It has been working for over a century upon the principles of co-operation and voluntary service so strongly emphasized by this governmental Commission.

Twentieth Century Plans.—In a territory so vast as the United States, into which teeming millions crowded from every quarter of the earth so that the republic suddenly sprang into a world-wide power, the conditions were too varied for a score of persons alone to survey.   The problem called for as great a variety of expert training and observation as there were different sections in the Union.   The Society had investigations by special field workers who had gathered a mass of information— the result of minute surveys of hundreds of communities in different sections of the country.   This mass of accumulated facts was intelligently sifted and presented in carefully prepared papers by leaders representing the various districts or sections of the country at the "Diamond Anniversary" of the Society under its present name (the 82d from its origin), together with a similar collation of facts presented by national workers in allied and co-operative organizations engaged in promoting Bible instruction throughout the country.

The present generation cannot easily realize the marvelous territorial expansion of the United States in a century.   When the Sunday-School Union started, the inhabited part of the country covered only a little corner of the extreme east and a narrow fringe along the Atlantic Coast.   With the opening of the twentieth century that territory had expanded so that it reached from the St. Lawrence on the north to the Florida Keys and the Rio Grande on the south, and from the Atlantic coast to the Pacific, and shot upward in the northwest, like the Aurora Borealis, to the Aleutian Islands.   The population which was less than 10,000,000 at the origin of the Union had become well-nigh 100,000,000 at the opening of the century.

The character of this flowing tide of migration into the Middle and great West was as varied as the countries from which the immigrants came.   Roughly, they might be divided into two great classes: one sought wealth and personal glory; the other, with thrift, sought to be helpful to others and to promote a noble type of Christian character.   This surprising change in our republic was graphically sketched in an eloquent speech by William E. Dodge, a vice-president of the Society. Referring to the origin of the Sunday-School Union, he said:

What was this country then?   A fringe of population along the Atlantic seaboard of the colonies almost entirely failing in understanding each other, the primitive modes of conveyance making it difficult to get from one part to the other; not consolidated, not fully understanding the splendid future before it, and waiting for the providence which has led it so wonderfully ever since.   Shortly after the beginning of our country's life hardy pioneers, splendid fellows, the very pick of our eastern population, began to press into the wilderness and to make homes for themselves. They plunged into the forest, they cut down great trees, they ran risks from the Indians and from wild beasts, and they fought splendidly to make homes and a new civilization in the wilderness. And that process went on, and they made a strong, vigorous onslaught on the interior of the country until they reached the Alleghenies, and crossed them and went down the Ohio and around the great lakes, and crossed the Mississippi and the plains to the foot-hills of the Rocky Mountains; they passed through its defiles until they came to the Western Sea, where the three great Western States, which have so much meaning for the future, lie against the Pacific Ocean now. . . .

Schoolhouses were carefully built, and the traditions and religious questions from time to time discussed in these simple communities. Then it was that these sweet-hearted, strong, wise, and tactful missionaries of the Sunday-School Union began their work. Going quietly into these little settlements, they gathered the mothers and fathers together, stirred up and rekindled the flame of Christian life and memory, and brought them together in their little Sunday-schools, in their homes, and, if there were no schoolhouses to be had, under the trees and under the stars. The dear old Bible was brought out, and the hymns that were remembered from home were sung, and Christ was there with his love and tenderness, and the germs of religion were planted there. They grew, as the settlement grew, into churches, and they are now the strongest and most vigorous in all the various denominations of the whole country; and that was followed out all the way through this wonderful expansion. . . . We never shall know what we owe to these pioneer missionaries, just as we shall never quite understand what we owe the pioneers of civilization who carried the torch of American liberty and freedom through this whole great land of ours.

In this initial work, where you go among a primitive and small population, you meet sectarian influence. It is hard enough to carry the spirit of the Sunday-school and the spirit of the church, of any kind of religious work, among this simple people, but if you handicap it by sectarian bias you are making it very much harder, and I thank God with all my heart that this Society continues now, as it always has, to bring simply Christ and God's Word to a simple people, as the one thing that can make their lives sweeter, better, and more helpful to the whole community.[1]

Of the sacrifices in this work, Morris K. Jesup of New York feelingly declared: "Little do you know—little do I know—of the sacrifices that these good men are making out on the plains of the West and of the South; of their privations, their poverty, and all that they do in the service of the blessed Master, that His name may be carried to those who otherwise, perhaps, would not hear of it."[2]

[1] *Anniversary Report*, 1899, pp. 86–88.   [2] *Ibid.*, p. 81.

The problem confronting the Union and its missionaries in the pioneer settlements of the Middle West was vividly portrayed by the Rev. Dr. Newell Dwight Hillis—himself a native of Nebraska and once a scholar in one of the Sunday-schools of the Union—in an impassioned speech:

It has been my fortune to spend most of my career in the West. I know its people, its institutions, its homes, its churches. I know something of its rapid growth in population and in wealth—a growth that gives promise of a mighty empire, and I know also that there is no institution that has done more for the instruction of our children and our youth in the remote rural districts than Union missionaries, who are literally our springs of liberty and architects of civilization.

When we study the career of the great men in our cities we find that the leaders are country-born, country-bred, and village raised. . . . A recent canvass of one hundred prominent men in a metropolis showed that 85 per cent. of lawyers, bankers, journalists, and merchants had been brought up either upon a farm or in a country town.

So you will find that the great rural districts of the West, to which foreign populations are going, are the places that are rearing our leaders, and this is the work of the missionaries from this Society.

Men in this part of the country (East) do not understand the problem at all, as to what is going on in the West, until they have gone there, as I have, and journeyed for a day and night through the great corn belt of Iowa, and another day and night through the great Red River wheat country, and then have gone on to the foothills of the great mountains, rich in minerals, full of treasures, which are the gift of God to man. Following one of these lines, as I did myself, and spending a year and a half of the happiest of my life as a missionary for the Sunday-School Union, you see homes spring up as if by magic. Going out to the end of the little railway, I saw the farmers and settlers pushing on with their teams into the country, traveling for a week at a time until they came to their destined point; thirty or forty families, including perhaps three or four Presbyterians, four or five Baptists, and three or four Methodists. At a central point they all come together, build a little schoolhouse, and, clubbing together, they hire a teacher for their children. With half a dozen denominations represented in the forty or more families, it is obviously impossible to found a denominational Sunday-school, but it is easy to sustain a Union Bible school. This Union school is their social, literary, and religious center, their college, their university. The missionary purchases for them a circulating library, he founds their literary club, he helps them in a series of meetings. During their long winter nights they get together in their religious meetings, and I have seen such a revival as we read of in the days of Finney and of Moody. Literally the whole community was touched and regenerated by the breath of God.

Here is the basis for the movement that will be a power in the work of the church of Jesus Christ. And this is the work of the Society. This is the nature of its influence, and this is its relation to our great civilization.

Of the changes in character which it accomplishes he gave this characteristic illustration:

> One woman was asked how she brought up her boys, and she replied, "In the fear of the Lord and of the horsewhip." A far better method was started among these people by the teaching of the Sunday-school, so that foreign people are Americanized and Christianized, and all become good citizens, scarcely understanding at first the spirit in which it is accomplished. . . . *There is no institution in the West doing so much for church unity, and there is no institution in the West doing so much to save the Sunday to the great West, as the American Sunday-School Union.*[1]

The Sunday-School Union Not Building for Itself.—Moreover, the American Sunday-School Union is eminently Christlike in that it aims to do good to all men, and especially to the young. It lays the foundation for multitudes of churches, not of any one denomination, but of every evangelical faith. It brings the gospel to all alike, and whenever those whom it instructs become followers of Christ, it leaves them to unite in or with any local church of whatever evangelical creed they may prefer. Thus its work strengthens all denominations. *It erects no church of its own.* This point was forcibly stated by Superintendent F. G. Ensign of Chicago:

> Keep in mind that this Society builds nothing for itself. All its labor has been for the building of the churches, and strengthening the nation. Its work stands out as one of the bright lights in the moral horizon of the nineteenth century. It has built no monuments of marble. No part of its fund has been hidden in temples of stone—only upon the imperishable tablets of human hearts has it made its records. This it will continue to do until the end of this era. Its instruments are the Word of God and the living missionary; and its field of operation is the children and youth, and the homes in the neglected settlements of our beloved land, and in the rural districts from which 75 per cent. of the men and women of power and influence in the church and nation are to come in the future as in the past.[2]

Confirming this statement, the Society during the previous decade reported 69,988 professed conversions, besides many more who had been led to Christ in its schools, of which no report had been made. These had gone into the churches and,

[1] *Anniversary Report*, 1899, pp. 96–98.   [2] *Ibid.*, p. 91.

in communities where there was sufficient strength, into new churches, which had been the case in 1,359 places.

Of the outlook for the Union in the twentieth century Mr. Ensign impressively affirmed:

> This Society occupies one of the ripest mission fields in the world, and its work reinforces every church and missionary society. It fortifies every good institution, and strengthens the government in every advance toward righteousness and justice and the preservation of the rights of the common people.[1]

Furthermore, it was made clear that the splendid achievements of the past were a wonderful inspiration for accomplishing greater things in the twentieth century. This was admirably and vigorously set forth in a brief but fervent testimony by H. Clay Trumbull, a Christian worker of national fame. His surveys and observations not merely covered New England and the East, but extended to nearly every state in the Union, from Maine to California and from Minnesota to Florida. Speaking of his lifelong service in religious education with this Society and other institutions, he tersely asserted:

> In view of these experiences and of my special historical studies since then, I desire to speak with emphasis and earnestness of our indebtedness in this country to the idea and agency represented by this Society, for most of what we have in our peculiar civilization, and of our social, moral and religious prosperity among the nations of the earth.

Of the problem of immigration he added:

> With all the various nationalities and the multiplied phases of religion and of irreligion represented in the horde of newcomers to our land, from the older countries of Europe, Asia, and Africa; swarming as they swarm to our shores, and packing more closely our closely packed cities, and moving out on our borders with the advancing wave of population, there would be small prospect or hope of winning to Christianity every new neighborhood thus formed, through pulpit efforts in behalf of non-churchgoing parents, in godless households, or through the printed page addressed to those who either cannot or will not read what is designed for their benefit. The one feasible, the one hopeful way is by winning the children, and those who would be as children, in an undenominational neighborhood Sunday-school. From this beginning there comes a readiness and a desire for other agencies and then the field is ripe for a missionary preacher of one denomination or another. A congregation is gathered, a church or churches follow in due order.[2]

[1] *Anniversary Report*, 1899, p. 93.   [2] *Ibid.*, pp. 69, 70.

Surveys by Sections.—The Union did not content itself with general statements and surveys of the country as a whole. The managers diligently sought for specific information in regard to each of the great sections. The republic had become too vast in its territory, and the population too varied in language, in race, in occupations and in religion to be taken in at one view. Each section had problems peculiar to itself. The elements of these problems must be ascertained, carefully considered and weighed, and measures adopted for efficiently meeting their respective needs. Thus in the New England, the Middle Atlantic, and the Middle Western States immigration brought increasing diversity of the population, in language, in religion and in social and economic conditions that must be carefully and wisely blended for peaceful homogeniety and good citizenship.

In the great section of the South Atlantic and Gulf States the racial problem continued vexatious and very complex. Even the white races are not homogeneous. There are the mountaineers or highlanders in the very heart of that section, a hardy, naturally hospitable, home-loving race, of noble ancestry. Denied means of public worship because of the rough, mountainous, sparsely settled country, they became indifferent to religion. In the lower strata is another class of "crackers" and "sand-hillers." These classes, with the better conditioned portion of the white race, are inextricably mixed, dwelling also with an increasing negro population, making the most difficult problem of our American life. These diverse peoples and races, living in the same section as they have for generations, must somehow find the way to dwell peaceably side by side in the same nation and under the same laws. Each must contribute its quota of support toward the making of a prosperous and virtuous community.

In the Rocky Mountains and Pacific Coast—a great section—are also peculiar problems. The red men and the yellow men and the white men settle side by side, and the problem there, as in other sections, is to find a way by which these varied races, so far as they come to this country as residents, may be absorbed, assimilated, Americanized, and Christianized.

Here are problems as difficult as they are abundant which

the American Sunday-School Union should aid the Christian patriot in solving, especially for those scattered widely throughout the country and denominated "the rural population" of our republic.

Our concern relates not so much, primarily, to the economic or the material phases of the problem as to discover some efficient plan for the moral and religious elevation of these various peoples. Furthermore, the conditions of the problem in any particular section are constantly changing. The historian should honestly report the surveys and information furnished by competent observers of the conditions that existed at the opening of the century. He is not required to prove that there were no exceptions to these statements; for it is quite likely that the exceptions would be held by the original investigators to prove the rule.

At the Anniversary in 1899 a mammoth map of the United States was exhibited, depicting the eight districts into which the country was then divided by the American Sunday-School Union for its missionary work; each district having a superintendent. These districts were shown in different colors, presenting their extent and character to the eye. In each state there were figures showing the number of children in Sunday-school, and the percentage of the entire population under Bible instruction. This map was compiled by the Society under the supervision of E. B. Stevenson, and was a telling object lesson at the Anniversary.

Thus it was shown that the percentage of Sunday-school membership for the whole United States was 17.4; Pennsylvania, 21.9; Colorado, 7.7; Utah, 3.3; etc.—the latest facts accessible in regard to every state being noted thereon in conspicuous figures.

New England and Oldest Sections.—Rev. Dr. Addison P. Foster, a native of New England and in charge of that district, called attention to a proclamation by Governor Rollins of New Hampshire, in which he used startling language concerning the condition of the rural portions of that state:

> There are towns where no church bell sends forth its solemn call from January to January; there are villages where children grow up to manhood unchristened; there are communities where the dead are laid away without the benison of the name

of Christ, and where marriages are solemnized only by justices of the peace. . . .

The Granite State is not a sinner above all others. The influences which have shaped its present religious condition have been in operation throughout New England. Maine, New Hampshire, Vermont, Massachusetts, Rhode Island and Connecticut are by history, by blood connections, and by business ties blended into one life. . . . The influences that are making New Hampshire what it is are at the same time making Massachusetts what it is. Throughout New England the urban populations are engorged, and religious conditions there are constantly seeking adjustment to new centers of life, while the rural populations are depleted and often in deplorable need.

Among influences working against religious progress in the rural districts in older sections were and are:

(1) The movement of the population from the country to the city; (2) adverse religious conditions due to the change going on from native to foreign born—a change which was affecting the people both in the city and in the country; (3) and last, but not least, "the division into a great number of denominations, largely working on individual lines and without coherence or co-operation." In Maine there were 27 denominations; New Hampshire, 22; Vermont, 24; Massachusetts, 38; Rhode Island, 28; Connecticut, 32, and in some of these denominations, counted as one in the census report, there were often from two to six different bodies. Thus, in New England, the Adventists were of six different kinds; the Free Baptists of two, the Christians of two, and so on.

The result of all this division of feeling is that denominational rivalry is strong. . . . In Maine, at a preaching service in a Union Sunday-School, in the small congregation eleven different denominations were represented. The whole countryside was similarly divided. . . . People could not be persuaded to sink their differences and unite in churches. In consequence church organizations in that part of the country are few, and those that exist are generally weak and often unable to maintain preaching. . . .

Similar conditions exist largely in all rural New England. There are far too many churches in a community; they find it extremely difficult to live; have to call on outside aid for support; pay their ministers very small salaries, and in consequence are obliged more and more to accept uneducated ministers.

Professor Henry T. Fairbanks of Vermont, after careful inquiries in his own state, affirmed that "290 churches had ceased to exist, and that in a population of 332,000 about

184,000 were not in the habit of church attendance, while on any pleasant Sunday not more than 75,000 were probably in the house of God." Yet Vermont is not exceptionally deficient.

Dr. Foster added:

> The effect of all these adverse influences on the morals and religious life of the people in the rural districts is marked. . . . Where there is no preaching, no Bible, no sacrament, no Sabbath, no prayer, no thought of God, no knowledge of Christ, what else can be expected than a weakened moral sense and an occasional outbreak of passion?

These conditions in New England attracted the attention of others outside. Thus the Rev. Dr. E. K. Bell, of the Lutheran Church in Ohio, noted that the problems in evangelization were becoming particularly prominent. Referring to the statements of Governor Rollins already quoted, he noted that the public press and great religious newspapers had taken up the inquiry and found that the conditions elsewhere were quite as grave as those reported of New Hampshire and of Vermont. He added:

> During the past twenty-five years the church has been concentrating her energies in the rapidly growing cities, making heroic efforts to save the urban population from moral and spiritual decay, in localities where results are more promising and conditions more inviting. The American Sunday-School Union never had a more urgent call than that which comes from the neglected districts in the country today.

Dr. Trumbull asserted at the beginning of the twentieth century:

> Forty years ago I first became aware of the religious destitution and needs of back-country districts and scattered rural communities—not in the extreme West and South, but in the heart of favored New England, where I then resided.

Many other competent observers testified to the destitution then existing, and to its rapid increase in this section. They confirmed the fact already stated that French Canadians and other alien races swarmed over the northern border into the lumber districts of Maine and into the agricultural districts of the other New England States, seizing upon the farms that were being forsaken by the sons of Pilgrims and Puritans. Owing to the influx of this alien population, many of the rural churches of that section were closed, the congregations being so weakened from depletion as to be unable to reopen them.

Furthermore, these conditions were made more difficult to meet by a tendency to place education as of equal or greater importance than religion in national life. Alluding to education as a proposed remedy for national diseases, Bishop Cyrus D. Foss of the Methodist Episcopal Church affirmed that they who tell us about the troubles which threaten us and urge: "Educate the people; give them knowledge—they do wrong because they know no better—give them knowledge and they will be better," illustrated his belief that great intellectual culture was not a panacea for national difficulties. He cited the instance of a great jurist in Massachusetts who was cross-examining a witness, when the witness appealed to the court for protection, saying that he was a professor of Harvard College. The jurist replied, "We hung one of them the other day," which was true.[1] He strongly affirmed that culture of the human intellect does not give assurance of a moral foundation and of security. The one panacea for it was to teach the gospel.

Eastern Middle Section.—In the Middle States a similar increase of destitution in the rural districts existed. The Hon. William E. Dodge referred to an examination of several counties in New York and of one or two counties in Pennsylvania and New Jersey where it was found churches had been closed. On one country road, running out of Utica, New York, there were seven churches found nailed up, two of which had been turned into cheese factories with "No Admittance" on the doors. On the Western Reserve in Ohio, in a center where there had been two or three churches, W. A. Hillis, of that state, found that because of change of population the churches were closed and in a tumble-down condition. He stated that there were over 565,000 children of school age in that state outside of Sunday-schools (2,000 more of that age than were outside of Sunday-schools in twelve of the great states of the Northwest). This excess was due to the greater density of the population in the rural sections of Ohio than in the frontier states. He discovered many districts in that properous state

---

[1] The allusion was to the celebrated Parkman-Webster case.

without Sunday-schools, and young men and women by the score who had never been in a Sunday-school in their lives. In another section of the state he said whole rural townships were without a church or Sunday-school.

Somewhat later similar conditions in western Pennsylvania were discovered by George J. Henderson. One rural county, formerly practically free from crime, recorded fourteen murders, twelve criminals sent to the penitentiary, thirteen to reformatories, fifty-three to workhouses, and 159 in jail in one year. Sixty-six per cent. of these were aliens. In another county of the same state, which for a generation had been in good repute for its virtue, $79,000 had been spent in one year in prosecuting criminals, most of whom were ignorant of our institutions and laws. A survey in another county revealed the fact that $2,000,000 had been spent for intoxicating liquors in about a year, and the immigration for industrial and mining purposes in the ten previous years was equal to the normal population of seven of the largest states in the South. These changes called for great activity, and new adjustments of every form of religious effort, including the redistribution or reorganization of many local churches. Moreover, in Michigan the missionary superintendent reported that it was each year becoming more difficult to maintain schools, due to several causes. The lumber business distributed millions of dollars in wages and often there were workers in camp ready to help; lumber operators were willing to put a missionary on the pay roll, yet so many of the lumbermen were either foreigners or were indifferent to religion that the places were steadily becoming more needy. Many lumber districts had been devastated by disastrous fires.

Central Northwest.—In the Northwestern District of the Society, comprising the great empire of the Middle Western States, where for two generations the American Sunday-School Union had been concentrating one great division of its forces for the establishment of Bible schools, so rapid had been the growth of population and the development of that vast territory that all the agencies, union and denominational, had failed to keep pace with the amazing increase and needs. There, as everywhere, the advance in material things had been far greater than in spiritual things. Even the magnificent provision made in those newer states for education had failed to master illiteracy and to reach the children of the incoming populations and train them in elementary education.

F. G. Ensign, then superintendent of that section, pointed out how hard it was to realize the rapid growth of the rural settlements in that vast territory.   In forty years the area of farms put under cultivation in virgin soil was 245,000,000 acres, the average migration into the section being 100 families a day, or 700 a week.   The new farms thus occupied and improved were, prior to 1850, buffalo and deer runs, and the area thus settled in a generation was greater than the German Empire, England, Ireland, Scotland, Holland, Belgium, Denmark and Switzerland combined; countries from which many of these settlers of varied tongues and nationalities had come to be transformed into American citizens.[1]

Considering the means at its command, the American Sunday-School Union had achieved marvelous results, of which Mr. Ensign gave a striking illustration.   A Union missionary founded a Sunday-school in Nebraska, in a new town. A young man, profane of speech, was made secretary because he was sufficiently interested to be present at its organization.   A revival followed, two churches grew out of the Sunday-school, the young man became a Sunday-school missionary, had started 210 other schools, with a membership of nearly 10,000, and already twenty-one young people's societies and fifty churches had grown out of these schools.

Beyond this, many people had been induced under his ministry (although he was not a minister) to prepare for Christian work through higher education.   Two from the schools he had planted had become missionaries in Africa, three in China, four in India, seven in Japan, two in South America, and five to the Indians, while five were Sunday-school missionaries and twelve were pastors or ministers in our own land.

Dr. Cuyler's Testimony.—The Rev. Dr. Theodore L. Cuyler also bore witness with burning eloquence to the achievements of the Society in this vast Middle West.   Referring to the heroic missionaries of the Union who wrought such priceless benefits in our beloved land, he exclaimed:

[1] *Anniversary Report*, 1899, p. 91.

I would like to summon from the realms of glory that typical representative Sunday-school missionary, grand old Benjamin Chidlaw. Put your eye on him—a boy in an Ohio log cabin that could not afford even glass in the windows. The boy learns to write on paper he has bought by selling raccoon skins, starts out and foots it forty miles to Granville to get his teaching, and then travels on foot 120 miles farther to a Buckeye college—and for the training for the magnificent work God had in store for him that is a far better discipline than to have swung in a hammock of a luxurious university. I tell you when Almighty God wants to train a pioneer for Christian work like Chidlaw, or train a pilot for a nation's tempests like Abraham Lincoln, he cradles them on the rock. . . . I might put alongside of Benjamin Chidlaw that kindred spirit so familiar to many of you— Stephen Paxson. It is just that rude, rough material in which the sturdy early church members all through that mighty West and Southwest found a field. In fact, if you could put your finger on the churches that have sprung out of the Sunday-schools planted by Chidlaw and Paxson I verily believe they would outnumber all the churches in your beautiful city of Philadelphia. Their dead hands are ringing church bells over the Western prairies, through the defiles of the Rocky Mountains, until the silvery music is lost in the murmur of the Pacific Seas. The grandest thing about the missionaries of this noble Union— the grandest thing they have done—has been to supply to this nation what is the very salt of its salvation, and that is a Bible conscience. We need it and shall need it in these days when we are confronting some great problems and perils to which we cannot shut our eyes. I tell you yonder over that Southern sky we detect the murky clouds of the race problem, and the only solution to that great question is a Bible conscience that shall educate and elevate the weaker class—a Bible conscience that shall make the stronger class just and generous.[1]

The Southwest Section.—If the moral and religious needs of the Northern belt of states were great, those of the great Southwest Section far exceeded them. This section comprised all the southwestern states from the Mississippi River to the Rocky Mountains.

"This territory," said Rev. Dr. W. R. King, then in charge of the district, "is so great that the entire population of Russia, Germany, and France could be placed within it and not be as densely populated as Holland."

Rich in mines, in cattle, in cotton, in fruits, in coal, and in its salubrious climate, it then contained upward of 7,500,000 people; four-fifths of them living in rural communities. Energetic young people from the older states, and great hordes of others from the frigid climate of the north flocked into this

[1] *Anniversary Report*, 1899, p. 83.

land of sunshine. The birth of Oklahoma was phenomenal and a prophecy of what the Southwest was to be in a few years. Of the immigrants, Mr. King said:

> The people who are coming into this section are coming out of good homes—many of them—they are getting away from the influence of godly parents and Christian churches, and there is nothing harder on a man's moral and spiritual life than the breaking up of home ties and the getting away from the restraints of home environment. They go into this new section, away from the church and the Sunday-school, plunging headlong into the race for wealth. They forget their God and soon learn to use his holy day for pleasure, if not for work. They seldom hear a gospel sermon, except as some faithful missionary comes as a light into the darkness, and carries the gospel by tract and paper and word of mouth into these homes. The people are isolated, the country is sparsely settled; in many places the people are very poor and the religious destitution is alarming. There are whole counties in Arkansas and Missouri and Texas without a single Sunday-school, except possibly in one or two cases at the county seat. In many of these places our missionaries do well if they succeed in getting enough money out of a newly organized Sunday-school to supply it for a month. The people have no money, and if they are to get religious literature and Bibles they must be supplied by the generous gifts of the people who are better favored. . . .
> The population is heterogeneous and unsettled. The people are always moving. Our missionaries may establish a Sunday-school or a church today, and tomorrow the thing may go off in a covered wagon. Doing missionary work in Oklahoma and the Indian Territory, Texas and Arkansas is like quail shooting on the prairies—we have to take them on the fly. . . . There is a glorious opportunity for this Society in the Southwest. . . . Here are 2,500,000 children who have no gospel privileges.

The South Section.—The Southern District, comprisng eleven South Atlantic and Gulf States—a territory 1,000 miles long and 700 miles wide—has a population of upward of 17,000,000; over one-third of whom are colored. It presents, perhaps, the most difficult problem of all. The condition of that field was forcibly stated by Rev. J. H. McCullagh, who succeeded his distinguished father in charge of the district.

The population is scattered, though some of the states are the oldest in the Union. There are only thirty-three inhabitants to the square mile, as against seventy-one in New England and 121 in the Middle States. The South has no large cities; 75 to 85 per cent. of the population are in the rural districts or small villages. They are split up into numerous denominations. The rural population as a whole possess very limited means. Thus, at the opening of this century, the taxable wealth of New York or Massachusetts would exceed that in all the eleven South Atlantic States combined. In face of the work done by the American Sunday-School Union and all denominational agencies in the South, and partly in consequence of the terrible devastation of the Civil War, there are still 3,500,000 children and youth in that district not in Sunday-school. The chief destitution is in the rural communities.

Mr. McCullagh declared that the line of separation between town and country became more marked every year. Many who live from one to three miles from a town never send their children to the Sunday-school. Among good people in the country the mistaken idea prevails that because they cannot have a denominational school, they cannot have any. When the missionary demonstrates that they can have a good Union school, it takes them a month to get through wondering why they never thought of it before.

Great destitution also prevails among the poor whites in the pine woods section. The destitution among the colored people and the great difficulty of meeting it are facts too conspicuous to need special description here. The destitution in the mountain region of the South, among the Highlanders, has deservedly attracted the attention of Christian missions. This is "Appalachian America," and "comprises the mountainous portion of eight states, with about 200 large counties and a population of about 3,000,000 souls. In area it is about as large as the German Empire. These highlanders have been isolated for over a century. The line which divides the mountains from the Blue Grass region is as distinct as if it were a river. Start from this line and go a mile in one direction—you will find land worth $100 an acre and people living in comfort; go a mile in the opposite direction—you find land nominally worth five dollars an acre and people living in cabins, perhaps their whole household goods not worth ten dollars." These people have lived a separate and distinct life, with little or no social communication. One writer says, "they seldom meet except in the state legislature and the state prison." When we read accounts of their lawlessness and feuds, many would infer that they were hopelessly depraved or inexpressibly stupid. A greater mistake could scarcely be made.

The sad fact remains that they are perhaps the poorest white people in the world. Visit thousands of their homes and you will not find a newspaper of any kind or date. A handful of primary, ragged school books for the children is the library. Nothing to beautify the home or refine the taste. Grim, ghastly, abject poverty on every hand! Their disregard for human life is largely owing to the lax execution of law and the customs of a hundred years.

> They are very hospitable and kind. A gentleman was invited home to take dinner with one of these mountaineers. When he sat down to the table, the gentleman's face, perhaps, indicated some surprise at the scanty bill of fare: there was nothing upon the table except potatoes. The host was not the least disconcerted, but said, "Have a tatur; take two taturs; why, take darn near all the taturs!" They will give you the best they have, and that is true hospitality.
>
> A missionary visited eighteen out of twenty-one families along one of the little mountain streams, and there was not a Bible in any of these homes. One man had reared eleven children, nine of whom were married, and he never had a Bible in his house. A college president who visited this region said, "There is not a Protestant population on the globe so destitute of educated, religious teachers!"

That these people are susceptible to evangelical influences Mr. McCullagh and his father gave abundant testimony. Thus, from one of the little country schools in Kentucky came a candidate for vice-president of the United States, a lieutenant governor of Kentucky, a leading book publisher in New York, three ministers of the gospel, one missionary of the American Sunday-school Union, fifty-six school teachers, ten physicians, seven lawyers and one judge. This is the testimony of Rev. Joseph H. McCullagh, familiar with the region all his life.

The Negro Race.—What can be said of the great problem of reaching with the gospel the 9,000,000 negroes of the South and their dark brethren in the islands under the protectorate of the United States? We confront a hard problem! Some Christian philanthropists said concerning these classes, as voiced by Rev. Dr. R. H. Conwell: "Many think we cannot civilize the Cuban bandits and the Philippine negritos." But he urged: "Introduce your school into every benighted community and establish a Sunday-school in which the children will learn the gospel and from which they will take the gospel home; then the bandits will disband, and savages will become civilized."

On this racial question, Dr. E. K. Bell confessed:

> Too long has American Christianity been neglecting the black children of the South. If the means were placed in the hands of the American Sunday-School Union to enable it vigorously to prosecute its work among the negro children, preparing the way for the Church to nurture them, within ten years the crimes of rape and murder, the crimes of lynching by burning and mutilation, would practically cease. There is no other remedy. The old blacks can be helped some, the work of evangelization must not cease among them, but the regeneration and rehabilitating of the race can only be accomplished by getting the Word of God into the hearts of the children, by putting the gospel where the Holy Spirit can work before the flesh and the devil have pre-empted the occupancy.

The Christian people of America must address themselves to this great problem. As John H. Converse foretold: "If as great progress can be made in the next seventy-five years, what may we not look for? In this movement more than in any other we have the development of what is called church-comity."

Rocky Mountain Section.—At the opening of the century the area of the Rocky Mountain District comprised four states and one territory—a region about seven and a half times as large as New England, but sparsely settled. Yet it was said to have not less than 500,000 youth unreached by the gospel. While this vast territory is crossed by transcontinental railways, there are hundreds, perhaps thousands, of valleys between the great mountain peaks of that region reached only by a wagon route or trail. W. L. De Groff, then in charge of that district, describes a valley containing 6,000 souls where there are no railroads and no tourists are found on the trail. It had been settled for twenty-five years and no religious services held there except by some followers of Joseph Smith. There were men and women with families who never had heard a sermon or learned anything of religion except Mormonism. There were a few timid and anxious souls awaiting a better day, and a school was planted in the little village. A Christian woman was superintendent. With her husband she spoke feelingly of what it meant to them to hear the gospel once more, after a quarter of a century of waiting!

Added information was presented to the Society as a result of a tour and survey through five of the Rocky Mountain States and along the Pacific Coast by Edwin W. Rice, Editorial Secretary, and two life members. The mass of facts he collected relating to the conditions in this region confirmed the glimpses of increasing destitution just mentioned. One of the greatest difficulties in the problem of this wild country, approximating 1,200 miles from north to south and 1,000 miles from east to west, is the mountainous character of it. The Great Cordilleran Plateau is crowded by high peaks, while the range is broken into a northern and a southern group.

The southern group is again split into a series of ranges running nearly north and south, and comprising great mountain valleys enclosed between the high ridges or vast mountain peaks, some rising to the height of 15,000 feet. These enclosed valleys are called parks—great parks of Colorado at an altitude of from 7,000 to 9,000 feet. It is said there are three hundred mountain peaks in Colorado alone, any one of which would be famous even in Switzerland, and not half of them have yet received appropriate names! Nestled among these great peaks are nearly 900 lakes, fed and drained by sixty rivers and mountain streams and by three times as many rivulets. The irrigated valleys may be covered over with grain, the mountain peaks are clothed in garments of snow, from which cool breezes sweep down at night to refresh the weary laborer on the hot plain. The dwellers in these altitudes delight to assure the newcomer that over three hundred of the three hundred and sixty-five days of the year are days of joyous sunshine. The high plateaus are usually green and fertile, covered with pines, spruces and green grasses, and often decked with rich and gaily covered flowers. Descending from the high plateau, the spruces, aspens and waving grasses are displaced by the cedars and pinon pine, and then by the cactus and yucca, until, on the low plain, little vegetation is found except where irrigation has spread fertility. The little mountain streams, fed by melting snows, possess a peculiar and ever-varying charm to the lover of nature. Helen Hunt Jackson, who had a delightful summer camp on Cheyenne Mountain, at the head of its wonderfully picturesque and awe-inspiring canon, has felicitously described a mountain stream: "It foams and shines and twinkles and glistens, and if there is any other thing which water at its swiftest and sunniest can do, that it does also."

Each tiny cascade has its melody and blends with the others without loss of its individuality. "It is the symphony of the streams, with big basses in front and airy violins softly chiming in at a distance, rising and falling in orchestral sweep, while feathered songsters from the neighboring tree-tops join in the harmony with their solos of flute-like trills."

The inhabitants might be classed in three groups: first, miners and mining population; second, the tillers of the land which include the cattlemen and ranchmen of mountain and plain, and the fruit and grain growers; third, the commercial, manufacturing and professional classes of the towns and cities in the region. The earliest mining class were adventurers or prospectors, restless, roving beings, with no settled purpose beyond the love of adventure or desire to chance upon a fortune in an hour. The later mining population belonged to a steadier class that came to dig out a fortune by patient toil. A few succeeded. Cripple Creek district alone yielded $25,500,000 worth of gold in one year and $120,000,000 in ten years.

The intellectual and religious life of the communities in the Rockies was not conspicuously strong. The ranchman and his cowboys had a frontier roughness typical to cattlemen of the plains. Widely scattered over large areas, a single ranch sometimes absorbed 500 to 5,000, and even 50,000 acres, making community life for educational and religious purposes very difficult. In the rural sections, where natural streams of irrigation turned the arid plain into fertile fields, the problem of religious worship and instruction was in process of slow solution. The Bible school seemed especially fitted to do a good work under these conditions. But the total membership of all the organized schools then in the Rocky Mountain region did not equal one-third of the youth of school age in it. Indeed, hardly one-fourth had been reached.

The difficulties of evangelizing this region are obvious to any observant Christian worker. Besides the broken character of the country, and the isolation of the people in the communities, are the great variety of diverse occupations and of religious prejudices. These were conspicuously illustrated in an extemporized Sunday service conducted by Editorial Secretary Rice, in a log cabin on a ranch upon a plateau on the shoulder of Bald Mountain, about thirty miles west of Denver and about 8,000 feet above the sea.

The little audience was made up of ranchers, miners, campers and hunters, dwelling in a circuit of from two to ten miles around the mountain. Notified the previous day by a ranchman's boy riding to the settlers, they promptly found their way to the cabin one Sunday morning; some, no doubt, out of curiosity, not having heard a service in that region for months, and some had never attended one. They represented Adventists, Baptists, Congregationalists, Methodists, Presbyterians, two kinds of Mormons, Roman Catholics, Socialists, Theosophists, Ethical Culture, and other rare 'isms. Their occupations were as varied as their religious prejudices. There were ranchmen and ranchwomen, cattlemen, cattlewomen, and a cowboy, farmer, gardener, miner, hunter, tourist, teamster, physician, missionary, engineer, assayer, and a professor in a university. They gave respectful and, some of them, earnest attention to the simple message of the Christ as the Saviour from sin and the Revealer of the glorious and redeemed life here and hereafter.

A peculiar difficulty, almost insurmountable, in this Rocky Mountain region is that of carrying the gospel to the Mormon population. There are two or more kinds of Mormons, but the largest class is counted followers of Joseph Smith and Brigham Young. The Mormon hierarchy establish schools of their own as rivals to those of the "Gentiles." Wherever an evangelical or Gentile school was established, either in one of their communities or on its border, the Mormons would straightway form a school of their own. If, however, from any cause, the evangelical school ceased to exist, the Mormon Sunday-school very soon languished, and, unless there were apprehensions of the Gentile school being revived, it also would cease. This was true however of the rural sections and not of the larger centers of Mormonism. In the present generation they have sustained such schools of religious instruction in every strong center, using a Mormon catechism, Mormon hymn books, and lessons referring to the Bible, but generally based upon the book of Mormon or some accepted work setting forth the teachings of the Mormon apostles. The chief hope of redemption of the Mormon people is to displace the teachings of the book of Mormon by the pure and simple teachings of the New Testament.

The Pacific Coast Section.—The Pacific Coast states present a problem peculiar to themselves. With a coast line on the Pacific of from 1,200 to 1,500 miles, with immense fertile and rich valleys between the coast range of mountains and the Sierras, like the San Joaquin, Sacramento and Santa Clara Valleys, and other vast stretches of country, with every variety of climate, rich in fruits, grains, and vegetation—far more rich thus than in its gold and silver—its people delight to call it "The Sunset Land."

Moreover, in this section many varieties of religion— Christian and pagan—confront the eye. It is full of sharp contrasts and sudden surprises. Old Spanish missions, side by side with modern Protestant churches, and, hard by, a Chinese temple; so that, in the Pacific cities, Protestant, Catholic, and Pagan worship strangely commingle. Japanese, Chinese and Spanish, American and Australian shops are so crowded together that store, shop, bazaar, and antique collector appear to have been hurled into one scarcely distinguishable melee by some earthquake. The passion for getting rich quick which attracted the gold prospectors to California in crowds, and the craze for extravagant indulgence in pleasures and pastimes, still largely dominate the multitude. Religion fails to attract. Faith is trodden underfoot, unheeded, by the rush for riches and sports. The need for Bible schools in the country districts is alarming. Most of the existing schools are in the cities and villages. If the testimony given by residents can be trusted, the public schools of this region interpret their laws as against teaching religion therein, and leave moral instruction without adequate Christian sanction or basis. Such teaching must be done in the church, the Bible school, or the home. If the parents are unbelievers (and reports indicate that in this region four out of five are) little religious instruction can be expected in the home. Many churches are struggling for existence or are crippled, and cannot undertake evangelism in remote rural districts.   The burden of this mission work must fall upon some interdenominational agency like the American Sunday-School Union.

Southern California was early settled by Mexican-Spanish people.   But these settlers were nearly lost in the tide of energetic and thrifty people from the East, for the population of Southern California increased about six-fold in twenty years (1880 to 1900).

The same neglect of general education which characterized the Roman Catholic religion of the Spanish type in Cuba for two centuries prevailed with its Mexican followers on the Pacific slope.   General education, better homes for the people, better economic conditions are not watchwords of the Roman friar; they are not found in his vocabulary.

A tour into the great oil regions of that section of the country, through the charming San Gabriel Valley, illustrated this fact.   Descendants of the old Spanish settlers had cattle and sheep ranches and fruit orchards.   Two Spaniards, brothers, in one part of that valley held 5,000 acres each, and their holdings obstructed the progress and improvement which small farms would give to the country.   Far up on the mountain crests, above this valley, were multitudes of oil wells hidden away among the hills of the high mountain ranges.   The people were intelligent, earnest; with humble homes made cleaner, sweeter, and more joyous by the message of the gospel which they had received through the Union Bible school.

A generation ago California was the "Land of Gold."   It is still in the front rank of gold-producing states, but gold is not now its largest product.   The annual output at the beginning of this century was about $15,000,000, while the value of agricultural products for a year exceeded $95,000,000.

I have already alluded to the variety of climate in California, Oregon and Washington; it is not one, but many.   The climates of the world are crowded into this strip of country on the Pacific, just as the world is there in miniature.   It is a splendid moving-picture show of the habits, customs, peoples and institutions of the globe.   It is the gateway to the Orient, and it has gained a new name, "The Land of Sunshine and of Flowers."   California claimed to lead all the states in the production of barley, beet-sugar, prunes, grapes, oranges and semi-tropical fruits, and to be in the front rank of the wool-growing states.

In the face of the passion to get rich quickly and the craze for extravagant pleasures, education has been given a prominent place in the Pacific states. The Leland Stanford, Jr., University and the University of California are in the front rank of educational institutions in the country, in magnitude of foundation, richness of endowment and in scientific attainments.

At the beginning of this century, the states bordering on the Pacific had about 8,000 (7,799 in 1900) buildings for public schools, to accommodate 612,825 persons of school age. California had 361,153 of these persons—the school age in that state being between five and seventeen years. In Oregon the school age is from four to twenty, and the school population in the same year numbered 133,181, and in Washington the school age is five to twenty-one, and they numbered then 118,491 youth of school age. As indicating the lack of Bible schools, Oregon had 2,070 school buildings, but only 1,092 organized Sunday-schools. These included schools in churches as well as those in the rural districts. While Washington appeared the best provided with public schools for youth, California and Oregon had the largest proportion of professed Christians —23 per cent. against Washington's 18 per cent. Of course, these figures are for all denominations, including Roman Catholic and Greek Catholic.

In this tour of the Pacific, Union Bible schools were described to us as being from ten to thirty-five or forty miles from the nearest church. A list was given us of thirty-five towns remote from railways but reached by stage, and only one of the thirty-five had a church. The development of dry farming in recent times has increased the difficulty of supporting religious service. The people around the dry farming regions are migratory and are not disposed to sustain religious services. Churches must be sustained by mission gifts. To maintain a regular preacher in a church or station is too expensive, and yet the country people need the gospel. They ought to have the gospel, but, living on farms here and there, many must be reached "on the fly." Experience shows that the Bible-school work is more effective in lonely homes on the plain than in the busy, distracting towns. The rapid increase of agriculture is increasing the population in the country districts beyond the reach of churches, and immensely increasing the demand for a flexible economic gospel agency to supply the religious needs of such rural communities. Missionary agencies, therefore, must be on the alert to keep pace with the phenomenal growth of the states on the Pacific coast.

After the Century—What Next?—America is proud of its Sunday-school achievements and forces. From a feeble, despised little band of a century ago, it now enrolls, in round numbers, nearly 200,000 schools (the denominations count 190,846) having upward of 21,000,000 members (the denominations claim 21,195,250 (*Encyclopædia of Sunday-Schools*, pp. 1198, 1199). These statistics by denominations are from reports of about 165 religious bodies in the United States, including Protestants, Roman Catholics, Jewish congregations, Latter Day Saints, Salvation Armies, Spiritualists, Ethical Culturists, Theosophists, and two bodies of Buddhists. But these "statistics of Sunday-schools by denominations" do not include Union schools unless under the control of and attached to some local church. The majority of evangelical Union schools are in rural districts too remote from churches, or in places of too many diverse religious prejudices to be so attached, even if churches were near and strong enough to sustain them. After a time revivals occur, professed disciples are multiplied, and they unite to form themselves into a church of their own choice.

The American Sunday-School Union, with its upward of 200 trained field workers, in ten years (1905 to 1915) organized 17,187 new Sunday-schools in communities that were without religious services, and reorganized 6,994 schools in other places (besides aiding thousands of feeble country schools), a total of 24,181 schools.

Adding these to the Sunday-schools reported by denominations increases the Sunday-school forces (1917) in the United States approximately to 215,000 schools, with not less than 25,000,000 members. Or, as the evangelical Union schools nearly equal in numbers and members those of the Roman Catholic and other non-Protestant schools combined, as reported in the "statistics by denominations," it appears that the Sunday-school forces of this country, using the *Bible* as the chief text-book for instruction, exceed 20,000,000.

Union Schools Strengthen Churches.—These evangelical Union schools are among the richest tributaries to the strength of American churches, for in ten years, preceding 1915, these Union schools reported 98,556 who confessed Christ through their mission work, besides others not counted in many schools; and 862 churches of different denominations were formed in as many places, where the same Union schools had prepared the way. The chief teaching in these Union Sunday-schools is the Bible doctrines that are essential to salvation—a teaching never in vain. The Holy Spirit uses it to convince and convert souls. As the workers view the marvelous results of this movement they may well exclaim, "What hath God wrought!"

Forty Million Unreached.—What of the 75,000,000 to 80,000,000 in the United States not enrolled in Bible or Sunday-schools? It is reported that upward of 38,000,000 are communicants or members of various religious bodies. About 15,000,000 of these members are in Catholic or non-evangelical and non-Protestant bodies, where the Bible, if not neglected or rejected, is not the supreme rule of life and conduct. But admitting that 50 per cent. of these 80,000,000 are under religious instruction, added to the 20,000,000 or more in Sunday-schools—and deducting none for the large number in these schools who are also counted again as church members—and there are yet 40,000,000 of souls left. When this vast multitude—40 per cent. of the total population of the Unites States alone that are not enrolled in the churches or Sunday-schools of any kind—are seriously considered, many trained workers must be alarmed for the future of our country. What have Christians been doing—playing at Mission and Bible-school work? After a century of boasted achievements, unparalleled in the history of Christianity, and in a land like America, all this work yet undone! This reveals the mighty task before us.

The Next Great Task.—After a century of achievement the work is scarcely half-done. There remain 40,000,000 or more people in our country not in the churches nor in the Sunday-schools who are unreached by religious instruction. How shall they be reached? Where are they? What forces are seeking them? Are the forces adapted to meet the conditions confronting them with any measure of success? These are fair questions. They ought to be thoughtfully considered and answered in Christian candor.

What have the 200 or more workers of the American Sunday-School Union to say, in view of the century of experience and recent surveys of the religious conditions of rural America? A questionnaire was sent them respecting the population, reached and unreached, by all forms of Bible instruction; any overlapping of Christian agencies; their attitude toward one another; and how they were meeting the religious conditions in rural communities. Scattered in all parts of the country, they responded by full and specific information in regard to the different great sections.

New England.—These detailed facts relate chiefly, no doubt, to the conditions in rural communities, where the majority of the population in the United States still reside.

As a result of long service and of recent surveys in the New England States, Warner L. Carver and his co-laborers state that about 18 to 20 per cent. of the people are under some form of stated Bible instruction, and from 78 to 80 per cent. are not. Thus, *The Maine Sunday-School Star* (May, 1912) claimed a Sunday-school enrolment in that state of 128,077 in 1,656 schools, of which 133 were Catholic, but there were 174,529 youth under twenty years of age not in Sunday-school, and 255 churches without Sunday-schools, 24 of them Catholic churches. In northern and eastern Maine the proportion unreached is greater than in the southern and western part of the state. The extent to which the rural sections are reached by other than Union religious agencies may be indicated by the number of teachers in Union rural schools reached by denominational or county teacher-training schools. The experienced Union missionaries in the state agree that barely 15 per cent. of the teaching force in the rural Sunday-schools are so reached, leaving fully 85 per cent. to be trained by the Union's workers. The overlapping is a negligible quantity, not exceeding 5 per cent. in any surveyed section.

In New Hampshire the conditions are very similar to those in Maine. Thus, in the southern part of the state, W. C.

Landis states that approximately 15 per cent. of the total population is reached by Sunday-school instruction, and 85 per cent. is not reached. He estimates that from 5 to 7 per cent. might be reached by denominational influences if Union agencies were not in the field. In Northern New Hampshire about 80 per cent. are not in Sunday-school, and, if the Union schools were closed, only about "one family of three members, of every forty scholars now in those schools, would receive Bible instruction in village schools." This does not indicate very serious "overlapping" in that section.

In Vermont, with a population of 355,956, it is estimated, E. C. Kinney states, that about one-third attend some church service and about 22 per cent. attend Sunday-school. Recent discussions of the rural church problem have surprised the people by the conditions that are alleged to exist. A minister said to the Union missionary, "You have done a wonderful work in revealing the conditions and needs of the rural districts." No great overlapping of religious agencies is noticed in that state.

The conditions in Massachusetts, Rhode Island and Connecticut are quite similar. From 18 to 20 per cent. are under some form of Protestant Bible instruction in Sunday-schools, and approximately 80 per cent. unreached, except the adult portion of the population that may attend church services. H. G. Wellington believes the overlapping is too small, generally, to be worthy of note.

Eastern Central States.—In New York and New Jersey the proportion of the total population under Sunday-school instruction is slightly less than in New England. The largest number yet unreached in New York will be found in the regions of the Catskill and Adirondack Mountains. Southern New Jersey is the poorest supplied section of that state. Neither of these states has one-half of the youth under twenty years of age in Sunday-school, and about 16 per cent. of the total population of New York and scarcely 12 per cent. in New Jersey are found in Sunday-schools. Delaware is far better supplied, having well-nigh 25 per cent. of its population under Bible instruction.

Pennsylvania has been called "The banner Sunday-school state." It has more than one-half of its youth under twenty years of age in Sunday-schools, with 25 per cent. of its total population under such Bible instruction. The eastern part of the state has a much larger proportion of its people under such instruction than the western section. The manufacturing and mining industries (coal, iron and steel) of the latter section have attracted a large alien population that are unreached by evangelical teaching. Were it not for these conditions Pennsylvania would show a much better Bible-school record. Vigorous and successful Union agencies are bringing that end of the state nearer to the high standard maintained in the eastern section.

In other central states—Ohio, Indiana and Michigan—George J. Henderson and his co-workers find that the number under Sunday-school training varies from about 23 per cent. of the population in Ohio and Indiana to about 18 per cent. in Michigan. The latest International Sunday-school Association statistics also indicate that over 2,250,000 of youth, under twenty years of age, in these prosperous states are yet unreached by Sunday-school instruction.

The impression prevails in these states, as elsewhere also, that the great influx of alien peoples have accentuated the desire for some effective form of co-operation or federated movement in country communities, and for some new or modified methods in country church work, adequately to cope with the situation. Meanwhile the Union Sunday-school continues to point out one efficient method for meeting the religious needs of the multitude of small communities in country sections.

The Northwest.—In Illinois and Wisconsin, with Chicago as the great center, about 17 to 18 per cent. of the total population are enrolled in Sunday-schools. Dr. W. W. Johnstone, of Chicago, places the number of youth under twenty years of age unreached in these states at over 2,000,000, exclusive of those in Roman Catholic and other non-evangelical families. The few denominational agents in these states work mainly along the railways and main lines of travel, and therefore do not overlap the Union's work. While the former render good service, much of it is on a quasi-union basis, and they call their schools "Community Schools." In teacher training the Union rural schools are, for the most part, unreached by other agencies, and look to the Union for aid in improving teachers and schools.

From 12 to 16 per cent. of the people in North Dakota, Montana and Minnesota are in, and about 85 per cent. are yet outside, the Sunday-school. Not one-half of the youth under twenty years of age are enrolled in Sunday-schools in either of these three states. The Rev. John O. Ferris and his associates observe that denominational and associational educational work overlap to some extent, but Union Sunday-school work does not overlap any other agencies.

A recent survey of 140 counties in Iowa, Nebraska and South Dakota discovered 1,659 church buildings of all denominations, 246 of which were abandoned or were without preaching services. If all the other counties of these states have similar conditions, it would indicate that the denominations are not reaching more than 25 per cent. of the country population. The Rev. Joseph Wells and the trained co-workers with him, in this group of states, place the total number statedly reached by all forms of Bible instruction at about 1,350,000, and state that about 2,750,000 youth are yet unreached. They report that the overlapping of agencies in rural religious efforts there is so insignificant as not to be worth counting. Some persons are counted twice because they are members of denominational schools and also aid in sustaining Union rural schools. The United States census credits Iowa with having 22 per cent. of its population in Sunday-school, including Roman Catholic schools; Nebraska with 20 per cent.; South Dakota with about 15 per cent.; and Wyoming with over 12 per cent. Iowa and Wyoming are further credited with having over one-half of their youth, under twenty years of age, under Sunday-school instruction. The alien population and their children are increasing rapidly in many sections of this group of states, as elsewhere throughout the interior west and on the Pacific coast, and are correspondingly increasing the magnitude of the task confronting all the Sunday-school and religious forces in the field.

The Rocky Mountain and Pacific States.—The conditions in the Rocky Mountain and Pacific Coast States may be inferred from the fact that Idaho and Washington more than doubled in population from 1900 to 1910. All the religious agencies find that their combined efforts have proved inadequate to keep pace with the abnormal increase of population and rapid multiplication of rural communities. In California the percentage of the population under Sunday-school instruction is still less than in her sister states, Washington and Oregon, according to the United States census, and the total includes Roman Catholic and all forms of non-evangelical schools held on Sunday. In Arizona, as in New Mexico and southern California, the alien population, especially those of Spanish descent, has proved a serious handicap to the progress of Bible instruction. The entire group of states west of the Rocky Mountains now offer the greatest opportunity for extending Bible instruction, and one which demands prompt and enlarged efforts to meet.

Nevada, the silver mining state, is at the foot of the list, having the smallest population of any state, and the smallest proportion (less than 7 per cent.) under Bible instruction in Sunday-school, with New Mexico and Arizona very near to her in the percentage of population unreached by the gospel.

The Southwest.—The eight great states of the Southwest— Missouri, Arkansas, Louisiana, Texas, Oklahoma, Kansas, Colorado and New Mexico—form a vast empire in territory, with 15,000,000 population, but destined to have 50,000,000 in the near future. They invite the gospel worker to enter and reap an abundant harvest. Excepting Spanish New Mexico, a good beginning has been made by bringing from 15 to 20 per cent. of the population under Bible-school instruction. E. B. Stevenson ranks as the veteran among the Union's workers there, having seen more than thirty-five years of service. He and his efficient company of missionaries should be fully competent to give trustworthy information regarding the conditions and prospects of the great task facing the Bible instructing forces in this empire of the Southwest.

Somewhat less than 3,000,000 are enrolled in Sunday-school in these eight states. Union workers think that denominational efforts are not more efficient now than twenty years ago in reaching rural districts. Thirty-five years ago Mr. Stevenson recalls that the Methodists were using the circuit rider, "and at each point reached insisting that the people have a Sunday-school." Other denominations had ministers also

[1] Rev. E. R. Martin and associates; *Annual Reports*, 1913–17.

preaching in two or more churches in country neighborhoods. "It is rare," he says now, "to find ministers doing much of this sort of work in country districts. . . . The Union Sunday-school is a more *permanent* factor in the average country community"; perhaps from necessity. If the Union forces were not in the field "thousands of these communities would not be reached at all."

Then there are extensive lumber, oil, and mining industries, calling for individual treatment, to meet the peculiar conditions of language, religious views, and habits of the wage earners. Some flexible policy in Union Sunday-school work, adapted to their needs, would enable the Union workers more effectively to reach these otherwise unreached classes. The great hope for this vast empire of the Southwest, workers declare, is in sending the living missionary to the homes of the people, establishing Sunday-schools, providing them with Christian literature, arranging to have it come regularly, and seeing that it is distributed Sabbath by Sabbath. This will surely reform and redeem the dwellers in the homes wherever it is faithfully, persistently and prayerfully done.

The New Old South.—The religious condition of that great section of our country, the South—comprising eleven states—Maryland, Virginia, West Virginia, Kentucky, Tennessee, North Carolina, South Carolina, Georgia, Florida, Alabama and Mississippi—as indicated by the United States census, is that about 40 per cent. of the population is under some form of Bible or religious instruction and about 60 per cent. is not. The Rev. Joseph H. McCullagh has had the oversight of Union Sunday-school work in the South for over thirty years, succeeding his father, the Rev. John McCullagh, in this responsible service. Their combined labors extend over more than seventy years, or from about 1842 to the present. Joseph H. McCullagh has thus inherited the accumulated knowledge and experience of his father and added to it his own long observation and study of the great religious problems in the South. It is the belief that the Census Bureau report is fairly complete and approximately accurate for the southern section. The percentage of rural population reached by the Union twenty years ago which is now reached, or would be reached by other agencies, he affirms, is exceedingly small, "not more than 1 per cent."; hence there is little chance for "overlapping" in rural districts in the South.

The Southern people are intense in everything, and so by nature are ardently denominational, yet, as the McCullaghs testify, the people have always cordially approved of the Union's work in rural communities. The condition of many churches in that section is such a struggle for existence that denominational work absorbs their energies and about all they have to give. The splendid achievements of the past, however, give promise of yet greater results in this century. The American Sunday-School Union has had a goodly share in the work so far done. In thirty years past it has established on an average over 400 new Sunday-schools annually in this section alone, providing Bible instruction for about 1,000,000 persons. Seventy thousand conversions have been reported, besides large numbers uncounted, and 800 churches have been erected or organized to strengthen the denominations as the partial fruit of these Union schools in the South. There never were so many youth in Sunday-schools in the South as there are now. But the renewed material prosperity of that section, added to the natural increase of population, especially of the negro race, has outrun the efforts of all religious agencies there, so that in the rural districts of the "new old South" there are more youth unreached by Bible instruction than have yet been reached. As the largest portion, by far, of the population of the South is rural, it follows that a large percentage of those unreached youth and adults are in country communities, and it is the judgment of Mr. McCullagh (in which a large number of trained workers and observers concur) that Union schools can be more efficiently maintained than others in these country districts.

There are many diverse classes in this great section. Besides the comparatively well-to-do white people, the "black belt" of negroes presents a grave problem for Bible-school laborers. That negroes are "naturally religious" is a common view. This view is sharply challenged by some trained observers. Thus Mr. McCullagh gives it as the result of his observation that "the negroes as a race do not attend religious services now as much as they did thirty years ago." And "the condition of the young colored people in the South is very sad. About 80 per cent. of them are in the rural districts, and, owing to the extreme poverty of many and to their improvidence, they rarely have Sunday-schools." This view is confirmed by the experienced Union missionaries in the South after many years of investigation and field service. Then the long neglected, but home-loving and sturdy mountaineers, the highlanders of the South, respond to evangelical instruction with a most unexpected cordiality. The poorer white classes of some sections—the "sand-hillers" and "crackers"—should not be overlooked in their abject poverty and ignorance, for they too have souls. These must be reached chiefly through an economical, efficient Union evangelical agency—one that will combine all the religious sentiment, and foster every spark of holy aspiration that may be latent in the soul. Here then is a mighty task—to give Bible instruction to the "New South" such as will saturate its material prosperity with a new heart and a blessed service for God and man.

How Master the Mighty Task?—Obviously, more vigorous efforts must be put forth to establish new Bible schools in all the unreached portions of America and the world. But existing schools must also be made vastly more efficient, in every way, especially in winning the neglected people at their very doors. The church and the Sunday-school alike must obey the Master's command: "Make disciples (learners) of all the nations."

There are large sections where, owing to the many divisions in creed, the agencies are crowding upon one another, yet are leaving masses unreached in the very fields they each and all claim to occupy. This conspicuous weakness of a divided Christianity must in some way be overcome if it is to conquer the world or even to make disciples of one great nation. The efficient co-operation and federation of Christian forces can come permanently only through the cultivation of the spirit of Christian unity for which Christ prayed (John 17 : 21).

Viewing continental United States alone, it is humiliating to find great sections of cities in which the population is massed in abject poverty—badly congested portions—abandoned by churches. Nor are they reached, except in a fragmentary way, by any Christian agency. Vastly greater areas in the country, over which are scattered yet larger numbers of people, as the surveys reported above abundantly show, are also without churches or Bible schools.

The extension of missionary work into destitute rural regions will require to be prosecuted with even greater energy than heretofore to keep pace with the incoming and increasing population, and that for an indefinite future. Federation may help greatly in the congested sections; in others there is nothing to federate—frontier and outlying communities that are wholly without Christian organizations or Bible schools. In and around cities having congested population centers much can be done by better distribution of Christian educational agencies. This must be done more systematically than in the past. Christian laymen are demanding it, irrespective of denominational relations, in order to prevent needless waste in the Lord's work. In new work also churches and Sunday-schools in city and country must be so formed and located as not unnecessarily to duplicate organizations in the same territory. Three or four or more evangelical agencies in a small community of ten, twenty, or forty families prove too great a burden, and must either be sustained from outside or maintain a feeble existence; when one organization, upon a basis that heartily unites them all, would render a well-supported and blessed service. The same principle must eventually be applied, on some broad plan, to all the religious organizations in the entire country if they are to produce economic and effective fruit. The total area of the United States comprising both land and water is about 3,000,000 square miles, exclusive of Alaska and outlying possessions. The great lakes and rivers and snow-capped mountain peaks that are neither arable nor habitable occupy quite a fraction of this total area. Were 200,000 to 250,000 Sunday-schools uniformly distributed over the United States, every family or person in the country would be within two miles of some Bible school. And, if that number of schools were limited to the actually habitable area of the country, every inhabitant would find a Bible school within about a mile to a mile and a half of his home. This points to a great problem of the near future, namely, the readjustment of many existing Bible schools and their better redistribution, so as to be located at points more accessible to the population they are aiming to serve. It would, of course, be ridiculous to attempt to distribute them with mathematical precision, like pawns on a chess-board, over the face of the country, but much better distribution can be made to promote economy and efficiency. Nor will those who support the Christian forces of America be satisfied until this is systematically and thoroughly accomplished.

Spiritual Character.—Moreover, the Sunday-school must become a dominating spiritual power in every community. Is any reform needed? It should lead in that surely. But the Sunday-school ought also to stand for something far deeper and higher than any reform. It should aim to re-create and renew the human source of all reforms; to lead to a new birth, a spiritual life. This creates the strongest motive for every reform and for the betterment of every community and of every life therein. Its chief mission is to have the heart of every member of the community filled to its utmost capacity wth the highest spiritual power. The meeting together in any place of persons blessed with an infilling of the Holy Spirit reveals a spiritual power which the world recognizes as from God.

In the formative period, for more than a generation after Raikes, the field, scope and fundamental principles of the institution engrossed the attention of the founders. Following that period the religious atmosphere and spiritual power of the Sunday-school had foremost consideration. But soon the general desire to gain popular favor and have the institution sweep over the whole of Christendom unintentionally seems to have relegated the cultivation of its spiritual power to a secondary place. Before and since the beginning of this century the watchword of many has been, "organize, organize." This has caused more emphasis and unusual attention to be given to the machinery of the institution. Enthusiasts tend to extremes, producing too complex organizations and too cumbersome machinery when their zeal starts in that direction. This more frequently occurs in conventions and associations of schools than in single or isolated schools. The organization, in such a case, exhausts too much of its energy in keeping the machinery in motion, and simply "marks time" as to any productive results. Many such organizations have had periods of suspended animation, or have died outright.

Another class of religious educators in Great Britain and America have insisted upon the introduction of more complete school methods into all phases of Sunday-school work. Where this view prevails, the objection has been made that it accentuates too strongly the intellectual and the academic features, and that it practically exalts "culture" into the foremost place, rather than primarily seeking to make and develop disciples of Jesus Christ. The effect, it is alleged, is rather to study and treat all forms of religion as "cults," to be investigated. Christianity is thus taught as one of the great religions, the best, it may be, but a "cult" in its essential nature rather than a life. This misplacing of emphasis has not escaped the severest criticism in some quarters, and it is rejected as unscriptural and unscientific.

Some series of lessons have been condemned for their bias, as supporters of the "cult" theory of Christianity. Allied to this, came also the charge that the new Graded Lessons were intellectual and academic, and either rejected or minimized the evangelical doctrines of the new birth, the resurrection, and the supernatural character of the spiritual life. The intellectual was exalted to the place of the spiritual, it was charged, and the spiritual birth and life practically denied or ignored. This criticism has been disputed. The advocates of the completer school methods assert that they center in Jesus Christ, and are as promotive of the Christ life as is the other.

The controversy regarding correct educational theories and the best system of Sunday-school study has been going on for a century, and while many related obscurities have been cleared up, the main questions are yet open and far from settled. Looking at the two systems, the International Uniform and the Graded Lessons, after years of testing, what do we see? Broadly, that the claims of the ardent supporters of the Uniform System, in securing a comprehensive knowledge of the Bible, have not been fully realized. Nor have the prophecies of its critics, of great disaster from its inherent weakness, been fulfilled. The Uniform Series created marvelous enthusiasm and a co-operation and unity of spirit that astonished even its friends. But in practical working it revealed defects and weaknesses that prevented it from attaining the rich harvests

that some predicted.   This, its friends assert, is merely to confess that it has imperfections such as belong to all things
human.

For the "New Graded Systems" (special grading of lesson
texts) it is claimed that they are scientific, putting the child
first and the teaching material second, and giving a more
comprehensive and exact knowledge of the Bible.   It is conceded that better teachers and some specially trained ones
may be required; that the enthusiasm which arises from numbers in mass may be lost; that separate rooms are more essential than under the Uniform plan.   But it is affirmed that all
these difficulties are overbalanced by the closer adaptation of
the material to be taught in the distinct periods of child development.

On the other hand, biblical scholars and some prominent
educators have criticized the "new graded lessons" as defective
at the very point where its advocates claim them to be perfect;
to wit, in minute grading to fit every successive step in child
growth.   It was noted that British and American workers did
not agree upon the extent to which the grading of the material,
or grading of the teaching even, should be carried.   The
Americans went to the extreme of seventeen or more grades of
lessons between the Cradle Roll Department and that for the
adult of twenty years.   This implied that a well-graded school
might be studying seventeen different passages of Scripture in
seventeen classes of the same school at the same time.   Practical teachers have asked if this does not assume that the
children of the present generation are of equal capacity (on
the average) at a given age.   They question this assumption.
They further inquire how it is possible, without violence and
risk of disaster, to chop child and adolescent life into so distinct periods, terminating at a uniform, definite age: as the
Primary at eight, the Junior at twelve, and the next at sixteen.
Experience indicates that the children of one community, in
one set of circumstances, might be further advanced at twelve
years of age than those in another community, under a different
environment, might be at sixteen years of age.   To determine
grading by an arbitrary age limit, it is alleged, is contrary to
the best educational experience and to pedagogical methods.
When this scheme is carried arbitrarily into yearly grading, the

system is declared to be destitute of good sense and often positively ludicrous in practice. It is further affirmed that it tends to increase the number of backward pupils instead of promoting progress. The theory also puts the emphasis on the wrong part of education—the mere acquisition of knowledge. The essential thing in true education is not knowledge, but right thinking and good character. Serious difficulties have been met at every stage of progress in the Graded as in the Uniform Series of lessons. For years schemes of lessons have been freely thrown open to the entire Sunday-school world to test. The ideal system, or one that approaches general satisfaction, has not yet emerged from these long testings.[1]

Preparedness for the Task.—The past history of the Sunday-school movement enforces the need for preparedness for the task yet before it. Viewing the great work that has been done, with the many diverse forces engaged, and the vaster task yet to be done to bring the masses under Bible instruction, it is evident that all the agencies hitherto employed must be greatly enlarged, their efficiency and support immensely increased, to win the field for the Church and for Christ.

The average Sunday-school must be far better organized in city and country, and the form of organization made more flexible and better fitted to the conditions of the people it aims to serve. It should be housed better in buildings suited to the work required. The very meager equipment now widely prevalent is a disgrace to our Christianity; it should be promptly remedied by providing the best manuals of methods, the simplest but best handbooks, dictionaries, and reference libraries of biblical exposition and interpretation, the most approved and standard treatises on child nurture and development, the latest and sanest suggestions on social service, recreation, play and work, and, above all, the best inspirational periodicals and books on the spiritual life—no dull, dyspeptic meditations of doleful tone, but cheery, bright, burning spiritual truths, hot from a heart on fire with love to Christ.

If the history of this enterprise reveals any one thing more clearly than another, it is that the best organized, best housed,

---

[1] See Prof. J. R. Sampey, *International Lesson System;* Prof. Ira M. Price on Graded Lessons, in *Encyclopædia of Sunday-Schools,* pp. 465–467; Frank Johnson, *British Graded Lessons,* pp. 465–467; *Sunday-School World,* 1912, pp. 6, 7, and 1914, 1916; *Handbook of the International Lessons,* 1872–1917, revised edition, by Edwin W. Rice, D.D.

and best equipped Sunday-school, without spiritual power and the inspiration of the Holy Spirit, is like a professing Christian without love—"sounding brass and a clanging cymbal."

Furthermore, the early historic efforts to unite all in this supreme task must be renewed with ten-fold energy and consecration. The training of teachers and of capable leaders for all the forces should become universal, deeply imbued with the consuming desire to win every life in its every phase, and to have it educated, trained, and fully consecrated to the Lord Jesus Christ.

SKETCHES OF PROMINENT WORKERS

Morris Ketchum Jesup (1830–1908), **Sixth President of the American Sunday-School Union** (1896–1908).

"The American Sunday-School Union took hold of my heart when I was a boy," said Mr. Jesup in 1896. "I remember very well—one of the earliest recollections of my life—when my father told me about this Sunday-School Union, and he became so interested in its work that he contributed toward the expenses of a missionary in Virginia. I like this work also because it is so catholic. It is a type of what we want as Christian unity. I like it also because it is so thoroughly evangelical. I like it also because it has stood the test of these seventy-two years and has never been found wanting. . . . I like the Sunday-School Union because it has fixedness of purpose, and because it has principle behind its work." [1]

Mr. Jesup was born in Westport, Connecticut, June 21, 1830, and when he was eight years old the family moved to New York. Soon after his father died. At an early age he began a business career, in which he developed signal ability, sagacity and a capacity for managing large mercantile and railway enterprises. It would take a volume to give an adequate notice of the many business, civil, philanthropic, and Christian institutions with which Mr. Jesup was connected, chief of which were the New York Chamber of Commerce, Young Men's Christian Association, Metropolitan Museum, and the American Sunday-School Union. Numerous colleges—Princeton, Yale, Williams, and Union Theological Seminary—were recipients of his generous gifts. The Museum of Natural

[1] *The Sunday-School World*, 1896, p. 229.

History of New York received $1,000,000 from him, and he was a generous patron of art and a liberal contributor toward Arctic and other exploring expeditions.

To the institutions of which he was president it has been justly said he gave four things—time, money, thought, and enthusiasm. In his generous gifts to the American Sunday-School Union there was an added graceful personal touch—for years he was accustomed to send $1,000 to be distributed as a special gift to the missionaries of the Society. He and Mrs. Jesup supported one or more missionaries of the Union for many years; their gifts, during life, amounting to over $35,000, and a bequest of $150,000 was made by Mrs. Jesup.

Mr. Jesup was vice-president of the Union for about ten years and president for nearly twelve years. The Hon. Seth Low happily voiced the esteem in which Mr. Jesup was held in business circles: "Like the flower of the century plant, his life has come to an end, simply because it had reached its perfect bloom, and we thank God that it was given to us to see it in all its beauty." [1]

James M. Crowell, D.D. (1827–1908), Secretary of Missions (1883–1908).

With great practical wisdom, suavity and efficiency Rev. Dr. James M. Crowell served as Secretary of Missions for the American Sunday-School Union about twenty-five years. His success as pastor, his ability as a speaker and his familiarity with, and frequent advocacy of, the work of the Union during this period, added to the fact that he had caught the spirit of the work from a former secretary who was an influential officer in his church (Maurice A. Wurts), led a friend and prominent manager, B. B. Comegys, to propose him for the responsible position.

A plan had been formed for removing the heavy debt of the Society and adding to its capital, so as to enlarge its operations. Some one able forcibly to present its claims to assemblies as well as to conduct its missionary operations was needed at the head of the Missionary Department. Dr. Crowell heartily threw himself into these plans and contributed his full share

---

[1] See also William Adams Brown, *A Character Sketch, Morris Ketchum Jesup*, New York, 1910.

toward the successful placing of the Society and its work upon an improved financial basis. He won friends for the Society by his sincerity, his affable manners, and his delicate courtesy, which are characteristic of a refined Christian gentleman. A clear thinker, firm in his convictions, he was tactful in promoting cordial co-operation in the co-ordinate departments of the Society's work, and in securing the highest efficiency. While having essential views of his own, he could gracefully respect the views of co-workers. With true magnanimity he perceived that the effort to remove the Society's indebtedness would, in the end, not diminish but increase the income for its missionary work, and this proved to be true.

His keen sense of humor and his cheerfulness, which always looked at the bright side of every difficult problem, cheered his co-workers in the field; for this characteristic was reflected in all his communications, even with the discouraged missionaries. The efficiency of the Society's work during his administration is shown in part, at least, by the record of 43,964 new schools, with 179,632 teachers and 1,552,850 scholars, besides 8,240 reorganized schools and 2,047 churches grown from the Sunday-schools organized, and 143,281 hopeful conversions reported among the scholars. His genial and efficient administration is a red-letter chapter in the Society's mission history. The field workers all respected and loved him because he knew how to give instructions pleasantly, to correct mistakes kindly, to rebuke when necessary, in love, and to cheer the discouraged and unfortunate and inspire them with fresh courage and new hope. His services during the constructive period at the close of the last century were of immense value in the work of putting the Society upon a strong financial basis. He keenly appreciated the advantage of good "team work" with his associates and heartily enjoyed it, and contributed his full share toward success until the Master called him to receive his reward.

APPENDIX

Raikes' Record.—The notice in the *Gloucester Journal*, November 3, 1783, of Raikes' schools was as follows:

Some of the clergy, in different parts of this county, bent upon attempting a reform among the children of the lower class, are establishing Sunday-schools, for rendering the Lord's Day subservient to the ends of instruction, which has hitherto been prostituted to bad purposes. Farmers, and other inhabitants of the towns and villages, complain that they receive more injury in their property on the Sabbath than all the week besides; this, in a great measure, proceeds from the lawless state of the younger class, who are allowed to run wild on that day, free from every restraint. To remedy this evil, persons duly qualified are employed to instruct those that cannot read; and those that may have learnt to read, are taught the Catechism and conducted to church. By thus keeping their minds engaged, the day passes profitably, and not disagreeably. In those parishes where the plan has been adopted, we are assured that the behaviour of the children is greatly civilized.

The barbarous ignorance in which they had before lived, being in some degree dispelled, they begin to give proofs that those persons are mistaken who consider the lower orders of mankind incapable of improvement and therefore think an attempt to reclaim them impracticable or, at least, not worth the trouble.

Colonel Townley of Lancashire, near Liverpool, saw this notice and wrote Raikes, who recounted the beginning of his enterprise to Townley more fully, November 25, 1783:

The beginning of the scheme was entirely owing to accident. Some business leading me one morning into the suburbs of the city, where the lowest of the people (who are principally employed in the pin manufactory) chiefly reside, I was struck with concern at seeing a group of children, wretchedly ragged, at play in the streets. I asked an inhabitant whether those children belonged to that part of the town, and lamented their misery and idleness. "Ah! sir," said the woman to whom I was speaking, "could you take a view of this part of the town on Sunday, you would be shocked indeed; for then the street is filled with multitudes of these wretches, who, released on that day from employment, spend their time in noise and riot, playing at 'chuck,' and cursing and swearing in a manner so horrid as to convey to any serious mind an idea of hell rather than any other place. We have a worthy clergyman, [the Rev. Thomas Stock], curate of our parish, who has put some of them to school; but upon the Sabbath they are all given up to follow their own inclinations without restraint, as their parents, totally abandoned themselves, have no idea of instilling into the minds of their children principles to which they themselves are entire strangers."[1]

Voluntary Plan.—That Raikes conceived and applied the voluntary principle is fairly implied by the letter of November 5th, 1787, to Mrs. Harris. In answer to her queries, he says:

I endeavour to assemble the children as early as is consistent with their perfect cleanliness—an indispensable rule. The hour prescribed in our rules is eight o'clock, but it is usually half after eight before our flock is collected. Twenty is the number allotted to each teacher; the sexes kept separate. The twenty are divided into four classes; the children who show any superiority in attainments are placed as leaders of the several classes and are employed in teaching the others their letters, or in hearing them read in a low whisper, which may be done without interrupting the master or mistress in their business. . . .

To those children who distinguish themselves as examples of diligence, quietness in behaviour, observance of order, kindness to their companions, etc., I give some little token of my regard, as a pair of shoes, if they are barefooted, and some who are very bare of apparel I clothe. . . . Besides, I frequently go around to their habitations to inquire into their behaviour at home and into the conduct of the parents, to whom I give some little hints now and then, as well as to the children. . . .

The stipend to the teachers [masters] here is a shilling each Sunday; but we find them firing, and bestow gratuities as rewards of diligence, which may make it worth six pence more. . . .

He throws a bit of personal history into this letter to Mrs. Harris. I must now tell you that I am blessed with six excellent girls and two lovely boys. My oldest boy was born the very day I made public to the world the scheme of Sunday-schools in my paper of Nov. 3, 1783. In four years' time it has extended so rapidly as now to include 250,000 children; it is increasing more and more.

The employment of paid teachers and their gradual supersession by voluntary teachers has, not unnaturally, given rise to popular misconception. The most important, indeed vital, working principle of the Sunday-school was, from the first, voluntaryism; and the initial impulse for the formation and support of schools always came from some individual or committee undertaking their general management. The "Master" or "Mistress" was often the tenant in whose kitchen the school was held, and was paid partly for services rendered and partly for rent; when the school grew and assistants were needed, they were also paid. This was the rule. Behind the "master,"

[1] *Gentleman's Magazine*, June, 1784.

"mistress," and "assistants" there was the patron or committee, and it seems to have been the custom for one of these to give directions to the "master" or "mistress," and personally superintend the religious instruction given to the children. . . . The paid teacher, at first, was made responsible for the good behaviour, cleanliness, and ability of the children to read and repeat their lessons; then the work of the Sunday-school, as a religious agency, passed into other hands whose work was purely voluntary. . . . The school with which Robert Raikes was most closely identified (the St. Mary de Crypt) had only one paid teacher; the most promising of the scholars assisting her as "monitors." He charged himself with giving religious instruction, and the work fascinated him, so that what at first was a duty became a pleasure, and then a passion. . . . We can, however, hardly appreciate the great services rendered to humanity by those who received into their kitchens and instructed the evil-smelling outcasts sent to them; but, to be accurate, we must separate them from an institution founded in voluntary effort as something foreign to its spirit, otherwise we may regard the general presence of the voluntary teacher as a later development instead of part of the original design.[1]

Discipline in Raikes' Schools.—Of the discipline in Raikes' schools, William Brick, a Sunday scholar, who attended the funeral when Raikes died and received a cake and a shilling along with the rest, says:

I can remember Mr. Raikes well enough. I remember his caning me. I don't suppose I minded it much. He used to cane boys on the back of a chair.

Some turrible bad chaps went to school when I first went. There were always bad 'uns coming in. I know the parents of one or two of them used to walk them to school with fourteen pound weights tied to their legs. . . . Sometimes boys would be sent to school with logs of wood tied to their ankles, just as though they were wild jackasses, which I suppose they were, only worse. . . .

When a boy was very bad he would take him out of the school, and march him home and get his parents to "wallop" him. He'd stop and see it done, and then bring the urchin back, rubbing his eyes and other places. Mr. Raikes was a terror to all evil doers and a praise to them that did well. Everyone in the city loved and feared him.[2]

Raikes a Bible Student.—Recent researches have shown that Robert Raikes was not only a Christian philanthropist, he was also a reader and a loving student of the Bible. Writing to the Rev. William Lewelyn, whose expositions of the book of Revelation he had printed, he says:

There is some pleasure in printing works that purify and elevate the heart and fit it for an intercourse with the mansions of eternity. . . . You seem to draw back the veil that conceals

[1] J. Henry Harris, *The Story of the Sunday School*, pp. 50-52.
[2] J. Henry Harris, *Robert Raikes: The Man and His Work*, pp. 37, 38.

from mortals the hidden things of God. . . . There are two or three passages that strike me very forcibly. They dart a degree of illumination into the mind that comes very nearly to what I have felt when perusing the pen of inspiration.

Citing these and many other similar expressions of Raikes, his biographer, Harris, remarks: "If Robert Raikes was such a Bible student and such a firm believer in the divine love, and mercy, and promises, is it not true that his was a religious life; and that the Sunday-school, through him, is Bible-rooted?"[1]

Fox's Wish for the Bible.—William Fox, leading co-worker with Robert Raikes in the founding of Sunday-schools, also expressed his desire "that every poor person in the kingdom might be able to read the Bible." In his address to his friends at the founding of the Sunday-School Society, among other things, he said:

> Great however as the temporal evils of the poor are and numerous as their wants appear, for these I ask no relief, but I do ask, nay I entreat, your aid for the support of schools, that while the poor remain destitute of the comforts of this life they may not be altogether unacquainted with that which is to come. . . . Without a Bible in their houses—and if they had, without ability to read it—too much neglected by the clergy as well as deserted by others, the poor live as the beasts that perish. What an opportunity there is here of displaying that generosity for which the heathen were so renowned.

Then, referring to the society for promoting religious knowledge among the poor, he adds:

> Suffice it to say there is but one thing wanting to make it one of the most benevolent institutions that has yet been established. You will readily perceive the one thing to which I allude is that now submitted to your consideration—for what use are Bibles to those who cannot read them?
> This was his plea for the organization of a Sunday-school society.[2]

Joseph Lancaster also, another of the influential supporters of Sunday-schools, was well known to have insisted upon the Bible as a chief text-book rather than the creeds and catechisms in the schools which were founded by him and his followers.

We have here the testimony of three of the leaders in the early movement who insisted upon the Bible as the chief text-book in Sunday-school.

Opposition to Sunday-Schools.—Robert Raikes' Sunday-school movement did not escape opposing forces from its beginning. "How long adverse forces were gathering strength we cannot say." But in 1797,

---

[1] J. Henry Harris, *The Story of Robert Raikes*, pp. 94–97.
[2] Powers, *Rise and Progress of Sunday-Schools*, pp. 62–68.

when the system was supposed to be secure from malicious opposition, the *Gentleman's Magazine*, of London, which had spoken in favor of the movement, opened its columns to an old and valued contributor to make a "slashing onslaught on the Sunday-schools and their founders." This article was written over the signature "Eusebius," a clergyman who voiced the growing apprehension that the education of the poor would unfit them for menial service, raise discontent, and foment rebellion. His long article concludes in these severe terms:

> We may, therefore, conclude that the Sunday-school is so far from being the wise, useful, or prudential institution it is said to be, that it is in reality productive of no valuable advantage, but, on the contrary, is subversive of that order, that industry, that peace and tranquility which constituted the happiness of society; and that, so far from deserving encouragement and applause, it merits our contempt, and ought to be exploded as the vain chimerical institution of a visionary projector.[1]

For persecutions, prosecutions, and false charges against Hannah More and her Sunday-schools and Sunday-school work, the reader is referred to Memoirs of Hannah More by William Roberts, 2 vols., New York, 1835.

Furthermore, a strong opposition to Sunday-schools came from Scotland. In 1798 the Rev. Thomas Burns preached two sermons against the introduction of the system into Scotland. He declared:

> I can see no necessity for the institution, and I am afraid men do not consider the effects that are likely to follow. . . . From the wise institution of parochial schools, every parish in Scotland is provided with the means of instruction. . . .
> Sunday-schools, then, are reflections on every parish where they are appointed; nay, more, they are reflections upon every parent in that parish.

He closes one of his sermons as follows:

> My great objection to Sunday-schools is that I am afraid they will in the end destroy all family religion, and whatever has tendency to do this I consider it is my duty to guard you against. I might also show that these schools are hurtful to public religion, for it consists with my knowledge that children stay at home from church to prepare their questions for the even; and their families are divided when they ought to be together.[2]

Sunday-Schools Before Robert Raikes (1780).—The places and persons claiming to have had a Sunday-school previous to that of Raikes, in Gloucester, 1780, are very numerous. A controversy in regard to these rival claims has been long continued and is still an unsettled ques-

---

[1] J. Henry Harris, *Robert Raikes: The Man and His Work*, p. 92.
[2] *Ibid.*, p. 98.

tion. The question is not simply one of priority of date, nor is it one alone of the particular form of either of these schools, although both the date and the form are elements in this dispute. Behind these is the more fundamental question in regard to which, if any, of these schools had a sufficient number of features of the modern Sunday-school movement to be recognized as similar to Raikes' movement. Sometimes the disputants seem to us to raise technical objections which amount to little more than quibbles.

One writer objects to the claim of Ephrata, Pennsylvania, because that school was held on the seventh day [the rest or Sabbath observed by that religious sect] rather than on the first day, or Sunday. This Episcopal writer (Rev. O. S. Michael), perhaps, has overlooked the fact that one of the bishops of the Church of England suggested that a Sunday-school, following Raikes plan, be held on Saturday instead of Sunday, to avoid certain objections made in his church.

Other writers claim that the so-called Sunday-schools in New England, previous to 1780, were catechetical classes, or were essentially day schools, having neither the form nor the methods of the modern Sunday-school.

Of the reputed Sunday-school in Christ Church Parish, Savannah, Georgia, said to have been begun by John Wesley, 1737, one writer asserts, "Nothing is better authenticated than that the institution which has given rise to this chronicle was the ordinary parish day school, taught by one, De La Motte." This seems to be corroborated by the fact that Wesley does not appear to have known of Sunday-schools or noted them earlier than 1783 or 1785, when he wrote in *The Arminian Magazine*, "Who knows but that some of these schools may become nurseries for Christians." This is taken to imply his first knowledge of Sunday-schools.[1]

It is clear, however, that some of the so-called schools that existed many years before the movement of Raikes had a school system in several respects similar to that planned by Raikes. The main point is whether they were schools teaching the catechism, or were also teaching direct from the Bible.

I investigated, at first hand, some of the early schools on this point. The Sunday-school at Bethlehem, Connecticut, under Dr. Joseph Bellamy, from 1740 on, is thus described by Dr. Joel Hawes in *Ecclesiastical History of Connecticut:*

> Dr. Bellamy, pastor of the church in Bethlehem in this state from 1740 until the time of his death, was accustomed to meet the youth of his congregation on the Sabbath, not merely for a catechetical exercise, but for a recitation from the Bible, accompanied with familiar instruction suited to the capacities of the young. In this exercise, too, he was often assisted by the members of his church.

[1] *The Arminian Magazine*, January, 1785.

What better language could be used to describe an ordinary Sunday-school of the present day? It was further asserted by another pastor of the church "that he had reason to believe they had never been without a Sabbath-school from the earliest settlement of the town." In confirmation of this fact, it is said that the colony, from its early settlement, had a law requiring "heads of families to teach their children and servants to read well," and fining every family twenty shillings for neglect of it.[1] Schools similar in form and with like instruction, held on Sunday, were quite wide-spread in New England in the early part of the eighteenth century.

In regard to the school at Ephrata, Pennsylvania, I made a careful investigation of its history in company with the Rev. C. Reimensnyder who was versed in their language (Pennsylvania Dutch) and spoke it fluently. This school was under the direction of a German Community, which separated from the Dunkards or German Baptists in 1728 and were led by Conrad Beissel, who observed the seventh instead of the first day of the week as the Christian Sabbath. They had a secular school, but in 1739 "Brother Obed"—a title given to Ludwig Haecker—became teacher of the school and immediately began a Sunday-school also in the afternoons of every Sabbath "to give instruction to the indigent children who were kept from regular school by employments which their necessities obliged them to be engaged at during the week, as well as to give *religious* instruction to those of better circumstances." This much I learned from reading and translating the original records, which I found in the "Brothers' House." These ancient records were freely and fully shown to us and we were given ample opportunity to read and translate them.

Dr. Fahnestock, in 1835, writes: "This school flourished for many years. It produced an anxious inquiry among the juvenile population, which attended the school, which increased and grew into what is now termed a 'revival' of religion. The scholars in the Sabbath-school met together every day before and after school hours to pray and exhort one another under the superintendence of one of the brethren." When the Revolutionary War broke out these buildings were needed for a hospital, and the one where the Sabbath-school was held was given up for this purpose. The Sunday-school was revived by Mr. Reimensnyder about 1870, not in the old buildings, but in the large room of a hotel. This new school awakened so much interest among the people that they cheerfully built a house of worship for its accommodation and for church service. The early Sunday-school, however, accomplished much good during its thirty years' existence, as the records of it prove, and on this account is entitled to the prominence which has hitherto been given it.[2]

---

[1] *The Sunday-School World*, 1875, p. 78.
[2] *Ibid.*, 1876, pp. 17, 18.

From this and many other similar instances which could be cited it is clear that there were some Sunday-schools in America previous to the movement under Raikes in England, and that these schools were similar in form, had a similar object, and that a prominent feature of some was instruction directly from the Bible. These facts identify them as forerunners of the modern Sunday-school movement.

The first efforts of these philanthropic persons were apparently quite independent one of the other. They evidently were moved by similar conditions and by a vision of similar fundamental principles in the making of Christian character. Their plans were clearly similar to those in British communities, but there is no record or intimation that they imitated the plans or had heard of the organizations in England before they commenced a similar movement in this country.

Robert May.—The record of Rev. Robert May's Sunday-school and evangelistic work in Philadelphia has confused writers of Sunday-school history in America. Some have held that he had no proper Sunday-school, but only a children's evangelistic service, basing their statements upon the records of the Evangelical Society of Philadelphia. The facts are clear that he held a Sunday-school as well as children's evangelistic services. The Sunday-school was held on Sunday from October, 1811, until late in January, 1812. His evangelistic services for children were held on week days. His record for November 17, 1811, makes it clear that he had classes and lessons on the Sabbath, as in the modern Sunday-school.

Thus, after the meeting was opened by prayer and singing on November 17, 1811, he says:

> We then proceeded to call and teach our different classes which were somewhat more regular and orderly than at first. We begin to know our children and they to know us. The children said their hymns very well in general; some said six verses in the Scriptures. Mr. Green, unable to attend from indisposition, Mr. Smith heard his class. After the classes were all heard, Mr. Erringer read the Scriptures and Mr. Smith engaged in prayer. A hymn was then sung and an exhortation to the children from Col. 3 : 20, the duty of children towards their parents. A few words were spoken to parents. About 210 children were present.

A similar record follows in regard to the sessions on November 24th and December 1st, and most of the following sessions of the school. On November 25th he records that there was a committee meeting which examined the proceedings as well as the bill for expenses, and adds,

> The number which attend on a Sabbath evening was found, upon examination, to be as follows: First class of girls, 31; second class of girls, 34; third class of girls, 36; fourth class of boys, 52; fifth class of boys, 51; sixth class of boys, 51.

A similar record of the different classes and their teachers occurs more than once in Mr. May's own handwriting in the record.

On December 30, 1811, there was a report to the committee as follows:

> First class of girls 30, from which 11 have been erazed [because of removal]; second class of girls 32, from which 7 have been erazed; third class of girls 33, from which 11 have been erazed; fourth class of boys 50, from which 9 have been erazed; fifth class of boys 50, from which 10 have been erazed; sixth class of boys 51, from which 8 have been erazed.
>
> Since the opening of the school, October 20, 1811, we have received upwards of 300 children; 56 have been erazed for non-attendance, and 246 remain in the school. Catherine Side left the school last Sabbath, being about to remove to Montgomery County. She appeared very thankful for instructions that she had received, and suitable advice and books were given her by the secretary on this day. Mr. Ely gave a good testimony in favor of the conduct of such of his boys as attended at our school. Mr. Ely is teacher of the Adelphi school in this city.

His record contains an alphabetical list of scholars and a memorandum of eight scholars from the school who had made a profession of religion and had joined different churches; the Presbyterian, Baptist and Methodist are especially noted. The manuscript records by Mr. May were found with the American Sunday-School Union.

WHO IS THE SECTARIAN?

He alone is the true sectarian who forgets that there is a common Christianity as well as a Christianity under the modification of his own party; who forgets that his duties to this common Christianity are of a higher obligation than those he owes (and some he does owe) to his own peculiarities; and who would see a soul of man left to perish without concern, if not saved by the application of a process of his own. In whatever religious body that man is found, he and he alone is the true sectarian.[1]

> **Mr. and Mrs. Divie Bethune.**—About the year 1812 (the precise date cannot here be given) the attention of Mr. and Mrs. Bethune was called to the blessed effects of the Sunday-school system established in England by Robert Raikes. Their pious correspondents in England, particularly Stephen Prust (?), Esq., of Bristol, sent them many reports and documents illustrating the work, and they endeavored to awaken the Christian public to that great means of usefulness, but for a time with little success. Pious people and some eminent ministers even doubted the propriety of so occupying the Sabbath day. Mr. Bethune, weary of delay, at last said to Mrs. Bethune: "My dear wife, there is no use in waiting for the *men*, do you gather a few ladies of different

[1] Richard Watson, quoted in *Sphere and Office of the American Sunday-School Union*, p. 6.

denominations and begin the work yourselves." Mrs. Bethune had already made encouraging experiments in two schools, one during the winter near her city residence within convenient distance of Dr. Romeyn's church, the other in the basement of her country seat between Bank and Bethune streets, Greenwich, besides starting others as she had opportunity during her summer travels in different parts of the country between the Hudson and the lakes. Intent upon a wider diffusion of the blessing, she determined to call a public meeting of ladies of different denominations in Wall Street Church, which she addressed from the clerk's desk, and, aided by many noble women, among them may be noted Mrs. Francis Hall of the Methodist, Mrs. William Colgate of the Baptist, and Miss Ball of the Dutch churches, she had the happiness of seeing put into successful operation *"The Female Union for the Promotion of Sabbath Schools,"* which continued, by its publications, and its schools containing 7,000 or 8,000 children, to exert a large usefulness, until it was absorbed by the New York Branch of the American Sunday-School Union. There had been Sunday-schools of various kinds in various places before this. Mrs. Graham, as early as 1792, had an adult Sunday evening school in Mulberry Street, and Mrs. Bethune in subsequent years had made several similar efforts; but this may be regarded as truly the first introduction of the Raikes system, as will be shown on some future occasion when time is had for proper research.

Mrs. Bethune's greatest delight was in the education of the young. She loved education as a science as well as a charity. Hence she was always personally attentive to that department of the orphan asylum, and taught her Sabbath class until she had long passed her 80th year. It is not surprising therefore that the infant school system, as organized by Wilderspin on the basis of Pestalozzi's plan of development, should have deeply interested her. On receiving the necessary books from England and Switzerland, she succeeded in establishing a society for advancing that method of instruction, aided by the late philanthropist, John Griscom, and also by Mr. Seton of this city, the lover of youth. Several schools were put into successful operation, which Mrs. Bethune actively superintended, and one of which she taught herself almost entirely, in the tough neighborhood of the Five Points—this more than 30 years ago. The Infant School plan was soon adopted as supplementary to the larger classes in Sunday-schools, and in the Primaries of our Public Schools, so that the good, thus begun, has been and will be perpetuated on a more extended scale. Several books of Infant School instruction, written and edited by Mrs. Bethune, are still highly prized.

From manuscript historical sketch in the possession of the New York Historical Society, a photographic copy of which is in the possession of the American Sunday-School Union.

List of Sunday-Schools and Societies Connected with the Sunday and Adult School Union Which, Therefore, Assented to its Change of Name to the American Sunday-School Union in 1824.

Name of School.	Number of Schools.	Officers and Teachers.	Number of Scholars.
Male, St. Paul's Church, Philadelphia	2	15	160
Female, St. Paul's Church, Philadelphia	3	45	260
Male, Christ Church and St. Peter's, Philadelphia	2	9	130
Male, Trinity Church, Southwark, Philadelphia	1	10	90
Female, Trinity Church, Southwark, Philadelphia	1	24	145
Male, St. John's Church, N. L., Philadelphia	1	6	50
Female, St. John's Church, N. L., Philadelphia	1	13	133
Berean Society, Philadelphia	2	6	130
First Presbyterian Church, Philadelphia	1	14	50
Adelphian Union, Philadelphia	7	81	548
Fourth Presbyterian Church, Philadelphia	2	12	150
Fifth Presbyterian Church, Philadelphia	2	15	220
Sixth Presbyterian Church, Philadelphia	2	23	90
Seventh Presbyterian Church, Philadelphia	2	14	110
First Baptist Church, Philadelphia	1	20	140
Second Baptist Church, Philadelphia	1	10	80
New-Market Street, Baptist, Philadelphia	1	14	170
Methodist, Kensington, Philadelphia	1	35	261
Methodist Episcopal Union, Philadelphia	1	22	193
Methodist, Ebenezer, Southwark, Philadelphia	1	24	268
German Reformed Church, Philadelphia	2	18	160
Female, First Reformed Dutch Church, Phila.	1	18	60
Union Sabbath School Asso. of N. L., Philadelphia	5	44	500
Combined Sabbath School Assoc. of N. L., Phila.	5	26	360
Auxiliary Evangelical Society, Philadelphia	4	26	300
Canaan Society, Philadelphia	1	9	70
Hope, Philadelphia	1	11	110
Samaritan, Southwark, Philadelphia	3	35	388
Mariners', Philadelphia	1	13	160
United Brethren, Philadelphia	1	10	70
Kensington, Philadelphia	1	20	100
Union Adult Society, Philadelphia	3	20	253
Sansom Street Baptist, Philadelphia	2	26	193
Bethlehem, Spring Garden, Philadelphia	1	13	100
First Reformed Church, Philadelphia	1	10	52
Oxford, Philadelphia County	1	12	60
Blockley, Philadelphia County	1	12	70
Frankford Union, Philadelphia County	3	15	185
Male, St. Luke's, Germantown, Philadelphia Co.	1	6	100
Hamiltonville, Philadelphia County	1	12	146
Bustleton, Philadelphia County	1	11	80
Holmesburg, Philadelphia County	1	14	115
Penn Township, Philadelphia County	1	5	60
Union, of Kingsessing, Philadelphia County	1	21	60
Lower Dublin, Philadelphia County	1	11	65
Ridge Road, Philadelphia County	1	10	71
Falls of Schuylkill, Philadelphia County	1	3	30
Radnor, Delaware County	1	8	67
Union S. S. Association, Delaware County	11	63	554

Name of School.	Number of Schools.	Officers and Teachers.	Number of Scholars.
Union, of Darby, Delaware County	1	18	46
Presbyterian, of Norristown, Montgomery County	1	8	60
Norriton, Montgomery County	2	14	100
Huntington, Montgomery County	1	5	40
Montgomery, Montgomery County	1	6	61
Evansburg, Montgomery County	1	7	70
United Upper Merion, Montgomery County	1	10	80
Pottstown, Montgomery County	1	25	90
Bristol, Bucks County	1	15	136
Neshaminy, Bucks County	3	29	150
Hilltown Lord's-Day, Bucks County	2	30	165
Buck, Bucks County	1	8	54
Newport, Bucks County	1	11	86
Doylestown, Bucks County	3	20	200
Newtown, Bucks County	1	26	98
Bensalem, Bucks County	1	17	77
Warwick, Chester County	1	12	50
Westnantmeal, Chester County	1	18	69
French Creek, Chester County	1	24	108
Upper Octarora, Chester County	9	93	446
Female, of New London, Chester County	3	17	134
Presbyterian S. S. S., Lancaster County	1	20	215
Female, St. James' Church, Lancaster County	1	15	100
Male, St. James' Church, Lancaster County	1	15	100
Lancaster, Lancaster County	1	6	30
Evangelical Lutheran, Lancaster County	1	68	480
Marietta, Lancaster County	3	25	213
Methodist, of Beams Meeting House, Lancaster Co.	1	10	93
New Holland, Lancaster County	1	12	90
Methodist, Lancaster County	1	12	55
Columbia, Lancaster County	2	16	139
Cedar Grove, Lancaster County	2	10	80
Strasburg Female, Lancaster County	1	14	107
Christ Church, of Leacock, Lancaster County	1	26	74
Pequea, Lancaster County	1	22	110
Compass, Lancaster County	1	21	80
Soudersburg, Lancaster County	1	19	75
Reading, Berks County	1	23	380
Womalsdorf, Berks County	2	20	149
Harrisburg, Dauphin County	2	30	260
Evangelical, of Harrisburg, Dauphin County	1	25	250
Methodist, of Halifax, Dauphin County	1	14	114
Allen Township, Dauphin County	1	19	75
Easton, Northampton County	3	25	220
Greenwich, Northampton County	1	5	50
Upper and Lower Mount Bethel, Northampton Co.	8	49	491
Evangelical, of Carlisle, Cumberland County	1	8	70
Newburg, Cumberland County	1	6	43
Silver Spring, Cumberland County	3	21	267
York, York County	2	23	205
Female, of Northumberland, Northumberland Co.	2	16	77
Northumberland, Northumberland County	1	5	28

Name of School.	Number of Schools.	Officers and Teachers.	Number of Scholars.
Female, of Sunbury, Northumberland County....	1	15	154
Female, of Shippensburg, Northumberland County.	1	12	50
Bridgewater, Susquehanna County..............	3	17	100
Lehigh, Lehigh County........................	1	4	43
Cattawissa, Columbia County..................	1	10	52
White Spring, Columbia County................	1	8	96
Berwick, Columbia County....................	5	53	229
Columbia, Columbia County...................15		187	796
Cattawissa Ridge, Columbia County............	1	8	46
Douglass Mills, Perry County..................	1	12	60
Germantown, Perry County....................	1	13	60
Upper Buffaloe, Perry County..................	1	9	50
Andersonville, Perry County..................	1	11	45
Petersburg, Perry County.....................	3	14	130
Wayne, Wayne County........................	1	7	57
Salem Congregation, Westmoreland County......	5	28	250
Lewistown, Mifflin County....................	1	12	99
Lewisburg, Union County.....................	1	20	120
Alexandria, Huntingdon County................	1	11	86
Gettysburg, Adams County....................	3	32	258
Bellefonte, Center County....................	1	11	162
Bellefonte, Methodist, Center County...........	1	8	80
Pine Grove Mills, Center County...............	1	10	50
Mount Pleasant, Center County................	1	10	50
Harmony, Center County.....................	1	15	141
Waynesburg, Franklin County.................	1	29	133
Chambersburg, Franklin County...............	1	22	200
Elkland, Lycoming County....................	2	26	72
Female, of Williamsport, Lycoming County......	1	12	40
White Deer, Lycoming County.................	2	50	147
Wilkesbarre, Luzerne County..................	1	26	181
Conyngham, Luzerne County..................	1	4	50
Washington, Washington County...............	1	21	182
Caernarvon, of Churchtown, Washington County..	1	15	81
Jefferson College, Washington County...........	2	13	85
Sunday-School Union, Crawford County.........47		255	1,362
West Union, Indiana County..................	5	63	255
Pittsburgh Union, Allegheny County............21		320	2,000
Methodist Association of Pittsburgh, Allegheny Co.	6	50	450
Dig Spring, Pennsylvania.....................	1	6	40
Brownsville, Pennsylvania....................	1	21	98
Middle Spring, Pennsylvania..................	2	14	66
Female Charity, Somerville, New Jersey.........	2	10	100
Union, New Mills, Burlington County, New Jersey.	1	11	60
Great Cross Roads, New Jersey................	1	11	86
Bordentown, New Jersey.....................	1	8	60
First Camden, New Jersey....................	1	15	97
Methodist, Bordentown, New Jersey............	1	11	61
Trenton and Lamberton, New Jersey...........	2	19	153
Birmingham Female, New Jersey...............	1	10	49
Flemington and Amwell, New Jersey...........	9	79	380
Union, Salem County, New Jersey..............	9	69	537

Name of School.	Number of Schools.	Officers and Teachers.	Number of Scholars.
Orange, Essex County, New Jersey	4	39	296
Cape May, New Jersey	1	5	60
New Brunswick, New Jersey	3	48	351
Cumberland Union, New Jersey	5	45	300
Osford and Harmony, New Jersey	5	30	361
Allentown, Monmouth County, New Jersey	3	25	244
Harbourton, New Jersey	2	6	90
Pohatcong Valley, New Jersey	5	39	361
Washington Female, Morris County, New Jersey	11	131	816
Woodbury, New Jersey	1	9	82
Black Horse, Burlington County, New Jersey	1	9	96
Hardwick, Sussex County, New Jersey	7	54	539
Basking Ridge, Somerset County, New Jersey	10	58	390
Springfield, New Jersey	6	32	255
Newhope and Lambertsville, New Jersey	4	35	248
Hackettstown, Sussex County, New Jersey	5	31	162
Princeton, New Jersey	18	136	1,000
Lawrence, New Jersey	4	9	136
Benevolent, Pennington, New Jersey	2	20	87
Trenton, New Jersey	3	29	250
Female, Bridgewater, New Jersey	1	15	93
Amwell, New Jersey	2	22	150
Buddtown, New Jersey	1	9	56
Lebanon and White House, New Jersey	11	57	431
Crosswicks, New Jersey	1	90	60
Laurel, Delaware	1	14	82
Wilmington, Delaware	10	86	567
Wilmington, Male, Delaware	1	7	100
Wilmington, of First Presbyterian Church, Dela..	1	12	65
Indian River, Delaware	1	5	41
Brandywine Manufacturers', Delaware	1	6	100
Union, of Lewis, Delaware	2	5	100
Newark, Delaware	6	28	275
Female Episcopal, of Wilmington, Delaware	1	10	120
Mathenian Assoc. of Fredericktown, Maryland	1	50	263
Female, of Easton, Maryland	1	10	25
Uniontown, Maryland	4	33	310
Union, of West Nottingham, Maryland	4	67	224
Christ Church Parish, Maryland	2	38	141
Female, of the Rock Church, Maryland	1	4	39
Frederick County, Maryland	1	8	70
Taneytown, Maryland	1	12	108
Salisbury, Maryland	1	11	58
German Reformed Church, Maryland	1	22	130
Union, of Cumberland, Maryland	2	9	99
Bear Branch and Pipe Creek Union, Maryland	1	6	73
African Female, Georgetown, D. C.	1	13	150
Washington Union, District of Columbia	14	174	1,279
Georgetown Union, District of Columbia	5	58	393
Alexandria Union, District of Columbia	5	40	300
Fredericksburg Evangelical, Virginia	4	50	265
Lynchburg Union, Virginia	2	23	110

Name of School.	Number of Schools.	Officers and Teachers.	Number of Scholars.
Winchester Union, Virginia	1	32	180
Presbyterian, of Fredericksburg, Virginia	5	35	300
London County Union, Virginia	3	24	152
Wheeling Union, Virginia	1	14	129
Timber Ridge, Virginia	1	1	55
Episcopal, of Winchester, Virginia	2	9	130
Culpepper, Virginia	1	8	31
Union, of Shepherdstown, Virginia	1	18	126
Fork Church, Hanover County, Virginia	1	22	80
Lewisburg, Greenbriar County, Virginia	1	9	95
Murfreesborough, North Carolina	2	8	85
Hillsborough, Orange County, North Carolina	12	60	50
Bethesda, Caswell County, North Carolina	1	3	60
Guilford, North Carolina	5	72	439
St. Mary's Chapel, Hillsborough, North Carolina.	1	7	100
Methodist, of Wilmington, North Carolina	1	10	55
Greensborough, North Carolina	2	51	307
Pendleton, North Carolina	7	34	242
Columbia, North Carolina	1	12	50
Charleston Union, South Carolina	10	138	895
Female Union, of the City of New York, New York.	43	487	2,377
Painted Post, Steuben County, New York	3	18	150
Hudson, Columbia County, New York	1	35	175
Hudson Baptist, New York	5	24	336
Guilford, Chenango County, New York	10	54	208
New Haven, Connecticut	2	50	270
Union, of Providence, Rhode Island	2	32	206
Society for Moral and Religious Instruction of the Poor, Salem, Massachusetts	4	110	550
Monroe, Chickasaw Nation, Mississippi	1	6	53
Natchez, Mississippi	1	18	130
Chariton, Missouri	1	9	31
Madison, Indiana	1	15	87
M'Chord's Church, Lexington, Kentucky	1	18	100
Maysville, Kentucky	2	9	260
Flemington, Kentucky	1	4	52
Louisville, Kentucky	1	20	200
Union, Kentucky	5	15	150
Kingsport, Tennessee	1	16	123
Union of Cincinnati, Ohio	8	162	1,185
Steubenville, Ohio	1	18	177
Salem, Harrisburg, Pennsylvania		...	.....
Lebanon, Pennsylvania		...	.....
Rye Township, Perry County, Pennsylvania		...	.....
Richmond Union, Virginia		...	.....
Petersburg Union, Virginia		...	.....
Dividing Creek, New Jersey		...	.....
Lebanon, New Jersey		...	.....
Cold Spring, Sussex County, Delaware		...	.....
Nashville, Tennessee		...	.....
Baptist, Providence, Rhode Island	22	175	1,200
	723	7,300	49,619

1817–1917, Date of Beginning of the American Sunday-School Union.— Representatives from ten or more local Sunday-school unions or societies met in Mr. Gartley's school-room, northwest corner of Fourth and Vine Streets, Philadelphia, May 13, 1817, to consider the formation of a general Sunday-school union.

They unanimously agreed that it was expedient to form such a union, and framed and printed a constitution. These delegates held three meetings in May, and promptly began work, while deciding upon the objects, basis, and title of the society. The records indicate that this movement was begun by laymen; clergymen not attending the meetings.

The title first proposed was "The Sunday and Adult School Association of ❡hiladelphia," but before the plans were completed it was changed to "The Sunday and Adult School Union."

While it was popularly called "The Philadelphia Sunday and Adult School Union," to indicate its headquarters, *Philadelphia* is no part of the title as given in the printed constitution of 1818, nor in the Act of Incorporation of 1819, nor is any limit indicated to its field of operations.

The direction of its affairs was committed to a board of twelve managers, chosen annually by ballot, together with two representatives from each connected school union. Clergymen, whose "school societies "were attached to the Union, were admitted as honorary members, with a right to vote.

The Sunday and Adult School Union was incorporated by decree of the Supreme Court of Pennsylvania in 1819.

The scope of operations which the founders had in view is confirmed by records which show that the Union formed and recognized auxiliary unions from ten states and the District of Columbia in the first three years of its existence, and by the seventh year it had unions and schools in seventeen states and the District of Columbia.

In view of this growth, suggestions that the Society become national in name, as well as in fact, came from various sections of the country, similar to this from New Jersey:

> Permit us to express the wish that the association (Union) of which it is our privilege to form a part, may continue to flourish and extend its genial influence till that happy day shall arrive when one mighty union shall be formed, embracing in its limits the people of every language and of every land.

A proposition from the New York Sunday-School Union Society in 1820 pointed to the magnitude of the work already accomplished by the Sunday and Adult School Union, and proposed a union general in name, to which other unions would become auxiliary. This implies that they did not contemplate becoming constituent bodies in a *new* organization, but that the Union located at Philadelphia should become national in name, and others become auxiliaries.

Influenced by these suggestions, the managers of the Sunday and Adult School Union, November 13, 1823, 29 members present, framed a constitution proposing to change its name to the American Sunday-School Union. Copies of this constitution were furnished to Sunday-school unions in different sections of the United States for consideration and approval. The basis and objects stated in this constitution of the American Sunday-School Union were essentially the same as those in the Sunday and Adult School Union:

> To concentrate the efforts of Sabbath-school societies in the different sections of our country; to strengthen the hands of the friends of pious instruction on the Lord's Day; to disseminate useful information; circulate moral and religious publications in every part of the land; and endeavor to plant a Sunday-school wherever there is a population.

This constitution, with a few suggested changes, was approved by the Society December 11, 1823, and referred to the Board of Managers to carry its provisions into effect. The Board of Officers and Managers, as instructed by the Society, presented the Constitution of the Society under its new name, the American Sunday-School Union, at the anniversary meeting, May 25, 1824. This anniversary was attended by distinguished representatives from various parts of the United States. The change of name to the American Sunday-School Union and the Constitution were ratified; the funds, books, and other property were transferred to the American Sunday-School Union; and the President, Treasurer, and other officers of the Sunday and Adult School Union were elected to similar offices in the Society under its new name.

Having changed its name, the law required a new Act of Incorporation. Repeated applications for such incorporation were presented to the Legislature of Pennsylvania between 1825 and 1829, and an Act of Incorporation was finally granted to the Society in 1845.

The phrase, "American Sunday-School Union organized in 1824," found in circulars and various publications of the Union, meant only the American Sunday-School Union organized *under its present name* in 1824.

That the American Sunday-School Union was not a new society in 1824 (but a change of name) is recognized and confirmed by subsequent records, as in circulars and in petitions to the legislature. In 1826 it is said, referring to the Sunday and Adult School Union: "The Society being thus in fact a great national institution, . . . it became proper to call it so, and by an alteration of the constitution it was styled the American Sunday-School Union." A similar statement was made again in 1828.

In another historical statement referring to the change from the Sunday and Adult School Union to the American Sunday-School Union is this phrase: "It is evident that this was simply a change of name and an enlarging of the powers of the former society." [1]

In an official address made in 1907 and placed in the corner-stone of the Society's present building is this statement:

> The American Sunday-School Union has a memorable record of Christian service for ninety years, 1817–1824–1907. Beginning as the Sunday and Adult School Union in 1817, it speedily became national in breadth and scope. . . . The friends . . . recognized its national character by reorganizing and renaming it the American Sunday-School Union.

Thus the Society under its two names—The Sunday and Adult School Union and the American Sunday-School Union—has had a continuous existence since May, 1817.

The origin of the Society may hereafter be briefly stated:

> American Sunday-School Union, instituted May 13, 1817, under the title The Sunday and Adult School Union; the name changed to the American Sunday-School Union May 25, 1824.

The foregoing statement of the origin of the American Sunday-School Union was prepared from its records by a special committee (Edwin W. Rice, Honorary Editor, and William C. Stoever, Manager and Attorney of the Society), and was approved by the Board of Officers and Managers April, 1916, and ratified at the annual meeting of the Society May, 1916, and ordered to be published in view of the one hundredth anniversary of the Union, May, 1917.

The Basis.—In 1844 the managers said:

> We do not seal up the sacred volume and require our fellow-men to believe what we or other fallible men have said, or may say, of its contents. . . . We seek to put the Bible into the hands of all the children and youth in the country. . . . We do not put any human authority above it nor by the side of it, but *immeasurably* below it. . . . The Bible is the only rule of faith and duty, and every man is required, on divine authority and at the peril of his soul, to search the Scriptures, and see what they testify of Christ and his doctrines. Hence to open the Bible to all the rising generation of our country is the grand and glorious object of the American Sunday-School Union. We unite for this purpose, and blessed be God that we can unite; that as a body of Christians, without distinction of sect, or creed, or custom, we *can* and *do* kneel together before the throne of our common Lord and Saviour, and implore, with one heart and voice, upon ourselves and upon the work of our hands, His gracious favour. We *can* and *do* inculcate the great truths of the Christian faith on which we rely for our own salvation,

[1] Report of Anniversary, 1899, p. 5.

upon the minds and hearts of the ignorant, the neglected, the unthinking and vicious myriads that throng our cities and rise up, like a dense cloud, all over the newly formed settlements of the land. We *can* and *do* scatter far and wide—through the agency of thousands upon thousands of our teachers, and our millions of Bibles, Testaments, and other religious books, circulating from week to week among a million of children and youth, and through the families and neighbourhoods in which they dwell—the free and boundless blessings of the Gospel.[1]

In 1834 they said:

The principle of our union has been stated so often, and with so much clearness, that it seems as if there could be no room for misapprehension. We are associated as individuals, for the purpose of aiding in the establishment of Sunday-schools, and publishing libraries for their use. Some of us are Baptists; some are Methodists; some are Presbyterians; some are Episcopalians; some are Lutherans, and some are of other denominations. As an association, however, we have no connection whatever with any denomination, nor has any denomination any connection whatever with us.[2]

In 1838 the managers answered the allegation that the Society taught a weak, diluted gospel:

We disavow, also, the allegation that the principles of our Union are chargeable with encouraging neglect of the particular formularies of the various denominations, or with discouraging full investigation of any doctrine that is a subject of difference with Christians. . . . It is no part of our principles to discountenance the action of denominational schools or societies, or to attempt to widen their basis. . . . Nor has it ever been our desire to exclude the instruction peculiar to any one form of evangelical belief, in order to introduce a diluted and weakened course of instruction. . . . If the catechisms of the churches are less studied than they once were, it is not because we have pretended to furnish a substitute for them. . . . It must be owing to want of proper arrangement or provision, if the children of that church are not instructed in their own catechism or formularies, according to its wishes, although good faith may require that this should not be imposed on all. We would, therefore, once more earnestly call upon the Christian church and its ministers to give their most watchful attention to the Sunday-school system, both as it affects their own distinctive creeds, and as it regards the general state of ignorance and irreligion in our country. The former is no part of our duty, and the latter does not belong to us exclusively. Our books may be used in every school to inculcate instruction and saving truth, without keeping away any scholars on account of denominational peculiarities. . . . Will the principle be defended, that we ought not to go into the villages and neighbourhoods where there are no churches or schools, and form a Sunday-school, where the Bible shall be diligently read, and the attendants shall learn

[1] *Report*, 1844, pp. 57-59.   [2] *Report*, 1834, pp. 20, 21.

their duties to God and man, and be urged to repentance and faith in the Lord Jesus Christ—that this shall not be done, because of the few pious and intelligent teachers who are to be found in the settlement, one is a Baptist, another an Episcopalian, a third a Methodist, a fourth a Presbyterian, or Moravian, or Lutheran? Is this a fact that is to exclude religious teaching from that population until each of these denominations successively gains strength enough, in the course of many years, to have a church and Sunday-school of its own?[1]

On the same principle we would ask whether the help of our publications should be wholly declined by any school because they abstain from points controverted. . . . Cannot Christian character be exhibited in biography; or Scriptural history and antiquities be illustrated; or the duties of life enforced and its dangers warned against, without incorporating in the work the peculiarities of some one creed? The very statement of the question shows the fallacy of the objection to which it refers.[2]

Utica Union Sunday-School.—The Utica Union Sunday-School, of which Truman Parmele was superintendent, was composed of *three* denominations of Christians—Baptists, Methodists and Presbyterians.

The first formation of the school in Utica was in 1816. The union of the above denominations was affected in 1820. The effect of the union has been to promote harmony and friendly feeling between the different societies which compose it and has materially increased the usefulness of the school. It is divided into two departments, male and female, each under the care of a superintendent and assistant. A system of instruction has, during the past year, been pursued in this institution which has had an astonishing effect in exciting the interest of the scholars, awakening the activities of the teachers, and increasing their usefulness. This system is, briefly, to question the scholars closely upon the lessons given them by their teachers, first in their respective classes, and then by the superintendents. To this system we are indebted for that valuable work entitled *Questions Designed for Sabbath-Schools.* For more than four years the teachers of these schools have been accustomed to observe the monthly prayer meeting. . . . These meetings were found to produce a happy effect upon the teachers, who were the first to recommend "The Teachers' Monthly Concert." . . . They have perceived the benefit of limited lessons, well committed, and recommend the plan in the strongest terms.

The Rev. S. W. Grace, corresponding secretary of the Western Sunday-School Union, noted a monthly publication, *The Western Sunday-School Visitor,* which "proves a powerful auxiliary to the good cause." He also reported a second edition of five thousand copies of Parmele's Questions lately published, with two other publications, one on the internal government of Sunday-schools and the other on a system of instruction

[1] *Report*, 1838, pp. 19-22.
[2] *Report*, 1839, pp. 19-22.

designed principally for public examinations. The Union then reported about 200 schools, about 1,500 teachers and 8,000 scholars.[1]

First Yearly Course of Scripture Lessons for Sunday-Schools. Revised in 1826

First Quarter

Lesson 1. Luke, Chap. i. Verses 5-25. The appearance of the angel Gabriel to Zacharias, to foretell the birth of John the Baptist.

Lesson 2. Luke, Chap. i. Verses 26-38. The appearance of the angel to Mary, to foretell the birth of Christ.

Lesson 3. Luke, Chap. i. Verses 57-80. The birth of John the Baptist.

Lesson 4. Luke, Chap. i. Verses 1-20. The birth of Christ, and the appearance of the angels to the Shepherds.

Lesson 5. Luke, Chap. ii. Verses 21-38. The presentation of Christ in the temple, and blessing of Simeon and Anna.

Lesson 6. Matt., Chap. ii. Verses 1-23. Jesus sought by the wise men—the flight into Egypt, and the massacre of the children of Bethlehem.

Lesson 7. Luke, Chap. ii. Verses 40-52. Christ is taken to Jerusalem at twelve years of age.

Lesson 8. Luke, Chap. iii. Verses 1-22. Christ is baptized by John the Baptist, who is preaching in the country about Jordan.

Lesson 9. Matt., Chap. iv. Verses 1-11. Christ's temptation in the wilderness.

Lesson 10. John, Chap. i. Verses 1-14. The divinity of Christ.

Second Quarter

Lesson 11. John, Chap. i. Verses 15-34. The testimony of John the Baptist, concerning Christ.

Lesson 12. John, Chap. i. Verses 35-51. Christ obtains his first disciples, Andrew, Peter, Philip and Nathanael.

Lesson 13. John, Chap. ii. Verses 1-22. Christ performs his first miracles at Cana; goes to Jerusalem, and cleanses the temple.

Lesson 14. Matt., Chap. iv. Verses 12-25. Christ preaches in Galilee, calls several disciples, and performs miracles.

Lesson 15. Luke, Chap. vi. Verses 6-19. Christ heals a man with a withered hand; he chooses his twelve Apostles.

Lesson 16. Luke, Chap. vii. Verses 1-17. Christ heals a centurion's servant, and raises a widow's son.

Lesson 17. Matt., Chap. viii. Verses 18-34. Two persons propose to follow Christ; his answers; he calms a tempest; casts out devils.

Lesson 18. Mark, Chap. v. Verses 22-43. A woman is healed of an issue of blood by touching Christ's garments; the daughter of Jairus restored.

Lesson 19. Matt., Chap. x. Verses 1-16. Jesus instructs his twelve Apostles and sends them forth to preach.

Lesson 20. Matt., Chap. xi. Verses 1-15. John the Baptist sends two disciples to Christ to inquire if he is the Messiah; Christ's answer and testimony concerning John.

[1] Report *Oneida County Sunday-School Union*, in *Annual Report* of the American Sunday-School Union, 1826, *Addenda*, p. 88.

Third Quarter

Lesson 21. Mark, Chap. vi. Verses 14-29. John the Baptist beheaded.
Lesson 22. Mark, Chap. vi. Verses 30-44. The Apostles return to
    Jesus, and go with him to a desert place, where he feeds five thousand
    men with five loaves and two fishes.
Lesson 23. John, Chap. v. Verses 1-18. Christ heals a lame man at
    the pool of Bethesda.
Lesson 24. Matt., Chap. xvi. Verses 13-28. Christ asks his disciples
    whom they suppose him to be, and foretells his death.
Lesson 25. Matt., Chap. xvii. Verses 1-13. Christ's transfiguration
    on a mountain.
Lesson 26. Luke, Chap. xvii. Verses 11-30. Christ heals ten lepers,
    and speaks to the Phariseses about the kingdom of God.
Lesson 27. John, Chap. xi. Verses 1-27. Christ goes to Bethany to
    raise Lazarus.
Lesson 28. John, Chap. xi. Verses 28-46. Christ raises Lazarus from
    the dead.
Lesson 29. John, Chap. xii. Verses 1-11. Christ is anointed by Mary.
Lesson 30. Luke, Chap. xix. Verses 28-48. Christ enters Jerusalem,
    weeps over it, and foretells its destruction.

Fourth Quarter

Lesson 31. Matt., Chap. xxvi. Verses 14-35. Christ foretells his being
    betrayed, and institutes the Lord's Supper.
Lesson 32. Matt., Chap. xxvi. Verses 36-56. Christ in the garden of
    Gethsemane, and there betrayed by Judas.
Lesson 33. Matt., Chap. xxvi. Verses 57-75. Christ is tried before
    Caiaphas, and denied by Peter.
Lesson 34. Matt., Chap. xxvii. Verses 1-23. Judas hangs himself;
    Christ tried and condemned by Pilate.
Lesson 35. Matt., Chap. xxvii. Verses 24-44. Christ's crucifixion.
Lesson 36. Matt., Chap. xxvii. Verses 45-66. The burial of Christ.
Lesson 37. John, Chap. xx. Verses 1-18. The resurrection of Christ.
Lesson 38. Luke, Chap. xxiv. Verses 13-35. Christ appears to two
    disciples, going to Emmaus.
Lesson 39. John, Chap. xxi. Verses 1-25. Christ appears to his
    disciples, when fishing.
Lesson 40. Luke, Chap. xxiv. Verses 36-53. Christ's appearance to
    his Apostles and others, and his ascension.

The foregoing selections, embracing the history of our Saviour's life
and miracles, constitute the first of a series of courses intended to be
published yearly—each course to consist of 40 lessons, with a book of
questions. The last Sabbath in each month should be devoted to reviewing the lessons of the month, and such other purposes as may suit the
circumstances of the different schools where this plan of instruction is
adopted. The second yearly course of lessons will embrace the public
and private instructions of our Saviour, and will complete the selections
from the gospels.

Scripture Lessons Selected for a Second Annual Course of Instruction.
Revised in 1826

Lessons for the First Quarter of the Year

Lesson 1. John, Chap. iii. Verses 1-21. Christ's conversation with Nicodemus.

Lesson 2. Luke, Chap. iv. Verses 16-32. Jesus preacheth in Nazareth from Isaiah, for which the Jews endeavor to cast him from a precipice.

Lesson 3. Matt., Chap. v. Verses 1-16. Christ's sermon on the mount—Christians called the salt of the earth, and the light of the world.

Lesson 4. Matt., Chap. v. Verses 17-32. Our Lord maintains the law, shows how an offending brother should be treated, and explains the seventh commandment.

Lesson 5. Matt., Chap. v. Verses 33-48. Swearing forbidden—kindness and benevolence enjoined.

Lesson 6. Matt., Chap. vi. Verses 1-18. Our Lord addresses his hearers concerning charity, prayer, and fasting.

Lesson 7. Matt., Chap. vi. Verses 19-34. Christ teacheth us where to lay up our treasure—shows that we cannot serve God and the world, and instructs us to trust in Divine Providence.

Lesson 8. Matt., Chap. vii. Verses 1-14. Christ forbids hypocrisy, encourages his hearers to pray, and to enter in at the strait gate.

Lesson 9. Matt., Chap. vii. Verses 15-29. Our Lord cautions his hearers against false teachers, and against making a false profession of religion.

Lesson 10. Matt., Chap. xiii. Verses 1-17. Parable of the sower.

Lessons for the Second Quarter of the Year

Lesson 11. Luke, Chap. xi. Verses 14-26. Christ accused of casting out devils by Beelzebub, and his reply.

Lesson 12. Matt., Chap. xiii. Verses 44-58. Parables of the treasure, pearl and net. The Jews offended with Christ on account of his low parentage and manner of life.

Lesson 13. John, Chap. v. Verses 17-30. Christ teaches that he is divine and the judge of all men.

Lesson 14. John, Chap. v. Verses 31-47. Our Lord speaks concerning the witnesses of his person and doctrine, and reproves the people for their unbelief.

Lesson 15. Matt., Chap. xv. Verses 1-20. Christ reproves the Pharisees, and shows to the multitude what things are defiling.

Lesson 16. Matt., Chap. xvi. Verses 1-12. Jesus answers those who require a sign from heaven, and warns his hearers to beware of the Pharisees.

Lesson 17. Matt., Chap. xviii. Verses 1-14. Jesus teaches humility, and shows his care for his people by the parable of lost sheep.

Lesson 18. Matt., Chap. xviii. Verses 21-35. Peter's question how often he should forgive his brother—Christ's instruction about brotherly love.

Lesson 19. Luke, Chap. x. Verses 25-37. A lawyer inquires what he must do to inherit eternal life. Jesus refers to the law of God, and shows him by the example of a good Samaritan, who is his neighbor.

Lesson 20. Luke, Chap. xi. Verses 37-54. Our Lord denounces woes against the Pharisees and lawyers.

Lessons for the Third Quarter of the Year

Lesson 21. Matt., Chap. xiii. Verses 24-35. Parable of the tares in the field—the grain of mustard seed and leaven.

Lesson 22. Luke, Chap. xii. Verses 1-21. Our Saviour teaches his hearers to have confidence in God—and warns them to beware of covetousness.

Lesson 23. Luke, Chap. xii. Verses 35-48. Our Lord teaches his hearers to be ready for his coming.

Lesson 24. Luke, Chap. xiii. Verses 23-35. Our Lord answers the question, whether there be few that be saved, and laments over Jerusalem.

Lesson 25. Luke, Chap. xiv. Verses 16-33. The parable of the great supper, and the terms of being Christ's disciples.

Lesson 26. Luke, Chap. xv. Verses 11-32. Parable of the prodigal son.

Lesson 27. Luke, Chap. xvi. Verses 1-13. The unjust steward.

Lesson 28. Luke, Chap. xvi. Verses 19-31. Parable of the rich man and Lazarus.

Lesson 29. Luke, Chap. xvii. Verses 1-10. Our Lord enjoins kindness to brethren, and the duty of faith.

Lesson 30. Luke, Chap xviii. Verses 1-14. The importunate widow. The Pharisee and Publican.

Lessons for the Last Quarter of the Year

Lesson 31. Matt., Chap. xix. Verses 13-26. Christ blesseth little children. The rich man's question what he should do to be saved.

Lesson 32. Matt., Chap. xx. Verses 1-16. Parable of the labourers in the vineyard.

Lesson 33. John, Chap. viii. Verses 12-30. Our Lord discourses to the Jews concerning himself.

Lesson 34. John, Chap. x. Verses 1-18. Christ the good shepherd.

Lesson 35. Luke, Chap. xix. Verses 11-27. The nobleman's kingdom.

Lesson 36. Matt., Chap. xxi. Verses 28-46. Parable of the two sons and the wicked husbandman. Our Lord is called the stone which the builders rejected.

Lesson 37. Matt., Chap. xxii. Verses 1-14. Parable of the wedding garment.

Lesson 38. Matt., Chap. xxv. Verses 1-13. Parable of the ten virgins.

Lesson 39. Matt., Chap. xxv. Verses 14-30. Parable of the talents.

Lesson 40. Matt., Chap. xxv. Verses 31-46. The last judgment.

The lessons for the third year in a similar way covered Old Testament history from the Creation to the Exodus, and the fourth year's lessons continued the Old Testament history to the death of Joshua. The fifth year took up the history of the Christian Church as recorded in the Acts of the Apostles, and the sixth year resumed the study of Old Testament history from the death of Joshua to the death of Samuel, and the seventh year the same history from the death of Samuel to the Captivity. In the eighth year the lessons were from the Epistle to the Galatians; in the ninth year they were on the history of the Israelites from the Captivity to the end of the Old Testament (Daniel, Ezra, Esther, and Nehemiah).

Two other courses were for Bible classes, as well as that on Galatians, to wit: one on the Epistle to the Romans, and the other on the Epistle to the Hebrews.

Simultaneously with these *The Child's Scripture Question Book* was issued for the younger classes.

Schools for Teachers.—The New York Sunday-School Union, auxiliary to The American Sunday-School Union, in 1827 reported:

> One of the greatest embarrassments attending the enlargement of Sunday-school operations is a deficiency of faithful and competent teachers; it is frequently the case that those who manifest a disposition to engage in this work are deterred on account of their ignorance of its duties. To obviate this last difficulty and to afford an opportunity to all teachers to become better qualified for their employment, the plan has been suggested of opening a school for teachers, on some week day or Sabbath evening, for the purpose of instructing in the practical duties of a Sunday-school teacher. A thorough acquaintance with the best plan of teaching a class, and a uniform system of instruction, so far as is practicable, appears to be very desirable. Your committee therefore highly recommend the establishment of a school for teachers, and the more so, because they have been informed that some of the oldest and most experienced among us are now ready to engage in it.[1]

Debate on Granting a Charter to the American Sunday-School Union.—Senator Duncan, from Philadelphia, took part in a debate on the granting of the charter to the American Sunday-School Union, and was opposed by Senator Jesse R. Burden in a speech covering eight closely printed octavo pages. Senator Powell made a similar attack upon the petition. Both of these speeches were printed in *The Christian Advocate and Journal* of 1828, with apparent approval of their general argument. A strong statement of the case by five managers of The American Sunday-School Union, who were prominent members of the Methodist Episcopal Church, pointed out the misapprehensions and misrepresentations of the senators, upon which the *Journal* had based its remarks. The managers say they did it from "a sense of justice to our brethren and ourselves." The character of this opposition is further indicated by articles in the columns of *The Episcopal Watchman* for 1827–28, *The Church Register* for the same year, *The Christian Baptist*, *The Christian Advocate* and other journals cited by Parson Brownlow in his address against Union Sunday-schools in 1831, and by a defence of the American Sunday-School Union made by Hon. Williard Hall, Justice of the United States Court, Delaware, 1828. As to the scope of the Union, the New York Sunday-School Society suggested in 1820 that it was national. There is no intimation in its records anywhere that the organization of the

[1] *Annual Report*, 1827, p. 7.

American Sunday-School Union was proposed by any outside of the committee of the New York Union composed of different evangelical Christians who held their business and annual meetings at that time in the John Street Methodist Church, New York. For further facts relating to the opposition and controversies, see *Vindication of Sunday-Schools*, by Archibald Alexander, 1832, revised edition 1845; *Union Principle Undenominational and Not Antidenominational*, by Henry A. Boardman, D.D., 1855; *Vindication of the Principle of Christian Union*, Stephen H. Tyng, D.D.; *The Union Principle*, by Stephen H. Tyng, D.D., New York, 1855; *Design and Importance of The American Sunday-School Union*, by Frederick A. Packard, LL.D., Philadelphia, 1838; *Review, etc., Sunday-School Quarterly Magazine*, October, 1831.

On the opposition to The American Sunday-School Union the Rev. Oscar S. Michael, in *The Sunday-School in the Development of the American Church*, asserts:

> The Methodists, as a class, bitterly opposed its progress on the ground that it was a propagating agency of Hopkinsianism or Calvanistic Presbyterianism to the detriment of other creeds. So powerful was the political influence of the Methodists that no charter could be procured for the Union from the commonwealth until 1845, or after a lapse of twenty years of hard work.[1]

It is true that many of the clergy and some of the journals in that church appear to have sympathized strongly with the remonstrants who opposed the granting of the charter in 1828. But, on the other hand, a large number of the laity in that church who had knowledge of the character and work of The American Sunday-School Union were not only friendly to it, but several of them signed a memorial answering the remonstrants and giving reasons why a charter should be granted.

Juvenile Literature, 1800.—Dr Packard, then editor of the publications of the Union, on March 5, 1850, addressed a letter to a number of leading educators and business people in various walks of life presenting this question:

> We are often asked by children and youth who have been accustomed all their short lives to a superabundance of books, What the people, who are now fifty or sixty years old, used to do for books when *they were children.* . . . What were the titles, size, price, and character of books which were then regarded as properly *children's* books? It would be a favor to us if you could describe the general character of such books and whether they were published in this country or abroad.

---

[1] See *The Charter*, A Plain Statement of Facts; also The Remonstrance and A Memorial, in answer to a Remonstrance, and Letter to the Editor of *The Christian Advocate and Journal*, 1828.

Answers were received from persons living in Braintree, Amherst, Springfield, Northampton, Massachusetts; Philadelphia, Pennsylvania; Wethersfield, Norwich, East Windsor, Hartford, Connecticut; Keene, New Hampshire, and from several other places, some of whom furnished quite an extended list of books current in their childhood, a very few of which could be properly called children's books.[1]

The "Horn" books and the "Chap" books, which were popular in the first half of the nineteenth century, had a wide circulation for a time, but were not conspicuous for their religious tone. Thus it is claimed that "Every phase of human nature was served up for a penny. . . . There were to be had primers, song books and joke books; histories, stories, and hero tales. They were printed in type to ruin the eyes, pictured in wood cuts to startle fancy and to shock taste—for they were not always suited to childhood." Moreover, the chap books were very rudimentary literature, if we may believe the literary critics of that period.

English Works vs. American.—A few years since, our chief dependence in this department (for reading books) was on English books, which we reprinted with such illustrations and modifications as suited them to our purpose. "It is no longer necessary, however, to resort to this means of supply. The number of American pens occupied in preparing religious reading for children is already large, and is continually increasing; and the change in the character of juvenile books, both in moral and natural science, is very obvious."[2]

Revision of Publications.—This practice of the Union to revise all works bearing its imprint, and to omit, as a rule, the names of the authors thereof led some of its critics to charge it with "disingenuousness" at various periods of its history. Thus a writer in the Protestant Episcopal Church ascribes disingenousness to the American Sunday-School Union "in mutilating books to fit its union principle," instancing the *Dairyman's Daughter* as having suffered such mutilation apparently, on the ground that those mentioned in it were not given their full title, thus robbing them of some dignity.[3] But, as a matter of fact, the Rev. Legh Richmond wrote the story of *Dairyman's Daughter*, as published first in book form, when he was honorary secretary of the London Religious Tract Society. That being an undenominational society, he wished the book to be acceptable throughout all denominations. He himself therefore in his original edition made whatever omissions were found in the editions by the American Sunday-School Union. Curiously enough, this charge of disingenuousness was made early in the history of the Society, and this same book was instanced as proof of it. But the Rev. T. S. Grimshawe, the friend and chosen biographer of Rev. Legh Richmond, in England,

[1] *Report*, 1850, pp. 53–69.
[2] *Report of American Sunday-School Union for 1833*, p. 16.
[3] O. S. Michael, *The Sunday-School in the Development of the American Church.*

examined the edition issued by the American Sunday-School Union and pronounced it "in every respect conformable to the original," and Dr. G. T. Bedell also said that the Union's edition was an exact copy of the original.[1]

There were "mutilated editions" issued by private publishers, chiefly abridgments of the original work, but not by the Union.

Therefore it is clear that the managers of the Union were consistent in their course, and aimed not to credit a work to the author unless it had his full approbation. It further accounts for their almost universal custom of omitting the names of authors in their books—a custom which prevailed for upward of forty years.

The managers expressly declared that the Union was responsible for whatever publications bore the impress of the Society in full, but not responsible for any other. They said:

> The declaration which the title page of each of our publications makes, shifts the burden of responsibility for every line and letter upon the Society, whether the name of the original author is retained or expunged. And while we regard, scrupulously, the rights of authors, and the provisions of law by which they are secured from violation, we esteem every book which is given to the world, without this protection, as common property, and claim the liberty to use it in whatever way will best subserve the purposes of religious education.

They added:

> This right of revision is enjoyed to its fullest extent by all others, without molestation and complaint, and there seems to be no good reason why it should be denied to those whose only object in exercising it is public advantage.[2]

Anniversary Hymns.—W. B. Tappam composed original hymns which were sung at the anniversary of the American Sunday-School Union for each year from 1825 to 1828 inclusive; six or seven hymns. Dr. W. A. Muhlenberg composed two similar hymns for 1831. Willis Gaylord Clark composed a hymn for 1832. Later the use of special collections of hymns on anniversary occasions was resumed, about 1859 or 1860, and several such collections were prepared and issued by George S. Scofield, agent of the American Sunday-School Union in New York. Several of these hymns found their way into more permanent collections also issued by this Society.

[1] G. T. Bedell, *Life of Leigh Richmond*, p. 102.
[2] *Report*, 1831, pp. 16, 17.

Fivefold Treatment and Expositions of the Sunday-School Lessons of
1830, an Adaptation of Gall's Lesson System

SECTION XVII

Parable of the Sower.—Luke viii. 4-15
See also Matt. xiii. 1-23, *and* Mark iv. 1-25

NARRATIVE

Jesus and his disciples, soon after the circumstance which took place
at the pool of Bethesda, passing through the corn fields on the Sabbath
day, and being hungry, plucked the ears of corn, by which they gave
offence to some of the Pharisees, (Matt. xii. 1-8. Mark ii. 23-28. Luke
vi. 1-5.) A few days afterwards, he cured the man with a withered hand;
and because of the opposition and persecution of the Jews on that account,
he withdrew himself from them, (Matt. xii. 9-21. Mark iii. 1-12. Luke
vi. 6-11.) After having his miracles again ascribed to Belzebub, which
he refuted, he was visited by his mother and brethren, who were become
exceedingly anxious for his welfare, but they could not come in for the
crowd, (Matt. xii. 22-50. Mark iii. 22-35.) Jesus then came out of the
house, which could not contain the multitude, and went to the sea side,
where he delivered the parable of the Sower, and afterwards interpreted it.

EXERCISE

Ver. 4. Who were gathered together? From whence did they come?
To whom did they come? How did Jesus speak to them?—5. Who
went out to sow? What did he sow? Where did the first portion of seed
fall? What became of it? By what was it devoured?—6. Where did
the second portion of seed fall? What became of it? When did it wither?
What made it wither?—7. Where did the third portion of seed fall?
What sprang up? With what did the thorns spring up? What was
choked? By what was the seed choked?—8. Where did the fourth
portion of seed fall? What became of it? How much fruit did it produce?
Who cried? When did he cry? Who were to hear?—9. Who asked
for an explanation? Of what did they ask an explanation?—10. What
mysteries were given them to know? How were others instructed? Why
were they so instructed?—11. Who explained the parable? What is
meant by the seed in the parable?—12. What is meant by the way-side?
Who cometh? What does he take away? From whence does he take it
away? Why does he take the word from their hearts? What would
happen were they to believe?—13. What is said of the rock, or stony-
ground hearers? When do they receive the word? How do they receive
the word? What is that which they have not? What do they do for a
while? When do they fall away?—14. When is it said the thorny-
ground hearers go forth? What becomes of them when they go forth?
With what are they choked? What do they not bring to perfection?—
15. What kind of heart have the good-ground hearers? What do they
do when they hear the word? How do they bring forth fruit?

EXPLANATIONS

Ver. 4. *Parable,* A continued comparison of one thing to another. A
picture of spiritual things, by means of sensible and external objects.
5. *A Sower,* A person who scatters seed in a field, or garden for the
purpose of its growing up and producing fruit. *Way-side,* Side of the
road. *Trodden,* Trampled upon with the feet. *Fowls,* Birds.

6. *Lacked moisture,* Wanted water; was dry at the root.

7. *Choked it,* Kept it from the sun and air, so that it could not thrive, or bring fruit to perfection.

8. *Hundred-fold,* A hundred times as much as the quantity at first sown.

10. *Mysteries,* things not easily understood.

13. *Time of temptation,* Times of trial, persecution, or enticements to sin and apostacy.

14. *Perfection,* To a complete state.

Patience, With calm submission and constancy.

EXPLANATION OF THE SYMBOLS

Seed, The word of God, or the truths of the gospel which ought to be kept pure, and liberally sown in every part of the *field* of this world.

Sowers, Ministers, teachers, parents, and all who communicate the truths of the gospel to others. The *hearers* are represented as ground of different kinds, receiving this seed according to the state of their hearts, and circumstances in life.

Way-side hearers, (1.) Those who, by inattention, wandering thoughts, or drowsiness, are prevented from hearing or understanding the word when it is delivered or read. (2.) Those who are so allured by the deceitfulness of sin, that they will not allow the truths of the gospel to have any impression on their hearts. (3.) Those whose violent prejudices, wicked lives, and unruly lusts and passions, induce them to contemn and trample upon the truths of the gospel.

Stony-ground hearers, Those whose imaginations are easily excited, and who are induced, without due consideration, to receive the word with joy, and for a while to make a promising profession; but not having their religion placed on a proper foundation, give it up whenever they are called to suffer persecution, or when any sufficiently powerful temptation occurs.

Thorny-ground hearers, They who make, and continue to maintain an outward profession of religion; but who permit themselves to be so absorbed by the business or the pleasures of life, that religion is neglected, becomes a mere name, and brings forth no fruit to perfection.

Good-ground hearers, Those who, having their affections set more on the things of God, than the things of the world, having their hearts renewed by the operation of the Spirit of God, receive and nourish the seed of the word; which brings forth fruit in their lives, to the praise and glory of God.

LESSONS

From this Section we learn,

That we should embrace every opportunity of having our knowledge increased, and the things of God made plain to our understanding, ver. 9.

That the *desire* for wisdom is the way to get wisdom. They who apply to Christ for knowledge shall not be disappointed; while others who are careless, shall hear without understanding, ver. 10.

That a mere attendance on the preaching of the word, or the means of grace, is no sure sign of true religion, ver. 12.

That wandering thoughts and inattention in hearing the word, are invitations to Satan to render it useless, ver. 12.

That there may be many fair appearances and even zealous affections in the profession of religion, without true and saving faith, ver. 13.

That they who trust in their own strength, lean on a broken reed. Temptation or persecution will dissipate all those resolutions which have not their foundation on the grace of Christ, and a sense of human weakness, ver. 13.

That indulgence in worldly pleasures is dangerous to true religion. Sensual gratification destroys the relish for holiness and heaven, and prevents the growth of humility and self-restraint, ver. 14.

That a medium station in society is that most favourable to the prosperity of true godliness. Affluence and want,—riches and care,—each in its own way choke the word, and render it unfruitful, ver. 14.

That legal observances, and rapturous emotions, though beautiful in the sight of men, will not be accepted of God, unless they bring their fruit to perfection, ver. 14.

That they who would receive the word effectually, and bring forth fruit, must have their hearts prepared, and made good and honest by the Spirit of God, ver. 15.

That an essential ingredient in true faith, is a patient continuance in well doing. They must not only ripen into fruit, but they must continue to bring forth fruit with patience, ver. 15.

Testimony of Henry Ward Beecher.—At the anniversary of the Society in 1848 the Rev. Henry Ward Beecher, then pastor of Plymouth Congregational Church, Brooklyn, New York, but recently from Indianapolis, Indiana, said:

There are continual demands made, and still making, on the East, in behalf of the West; and it is Give, give, give—Send send, send—Come, come, come—continually. Must the East, because it stands in the relation of an elder brother to the West, adopt and bring up the child? Must the East feed and clothe and educate the West, and pay all her bills? How long before the West will become of age, that we may dismiss her from our care? How many colleges must we found? How many ministers must we send out? How long must we stand as the guardians of the West? And how much of the funds of the American Sunday-School Union are to be expended before we have accomplished the work of building up and educating the West?

I confess that I sympathize with these querists; and were I a layman, as I am a clergyman, and if I was rich, as I am not, and certainly never shall be, I should like to know the end—if there be any end—to all these things. . . .

Every well devised system of benevolence should have this in view; that their aid should be so given that it shall not conduce to the *dependence* of those aided, but to their *independence*.

This principle is pre-eminently applicable to the West. She does not come here as a slave—she does not come here as a beggar. I speak of being of her, for, although temporarily transplanted, my heart is still there. . . . No; this is all we ask in the West: we ask, that as, in the beginning of the world, man received help from on high,—that as, in the beginning of our national existence, we received aid from abroad,—that as, in the beginning of every great enterprise, aid is necessary—that inasmuch as civilization always works from within outward, and never inversely,—inasmuch as civilization is indigenous to no soil, but is always transplanted—so we in the West ask, that in her juvenile days, while she opens roads, constructs cities and villages, digs canals and lays railroads, you should help her. She does not wish you to do all her other work, but to help her while she founds schools and colleges and theological seminaries and rolls the vast tide of civilization throughout her boundless extent. . . .

I look forward to the day when the West shall say to the East, "Come, we will help you to found new states, to build up other communities, and furnish them with schools, colleges, and churches."

CALL FOR A NATIONAL SUNDAY-SCHOOL CONVENTION AS PROPOSED BY THE AMERICAN SUNDAY-SCHOOL UNION, 1832

Circular to Sunday-School Teachers and Superintendents.—In pursuance of public notice,[1] a meeting of teachers, superintendents, and others engaged in conducting Sunday-schools was held in Philadelphia on the 23d of May last, at which were present persons from the following States:

Maine	Virginia
Massachusetts	District of Columbia
Connecticut	South Carolina
New York	Georgia
New Jersey	Ohio
Pennsylvania	Indiana
Delaware	Michigan Territory
Maryland	

At this meeting it was unanimously resolved that a general convention of persons actively employed in Sunday-schools should be assembled in New York, on the first Wednesday of October next. The object of the convention is to deliberate on the best plans of promoting the usefulness of this system of religious instruction, and, if possible, to adopt some means of rendering it more efficient than it yet has been. The mode of representation agreed upon at the meeting followed, as noted on p. 440.

The circular continued:

We trust that you will perceive at once the importance of the measure, and that you will take timely steps to have your schools represented agreeably to the above plan, and provide for the expense of your delegates. It is a subject in which we are all deeply concerned, the results of which will more than compensate for the expense that will be incurred.

A committee of arrangements was appointed, consisting of five gentlemen residing in the city of New York, who request the delegates to report themselves, on their arrival, at No. 140 Nassau Street.

[1] This notice was issued by the managers of the American Sunday-School Union May, 1832.

In order to collect the greatest amount of information and advice on the subject, the accompanying list of interrogatories was prepared, and a committee appointed to circulate them as widely as practicable, and to urge upon all those who receive them to communicate their views on the general subjects to the committee, who will condense the information received, and present it for the consideration of the convention.

Your serious and immediate attention to this service is most respectfully and earnestly solicited. It is not expected that your answers will be limited by the form of the questions, but that you will furnish your views in any shape, and to any extent you please, on any topic connected with the subject of our inquiry, and whether contained in the questions or not. Our great purpose is to procure a full expression of the opinions of experienced and intelligent teachers, and others, on all points connected with the system, so that the convention may be guided in their course by the information thus collected from the whole country.

As much time and labor will be required to examine and prepare the replies for the use of the convention, we hope you will send your communication so that we may receive it by the *first day of September*. You will please address it to JOHN HALL,

No. 22 Post-office,

Philadelphia.

INTERROGATORIES

I. *Schools*

1. Have you schools for infants?—for children?—for adults?
2. What is the total number of your learners?
3. How many of your young scholars are children of persons belonging to your congregation?
4. How many children belonging to the congregation are not in the schools?
5. What means have been used to increase your schools? What prevents a more rapid increase?
6. Are your schools suspended during any part of the year? If they are, for what reasons?

II. *Organization*

7. Are the children classed according to their capacity and progress?
8. What is the proper number for a class of children?
9. What is the proper size of a room for a given number of pupils, in reference to their health and the success of teaching? Should the classes be accommodated, if possible, in separated rooms?
10. How often in the day do the schools meet? How long are they continued each Sabbath? What is the order of exercises and time allotted to each?

11.　Are children enrolled or dismissed without the knowledge of their parents or guardians?

12.　Do you approve of having more than one teacher to a class, acting at different times?

III.　*Discipline*

13.　What is your system of discipline?　Do you require and secure punctual and regular attendance in teachers and scholars—every one taking their seats as soon as they enter the room, with order and stillness? How do you effect this?

14.　What are the proper modes of punishment?　Is corporal correction ever justifiable?　Should a scholar be expelled under any circumatances?

15.　What is the best mode of urging children to diligence and regularity?　What sort of rewards should be offered, if any?　Is it expedient to distribute premiums?　If so, how often, on what grounds, and in what manner?

16.　How do you dispose of the scholars during the time of public worship?　Should they be taken to the place of worship, or have services peculiarly adapted to them in some other place?

17.　What degree of conformity to the discipline and purposes of the school is considered necessary, on the part of a teacher, to maintain his station?

IV.　*Visiting*

18.　How often, and on what system, are your scholars visited at their homes?　What effect has it upon them and their families?　How can these visits be best conducted so as to render them agreeable and useful?

19.　Should committees be appointed to visit those whom any of the regular teachers may be prevented from visiting?

20.　Should committees be appointed to visit houses to procure scholars?　Is it desirable, where circumstances admit of it, to employ persons to perform these combined duties of visiting scholars and their parents, procuring new scholars, and advancing the cause generally?

V.　*Mode of Instruction*

21.　Please to state fully your views of the best method of instruction, whether orally by the teacher, by conversation with the class, or with the scholars individually, or by lectures; whether it is advisable to encourage the children to express their own sentiments, to discuss important points with them, and to gain their assent to truth by reason instead of authority.

22.　Mention any mode of communicating knowledge which you know or believe to be peculiarly adapted to the object.

23.　What is the best plan for instructing children who cannot read, and what are the best elementary books?

24. What is the most effectual method of engaging the attention of learners, and interesting them in religious and moral subjects?

25. Do you use maps, pictures, diagrams, etc.?

26. Do you impress the evidences of Divine wisdom, power, and providence by facts drawn from astronomy, natural philosophy, etc.? Would a manual furnishing the rudiments of natural science, and adapted to Sunday-schools, be proper to be introduced?

27. How much should children be required to commit to memory? Do they learn to repeat the Ten Commandments accurately?

28. Do your teachers see that the children who cannot read are placed at public schools, or are otherwise instructed during the week?

29. Have you any peridoical examination of the classes by the minister, or other person, in the presence of the congregation.

VI. *Union Questions*

30. Do you use the Union Questions? If so, please state how you use them—whether by asking all the questions as they stand in the lessons, or whether you select them according to the capacity and intelligence of the several members of the class, or ask questions of your own on the general subject of the lesson, without reference to the order or language of the book, etc.? Please mention particularly your views on this head, and the result of your experience or knowledge in regard to the plan of using the Questions.

31. Can you suggest any improvement in the construction of the Union Questions?

32. Do you put the questions to each class, or to each scholar individually?

33. Are the scholars required to be prepared to recite the lesson of the day before they come to the school? What are the best means of securing this object?

VII. *Other Books*

34. Do you use any other book than the Union Questions?

35. What is your opinion of the use of denominational catechisms?

36. Can you recommend any work not in general use which you believe to be adapted to the purposes of Sunday-school instruction?

VIII. *Libraries*

37. What is your plan of conducting the libraries? How often do you purchase books?

38. Do you appoint any person to examine books the character of which is not authenticated? How do you determine what books are fit for the library?

39.   What principle do you adopt with respect to the introduction of other than religious books?

40.   How do you regulate the giving out of books, and ascertain whether they are read?   If you know of a successful method, state it very particularly.

41.   What suggestions can you make respecting the character of the books published for the use of Sunday-schools?   Can you suggest improvements?   What kinds are most acceptable and useful?   What kinds are most wanted?   Are they adpated to adult classes?   What influence do they appear to exert on their readers?   Are they extensively read by the parents and families of the learners?   Are books needed in other languages than the English?

42.   Is it proper to publish fictitious books for Sunday-school reading?

43.   Have you a library for the express use of teachers in preparing themselves on the lessons?   What books are needed for their special use?

IX.   *Other Means of Success*

44.   Are direct efforts made for the spiritual welfare of your classes? Do you think the teachers labor, and pray for, and expect this as the great end of their exertions?

45. How many teachers and scholars are professors of religion?   Is there any peculiar seriousness among either?   What are the feelings of teachers on this subject?

46.   Do the teachers hold special prayer meetings on the Sabbath, or at other times, besides the regular one on the second Monday of every month?   Are any pains taken to make the Sunday-school Monthly Concert interesting?   Do you hold prayer meetings with the children who are willing to attend them?   What is the best plan of conducting such meetings?   Should seriously disposed or pious children be encouraged, under any circumstances, to hold prayer meetings among themselves?

47.   Has there at any time been any unusual attention to religion in your school, and what accession to the church has been the result? What circumstances have appeared to you to advance or hinder the progress of piety in your scholars?

48.   How do you account for the comparative want of interest in Sunday-schools on the part of many ministers and church officers? How shall members of churches and congregations be interested in them? How shall parents be induced to see that their children prepare their lessons?   Are Sunday-schools commonly mentioned in family prayers?

49.   What is the best plan of mutual instruction and study for teachers?

50.   Do teachers hold weekly meetings to study the lesson?

51.   Does your minister lecture on the lesson?   Should there be a uniformity in the explanations of passages of Scripture by all the teachers?

X. *Superintendents*

52. What are the duties of a superintendent?

53. Should he have a class? How often should he address the school?

54. How may he secure the union of the teachers with him in promoting the general interests of the classes? How often should they meet together to consult on the state of the school?

55. What should be the distinction between his authority and that of the teachers?

56. Is it in any case advisble to have more than one superintendent of a school at the same time?

XI. *Bible and Adult Classes*

57. Could not more be done for the establishment of schools for adults, both for those who cannot read and those who can, but are from any cause prevented from regular attendance on public worship?

58. Might not Bible classes be formed to include all ages and ranks in the congregation, but especially of youth who are above the ordinary age of Sunday scholars?

59. Is it expedient to use question books with such classes? Should they be required to recite Scripture lessons?

60. Have your instructions to Bible classes a direct reference to prepare the members for Sunday-school teaching?

61. What method of studying the Scriptures do you recommend to the scholars? Do you propose religious subjects to be written upon by your scholars?

62. At what age are Sunday scholars transferred to the Bible class?

63. Is it proper to instruct them on other subjects than those immediately connected with the Bible, such as history, natural philosophy, etc.?

64. Is there any particular advantage in having Bible and adult classes taught in the same apartment with children?

XII. *Infant Schools*

65. At what age should children be admitted into these schools? And what is the best mode of conducting them?

66. What is the proper discipline of an infant Sunday-school? What are proper subjects and modes of teaching? And what exercises are suitable?

XIII. *Miscellaneous*

67. What is the best plan of training scholars to become teachers? What is the result of your observation respecting the usefulness of scholars who have become teachers?

68.   What preparation is considered necessary to enable a teacher to meet his class?

69.   Have classes been formed in private houses when children cannot conveniently be sent to the school?

70.   What is the best system of organization of unions for towns or counties?

71.   What is your method of raising funds for the support of the school?

72.   Is it useful to have an annual meeting, or celebration, say on the Fourth of July, of the teachers and scholars within a convenient district? If so, what would be the appropriate services for such an occasion?

73.   What attention is given to the cultivation of sacred singing, and what measures should be taken to promote it more generally?

74.   What are the best means of retaining the elder scholars?

75.   Do you approve of encouraging the children to bring contributions from their own pocket-money for benevolent objects?

76.   By what means can all the intelligent adults of your congregation be afforded the opportunity of being actively engaged in giving instruction on the Sabbath?

77.   Do you provide clothing for those children who, for want of it, would be prevented from attending?

78.   Is any custom or personal habit indulged by teachers which their scholars might not with propriety adopt?

[The above circular was printed on eight folio pages, leaving large spaces for answers after each question.—Editor.]

Churches and Confessions.—As the American Sunday-School Union has not purposed to organize churches, it has never attempted systematically or regularly to preserve, collate or gather information in regard to the number of churches that followed the Union schools it has founded. Much less has it attempted to take note of the denominational relations of those churches.

Nor has the Union at any period been careful or concerned to have its workers note and report the number of persons who confessed Christ in its schools. A number of the schools and auxiliary societies that made reports direct to the Union in the early period of its history frequently but incidentally noted cases of persons who were led to confess Christ through the Bible instruction in Union schools. Rarely, however, was there any attempt to enroll or state the exact number in such cases. The frequency, however, of revivals and confessions occasionally reported and published attracted the attention of the friends and supporters of the cause. They recognized those so reported as an indication of the remarkable and conspicuous results, in part, of the evangelical message first given to the places unreached by other missions, and which made disciples of teachers and scholars, as well as of members of the families from which the scholars came. Most of the detailed reports from schools and auxiliaries from 1820 to 1835 repeatedly noted numbers that made public confession of Christ. Not only was this true of the members of the schools, but it included members of the families in the community. It was a marked evidence of putting emphasis on godly life in all the teaching. These evidences from confessions have continued through the entire century of work. Yet there was no systematic effort to collate and give a complete census of the confessions and conversions thus indicated. From time to time computations were made upon this phase of the work. These are often noted in the body of this book, as the reader will have already discovered.

Moreover, the reports of churches growing out of union schools, or following them, have been incidental rather than regular reports. Sometimes the workers told of the organization of a church in connection with the change of a Union school to a denominational one, when a church was organized where the pioneer school was located. Sometimes, too, these cases were noted in the reports of the Society, but no effort was made to tabulate even these reports. Only a very small portion of the whole number of first churches actually following from the Union schools were thus reported or noted.

An illustration of the extent to which churches have had the way prepared for their coming by a Union school may be given from the state of Wisconsin. Union Sunday-school missionary work was begun there some years before it ceased to be a territory and was admitted as a State. Mr. J. W. Vail was an early (but not the first) Sunday-school mission worker in Wisconsin under the Society. He wrote an account of the results of the Society's services there, which was published in a series of articles in the *Wisconsin Puritan* in 1866. He also furnished to the author of this work added details of some schools in centers that had become cities at that time. Mr. Vail compiled also a list of more than a score of new settlements that in 1866 had become cities or large towns in that state, and in which the first religious organization (preceding all churches in those places) was a Union Sunday-school, planted by this Society. Among the places so noted were Neenah, Menasha, Sheboygan, Sparta, Portage, Fox Lake, Columbus and Oshkosh .

A specimen record of one of these cases now a large town was where he organized a Union Sunday-school in a log house. "There were only three houses (all built of logs) then in the place. Mr. Strong, a young man from Boston, was chosen Superintendent. The people subscribed $2.50 and he doubled it as a gift from the Union, to provide a meager supply of literature to start the school." In another place, now a city, a school was started in a tavern, the only available place. A private room was freely granted by the tavern-keeper, who was, of course, not a

Christian, but was desirous of having his children study the Scriptures. Still another school was started in a carpenter-shop as the only available building in the place. Both of these places are now large towns having many churches. Similar facts in detail were given in regard to many other places by Mr. Vail at that time. They were copied from his original records concerning each of the places. These towns now have healthy churches belonging to leading Protestant denominations. In about a half a dozen extended articles in the *Wisconsin Puritan* Mr. Vail presented a summary of his work of fourteen years in Wisconsin. He stated that there were 65 Sunday-schools in the territory when he began. More than half of them were Union. Several of them were formed by a previous worker of the Society. Mr. Vail and his associates established 924 schools in 42 counties of Wisconsin, besides 24 schools in 5 neighboring counties in Illinois. He reported having distributed $26,500 worth of publications, of which about $8,000 ($7,874) were donated. The schools had, when organized, a membership of upward of 16,000. He notes the first religious organization in Beloit (now the seat of Beloit College) was a Union Sunday-school, which now has many prosperous churches. More than 50 first churches immediately grew out of or followed the planting of Union schools, and in as many cities and towns in Wisconsin. The membership of these first churches was largely composed of members from these same Union schools.

Another Union worker of the Society in that state, a few years later, ascertained that about 150 churches in Wisconsin and in eastern Minnesota had grown out of or followed Union schools. Similar facts might be given in respect to other states in the Middle West.

Churches Organized in Twenty-five Years.—The Rev. George P. Williams, D. D., Secretary of Missions, has collated the number of first churches organized from or immediately following Union Sunday-schools year by year for the past twenty-five years, as shown by the reports of the missionaries and records of the American Sunday-School Union. This list indicates that the number so reported varied widely in different years. That is doubtless due partly to the fact that the missionaries did not attempt to secure a complete report nor to ascertain the full number of churches that had followed Union schools in their respective fields. They only reported such as they knew or learned of in the pursuit of regular phases of their work. It may also be partially due to the extent of evangelistic interest prevailing throughout the country in different years. Thus, the number of churches so reported in 1892 was 216; in 1893, 186, while in 1894 no churches were so reported; but unquestionably many churches were so organized that year. In the year ending March, 1905, 138 churches were reported as organized. The least number for any of the years for the past twenty-five years has been 75 churches organized from Union schools. For about one-half of the past twenty-five years more than 100 churches have been reported as so organized each year. It is a matter of regret to some friends that the Society has not been more diligent in gleaning and collating the facts in regard to churches, as well as confessions resulting from its field work for the entire century.

Sunday-School Missionaries Who Have Formed 1,000 or More Sunday-Schools.—Some of the missionaries of the American Sunday-School Union have been spared for an exceptionally long service, and have been blessed of God with rare tact, skill, and devotion, so that each of them has founded 1,000 or more Sunday-schools in otherwise neglected districts of the United States.

There are many other of the Society's missionaries who have been as faithful and devoted and as self-sacrificing as these whose labors God has honored and blessed in this particular way of forming an exceptional number of new schools. But these are mentioned for the encouragment of workers and of friends of the Society, and to recognize the singular blessings of God upon the humble services of his servants in reaching the wandering and lost among the hedges, highways and byways of the country. Many persons thus reached were far beyond the sound of any church bell and the hearing of any preacher's voice.

Captain W. W. Bradshaw, of Kentucky, gave over thirty years of service to the Society, which he entered after winning the rank of Captain for his gallantry in the Civil War, and teaching in the public schools for twenty years. He was 6 feet tall, and straight as a pine tree, and had an impressive personality and a commanding voice. He founded 1,079 schools in 56 of the mountain counties of Kentucky. These schools provided religious instruction for over 100,000 children of the highlanders or mountaineers of that state. The schools reported over 10,000 conversions, and were the forerunners of over 80 churches. Out of the schools also came over 100 young men who entered the gospel ministry.

T. W. Dimmock, of Georgia, has been nearly forty years in the service of the Society. He has founded nearly 1,200 (1,161) Sunday-schools up to the present date, and is "still in the harness," diligent and faithful, bringing forth rich spiritual fruit in his advancing years.

Rev. Isaac Emory, of Tennesee, was over thirty years in service, which he entered after the Civil War. He wrought so faithfully and God so blessed his labors that he reported founding over 1,000 (1,010) Sunday-schools, enrolling more than 60,000 members, from which an unusually large number of conversions and churches resulted. After traveling over 100,000 miles on horseback, by stage, steamboat and railroad, he was instantly killed in a railway accident.

Rev. G. S. Jones, of North Carolina, was over thirty years also in the service, entering it after the Civil War. He organized 1,165 new Sunday-schools with a membership of 57,700 at their organization. A large number of these schools doubled their membership later, reaching over 100,000 persons. Out of these schools came 32 young men who became ministers of the gospel, and 130 or more churches were formed with the members of these schools as a basis, at their organization.

J. P. Lane, of Texas, has been over thirty-five years in service and has formed about 1,200 (1,196) new Sunday-schools, besides about 500 others re-organized.   Mr. Lane has not grown weary in well doing and continues to render faithful service, witnessing to the gracious blessings that God bestows upon faithful evangelists.

Martin B. Lewis, of Minnesota, gave over fifty (52) years to the service· He was a lay-evangelist, consecrated in soul, of deep spirituality, and gifted in a peculiar manner for winning souls by personal work.   He founded over 1,000 Sunday-schools, many of them among people of foreign birth and language, and which became the forerunners of over 150 churches.   He was ever welcome to the homes of the common people as a gospel messenger, always seeing the bright side of life and its events, so that his visits were uniformly welcomed as a benediction.

Rev. John McCullagh, of Kentucky, was in the regular service of the Society for forty-seven years, following a volunteer service of seven years. For he was first a Volunteer Missionary, then commissioned by the Society for a generation, was Superintendent of the Southern District, comprising from 9 to 12 states, and for four years later a General Missionary.   His services are remarkable in that he *personally* organized over 1,000 Sunday-schools, besides supervising the labors of a large number of missionaries in the southern district.   He retired from this supervision owing to impaired hearing and health in 1884, and four years later passed to the larger life in 1888.

Rev. G. E. Mize, of Alabama, has rendered twenty-five years of service, forming nearly 1,100 (1,089) Sunday-schools with a membership of over 70,000.   He knows of at least 15 young persons from these schools who have entered the gospel ministry, and of 133 churches that have followed and grown out of the schools.   Mr. Mize continues joyously and successfully in this service, a worker commanding the confidence and esteem of the people of all races in the State.

Stephen Paxson, of Illinois, devoted twenty years to the missionary service, and when worn by toil and travail in the field, he was transferred to the charge of the Society's Depository in St. Louis where he continued for thirteen years until called by the Master to his reward.   Mr. Paxson was instrumental in starting 1,314 Sunday-schools.   When a gentleman called on Mr. Paxson, saying that some people were a little suspicious of the report that he had actually organized 1,300 new schools with more than 60,000 scholars, and wanted to gain some proof of it, Mr. Paxson promptly answered, "Here are my books containing the name of each school, superintendent's name and post office address, and the number of scholars, set down upon the very day it was organized.   I never leave such things over night.   A duplicate is sent to the Home Office in Philadelphia, Pa." The questioner on examining the records was satisfied, and bade him good-bye.   It is said of "Father" Paxson that he once performed the feat or organizing "40 Sabbath-schools in 40 consecutive days."

C. B. Rhodes, of Arkansas, was for thirty years in service as the representative of Mr. and Mrs. Morris K. Jesup.   He formed over 1,000 Sunday-schools in neglected places of Arkansas with a membership of upward of 60,000.   He passed to the other life in 1909.

There are other missionaries of the Society who, by fidelity of service and the schools they have organized with other work, deserve honorable mention.   Among them may be noted the Rev. Thomas Lain, for about thirty-four years in the service, and who organized 908 schools with a membership of 50,800 (50,750), reporting conversions of about 4,850 (4,843). Also A. B. Norrell, of Texas, has organized 883 schools with a membership of 36,900 (36,825), out of which have grown 197 churches.

There are still other missionaries who have rendered efficient service in evangelistic work and in securing the support of faithful and devoted men who have entered the service. These have at the same time organized several hundred schools and therefore merit honorable mention were it possible to put the results of all their labors in a tabular form. It is surely remarkable evidence of the blessing of God upon this work of the missionaries that 12 workers have organized over 12,000 Sunday-schools which have been followed, it is believed, by more than 1,000 churches connected with from 20 to 30 different denominations.

Early Sunday-School Periodicals.—Before and during the first twenty-five years of the last century periodicals, whether scientific, critical, technical or theological, were rare. The number that began and survived for ten years of that period either in Great Britain or America were comparatively few. There were literary and political pamphlets of serial or periodic issue, but even they were irregular, ephemeral and short lived. Franklin's "General Magazine," 1741, Webb's "American Magazine," a rival of Franklin's, among others were started in America before the revolution, but came to an untimely end. "The Ladies' Magazine," 1792, Philadelphia, survived for a generation. "The Theological Magazine," 1796, soon expired. Of a carefully selected list of 275 periodicals, noted in the American Cyclopedia, including American, English, French, German and in other European languages in all fields of human learning that survived to 1860, scarcely eighteen were begun earlier than 1820. These, moreover, were chiefly journals of scientific societies, and not properly magazines or literary journals.

In America the "Teacher's Offering" for Sunday scholars was begun in 1823, bought by the American Sunday-School Union and continued under the title of "Youth's Friend" for upward of twenty-five years, when it was succeeded by the "Youth's Penny Gazette." The "Infant's Magazine" was also begun about 1828 as a small 32mo periodical, with stories and illustrations to interest the wee ones.

Great Britain issued periodicals for Sunday-schools at an earlier date than any in America. The London Sunday-School Union, in its early work, made larger use of pamphlets and serial publications than of books.

The "Sunday-School Repository or Teacher's Magazine" began in 1813 as a quarterly at a sixpence; changed in 1821 to the "Sunday-School Teacher's Magazine" monthly. It was chiefly for teachers, with some added matter for younger readers. W. F. Lloyd was the founder, editor and proprietor for several years. He was the first Secretary of the London Sunday-School Union. When he closed his editorial work, the Union assumed the responsibility of continuing "The Sunday-School Teacher's

Magazine." It was followed by the "Union Magazine," "The Sunday-School Teacher," and finally by the "London Sunday-School Chronicle," which is still issued. (See below.)

The "Youth's Magazine," a small monthly begun in September, 1805, was issued by private publishers in London. It was intended for the higher classes, and attained a large circulation.

The London Sunday-School Union approved the publication of the "Penny Magazine for Children," by William Gover in 1820.

The Religious Tract Society began the "Child's Companion" very soon after, and the "Penny Magazine" was issued by Mr. Gover for only two years. W. H. Watson reports that the "Youth's Magazine" and the "Magazine for Children" were started at the suggestion of the London Sunday-School Union.

Confirming what is stated above in regard to the issue of periodicals instead of books by the London Sunday-School Union, at the 9th Anniversary of that Society in May, 1812, which was held at the New London Tavern, Cheapside, London the only publications reported were the following:

"Plan for the Establishment and Organization of Sabbath Schools," one edition.

"Introduction to Reading," part 1, 85.000 copies.

"Milk for Babes," 38,000 copies.

"Selected Portions of Scripture," designed as a guide to teachers for a course of reading in Sunday-schools.

The "American Sunday-School Teachers' Magazine and Journal of Education" began in 1823 as a quarterly by private publishers in New York. It was soon transferred to the American Sunday-school Union and continued as the "American Sunday-School Magazine" and issued monthly under that title until 1831, when it again became a quarterly. It was succeeded in America by "The Sunday-School Journal and Advocate of Christian Education," a weekly started in 1831, in folio form, and was continued until 1834, when it was changed to a semi-monthly and later to a monthly publication. It was the first Sunday-school teacher's journal issued weekly. It was discontinued as a weekly for some time, but reappeared again under the title "The Sunday-School Times," in 1859; was transferred to private publishers in 1861, and still continues to be the leading teacher's journal in America.

The "Sunday-School World" in 1861 succeeded the "Sunday-School Magazine," 1823–33, and the "Sunday-School Journal" of 1834–1858.

"The Church of England Sunday-School Magazine" was issued quarterly in 1848, and later as a monthly, and is continued to the present time.

"The Sunday-School Chronicle" of London, 1874, is the first teacher's journal issued weekly in Great Britain, Benjamin Clarke, editor. "The

London Sunday-School Chronicle" continues to be ably edited by Rev. Frank Johnson. Each of the larger denominations maintaining a Sunday-school department or board, issues a periodical for teachers, monthly, under the direction of a strong editorial staff. These journals give special attention to principles and methods of instruction, and present series of lessons with helps for officers and teachers.

We append a list of the more important early juvenile periodicals for Sunday-schools.

JUVENILE PERIODICALS

1. "The Youths' Magazine; or, Evangelical Miscellany." Fourpence per number, monthly; begun in 1805, by G. W. Gurney, under the management of a committee.

The earlier volumes were adapted to younger children, and to less-informed readers, than the later volumes, which were intended to interest intelligent and well-educated young people. The early publishers were Hamilton, Adams & Co., London, England.

2. "Youths' Instructor and Guardian." Fourpence; issued by J. Kershaw, London; begun about 1817, under the auspices of the Wesleyans.

It was counted in 1825 "solid, serious and useful; the extracts being selected with great judgment," said a friendly critic.

3. "The Juvenile Friend." First issued as "The Family and School Magazine."

It had what a contemporary critic calls "good wood-cuts." The original and compiled material was not of the best quality. This was also issued by a private publisher, Mr. Souter, London, at fourpence per number.

4. "The Sunday Scholars' Magazine; or, Monthly Reward Book." Issued by B. J. Holdsworth, Oxford, 12mo 24 pages, illustrated; threepence; later at twopence a number.

This was begun about 1821, and at first devoted entirely to the infants in Sunday-schools. It was edited with much spirit; but the interest was not sustained after four or five years, so the price was lowered to twopence.

5. "The Child's Magazine." Edited by Mrs. Sherwood; published by Knight & Lacey, London; one penny; was begun about 1821; badly printed, and poorly edited at first; changed to new form January, 1823, with Mrs. Sherwood as editor.

A contemporary or reviewer says: "Mrs. Sherwood is well known and highly esteemed as an excellent writer for the young; yet, as the editor of a child's magazine, she does not excel"; a distinction which often appears in modern juvenile literature. Simplicity and variety are needed in a periodical.

6. "The Teachers' Offering; or, The Sunday-School Monthly Visitor." Rev. J. Campbell, editor. One penny; issued by Westley, London; be-

gun January 1, 1823, in its present form, but displaced an earlier and poorer magazine.

This new one needed great improvement in paper, print and cuts, in the opinion of a contemporary reviewer.

7. "The Sunday-Scholars' Magazine and Juvenile Miscellany." Twopence; issued by T. Albat, Hanley, Staffordshire; local in circulation.

8. "The Religious Instructor; or, Church of England Sunday-School Magazine." Fourpence; by Seeley, London.

This was at first designed partly for scholars and partly for teachers; later it was devoted to teaching and conducting Sunday-schools. It was begun about 1825.

9. "Wesleyan Sunday-School Magazine." Issued at York, England, from 1824, at one penny; chiefly local in circulation.

10. "The Children's Friend." Rev. W. Carus Wilson, editor; issued by Seeley, London, at one penny.

Mr. Wilson was also the editor of a popular monthly for adults, "The Friendly Visitor."

It was reported that half a million copies of these two magazines were circulated in 1824. The "cuts" were counted poor.

11. "The Child's Companion; or, Sunday-Scholars' Reward." One penny; issued by the Religious Tract Society, London, and gained about half a million circulation in 1824.

12. "The Child's Magazine and Sunday-Scholars' Companion." One penny; under the Wesleyan Conference; printed by Kershaw, London; intended to do for little children what the "Youths' Instructor" (No. 2) aimed to do for youth.

A reviewer counts it too old, and lacking in childlike simplicity of matter and manner.

13. "The School Miscellany." One penny; issued by Welton, London; begun March 1, 1824, and devoted to "moral rather than religious instruction."

14. "National School Magazine." One penny; issued by the Rivingtons, London, semi-monthly; also devoted to moral instruction.

15. "The Youth's Friend," formerly "Teachers' Offering." Issued by the Sunday-School Union, Philadelphia, Pa., 1823. 24mo, 16 pages.

16. "The Infants' Magazine." 32mo 12 pages, illustrated; issued by the American Sunday-School Union, 1826.

17. "Infant Scholars' Magazine." 32mo illustrated, 16 pages, monthly; January 1, 1827; John Stephens, London, England.

18. "Cottage Magazine." 12mo 36 pages; January 1, 1812; Sherwood, Neely & Co., London; threepence per number; without illustrations.

It was "for the exclusive use of the lower orders of society."

19. "Child's Magazine." Issued by the Sunday-School Union of the Methodist Episcopal Church, New York, 1827; 18mo, 16 pages.

20. "Genesee Sabbath-School Herald," April, 1828; 18mo, 16 pages, not illustrated; L. A. Ward, Rochester, N. Y.

21. "Family Visitor and Sunday-School Magazine." Issued by the General Protestant Episcopal Sunday-School Union, 1829, at 46 Lumber Street, New York.

22. "Sabbath-School Reporter." 18mo, 16 pages; vol. 1; Windsor, Vt.; date uncertain.

23. "The American Sunday-School Magazine." 12mo, 32 pages; July, 1824; the American Sunday-School Union.

This was for teachers, workers and adults, rather than for juveniles.

24. "The Sabbath-School Visitant," 1824; Utica, New York.

25. "Youth's Herald," 1829.

26. "Sunday-School Child's Repository in South London." Begun in 1815. In 1820 Gover, published a magazine of the same name, but only fourteen monthly numbers were issued.

27. "Child's Own Book" was begun as a ha'penny serial in 1821 and 1822. It was continued until 1850; was succeeded then by the "Child's Own Magazine."

28. "Bible Class Magazine and Penny Magazine for Senior Scholars and Junior Teachers," was begun in 1848 and was succeeded by "The Excelsior" and then by "The Golden Rule."

29. "Kind Words for Boys and Girls" was started by the London Union in 1866. It was issued as a monthly until 1880, when it was changed to "Young England." It is still published.

30. "Baptist Children's Magazine," 1827.

31. "Children's Catholic Magazine," 1838.

32. "Youth's Penny Gazette," 1843.

33. "Youth's Sunday-School Gazette," 1859; Philadelphia.

Books in Foreign Lands.—*Publications of the American Sunday-School Union in Foreign Countries.*—In the first twenty years of the history of the American Sunday-School Union large quantities of its literature were called for in foreign countries. The Hon. C. E. Trevelyan of Calcutta ordered a set of the Society's publications at his own expense because he became so interested in them from an examination of the list. The persons who received them wrote, "We have received your magnificent gift of books from America, which have delighted our hearts. They are indeed beautiful. The maps, picture cards, etc., are far superior to any we have ever seen in England. A physician in India, seeing this set of publications also ordered a supply for his own family.

The Rev. Dr. M. Winslow of Madras of the American mission there, in an application for publications said, "The American Mission at Madras, has not only the means of lending but of distributing gratuitously a great part of the books. They would be particularly useful in the schools.

They would be sought after and read with great avidity by many who would not read any religious work in their own language."

The Rev. Dr. Dwight of Constantinople wrote, "We can employ to great advantage sets of all your books adapted to children from eight to ten years of age: Dictionaries of the Bible, Bible natural history, Union Questions, Bible Geography, Maps, Cards and lessons on cards, or card pictures without the lessons. Particularly Scripture illustrations to almost any extent can be used by us, putting the lesson in whatever language we need. Many of the cuts in your books would answer well in our translations."

Rev. W. H. Pearce of Calcutta said, "I look with great interest to the translations of your books into the native languages. The salt which such books as these diffuse among the mass is what under God's blessing will prevent its moral putrefaction."

Another missionary of the Church of England was then translating the "Life of Daniel," issued by the Union, and still another was translating into Bengali the "Church History" issued by the Union. The Mission in Benares was using the "Life of Henry Martin," "The Life of Daniel," "The Life of Elijah" and the "History of the Orissa Mission" issued by the Union and were also translating them into Hindustanee.

The Rev. S. Wells Williams of China, applying for books of the Society said "I do not think of any more profitable present that could be made to the Library of a Missionary than these volumes," referring to the works issued by the American Sunday-School Union. He adds, "Some of the books on Natural History appear to be adapted to the knowledge of those subjects which the Chinese have already attained to, and would lead them on in the road of admiring and studying nature's works and nature's God."

The Rev. J. R. Campbell of Northern India applied for books for several English schools established in India. "I know you will not permit them to be raised up with mere scientific knowledge to become infidels, while you have it in your power to afford them Bible truth in the most simple and attractive form and exactly adapted to their capacities."

"The Life of Washington" published by the Union was translated into upward of twenty languages, and many other of its publications were issued in foreign lands as well as our own, from the "icy mountains of Greenland to the coral strand of India."

INDEX

Adams, John ("Father") (1772–1863), sketch of life and work of, 212
Stephen Paxson and, 272
work as an educator, 235
Adams, William, 214
Addison, 155
Africa, Sunday-schools in, 34, 35
Aids, Lesson, see Lesson aids.
Alden, Timothy, 69, 190, 219
Alexander, Archibald (1772–1851), American Sunday-School Union defended by, 134
author of "Vindication of Sunday-Schools," 143
graded instruction for Sunday-schools, 123
helped form Evangelical Society of Philadelphia, 51
treatise on vindication of Sunday-schools by, 122
sketch of life and work, 122
Alexander, James Waddell (1804–59), 353
sketch of life and work, 135
testimony for memorizing Scripture, 59
Alexander, Joseph Addison, author, 135
Allibone, Samuel Austin (1816–89), 97, 166
sketch of life and work, 181
America, attitude toward education, 41
attitude toward modern Sunday-school in, 43
condition of, in eighteenth century, 41
early Sunday-schools in, 43, 52
first attempts to introduce Bible study in, 42
housing of Sunday-schools in, 282
need of Sunday-schools in, 44
objection to Sunday-schools, in 19, 20, 41, 48
toleration and education in, 40
voluntary, mutual and monitorial system in, 48, 49
work of Robert May for Sunday-schools in, 52. See also South and Central America and United States.
Rural, influences against religious progress in, 403
religious condition of, 388, 402
American attitude toward the modern Sunday-school, 40
American Bible Society. See Bible Society, American.
American Christian Commission. See Christian Commission, American.
American Church Sunday-school Institute, 1875; 385, 62

American Education Society, 212
American missionary work for the modern Sunday-school, 39
American Revision Committee, 170
American Sunday-School Magazine, 1823; 91, 94, 110, 158, 370
American Sunday-School Union (1817–1917), administrative methods, 81, 236, 260
affiliation of First Day Society with, 48
aims of, 79, 84, 90, 188, 206, 261, 389
approves Uniform Lesson System, 300
as educator, 232
basis of, 80, 454, 456
bequests, legacies and gifts left to, 260, 261, 323, 326–331, 343, 347, 393
Bible study promoted in Europe by, 32
"Book Fund," 325
brief history of, 452–455
causes of indebtedness, 327
centennial year, 1917; 174
changes in editorial force, 1915; 173
charter finally granted to, 130, 132, 461
children's work of, 214
Church and Sunday-school, relations urged by, 89
churches following Sunday-school work of, 474
churches not formed by, 232
Civil War's effect upon, 241, 251, 325
claims by various denominations of establishing, 132
collection agencies abandoned by, 246
condition in 1900; 329
defended by Willard Hall, etc., 124, 134
defrauded of funds, 244–246
"Diamond Anniversary," 396
educational aims of, 86, 00 00
evangelistic work of, 263
family instruction aided, 89
financial history of, 194, 195, 240–246, 256, 260, 318, 320, 322, 392, 393
housing of, 285
"Interdenominational," 84
jubilee of, 257
limited Lesson System introduced by, 103, 106, 107
list of Green Fund Books, 479
list of Sunday-schools and Societies connected with the Sunday and Adult School Union who assented to changing name to, 447–451

AMERICAN EDUCATION:
ITS MEN, IDEAS, AND INSTITUTIONS
An Arno Press/New York Times Collection

Series I

Adams, Francis. **The Free School System of the United States.**
1875.

Alcott, William A. **Confessions of a School Master.** 1839.

American Unitarian Association. **From Servitude to Service.**
1905.

Bagley, William C. **Determinism in Education.** 1925.

Barnard, Henry, editor. **Memoirs of Teachers, Educators, and
Promoters and Benefactors of Education, Literature, and
Science.** 1861.

Bell, Sadie. **The Church, the State, and Education in Virginia.**
1930.

Belting, Paul Everett. **The Development of the Free Public High
School in Illinois to 1860.** 1919.

Berkson, Isaac B. **Theories of Americanization: A Critical Study.**
1920.

Blauch, Lloyd E. **Federal Cooperation in Agricultural Extension
Work, Vocational Education, and Vocational Rehabilitation.**
1935.

Bloomfield, Meyer. **Vocational Guidance of Youth.** 1911.

Brewer, Clifton Hartwell. **A History of Religious Education in the
Episcopal Church to 1835.** 1924.

Brown, Elmer Ellsworth. **The Making of Our Middle Schools.**
1902.

Brumbaugh, M. G. **Life and Works of Christopher Dock.** 1908.

Burns, Reverend J. A. **The Catholic School System in the United
States.** 1908.

Burns, Reverend J. A. **The Growth and Development of the
Catholic School System in the United States.** 1912.

Burton, Warren. **The District School as It Was.** 1850.

Butler, Nicholas Murray, editor. **Education in the United States.**
1900.

Butler, Vera M. **Education as Revealed By New England Newspapers prior to 1850.** 1935.

Campbell, Thomas Monroe. **The Movable School Goes to the
Negro Farmer.** 1936.

Carter, James G. **Essays upon Popular Education.** 1826.

Carter, James G. **Letters to the Hon. William Prescott, LL.D., on
the Free Schools of New England.** 1924.

Channing, William Ellery. **Self-Culture.** 1842.

Coe, George A. **A Social Theory of Religious Education.** 1917.

Committee on Secondary School Studies. **Report of the Committee on Secondary School Studies, Appointed at the Meeting of
the National Education Association.** 1893.

Counts, George S. **Dare the School Build a New Social Order?**
1932.

Counts, George S. **The Selective Character of American Secondary Education.** 1922.

Counts, George S. **The Social Composition of Boards of Education.** 1927.

Culver, Raymond B. **Horace Mann and Religion in the Massachusetts Public Schools.** 1929.

Curoe, Philip R. V. **Educational Attitudes and Policies of Organized Labor in the United States.** 1926.

Dabney, Charles William. **Universal Education in the South.**
1936.

Dearborn, Ned Harland. **The Oswego Movement in American
Education.** 1925.

De Lima, Agnes. **Our Enemy the Child.** 1926.

Dewey, John. **The Educational Situation.** 1902.

Dexter, Franklin B., editor. **Documentary History of Yale University.** 1916.

Eliot, Charles William. **Educational Reform: Essays and Addresses.** 1898.

Ensign, Forest Chester. **Compulsory School Attendance and Child
Labor.** 1921.

Fitzpatrick, Edward Augustus. **The Educational Views and Influence of De Witt Clinton.** 1911.

Fleming, Sanford. **Children & Puritanism.** 1933.

Flexner, Abraham. **The American College: A Criticism.** 1908.

Foerster, Norman. **The Future of the Liberal College.** 1938.

Gilman, Daniel Coit. **University Problems in the United States.**
1898.

Hall, Samuel R. **Lectures on School-Keeping.** 1829.

Hall, Stanley G. **Adolescence: Its Psychology and Its Relations to
Physiology, Anthropology, Sociology, Sex, Crime, Religion, and
Education.** 1905. 2 vols.

Hansen, Allen Oscar. **Early Educational Leadership in the Ohio
Valley.** 1923.

Harris, William T. **Psychologic Foundations of Education.** 1899.

Harris, William T. **Report of the Committee of Fifteen on the
Elementary School.** 1895.

Harveson, Mae Elizabeth. **Catharine Esther Beecher: Pioneer
Educator.** 1932.

Jackson, George Leroy. **The Development of School Support in
Colonial Massachusetts.** 1909.

Kandel, I. L., editor. **Twenty-five Years of American Education.**
1924.

Kemp, William Webb. **The Support of Schools in Colonial New
York by the Society for the Propagation of the Gospel in Foreign Parts.** 1913.

Kilpatrick, William Heard. **The Dutch Schools of New Nether-
land and Colonial New York.** 1912.

Kilpatrick, William Heard. **The Educational Frontier.** 1933.

Knight, Edgar Wallace. **The Influence of Reconstruction on Education in the South.** 1913.

Le Duc, Thomas. **Piety and Intellect at Amherst College, 1865-
1912.** 1946.

Maclean, John. **History of the College of New Jersey from Its
Origin in 1746 to the Commencement of 1854.** 1877.

Maddox, William Arthur. **The Free School Idea in Virginia before the Civil War.** 1918.

Mann, Horace. **Lectures on Education.** 1855.

McCadden, Joseph J. **Education in Pennsylvania, 1801-1835, and
Its Debt to Roberts Vaux.** 1855.

McCallum, James Dow. **Eleazar Wheelock.** 1939.

McCuskey, Dorothy. **Bronson Alcott, Teacher.** 1940.

Meiklejohn, Alexander. **The Liberal College.** 1920.

Miller, Edward Alanson. **The History of Educational Legislation
in Ohio from 1803 to 1850.** 1918.

Miller, George Frederick. **The Academy System of the State of New York.** 1922.

Monroe, Will S. **History of the Pestalozzian Movement in the United States.** 1907.

Mosely Education Commission. **Reports of the Mosely Education Commission to the United States of America October-December, 1903.** 1904.

Mowry, William A. **Recollections of a New England Educator.** 1908.

Mulhern, James. **A History of Secondary Education in Pennsylvania.** 1933.

National Herbart Society. **National Herbart Society Yearbooks 1-5, 1895-1899.** 1895-1899.

Nearing, Scott. **The New Education: A Review of Progressive Educational Movements of the Day.** 1915.

Neef, Joseph. **Sketches of a Plan and Method of Education.** 1808.

Nock, Albert Jay. **The Theory of Education in the United States.** 1932.

Norton, A. O., editor. **The First State Normal School in America: The Journals of Cyrus Pierce and Mary Swift.** 1926.

Oviatt, Edwin. **The Beginnings of Yale, 1701-1726.** 1916.

Packard, Frederic Adolphus. **The Daily Public School in the United States.** 1866.

Page, David P. **Theory and Practice of Teaching.** 1848.

Parker, Francis W. **Talks on Pedagogics: An Outline of the Theory of Concentration.** 1894.

Peabody, Elizabeth Palmer. **Record of a School.** 1835.

Porter, Noah. **The American Colleges and the American Public.** 1870.

Reigart, John Franklin. **The Lancasterian System of Instruction in the Schools of New York City.** 1916.

Reilly, Daniel F. **The School Controversy (1891-1893).** 1943.

Rice, Dr. J. M. **The Public-School System of the United States.** 1893.

Rice, Dr. J. M. **Scientific Management in Education.** 1912.

Ross, Early D. **Democracy's College: The Land-Grant Movement in the Formative Stage.** 1942.

Rugg, Harold, et al. **Curriculum-Making: Past and Present.** 1926.

Rugg, Harold, et al. **The Foundations of Curriculum-Making.** 1926.

Rugg, Harold and Shumaker, Ann. **The Child-Centered School.** 1928.

Seybolt, Robert Francis. **Apprenticeship and Apprenticeship Education in Colonial New England and New York.** 1917.

Seybolt, Robert Francis. **The Private Schools of Colonial Boston.** 1935.

Seybolt, Robert Francis. **The Public Schools of Colonial Boston.** 1935.

Sheldon, Henry D. **Student Life and Customs.** 1901.

Sherrill, Lewis Joseph. **Presbyterian Parochial Schools, 1846-1870.** 1932 .

Siljestrom, P. A. **Educational Institutions of the United States.** 1853.

Small, Walter Herbert. **Early New England Schools.** 1914.

Soltes, Mordecai. **The Yiddish Press: An Americanizing Agency.** 1925.

Stewart, George, Jr. **A History of Religious Education in Connecticut to the Middle of the Nineteenth Century.** 1924.

Storr, Richard J. **The Beginnings of Graduate Education in America.** 1953.

Stout, John Elbert. **The Development of High-School Curricula in the North Central States from 1860 to 1918.** 1921.

Suzzallo, Henry. **The Rise of Local School Supervision in Massachusetts.** 1906.

Swett, John. **Public Education in California.** 1911.

Tappan, Henry P. **University Education.** 1851.

Taylor, Howard Cromwell. **The Educational Significance of the Early Federal Land Ordinances.** 1921.

Taylor, J. Orville. **The District School.** 1834.

Tewksbury, Donald G. **The Founding of American Colleges and Universities before the Civil War.** 1932.

Thorndike, Edward L. **Educational Psychology.** 1913-1914.

True, Alfred Charles. **A History of Agricultural Education in the United States, 1785-1925.** 1929.

True, Alfred Charles. **A History of Agricultural Extension Work in the United States, 1785-1923.** 1928.

Updegraff, Harlan. **The Origin of the Moving School in Massachusetts.** 1908.

Wayland, Francis. **Thoughts on the Present Collegiate System in the United States.** 1842.

Weber, Samuel Edwin. **The Charity School Movement in Colonial Pennsylvania.** 1905.

Wells, Guy Fred. **Parish Education in Colonial Virginia.** 1923.

Wickersham, J. P. **The History of Education in Pennsylvania.** 1885.

Woodward, Calvin M. **The Manual Training School.** 1887.

Woody, Thomas. **Early Quaker Education in Pennsylvania.** 1920.

Woody, Thomas. **Quaker Education in the Colony and State of New Jersey.** 1923.

Wroth, Lawrence C. **An American Bookshelf, 1755.** 1934.

Series II

Adams, Evelyn C. **American Indian Education.** 1946.

Bailey, Joseph Cannon. **Seaman A. Knapp: Schoolmaster of American Agriculture.** 1945.

Beecher, Catharine and Harriet Beecher Stowe. **The American Woman's Home.** 1869.

Benezet, Louis T. **General Education in the Progressive College.** 1943.

Boas, Louise Schutz. **Woman's Education Begins.** 1935.

Bobbitt, Franklin. **The Curriculum.** 1918.

Bode, Boyd H. **Progressive Education at the Crossroads.** 1938.

Bourne, William Oland. **History of the Public School Society of the City of New York.** 1870.

Bronson, Walter C. **The History of Brown University, 1764-1914.** 1914.

Burstall, Sara A. **The Education of Girls in the United States.** 1894.

Butts, R. Freeman. **The College Charts Its Course.** 1939.

Caldwell, Otis W. and Stuart A. Courtis. **Then & Now in Education, 1845-1923.** 1923.

Calverton, V. F. & Samuel D. Schmalhausen, editors. **The New Generation: The Intimate Problems of Modern Parents and Children.** 1930.

Charters, W. W. **Curriculum Construction.** 1923.

Childs, John L. **Education and Morals.** 1950.

Childs, John L. **Education and the Philosophy of Experimentalism.** 1931.

Clapp, Elsie Ripley. **Community Schools in Action.** 1939.

Counts, George S. **The American Road to Culture: A Social Interpretation of Education in the United States.** 1930.

Counts, George S. **School and Society in Chicago.** 1928.

Finegan, Thomas E. **Free Schools.** 1921.

Fletcher, Robert Samuel. **A History of Oberlin College.** 1943.

Grattan, C. Hartley. **In Quest of Knowledge: A Historical Perspective on Adult Education.** 1955.

Hartman, Gertrude & Ann Shumaker, editors. **Creative Expression.** 1932.

Kandel, I. L. **The Cult of Uncertainty.** 1943.

Kandel, I. L. **Examinations and Their Substitutes in the United States.** 1936.

Kilpatrick, William Heard. **Education for a Changing Civilization.** 1926.

Kilpatrick, William Heard. **Foundations of Method.** 1925.

Kilpatrick, William Heard. **The Montessori System Examined.** 1914.

Lang, Ossian H., editor. **Educational Creeds of the Nineteenth Century.** 1898.

Learned, William S. **The Quality of the Educational Process in the United States and in Europe.** 1927.

Meiklejohn, Alexander. **The Experimental College.** 1932.

Middlekauff, Robert. **Ancients and Axioms: Secondary Education in Eighteenth-Century New England.** 1963.

Norwood, William Frederick. **Medical Education in the United States Before the Civil War.** 1944.

Parsons, Elsie W. Clews. **Educational Legislation and Administration of the Colonial Governments.** 1899.

Perry, Charles M. **Henry Philip Tappan: Philosopher and University President.** 1933.

Pierce, Bessie Louise. **Civic Attitudes in American School Textbooks.** 1930.

Rice, Edwin Wilbur. **The Sunday-School Movement (1780-1917) and the American Sunday-School Union (1817-1917).** 1917.

Robinson, James Harvey. **The Humanizing of Knowledge.** 1924.

Ryan, W. Carson. **Studies in Early Graduate Education.** 1939.

Seybolt, Robert Francis. **The Evening School in Colonial America.** 1925.

Seybolt, Robert Francis. **Source Studies in American Colonial Education.** 1925.

Todd, Lewis Paul. **Wartime Relations of the Federal Government and the Public Schools, 1917-1918.** 1945.

Vandewalker, Nina C. **The Kindergarten in American Education.** 1908.

Ward, Florence Elizabeth. **The Montessori Method and the American School.** 1913.

West, Andrew Fleming. **Short Papers on American Liberal Education.** 1907.

Wright, Marion M. Thompson. **The Education of Negroes in New Jersey.** 1941.

Supplement

The Social Frontier (Frontiers of Democracy). Vols. 1-10, 1934-1943.

D?   F